Jack Tar

Jack Tar

Life in Nelson's Navy

ROY and LESLEY ADKINS

Little, Brown

LITTLE, BROWN

First published in Great Britain in 2008 by Little, Brown

Copyright © 2008 Roy and Lesley Adkins

ISBN 978-1-4087-0054-9

Typeset in Caslon by M Rules
Printed and bound in Great Britain by
Clays Ltd, St Ives plc

Papers used by Little, Brown are natural, renewable and recyclable
products made from wood grown in sustainable forests and certified
in accordance with the rules of the Forest Stewardship Council.

Mixed Sources
Product group from well-managed
forests and other controlled sources
www.fsc.org Cert no. SGS-COC-004081
© 1996 Forest Stewardship Council
FSC

Little, Brown
An imprint of
Little, Brown Book Group
100 Victoria Embankment
London EC4Y 0DY

An Hachette Livre UK Company
www.hachettelivre.co.uk

www.littlebrown.co.uk

To Susan, Robin, Chris and Ali,
with love

CONTENTS

———•◆•———

LIST OF MAPS AND PLANS

———•◆•———

LIST OF ILLUSTRATIONS

———•◆•———

SECTION ONE

Section through a first-rate warship
The press-gang at work (a 1790 print in Robinson, 1911)
A 1782 caricature of the press-gang (Robinson, 1911)
Rear-Admiral Lord Nelson (*Naval Chronicle* 3, 1800)
Cuthbert Collingwood
Marine privates (Field, 1924)
A seaman heaving the lead
Seamen 'on a cruise' in Portsmouth (C. Beresford and H.W. Wilson, *Nelson and His Times*, 1897)
Leisure time below decks (a 1779 print in Robinson, 1911)
'Jack and his Money' (Robinson, 1911)
The 1801 mutineers of HMS *Temeraire* (*The Trial of the Mutineers, late of His Majesty's Ship Temeraire*, 1802)
The lower gun deck of HMS *Victory* (by kind permission of the commanding officer)
The Battle of the Nile

SECTION TWO

The *Victory* at the Battle of Trafalgar
The hold of HMS *Victory* (by kind permission of the commanding officer)
The hold of the *Phoebe* (by permission of Brixham Heritage Museum)
The galley stove of HMS *Victory* (by kind permission of the commanding officer)

JACK TAR

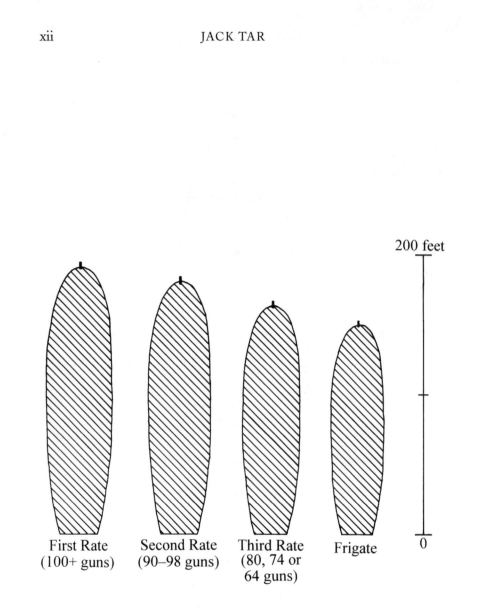

200 feet

First Rate
(100+ guns)

Second Rate
(90–98 guns)

Third Rate
(80, 74 or
64 guns)

Frigate

0

Approximate comparison of ship sizes

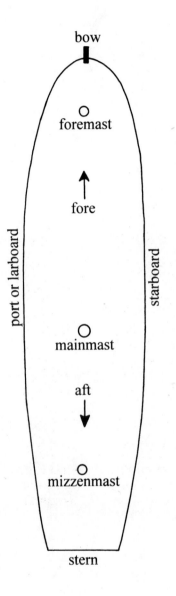

The parts of a ship

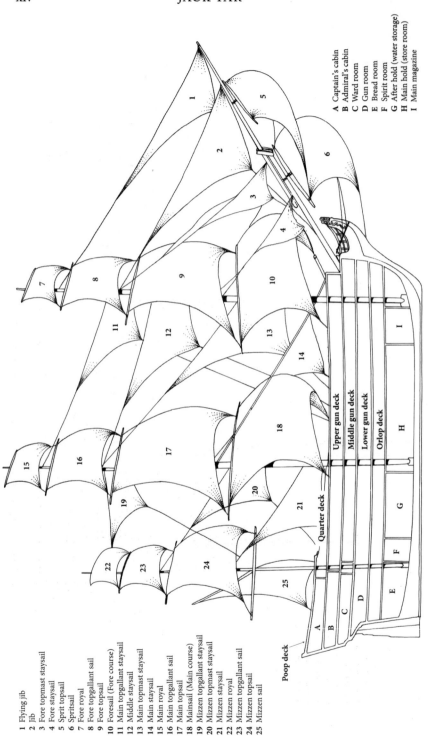

The pattern of sails on a 100-gun ship of the line

1 Flying jib
2 Jib
3 Fore topmast staysail
4 Fore staysail
5 Sprit topsail
6 Spritsail
7 Fore royal
8 Fore topgallant sail
9 Fore topsail
10 Foresail (Fore course)
11 Main topgallant staysail
12 Middle staysail
13 Main topmast staysail
14 Main staysail
15 Main royal
16 Main topgallant sail
17 Main topsail
18 Mainsail (Main course)
19 Mizzen topgallant staysail
20 Mizzen topmast staysail
21 Mizzen staysail
22 Mizzen royal
23 Mizzen topgallant sail
24 Mizzen topsail
25 Mizzen sail

A Captain's cabin
B Admiral's cabin
C Ward room
D Gun room
E Bread room
F Spirit room
G After hold (water storage)
H Main hold (store room)
I Main magazine

Poop deck
Quarter deck
Upper gun deck
Middle gun deck
Lower gun deck
Orlop deck

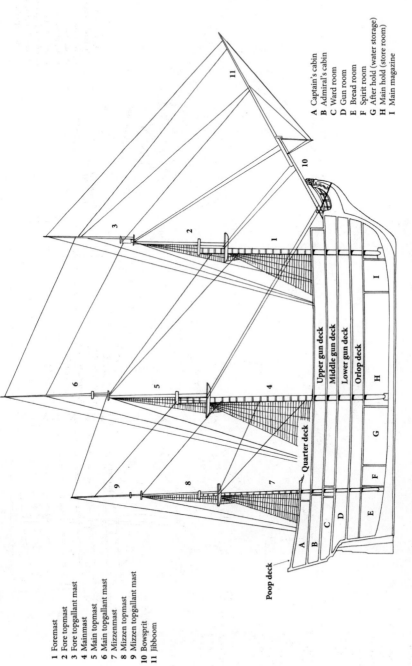

The standing rigging, masts and decks of a 100-gun ship of the line

1 Foremast
2 Fore topmast
3 Fore topgallant mast
4 Mainmast
5 Main topmast
6 Main topgallant mast
7 Mizzenmast
8 Mizzen topmast
9 Mizzen topgallant mast
10 Bowsprit
11 Jibboom

A Captain's cabin
B Admiral's cabin
C Ward room
D Gun room
E Bread room
F Spirit room
G After hold (water storage)
H Main hold (store room)
I Main magazine

Poop deck
Quarter deck
Upper gun deck
Middle gun deck
Lower gun deck
Orlop deck

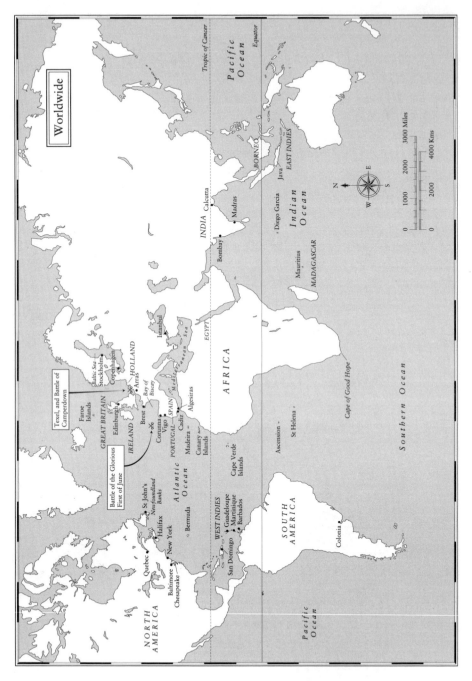

Major place-names worldwide

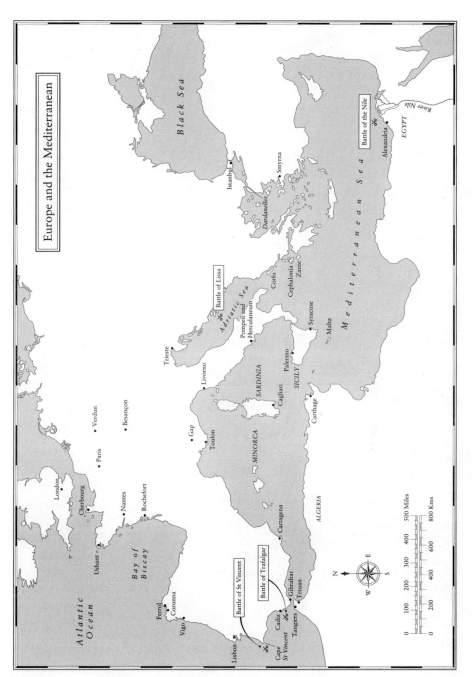

Europe and the Mediterranean

Major place-names of Europe and the Mediterranean

Major place-names of the British Isles

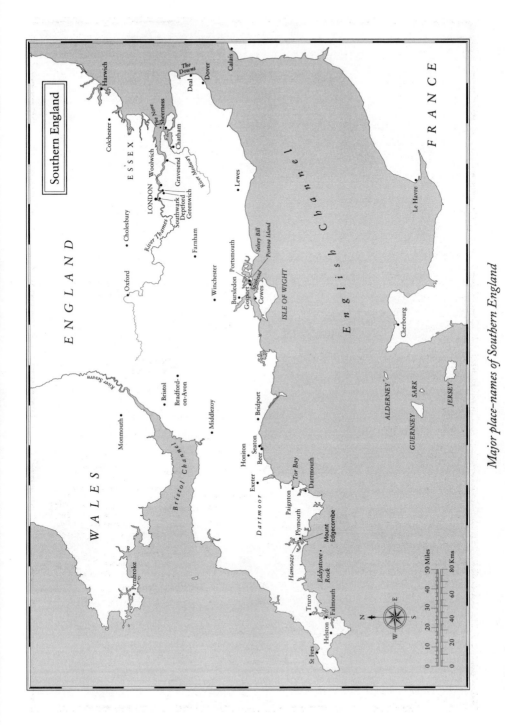

Major place-names of Southern England

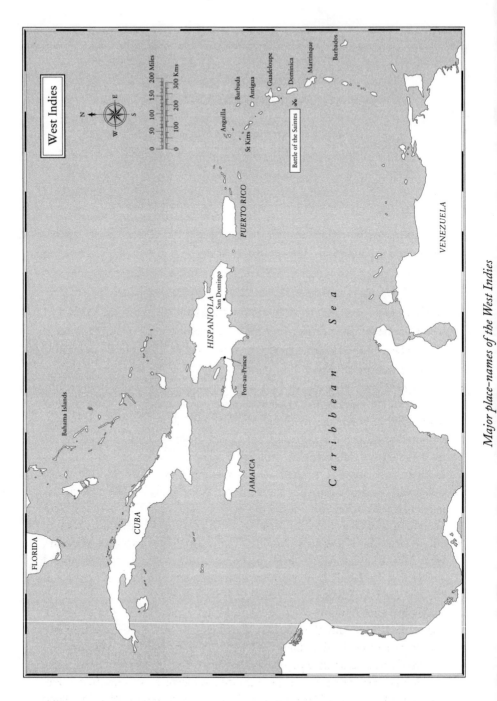

Major place-names of the West Indies

ACKNOWLEDGEMENTS

———•◆•———

It is a pleasure to acknowledge the help, enthusiasm and generosity of many people and organisations during the formation of *Jack Tar*, which was being researched and written during the publication of our previous book, *The War for All the Oceans*. Thanks are due to everyone who took the trouble to contact us about that book, some of whom provided information and leads that helped in the writing of this present book. Please keep that feedback coming! We can be contacted via the publisher, via our agent at AM Heath or by email from our website at www.adkinshistory.com.

For *Jack Tar*, we are especially grateful to all those people and organisations who gave unlimited access to their archives and publications, and permission to make use of the material in this book. We are particularly indebted to John and Francesca Upton, Peter Yule-Booth and Susan Lucas for so generously allowing us to see and make use of original manuscripts in their possession. The staff of many archives also gave us invaluable assistance, most notably at the Royal Naval Museum Library and Archives, particularly Matthew Sheldon, Heather Johnson, Paul Raven and Allison Wareham, as well as the Caird Library of the National Maritime Museum, where everyone is always so helpful, and at the Royal Marines Museum, where the archivist Matt Little spared no effort to ensure that we found everything we needed. As ever, we also received exemplary service from the National Archives at Kew and the British Library.

Many people in numerous other libraries and organisations also assisted in our research, especially the Local Studies Library of the Newcastle Libraries and Information Service, Diana Gregg at Portsmouth City Museum and Record Office, the South Tyneside Local Studies Library at South Shields, the London Library, Exeter University Library, the Devon and Exeter Institution, Bamstaple Library, the Newfoundland Historic Trust, and the Newfoundland

and Labrador Studies at the Memorial University of Newfoundland. Special mention must be made of Jill Hughes, Judith Prescott, Katie Forsey and Karen Lee of the St Thomas branch of the Devon Library and Information Services, as well as Lesley Salter and Hazel Skinner of Tiverton Library and Andrew Davey and Vera Wright of Exeter Central Library.

We are also very pleased to acknowledge the Special Collections of University of Miami Libraries for permission to use their Aaron Thomas journal, to Jean M. Murray for permission to use her Aaron Thomas journal, to Alistair Kennedy for permission to quote from his George Price letters, to Anne Yannoulis for permission to quote from the wonderful Major T. Marmaduke Wybourn letters and journals, to the Military History Society of Ireland for use of the Henry Walsh journal in the *Irish Sword*, and to the librarian of the Wellcome Library for the History and Understanding of Medicine for use of manuscripts. Philip Armitage of Brixham Heritage Museum very usefully alerted us to the existence of William Ffarington's logbook, and the staff of Tiverton Library tipped us off about a prisoner-of-war archive in their keeping, while the Tiverton War Memorial Trust gave permission to use that material. We are also grateful to Lieutenant Commander John Scivier of HMS *Victory* for allowing us to reproduce several photographs.

Various other people kindly shared their expertise or pointed us in the right direction, including David Clement of the South West Maritime History Society, Brian Stevens, curator of St Ives Museum, Ceri Boston of Oxford Archaeology, Steve Fuller of Devonport House De Vere Hotel, Alex Barter of Sotheby's, Tony Beales, Jerry Bryant of Old Fashioned Music, Alain Chappet, David Cordingly, Dr Mike Duffy of Exeter University, Dr Steve Fuller, Keith Gregson, Mick Davis and Patrick Marioné. Additional support was given by Kevin and Miriam Smith and Valerie and Richard Wheeler.

A special mention in dispatches was earned by Peter N. Lockyer who worked so hard in finding material and sources which had eluded us that we came to regard him as our Honorary Research Assistant. Extra grog for him.

We are grateful to Chris Mortimer of Blacksnow.co.uk for all the patient and expert internet/website/email support, which probably drove him mad at times, and to Sue and Tony Hall, Ray Hockin and John Barr for their practical help. We are also indebted to all the team at Little, Brown, including Richard Beswick and Zoë Gullen, as well as Merlin Cox for copy-editing, Celia Levett for proof-reading, indexer Sarah Ereira and John Gilkes for cartography. Our final and heartfelt thanks are due to Bill Hamilton at AM Heath, particularly for staying on board through some rather heavy weather.

AUTHORS' NOTE

———— •◆• ————

This is not a reference book, although all sources of quotations are provided for those engaged in family history, naval or other types of research, and who might wish to follow up a specific person, ship or incident. Instead, the purpose of the book is to give a taste of life on board the warships of Britain's navy at the turn of the eighteenth and nineteenth centuries, using eyewitness accounts from previously unpublished diaries, letters and other manuscripts, mixed with rarely seen accounts published in the nineteenth century, as well as a few familiar voices.

This was not a world of the proverbial 'rum, sodomy and the lash', but rather one of grog, women, occasional carnage, hopes, fears, dangers, hard work and boredom. The warships were not props in a costume drama, but working war machines, and they appear in scenes that do not always match our expectations. Frequently, the background cacophony of carpenters, blacksmiths and the other trades needed to keep the ship afloat and in fighting trim would drown out the sound of the wind in the rigging. Noisy animals kept for food were crammed into pens or roamed the decks, adding a farmyard flavour to the sea air, and on washing days lines were festooned with drying laundry. The seamen and marines were constantly at work, sailing, cleaning and repairing the ship, and shore leave was hardly ever permitted for fear of desertion.

The navy of this time has many names – *Royal Navy, British Navy, English Navy, King George's Navy, His Majesty's Navy,*

Nelson's Navy – but for the men, women and children in the war-ships it was, for a brief period of months or years, their home and close family.

INTRODUCTION

————•◆•————

SCUM OF THE EARTH

History, of all literary productions, is the most important, pleasing, and instructive, as it is the record of the manners, and customs of nations, with their religion and polity, and all their relative transactions. It also represents to us the actions of all those who have made themselves conspicuous on the theatre of the world . . . In short, everything calculated to interest us in life is contained in history.

George Watson, an able seaman from Newcastle, who wrote about his life in the Royal Navy[1]

Anyone making the mistake of referring to a sailor as being *on* a ship is often told that the term is *in* a ship, not *on* it – the same as saying *in* a house rather than *on* a house. Of all the military forces, the navy is the only one where large fighting machines are also the homes of their crews. During the Revolutionary and Napoleonic Wars, sailors of the Royal Navy were at sea for long periods, often several years at a time, and they were rarely allowed shore leave, not even for a single day, for fear of desertion. In 1811 James Wathen, who was about to sail as a passenger to India, was given a guided tour by boat among the warships anchored at Spithead:

'Each of those tremendous, though beautiful floating castles,' said my guide, – 'each of those first-rates, contain when at sea an active garrison of one thousand men, one hundred pieces of ordnance, with provisions and ammunition for six months; a burthen of between two and three thousand tons!' . . . Such are the effects of the skill and industry of man, excited by thirst of gain, the desire of protection, or ambition, and set in motion by the energies of a warlike and commercial nation.[2]

These warships were Britain's 'wooden walls' – meaning not the walls of a house, but the defensive walls of a town or city. The term originated in the fifth century BC, when the oracle at Delphi was consulted by the Athenians in the face of threats by the Persians. According to Herodotus, they were told to rely on their wooden walls. Most defensive walls in Greece were of stone, but eventually the prophecy was interpreted correctly – they should defend themselves with wooden warships. As a result, in 480 BC the Persians were defeated at the naval battle of Salamis.

In Nelson's navy, every warship was a community, comparable to a village or small town, and the history of naval warfare at this time is not just a record of battles and skirmishes, successes and failures, but the story of how the men and boys, as well as a handful of women and young children, lived from day to day. Many of these seamen were the nautical equivalent of those common soldiers described by a despairing Wellington as 'the scum of the earth'[3] in his dispatches from northern Spain in June 1813 after the Battle of Vittoria. Yet it was widely acknowledged that the navy, not the army, was Britain's foremost fighting force, and even Wellington relied on it to safeguard his supply lines. Marmaduke Wybourn, a marine officer, could not help being impressed by life on board one warship in 1801:

What an astonishing thing is a large ship, only conceive, we have 58 heavy guns, near 1100 men and baggage, camp equipment etc., for the whole regiment, with provisions and water for five months on board, and yet we ride securely in defiance of winds and waves over the most dreadful monsters of the deep and visit the remotest quarters of the globe? What man that is at all contemplatively inclined, can behold at night the Ship forcing her way through seas 'foaming with madness' in almost opposite directions to the winds, the changes and variety of colours, and the sparkling particles like fire, looking exactly as though we were sailing through a flaming phosphorus, without feeling sensations the most sublime and delightful?[4]

Nelson was born in 1758 – some two and a half centuries ago – and this book is about the everyday lives of the ordinary sailors and marines, as well as some of the officers, who served in the navy in Nelson's time – the navy that he joined as a captain's servant at the age of twelve in 1771 and the navy that he left behind after his death at the Battle of Trafalgar in 1805, up to the defeat of Napoleon in 1815. The story of these sailors and marines has a wide geographical sweep, in all seasons, right round the globe, at a time of social upheaval. In Britain the start of the Industrial Revolution was drastically changing the social, political and physical landscapes; in Europe and America the Age of Enlightenment was giving way to the Age of Revolution, as knowledge began to spread to the majority of the population, bringing disillusion with the established order. This historical setting encompasses the American War of Independence, the Revolutionary and Napoleonic Wars against France and much of Europe, and the 1812 war with America, but the famous battles were not won by Nelson and other officers single-handedly.

At the Battle of Trafalgar over 17,000 men were on board the twenty-seven British ships, and they faced a fleet that appeared overwhelmingly superior, with thirty-three ships carrying over 30,000 men, but they defeated them – not because of Nelson's leadership or innovative tactics, but through the skill, courage and tenacity of the sailors and marines that he had come to rely on and respect. It was men more than ships that made the difference between success and failure, but such superiority of skill did not appear overnight. The year after Nelson was born, the actor David Garrick wrote the celebrated song 'Heart of Oak', with its stirring refrain:

> Heart of oak are our ships,
> Heart of oak are our men;
> We always are ready, steady, boys, steady!
> We'll fight and we'll conquer, again and again.[5]

In the age of sail, the backbone of the navy was the ordinary seaman, the Jack Tar. The word 'tar' was in use by the 1600s, and became a familiar term for a sailor. It was particularly used by the officers to describe the men. At times it was prefixed by 'jolly' and it probably derived from 'tarpaulin', which was a sheet of canvas that was coated with tar to make waterproof cloth. Because it was black in colour, it is thought by some that the word 'tarpaulin' may have originated from 'tar' and 'pall', suggesting a similarity to a funeral pall. A sailor's waterproof hat was also called a tarpaulin, and the term 'tarpaulin' was applied to those few officers who rose from the ranks and so were not gentlemen.

The origin of 'Jack' – a familiar term for John – is disputed, but it was frequently a generic name given to anyone from the common mass of people. The term 'Jack the Tar' appears in an engraving of 1756 (the start of the Seven Years War with France) entitled 'The Invasion' by William Hogarth. The verses at the bottom of the engraving, also written by David Garrick, began:

> See John the Soldier, Jack the Tar,
> With Sword & Pistol arm'd for War,
> Should Monsir dare come here!!
> The Hungry Slaves have smelt our Food,
> They long to taste our Flesh and Blood,
> Old England's Beef and Beer![6]

In 1770 the playwright and essayist Francis Gentleman published a book of critical reviews, *The Dramatic Censor*, that he dedicated to David Garrick and in which one actor was described as 'stalking backward and forward, like a Jack-tar on the quarter-deck'.[7] 'Jack Tar' was applied to both American and British seamen, and one instance relating to the American War of Independence is a song that begins,

'Come brave honest Jack Tar, once more will you venture? Press war-
rants they are out: I would have you to enter.'[8] Known as 'Jack Tar',
this song was first published in 1776. The men would frequently call
themselves 'Jack' or 'Jack Tar',* while the officers also used the terms
'the Men' or 'the People'. The words 'sailor' and 'seamen' are now
interchangeable, but sailor once meant a person who managed the
sails.

The black substance known as tar was an intrinsic ingredient of life
at sea, since it was used for waterproofing and protection, and barrels
of tar were always stored on board. Up to the late eighteenth century,
a warship's outer hull was protected underwater from shipworm
attack by being coated with a mixture of tar and hair held in place by
thin sheets of planking. The gaps between planks (seams) of a ship
were also kept watertight by caulking, in which oakum (strands of old
rope mixed with tar) was forced into the cracks with iron tools, and
the seams were then sealed with tar. Tar was also used to try to prevent various ropes from rotting through the damaging effects of wind
and sea water – ropes were made from vegetable fibre, usually hemp
(wire ropes were then unknown). Tar therefore pervaded everything,
right down to the skin and clothing of the seamen, who would also
use tar to waterproof their hats and coats.

The Royal Navy obtained barrels of tar primarily from the Baltic,
with some from North America. It was manufactured by burning pine
resin in the vast forests of northern Europe, and was generally referred
to as Stockholm tar because Stockholm was the major exporting port.
The 9th Earl of Dundonald – the father of Thomas Cochrane, the
maverick naval officer – was a gifted scientist and in 1780 he developed
a new method of extracting tar from the coal that was mined on his
Culross Abbey estate. He could see that the tar would be beneficial in
ships and for coating iron to prevent rusting. While his discoveries
were brilliant, he was a disastrous businessman, and others successfully
adapted his work and made their fortune, especially the use of coal gas

---

* The jack was a small flag denoting the nationality of a ship that was flown from the
jack-staff at the ship's bow, with a different origin from the term 'Jack' that was applied
to seamen.

for lighting, which he thought was only a novelty. In fact, tar and coke became profitable by-products of producing gas from coal.

Tar can occur naturally as bitumen, and when his ship was patrolling the Ionian Islands in 1812, the seaman George Watson was allowed to land at Zakynthos, where, he said, 'there is a well, in the middle of a corn field, that produces tar, and all around the margin of it to some distance, is this bituminous substance, and by putting a ladle into this well . . . you may draw it up full, and it is so perfect in nature, it only requires boiling to be fit for use. I was at this place with some others, and got a barrel of its contents as a specimen.'⁹ These natural bitumen springs had been utilised for hundreds of years and were even mentioned by Herodotus. Another source occurs close to the River Severn in Coalbrookdale in Shropshire. It was known since at least the late seventeenth century and was believed to have medicinal properties. Dundonald became involved in the Coalbrookdale industries, including tar extraction, and in 1786 a further spring of bitumen was discovered when an underground canal was being dug. This 'tar tunnel' subsequently produced thousands of gallons of tar. The Admiralty and the shipbuilders, though, were reluctant to adopt Dundonald's tar for protecting hulls, and shortly afterwards coppering of ships became standard practice instead – covering the outer hull with thin copper sheets. This not only protected vessels from shipworm, but slowed down the encrustation of the hull and so made the vessels faster.

Within the close wooden walls of sailing warships, young boy volunteers, all kinds of civilian seamen from fishermen to smugglers, raw novices conscripted by the press-gang, and numerous foreign recruits were trained, disciplined and gradually absorbed into crews that formed the front line in the defence of Britain. Although from a seafaring island, these men in the Royal Navy were not always bred to the sea, nor were many of them willing volunteers, yet they lived, fought and sometimes died together as a real 'band of brothers'.

The marines are also part of this story. They were sea soldiers who served on board warships as sentries, forming a buffer between the officers and the seamen. In naval engagements, they provided small-arms fire with muskets, and they also took part in attacks on land, aided the press-gangs and frequently helped out on board. Since 1755 the marine regiments had been under the control of the government department known as the Admiralty, and in 1802 they became the Royal Marines. Two years later the Royal Marine Artillery was formed. Like army soldiers, the redcoats, the marines wore red tunics and were frequently called 'jollies' by the sailors. Naval officers wore a blue uniform, and although ordinary seamen did not have a uniform, blue was a preferred colour, and so they were nicknamed 'bluejackets', while soldiers and marines were 'lobsters'.

According to Daniel Goodall, who enlisted as a marine in 1805, there was a 'hereditary dislike popularly supposed to be entertained by the blue jackets for the "lobsters" – for Jack is declared on authority to "hate a marine as the Devil hates holy water"'.[10] While operating along the Adriatic coast in boats in 1812, the seaman George Watson said that they were accompanied by both marines and soldiers: 'You would have laughed to see the distinction [Lieutenant Augustus] Cannon, who always commanded the squadron, made when addressing them, and the marines, in discharging their muskets, as they generally fired alternately; he used to cry, "Well done, fire soldier!" then, "fire marine!" conformably to the idea which the Jack tars entertain of marines, viz. that they are, neither soldier nor sailor.'[11]

Captain Basil Hall gave a caricature picture of marines and seamen in order to highlight their differences:

The words Marine and Mariner differ by one small letter only; but no two races of men, I had well nigh said two animals, differ from one another more completely than the 'Jollies' and the 'Johnnies'* . . . Jack wears a blue jacket, and the Jolly wears a red one. Jack would sooner take a round dozen [lashes], than be seen with a pair of braces across his shoulders; while the marine, if deprived of his suspensors, would speedily be left sans culotte. A thorough-going, barrack-bred, regular-built marine, in a ship of which the sergeant-major truly loves his art, has, without any very exaggerated metaphor, been compared to a man who has swallowed a set of fire-irons; the tongs representing the legs, the poker the

* 'Johnny' was also used to describe the seamen as a body.

back-bone, and the shovel the neck and head. While, on the other hand, your sailor-man is to be likened to nothing, except one of those delicious figures in the fantoccini [puppet] show-boxes, where the legs, arms, and head, are flung loosely about to the right and left, no one bone apparently having the slightest organic connexion with any other; the whole being an affair of strings, and springs, and universal joints![12]

Now that air travel is the most common form of passenger transport overseas, it is too easy to overlook just how important shipping was in the past. Despite the Channel Tunnel, Britain is an island, and the vast majority of imports and exports still travel by sea. Without any trade by sea Britain might not starve immediately, but the problems of providing subsistence would prove immense. It was during the wars with France that Britain gained effective control of maritime global trade, after which navy and merchant ships became essential for the survival of the nation and the rise of the empire. Involvement with shipping spread far inland, and at the end of the war, one naval officer remarked that 'there are few families [in Britain] who either are not actually, or may not soon be, connected with the naval service'.[13] Anyone researching their family history in Britain today is therefore likely to find close connections with the sea, and most people have at least one Jack Tar in their ancestry.

A FEW FACTS AND FIGURES

I shall not use many nautical expressions, but when they occur, I will not divert you from the subject, by explanatory annotations, as, I think, terms used at sea, are so generally known, to you, and this commercial country at large, that it would only be a waste of time to illustrate them.

George Watson in the introduction to his memoirs,
published in 1827[1]

Although many people today are familiar with boats as a leisure pastime, very few are associated with the sea professionally, either directly or indirectly, and so Watson's words no longer hold true. Most people do not understand nautical terms, though they may use old naval expressions unwittingly in their everyday language (such as in 'the devil to pay!'*). The following paragraphs are therefore intended for those who are perhaps new to naval history or for those who want to be reminded of information that has slipped their grasp.

Nelson's navy was the Royal Navy, but was far more frequently referred to as the British Navy by officers and other writers of the time, and is still commonly referred to as such by historians today, especially when there is likely to be confusion with navies of other states that also had a 'royal navy'. It was occasionally described as the English Navy, just as the word England was used, even by Scotsmen,

---

* The seam at the very edge of the planking or close to the water-line was known as the devil, and caulking ('paying') these seams was very difficult, so the term came to be applied to a task that was unwelcome.

to describe Great Britain. Nelson in his correspondence calls the service 'the Navy', 'His Majesty's Navy' or 'His Majesty's Royal Navy' – his Majesty being King George III, who ruled from 1760 to 1820, although owing to severe illness his son the Prince of Wales (the future George IV) became Prince Regent in 1811.

Names of ships can be even more confusing, because some British ships had French-sounding names, such as the *Guerriere*, and some French ships had English-sounding names, like the *Berwick*. This arose when the original names of captured ships were retained. The *Guerriere* was a French frigate (*La Guerrière*) that was captured by the *Blanche* frigate in a fierce battle off the Faroe Islands in 1806 and was then incorporated into the Royal Navy with the same name, though French accents were usually dropped. *Blanche* was the name given to a frigate that was built in 1786 at Bursledon and wrecked through pilot error off Holland thirteen years later. The name *Blanche* was then given to another frigate that was being built at Deptford, but that vessel was captured in July 1805. A few months earlier the Spanish *Amfitrite* was captured off Cadiz and came into service with the Royal Navy in 1806. There was already an *Amphitrite* in the Royal Navy, and so the Spanish ship was renamed *Blanche* – it was this ship that captured the *Guerriere*. The *Blanche* was wrecked off Ushant eight months later, and the *Guerriere* was destroyed by the American frigate *Constitution* in 1812. The seamen also gave nicknames to their ships, especially when the official names were difficult to pronounce, such as Billy Ruffian for the *Bellerophon*. The men were often referred to collectively by their ship's name, such as 'the Shannons'.

Sailing warships depended on wind, which was harnessed by sails, for their power, and they were constrained by wind direction in their manoeuvrability. The warships were square-rigged, which meant that the sails in their neutral position hung from the three masts (vertical poles) across ('square to') the breadth of the vessel (whereas fore-and-aft vessels had the sails running down the length of the vessel). The sails themselves were not square, but rectangular or tapering, and they were made by sailmakers from lengths of canvas cloth. The canvas was manufactured from flax that was imported largely from the Baltic.

The three masts were the foremast (at the forecastle), mainmast (the largest mast, near the centre) and mizzenmast (on the quarter-deck). The bowsprit was a fourth mast that extended at an angle from the bow of the ship (the front or 'fore' end). Masts of warships were not a single piece of wood but comprised several sections. The lower mast was made up of pieces of timber fitted together. On top of the lower mast was a topmast, made from a single pole (tree trunk), which was in turn surmounted by a topgallant mast, also a single pole. In bad weather the topgallant mast and the topmast could be lowered – struck – to the deck to reduce the weight and exposure to the wind. The sails were supported by the yards, which were poles that were at right-angles to the masts and could be hoisted up and down. The yards were named according to their mast and their position on the mast, such as the fore topgallant yard right at the top of the foremast. The end of the yard was the yardarm, and the fore-yardarm was all too familiar as the place from which condemned men were hanged.

The standing rigging comprised shrouds and stays, which were ropes that were permanently in place to support the masts, yards and bowsprit. The shrouds prevented the masts moving sideways, and stays prevented forward and backward movement. The ropes known as running rigging were ones that passed through pulley blocks, and they were used to hoist and lower the yards and control the sails. A single ship of the line had about 40 miles of rope of different sizes, for rigging, anchors and guns, as well as about one thousand pulley blocks, and the sails covered over an acre in area.

In a battle the tactics of a sailing ship were dictated by weather conditions, even down to which side of an enemy vessel was attacked. Being downwind from an enemy was regarded as a defensive position, because a ship only had to hoist more sails to escape, while being upwind was an attacking position. Warships in Nelson's time were essentially floating platforms from which to fire cannons,* which were concentrated down each long side ('broad side'), as there was no

---

* The plural of 'cannon' is 'cannons' or 'cannon' – we use cannons to avoid confusion.

room to fire more than a few cannons from the bow or stern (the rear or 'after' part of the ship). The term 'larboard' for the left-hand side of the ship when looking from the stern towards the bow came to be replaced by 'port', because larboard was too easily confused with starboard, the term for the right-hand side of the ship. The traditional strategy of fighting at sea was for each opposing side to form their warships into a line, bow to stern, parallel with their opponent's line of battle. The two lines of ships would then pound each other at close range until individual ships surrendered or retreated, and the simultaneous firing of the guns along one side was called a broadside. The biggest ships were known as 'ships of the line' – so called because these were the battleships, carrying at least sixty-four guns (cannons), that traditionally formed the line of battle. The term 'battleship' is an abbreviation of 'line of battle ship'.

Ships of the line were rated according to the number of guns and therefore the number of gun decks – decks that were strong enough to support the weight of the guns. First rates (such as the *Victory*) had one hundred guns or more and three gun decks ('three-deckers') – three full decks that carried guns. These ships were usually flagships, as they were large enough to accommodate an admiral, who was a flag officer. Second rates also had three gun decks and ninety to ninety-eight guns. Third rates were the most common and had two gun decks ('two-deckers') and sixty-four to eighty-four guns. Fourth rates also had two gun decks, and fifty to sixty guns, but were not common. The heaviest guns were carried on the lower gun deck to prevent the ship being top-heavy. Frigates had one gun deck and were either fifth rates with thirty to forty-four guns or sixth rates with twenty to twenty-eight guns.

Other Royal Navy vessels such as brigs, sloops, gunboats and bomb vessels were not rated, and technically they were not ships, as that term tended to be restricted to vessels that were square-rigged and had a bowsprit and three masts. A brig, for example, was a two-masted vessel that usually had fourteen to eighteen guns and was mainly used for running errands. These unrated vessels were too small to have a full captain, but instead had a commander as a senior officer, with the courtesy title of 'captain'. The size of a naval vessel is often expressed by the number of guns in brackets after the name, such as *Raisonnable* (64), Nelson's first ship in 1771, and *Victory* (100), the ship in which he died at the Battle of Trafalgar.

Apart from the gun decks, warships also had armed quarterdecks and forecastles. The quarterdeck was a part-deck that ran from the mainmast to the stern and was the place from where officers controlled the ship, similar to the 'bridge' of a modern ship. Ships of the line also had a poop, the highest deck of the ship, which was above the quarterdeck and covered about half its length. The forecastle (or fo'c'sle) was at the same level as the quarterdeck, but was at the bow. The gap between the forecastle and the quarterdeck was the waist. The next deck down was the main deck, or upper gun deck, which ran the entire length of the ship. This was also called the weather deck, as it was open to the weather in the centre, at the waist. In a three-decker ship there was a main deck, middle deck and lower deck, which were all gun decks, though at times the term gun deck is used just to refer to the lower deck.

Access between decks was up and down ladders, which were difficult for those new to sea life, as Midshipman William Dillon admitted: 'I found the ladders communicating from one deck to the other rather awkward. Not being used to going down them, my feet often slipped, and my back, coming in contact with the steps, caused considerable pain.'[2] In bad weather gunports on the lower gun deck were closed to prevent the ship being swamped. The men ate and slept on the middle and lower decks, but the height of decks was dictated by the working space needed for the guns, not the comfort of the men. The headroom below decks was dependent on the design of the ship and on the need to balance the weight of the cannons on upper decks against the stores and ballast at the bottom of the ship for stability and good sailing qualities. Generally, the smaller the ship, the lower the headroom below decks. When the length of a ship is given, this refers to the gun deck. The *Victory* is 186 feet long and nearly 52 feet wide, but has an overall external length of 227 feet 6 inches.

Decks at or below the water-line did not carry guns, and had even less headroom. Below the lower deck (and below the water-line) of ships of the line was the orlop* deck, used for stores and the quarters of various warrant officers. The midshipmen had their quarters in the part of the orlop deck known as the cockpit, which in time of battle was taken over by the surgeon. Below the orlop deck was the hold, which was divided into compartments by partitions known as bulkheads. The hold of the *Victory* measured 150 feet long, 50 feet wide and 21 feet high. Compartments of the hold contained the ship's stores and gunpowder magazines. At the very bottom of the hold was ballast of shingle and iron pigs, above which were stored hundreds of wooden casks containing water, beer, meat and other provisions.

Ships also carried small boats of various kinds, such as jolly boats, cutters, yawls and barges, which were critical for the day-to-day operations. These were not lifeboats but were used for essential tasks, such as conveying officers and men from ship to shore or to other ships, transporting stores and water, moving the ship when in a confined space or with no wind, and in amphibious attacks. They were housed side-by-side on beams across the open space between the quarterdeck and forecastle – the waist – or were hung from davits on either side of the stern. They were lowered and hoisted back up with lifting tackle, and were equipped with sails and oars (sweeps) for rowing. They could also be towed behind the ship when not in use, something that was usually done in battles to prevent them being smashed, with splinters flying about the decks.

There are no precise figures for the number of ships in the service of the Royal Navy at any one time, but in 1776, not long after Nelson joined, there were around 373 ships, of which 58 were ships of the line and 198 were frigates. Many were laid up in ordinary – kept in reserve in rivers and harbours, without guns, stores and upper masts, without a full crew and not ready to sail. In 1793 there were 411 ships, of which 169 were laid up or being repaired, in 1804 there were 726

---

* 'Orlop' is from an Old German word meaning 'the deck above the hold', but was once incorrectly thought to derive from 'overlap'.

ships, including 216 ships of the line and 204 frigates, and in 1811 there were 1019 ships.

Sizeable crews were needed to man the guns and control the sails, though many ships did not have their full entitlement because of difficulties in finding enough men. First-rate ships were allowed a crew of 850 or more, second-rates 750 to 850 men, third-rates 500 to 720, fourth-rates 350 to 420, fifth-rates 215 to 295, and sixth-rates 120 to 195. No exact figures are available for the numbers of men who were serving at any one time in the Royal Navy, but in 1771 there were around 26,000 men in total, including marines, rising to about 95,000 ten years later. By 1786, after the ending of the American War of Independence, the numbers reduced to about 13,500, but after war broke out with France in 1793, the figure expanded to over 81,000. By 1801 there were more than 118,000 men. During the Peace of Amiens the numbers dropped to below 50,000, but grew to over 109,000 by 1805 and over 130,000 men by 1813. At the end of the war this diminished to fewer than 80,000 men.

In 1776 the complement of marines increased to just over 10,000, and rose to 25,000 by 1783, but with the conclusion of the American War of Independence the number of marines was slashed to fewer than 4500. After war began with France in 1793, the numbers increased to nearly 20,000, but they were reduced in the short-lived peace in 1803 to just over 12,000. By 1810 there were over 30,000 marines.

Individual fleets were given geographical names, according to their area of operation, the main one being the Channel fleet. This patrolled the English Channel from Selsey Bill in Sussex to as far south as Ferrol in Spain. Fleets could be divided into several squadrons that operated within a smaller area, while some squadrons were independent. The North Sea fleet was responsible for the eastern stretch of the English Channel as well as the North Sea up to Shetland, while other fleets and squadrons operated in the Baltic, Mediterranean, North America, West Indies, East Indies and Cape of Good Hope. There were also bases abroad, though which of these were occupied changed according to the territory that was held by the British and who was an ally of Britain at the time. 'The Fleet' could also refer to the Royal Navy as a whole, which was formerly divided into three squadrons (the red, white and blue), and each squadron was in turn divided into the van, middle and rear divisions. These divisions were commanded (in descending order of rank) by admirals, vice-admirals and rear-admirals. Admirals outranked vice-admirals, who in turn outranked rear-admirals, but the term 'admiral' was loosely used to refer to all three ranks. This particular squadron structure with the three colours had long been superseded, but the different ranks of admiral survived. At Trafalgar, Nelson was a vice-admiral of the white.

Sailors had various approximate measurements for distances that are no longer widely used: a pistol shot was about 25 yards, a musket shot approximately 200 yards and a gun (or cannon) shot about 1000 yards. A cable was 200 yards, a fathom was 6 feet, and a league was 6116 yards – equivalent to 3 nautical miles. A nautical mile was equivalent to 6116 feet, but is now a distance of 6080 feet. A knot was regarded as the speed of 1 nautical mile per hour, or just the distance of 1 nautical mile – speeds were still being recorded in knots per hour at this time and not simply in knots as used today. For those better acquainted with metric than with the imperial measurements of the time, the following may be useful:

12 inches (in.) = 1 foot (ft)
3 feet = 1 yard (yd)
6 feet = 1 fathom
22 yards = 1 chain
10 chains = 1 furlong
1760 yards = 1 mile
8 furlongs = 1 mile
6116 feet = 1 nautical mile (but now 6080 feet)
2 pints = 1 quart
4 quarts = 1 gallon
36 gallons = 1 barrel
54 gallons = 1 hogshead
16 ounces (oz) = 1 pound
14 pounds (lb) = 1 stone
8 stone = 1 hundredweight (cwt)

20 hundredweight = 1 ton
12 pence (12d) = 1 shilling (1s)
20 shillings = £1 (one pound)
£1 1s = 1 guinea

Some imperial–metric conversions are:
1 inch = 2.54 centimetres
1 foot = 0.30 metres
1 yard = 0.91 metres
1 mile = 1.609 kilometres
1 pint = 0.568 litres
1 gallon = 4.54 litres

The spelling in eyewitness accounts has been largely corrected and the punctuation and style modernised where needed, particularly the tendency to use dashes instead of full stops, ampersands (&) instead of 'and', and upper-case letters for the start of many words. Ship names have been italicised. Most quotations have only been altered slightly, if at all, and the words and meaning have not been changed. Some have been made more readable because lack of education did not necessarily imply lack of intelligence, and so leaving the original spelling serves no useful purpose. For example, James Bodie was barely literate and wrote in 1807 that 'it was aGreed among the offsers to Bord hir', which should read 'it was agreed among the officers to board her',[3] while two years earlier George Price wrote that 'I think it very hard that I Cannot Git no Letter from You and You Know I have no body Ells to Right Too', which should read 'I think it very hard that I cannot get no letter from you and you know that I have nobody else to write to'.[4]

Key Events

This list of dates is primarily a reminder of naval or navy-related events and social context from the time that Nelson joined the Royal Navy to the final defeat and exile of Napoleon.

1758
Nelson was born at Burnham Thorpe, Norfolk (29 September)

1760
George III became king (October)

1771
Spain ceded the Falkland Islands to Britain (January)
Nelson joined the Royal Navy as midshipman on board the
    Raisonnable (March)
The engineer Richard Trevithick was born (April)

1772
British case law established that a slave landing in England was a free
    person
Warren Hastings was appointed Governor of Bengal (April)
The poet Samuel Taylor Coleridge was born (October)

1773
The Boston Tea Party, when American colonists protested against
    the unjust taxation of tea imports (December)

1774
Accession of Louis XVI as king of France (May)
First Continental congress of the thirteen British colonies in America
    (September)

1775
War of American Independence began with the British defeat at
    Lexington (April)

1776
The painter John Constable was born (June)
American Declaration of Independence (July)

1777

War in America continued with successes on both sides. The Americans were defeated at Germantown in October and that same month the British were defeated at Saratoga

1778

The French became allies of America, and Britain declared war on France (February)

Ex-prime minister William Pitt (the elder), Earl of Chatham, died (May)

The engineer Humphrey Davy was born (December)

1779

Captain Cook was killed in Hawaii (February)

Spain declared war on Britain and laid siege to Gibraltar (June)

The first iron bridge, across the River Severn at Coalbrookdale, was completed

1780

Admiral Rodney defeated the Spanish at Cape St Vincent (the Moonlight Battle) and temporarily relieved Gibraltar (January)

First use of steel pens in England, but quills remained the standard writing implement

Britain declared war on the Netherlands (December)

1781

The engineer George Stephenson was born (June)

Spain captured Pensacola, Florida, from the British (July)

Following other British successes during the war in India, the Dutch settlement at Negapatam, Madras, was captured (November)

1782

The British captured Trincomalee, Ceylon, from the Dutch (January)

Admiral Rodney defeated the French at the Battle of the Saintes in the West Indies (April)

Spain completed the annexation of Florida (June)

The Spanish attack on Gibraltar ended in disaster and the Rock remained British (September)

Admiral Howe relieved the siege of Gibraltar (October)

1783

The Montgolfier brothers experimented with hot air balloons in France (June)

Simon Bolivar was born (July)

Peace of Versailles between Britain, France, Spain and America. Britain, France and Spain each recovered some of the territories they had lost during the war, and Britain recognised American independence (September)

The first manned flight of a hot-air balloon (November)

The first successful trial of a steam-powered paddle boat, built in France by the Marquis Jouffroy d'Abbans

1784

The British signed a peace treaty with Tippoo of Mysore (March)

Peace treaty between Britain and Holland (May)

The East India Company was placed under a government board of control to curb territorial expansion in India (August)

Dr Samuel Johnson died (December)

1785

A rotary-action steam engine, built by Boulton and Watt, was installed in a cotton-spinning factory at Papplewick, Nottinghamshire

Alliance between France and Holland (November)

1786

The explorer John Franklin was born (April)

Frederick the Great died (August)

Commercial treaty between Britain and France (September)

1787

The first convoy of convicts ('The First Fleet') sailed from Britain to begin the European colonisation of Australia (May)

Political unrest in France

1788

John Walter founded *The Times* newspaper (January)

The poet Lord Byron was born (January)

Alliance between Britain and Holland (April)

The foundation of a British settlement in Sierra Leone, as a sanctuary for slaves (August)

The painter Thomas Gainsborough died (August)

1789

George Washington became first president of the USA (April)

The storming of the Bastille in Paris (July)

The French Revolution began

J.L.M. Daguerre, inventor of the first practical photographs (daguerreotypes), was born (November)

1790

The revolution in France gathered strength, dividing political opinion in Britain

Benjamin Franklin died (April)

British alliance with the Mahrattas in India (June)

1791

Fearing a war with Russia, Britain began to increase the Royal Navy (March)

Samuel Morse, inventor of the Morse Code, was born (April)

The National Assembly in France made the country a constitutional monarchy (September)

1792

The architect Robert Adam died (March)

France began the Revolutionary Wars by declaring war against Austria (April)

France declared war on Prussia and Sardinia (July)

USA introduced its own coinage based on the dollar (October)

The trial of Louis XVI began (December)

1793

Execution of Louis XVI and Marie Antoinette (January)

France declared war on Britain and Holland (February)

France declared war on Spain (March)

Admiral Hood occupied the port of Toulon (August)

The British were driven out of Toulon by a young French officer, Napoleon Bonaparte (December)

The invention by Eli Whitney of the cotton gin for processing raw cotton led to a rapid growth of cotton exports from America

1794

The British defeated the French at the Battle of 'Glorious First of June' off Ushant (June)

Slavery was abolished in the colonies of France

1795

The Batavian Republic was established in Holland (March)

Spain signed a peace treaty with France (July)

The poet John Keats was born (October)

1796

Spain declared war on Britain (October)

The Royal Navy withdrew from the Mediterranean (November)

1797

The British defeated the Spanish at the Battle of St Vincent (14 February)

Mutinies aboard British warships at Spithead and the Nore (May–June)

Failed attack on Santa Cruz by Nelson in which he lost his right arm (July)
The British defeated the Dutch at the Battle of Camperdown (October)

1798
Napoleon's army landed in Egypt (July)
The French fleet was destroyed by Nelson at the Battle of the Nile (1 August)
Malthus published *Essay on the Principle of Population* – the start of his campaign to demonstrate that overpopulation inevitably leads to war, famine and epidemics

1799
Napoleon was defeated at Acre in Syria (May)
Napoleon escaped from Egypt and returned to France (October)
Napoleon and his allies seized control of France (November)
George Washington died (December)

1800
Britain captured Malta from France (September)
Spain sold Louisiana to France (October)

1801
The first Battle of Copenhagen (2 April)
Peace treaty (of Amiens) between France and Britain (October)
Robert Fulton, working in France, constructed the first practical submarine

1802
The Peace of Amiens was ratified between France and Britain (March)
Napoleon became First Consul of France for life (August)

1803
The hot press began (March)
USA bought Louisiana and New Orleans from France (April)
Start of the Napoleonic Wars between Britain and France (May)

1804

Diamond Rock was captured from the French (January)
Napoleon declared himself Emperor of the French (May)
Spain declared war on Britain (December)
Napoleon was crowned Napoleon I (December)
The future Victorian prime minister Disraeli was born (December)

1805

Diamond Rock was retaken by the French (June)
Battle of Trafalgar (21 October), when the French and Spanish were
    defeated by the British, and Nelson was killed
Strachan's action when he captured several French warships that had
    retreated from Trafalgar (November)
Napoleon defeated the combined Russian and Austrian armies at
    Austerlitz, leading to peace between Austria and France
    (December)

1806

The Dutch colony of Cape of Good Hope was captured by the
    British (January)
Funeral of Nelson (9 January)
Death of Prime Minister William Pitt (the Younger) (January)
The British defeated the French at the Battle of San Domingo (in
    San Domingo Bay) (February)
The engineer Isambard Kingdom Brunel was born (April)
Expedition to South America (from June)

1807

The unsuccessful Dardanelles expedition (February)
The South America expedition failed (July)
The British slave trade was abolished (March)
USS *Chesapeake* was attacked by HMS *Leopard* (June)
Giuseppe Garibaldi was born (July)
Bombardment of Copenhagen (August–September)

1808

USA prohibited the import of slaves from Africa (January)
The Spanish began to revolt against the French (May)
Napoleon abolished the Inquisition in Spain and Italy

1809

Retreat of the British army to Vigo and Corunna and evacuation by sea (January)
Land battle of Corunna in which Sir John Moore was killed (January)
Charles Darwin was born (February)
Attack on the French warships in Basque Roads (April)
Unsuccessful Walcheren expedition (July–December)
The future Victorian prime minister Gladstone was born (December)
Pall Mall in London was illuminated by gas street lights

1810

Guadeloupe was captured by the British from the French (February)
British captured Amboyna in the Molucca Islands (February)
British captured Mauritius (Île de France) (December)
Sweden declared war on Britain (end of year)
Severe winter in Europe (1810–11)

1811

George III was declared insane and the Prince of Wales became Prince Regent (February)
Battle of Lissa (March)
USS *President* attacked HMS *Little Belt* (May)
Java was taken by the British from the Dutch (August–September)

1812

Charles Dickens was born (February)
United States declared war on Britain (June, so-called '1812 war')
USS *Constitution* defeated HMS *Guerriere* (August)
USS *United States* defeated HMS *Macedonian* (October)
USS *Constitution* defeated HMS *Java* (December)

1813
USS *Hornet* defeated HMS *Peacock* (February)
David Livingstone was born (March)
Richard Wagner was born (May)
HMS *Shannon* defeated USS *Chesapeake* off Boston (June)
Giuseppe Verdi was born (October)
The first smooth-wheeled steam train was used to pull coal trucks at
   Wylam colliery, Northumberland

1814
Napoleon abdicated and went into exile on Elba (April)
USS *Wasp* defeated HMS *Reindeer* (June)
Battle of Bladensburg (August)
Washington was attacked and burned by the British (August)
The British unsuccessfully attacked Baltimore (September)
The failed British attack on Fort Bowyer at Mobile Point
   (September)
A peace treaty was signed at Ghent between Britain and America (24
   December)
British attack on New Orleans (December–January)

1815
Battle of New Orleans (January)
Emma Hamilton died (January)
The Treaty of Ghent was signed in America (February)
Napoleon escaped from Elba (February)
Napoleon landed in France (March)
Battle of Waterloo (18 June)

For more background to this book, please visit our website at
www.adkinshistory.com

ONE

— ◆ — ◆ ◆ — —

LEARNING THE ROPES

> He was also as much a sailor, as an hero; he knew every rope
> in the ship as well as a forecastle man, both how to put it up,
> and how to take it down.
>
> Able Seaman George Watson praising an officer in HMS *Eagle*[1]

Jack Tar, as a contemporary song had it, 'dances and sings, and is
always content, in his vows to his lass he'll ne'er fail her . . . Long-side
of an enemy, boldly and brave, he'll with broadside and broadside
regale her, yet he'll sigh to the soul o'er that enemy's grave, so noble's
the mind of a sailor.'[2] Songs about naval seamen as well as characters
portraying them were common in plays and musical performances in
Nelson's time, since they were regarded as heroes who kept the enemy
from the shores of Britain. The smart appearance and noble sentiments of these stage sailors doubtless inspired many with patriotic
fervour and a desire to volunteer for the navy and share their glory,
but the reality was quite different. The fourteen-year-old Scottish boy
Daniel Goodall, when volunteering for the Royal Navy at Greenock,
was appalled by the sight of his fellow recruits who were waiting to be
assigned to a ship:

> A more ruffianly, villainous-looking set of scamps I have rarely had the
> ill-fortune to fall amongst. True, they were seen to the very worst advan-
> tage, for they were dirty, ragged, and reckless. Many bore marks
> of violence received in resistance to the press-gang, and the moody

sullenness stamped on the faces of most of those victims of Government urgency was in the last degree forbidding. Traces of deep debauchery were visible on the faces of the majority, and altogether the picture was such that I had a strong feeling of having made a very serious mistake in the choice of a vocation. This impression did not, however, last long, and a more careful survey of my companions showed me that there were some honest men enough amongst them, and led me to the inference that the greater part of the physical material I saw before me would improve by time and favourable circumstances.[3]

The navy was always short of seamen and took whatever men were available, leaving the officers to make the best of it, as Captain Rotheram complained in one of his 'growls':* 'When arranging your Ship's Company which is just put on board of you by different draughts from all parts, Liverpool, Bristol, Hull, Leith, Dublin, Waterford, Cork and Ballyhack, discovering your First Lieutenant to be a lubber, your Boatswain a drunkard, your Purser an idiot and your Clerk a fool.'[4]

Not just the captain, but all the officers of a ship were periodically faced with sorting out a group of fresh recruits sent on board to man a newly commissioned ship, or to replace those who had died, been taken to hospital, discharged or deserted. These new men always ranged in skill from experienced seamen to absolute novices. They had to be given jobs that made best use of their abilities, or, in some cases, jobs where they would do least damage until, quite literally, they 'learned the ropes' – and became familiar with all the other working parts of a sailing warship. As Captain James Scott commented, 'a seaman cannot, like a recruit [into the army], be formed in six months; it requires more than that number of years to form a tolerably good sailor. It is a profession embracing such a variety of

---

* Edward Rotheram, who was captain of Vice-Admiral Collingwood's flagship the *Royal Sovereign* at Trafalgar, had a wry sense of humour. He filled pages of his notebook with jottings of various kinds, including the everyday problems of life at sea from the captain's point of view. Under the heading 'The Growls of a Naval Life' were sixty-four pithy grumbles, and this was number six.

incidental and novel circumstances, that unexpected knowledge may at all times be drawn from events by the oldest and most experienced seamen.'[5]

Most new hands found it quite a shock joining a warship – this was a strange and foreign place, completely beyond their previous experience. Well into the nineteenth century, when the spreading network of railways in Britain made travel easier, the majority of people seldom strayed beyond the bounds of their county, but spent their lives within a few miles of where they were born. Even those relatively close to the coast were unlikely to set foot in a ship unless they were connected to some seafaring trade. The Scottish officer Basil Hall, who began his life in the navy in 1802 as a midshipman in HMS *Leander*, summed up the experiences of many: 'In most other professions, the transition from the old to the new mode of life is more or less gradual, but in that of the sea, it is so totally abrupt, and without intervening preparation, that a boy must be either very much of a philosopher or very much of a goose, not to feel, at first, well-nigh overwhelmed with the change of circumstances.'[6]

This was certainly the experience of Henry Walsh, who was from an Irish farming family: 'I then being an entire stranger to the sea and unaccustomed to the ways of a seafaring life, you may judge how strange their manners and customs appeared to me'.[7] Walsh never wrote home to his parents because, he explained, 'I did not wish to write to them or let them know where I was least [in case] it augment their sorrow in knowing that I was in a man of war, as country people generally is unacquainted with the sea, and I have often heard say when I was at home that they would as soon see the death of a child than know of him going to sea.'[8] Indeed, when Aaron Thomas was staying at Wheatley near Oxford at the end of 1792, before he joined the navy, he found that sailors were regarded with suspicion, with one publican declaring that 'It is a foolish opinion we have got, but none of us country people feel a partiality for them.'[9]

The crew of a warship was very like a community in a town or village, which at that time would have been populated by all kinds of craftsmen – little work was mechanised, and much depended upon the skill of various trades. A warship was similarly filled with men from diverse backgrounds. Some time between 1805 and 1809, Captain Rotheram compiled a unique and detailed survey of his crew* on board the *Bellerophon* warship, of which he was in charge for two and a half years after the Battle of Trafalgar. Nearly four hundred men were in his survey, and Rotheram recorded their former occupations, which included shoemakers, hatters, barbers, watchmakers, snuff-makers, farmers, fishermen, glaziers, glassblowers, papermakers, wheelwrights and different types of merchant seaman. Some of these men were employed in the same trade on board the *Bellerophon*, but most had little use for their previous skills – though from time to time men such as shoemakers would have been useful to their messmates.

For most men and boys, the first navy vessel they boarded was a receiving ship, which usually acted as a clearing house for both willing recruits and pressed men. From here they were distributed to warships needing seamen, where they were sorted out by one of the officers – usually the first lieutenant. Once on board their allotted ship, they were recorded in pre-printed ledger books, known as muster books, which gave a list of the ship's company. These muster books, periodically submitted to the Navy Board (part of the Admiralty), were divided into several columns for entering the man's allotted number, the date of recruitment (pressed or volunteer), age when joining the ship, place and country of birth, name, and when discharged and why – D meant discharged, DD discharged dead and R run, meaning deserted. Further columns related to pay and provisions.

Detailed descriptions of each man were also compiled by the captains, but these books did not have to be submitted and so most have been lost. The seaman Robert Mercer Wilson observed the process:

---

* David Cordingly has analysed the survey in detail and suggests (2003, p. 209) that it may have been a deliberate scientific survey for his brother John, who was Professor of Natural Philosophy at St Andrews University.

On your first appearance on board you are summoned before the First Lieutenant, who interrogates you concerning your profession, your abilities as a seaman, place of nativity, and dwelling; name and age, length of time you may have been at sea, whether in ships-of-war or merchantmen, to which questions you are looked to for prompt answers. You are then rated on the ship's books according to your abilities, as the First Lieutenant may think fit – at the same time without prejudice or favour being shewn to anyone. Should it so happen that you are found not competent to the rating you had at first, you are disrated. But previous to being entered on the ship's books, you are examined by the surgeon to see if you are a fit man for His Majesty's Service . . . Your description is then stated down by the Captain's clerk, with the addition of your parents', relations', or friends' dwelling; in short, all your connections, in case of your desertion.[10]

This was an era before photography, and the physical traits of a person had to be written down. Only the officers could afford to have their portraits painted, often as miniatures for keepsakes to leave with their wives. Consequently, representations of these men survive at various stages of their career, and there were even busts and occasional commemorative statues. Some black-and-white photographs were taken of those officers who survived into the later nineteenth century, but these elderly men do not illustrate the character of Nelson's navy. Officers were also represented in paintings of battles, and it is in these scenes that ordinary seamen might be portrayed as well, but mostly not as likenesses of actual seamen. A few illustrations show real seamen, such as sketches in personal diaries and the portraits of the mutineers from the *Temeraire* that accompanied an account of their trial in 1802. Other illustrations show the seamen when much older, such as one of John Nicol at the age of sixty-seven.

Much more common are written descriptions of seamen, marines and officers, and these survive in memoirs, journals and letters, along with comments on character traits. An unflattering portrayal of the first lieutenant and the boatswain of the *Impetueux* was left by Private William Wheeler when he was waiting for the Walcheren expedition to set sail in July 1809: 'The first Lieutenant who goes by the name of "Ugly Betty" is a tall thin meagre ugly looking fellow, and what is worse than all, his mind is as evil as his person is disagreeable . . . The Boatswain if not a twin brother of Ugly Betty, seems to be possessed with the same evil genius."[11] A few days later, Ugly Betty broke both his legs, much to the joy of everyone on board. The first lieutenant's real name was John Jones, and the boatswain was William Hewitt.

James Anthony Gardner, from Waterford in Ireland, jotted down some lively character sketches of each of the officers he served with at various times, and those on board HMS *Queen* included: 'LOVE CONSTABLE, 1st Lieutenant. Dead. A commander; an excellent sailor and an indefatigable first lieutenant. The devil on board, but an angel on shore . . . GEO. MILNER, Midshipman. Dead. No man's enemy but his own . . . JOHN A. HODGSKIN, Midshipman. Dead. A lieutenant; called "Pig Hog" and "Hog's-flesh".'[12] The chaplain Edward Mangin, new to the navy in 1812, also noted many details that give valuable insights into the appearance and character of the people. Of the crew on board the *Gloucester*, he related that

> The third Lieutenant, Mr. Baikie, came from the Orkneys: he was a very peculiar person, and compounded of strange elements. He loved play, and wine exceedingly; and was not less fond of good eating; altogether a man of coarse feelings, and gross appetites . . . Mr. John Jones, the Master, was a Gloucestershire man: one of those kindly beings whom everybody loves, and no one envies . . . He was humble, modest, silent and sweet-tempered, without being either servile, sheepish, reserved or silly.[13]

Descriptions of seamen were also intended to prevent fraud, as in the certificates given out for pensions for injuries. William Warneck was awarded a pension because his sight was impaired by an accident. His certificate recorded that he was 'Aged about thirty four years, born at or near Ayr in the County of Ayr, Scotland, of light hair, grey eyes, swarthy complexion, stature five feet two and a half inches . . . marked with the small pock.'[14] When men deserted, descriptions of the offenders were circulated, such as those sent to the Admiralty by Captain Seator of HMS *Leyden* at Harwich in July 1803:

Enclosed I send you the descriptions of two Seamen who deserted last night from His Majesty's Ship under my command by swimming away from her . . . I can scarcely think it possible they could reach any vessel. They are both tall men . . . Samuel Cousins, Aged 27 years, 5 ft 11 in high. Strong black hair, dark eyes, long face, and black beard. Has four letters punctured on his left arm, *HN–SC 1797* and *AC* on the same hand. Was born at York, but married and did reside at Hull where his wife now lives in Trippett Street having allotted part of his pay to her – John Warsworth (a vol[unteer] and [was] paid the bounty). Aged 22 years, 5 ft 6¾ in high. Florrid open countenance, stout made, little or no beard, light sandy hair, tyed. Born in Kackington, Derbyshire. Single man but has a mother living at Draple, near Hull, to whom he had allotted a part of his pay.[15]

With many men entering the ship against their will as victims of the press-gang, it is likely that numbers of them provided false names and addresses. Knowing this, particular attention was paid to their physical appearance and distinguishing marks such as tattoos. The punctured letters on the left arm of Samuel Cousins were tattoos, and Captain Rotheram in his survey noted many distinguishing marks, with more than a quarter of the men having tattoos. Among his crew were 'Charles Brown: moon and stars on left hand', 'Daniel Cameron: anchor on left arm', 'William Fairweather: crucifix on right arm', 'Richard Grant: crucifix and mermaid on left arm', and 'Josh. Norman: tattoed on forehead'.[16]

The most popular designs were the sun, moon and stars, crucifixes, anchors and mermaids, but even more popular were sets of initials. Tattoos were frequently the subject of superstitions and thought to be charms against drowning, venereal disease and evil spirits, and individual designs may have been chosen because they were believed to guard against specific evils. These tattoos were done by the sailors themselves using a sharp point to break the skin before rubbing a colouring such as soot or gunpowder into the wounds – 'the pricking of a mermaid on the arm of his messmate'[17] is one of the leisure-time skills mentioned by Robert Hay – and so the artistry of the finished design depended on the wishes of the person being tattooed and the skill of his friend wielding the sharp point. On board the *Gloucester*, Dublin-born Edward Mangin was saddened by the death of the coxswain, Thomas Flynn, who was from Belfast. 'When stripped,' Mangin related, 'I observed that he had on the upper part of one arm, a drawing, not very rudely executed, of a female and a seaman parting, and a motto beneath "Thomas, come home to Ann". Marks of some kind, put on as his was, are common among sailors, and by a certain process are rendered indelible.'[18]

Rotheram also documented the heights of the men, and the average was 5 feet 5 inches, with several being under 5 feet and none over 6 feet.[19] Captain Seator described both deserters as tall men, though one was only 5 feet 6¾ inches; skeletons excavated at the cemetery belonging to Greenwich Hospital have a mean stature of 5 feet 6 inches, which is in accordance with Rotheram's data.[20] Nelson is believed to have been 5 feet 6 inches tall, maybe 5 feet 7 inches. There is evidence that many officers were of above average height, and that may have been due to their middle- and upper-class backgrounds, with better-quality and more plentiful food in childhood than the average sailor. Being shorter than today's average height, they would have found it easier to move about below decks.

Officers and many of the men were clean-shaven, like civilians – not even moustaches were fashionable, although fairly short side whiskers were common. The reference to the 'beards' of the deserters was a description of the colour of facial hair, rather than meaning they had full beards. On board the *Lapwing* in the West Indies in 1799, thirty-seven-year-old Aaron Thomas loathed the custom of some seamen tying their hair in a long plait – a pigtail or queue – and he joked that 'In the next war I suppose it will be the fashion for sailors never [to] shave but wear long beards, which they will tye into tails.'[21] With his sardonic humour he added: 'These chin tails will have its use, for when a man is ordered on the quarter deck to be started [beaten with the end of a rope or stick], the boatswain's mate, instead of laying hold of the collar of your shirt, will lay hold of the chin tail, to keep you too, while the thrashing [is] performed.'[22]

The pigtails were commonly bound with tape or strips of cloth, explained by Thomas with exaggeration: 'A sailor's head is . . . very friendly to tape makers, as he often has as many yards of tape lapped round his hair as would reach from England to Newfoundland, so that when the tape and hair are bundled up together behind, so far from its looking like a tail, it appears as if half the main topgallant mast had been cut off, then rolled up in coarse slips of canvas, and in this state stuck to the hind part of the head.'[23] Such pigtails were worn by seamen and officers alike, and Nelson's pigtail, bound in tape, was cut off when he died and is now in the National Maritime Museum. When writing to a former shipmate, Thomas remarked: 'I hope you will have followed my wishes; that is to wear your hair short and thin. That nasty custom of tying hair, is as bad as drinking your grog out of a piss pot. I now wear no hair on my head that is longer than the hair on your eyebrows.'[24] Some months before, he described himself as 'my hair curled close to my head, as I generally wear it'[25] – dressed in black, he was often mistaken on shore for a clergyman.

Pigtails were so fashionable that some men wore false ones. Marine Lieutenant John George wrote to his parents that 'I was obliged to get a false tail, my hair being too short to tie.'[26] On joining the navy in 1783, Jeffrey Raigersfeld's first captain was Cuthbert Collingwood. 'Now it so happened,' he related, 'that at this time it was a fashion for your bucks of the navy to wear their hair tied in a pigtail behind, close up to their neck.'[27] One day Captain Collingwood wanted to see all the midshipmen doing navigational observations of the height of the sun at noon, and many years later Raigersfeld had a feeling that short hair came into fashion because of what happened next:

> Only three or four out of twelve or thirteen could accomplish this with any degree of exactitude, so calling those to him who were deficient, he observed to them how remiss they were, and suddenly, imputing their remissness to their pigtails, he took his penknife out of his pocket and cut off their pigtails close to their heads above the tie, then presenting them to their owners, desired they would put them into their pockets and keep them until such time as they could work a day's-work, proper.[28]

Aaron Thomas thought long hair was dangerous: 'I have heard of a sailor, whose tail [pigtail] catched in the block [pulley], as the fall [ropes] was going, and had his head pulled out from between his shoulders. So also of a sailor, whose hair was long and loose; it blew in his eyes as he was going up the shrouds [ropes]; he put his hands to his face, to clear it, when he missed his hold, fell into the chains and broke his neck.'[29] Thomas also colourfully demonstrated that long hair was unhygienic and harboured lice:

A sailor who wears his hair tyed appears to me to be a very accommodating man; the queue which falls from his head down his back being well adapted to answer the purpose of a bridge, over which large bodies of lice may decamp from headquarters, when the napper is overstocked, and spread themselves in more commodious pasturage about the jacket, shirt and fork of the trowsers. The tail also well answers the use of a backstay, for it not only assists in keeping the head steady, but it affords the means of giving to every part of the body the same quantity of scrat,* for when the lice are all in the head, the general scrat is there also, but when they crawl down the tail, and disperse themselves, there then exists a general scrat from head to toe.[30]

As if to prove his point, Thomas recorded that on 16 May 1799, off Montserrat, they 'flogged the boy Joseph Hilliar on his bare bum for having scabby and lousy hair. Cut all his hair off, and *shaved* his head.'[31]

Despite cutting off his midshipmen's pigtails, Collingwood wore his own hair like this, as Midshipman Abraham Crawford, from Lismore in Ireland, observed on first meeting him: 'At the time I write [1806], Lord Collingwood was between fifty and sixty . . . He wore his hair powdered, and tied in a queue, in the style of officers of his age at that time.'[32] Hair was universally powdered by officers up to 1795, but the practice declined after a tax on hair powder was introduced, though in a list compiled a decade later of items a lieutenant needed to buy, Captain Rotheram included 'Six pound of hair powder

*He probably means scratching.

£0.6.0'.[33] Wigs were also worn by some officers, but gradually wigs, powder and queues became unfashionable, officers wore their hair much shorter, and in 1808 marines were ordered to crop their hair and cease using powder.

The nationalities of a warship's crew were even more varied than their hairstyles, and in 1803 the fourteen-year-old Scottish volunteer Robert Hay was amazed by the different backgrounds of the seamen in his first ship:

> It would be difficult to give any adequate idea of the scenes these decks presented to anyone who has not witnessed them. To the eye were presented complexions of every hue, and features of every cast, from the jetty face, flat nose, thick lips and frizzled hair of the African, to the more slender frame and milder features of the Asiatic. The rosy complexion of the English swain and the sallow features of the sun-burnt Portuguese. People of every profession and of the most contrasted manners, from the brawny ploughman to the delicate fop. The decayed author and bankrupt merchant who had eluded their creditors. The apprentice who had eloped from servitude. The improvident and impoverished father who had abandoned his family, and the smuggler and the swindler who had escaped by flight the vengeance of the laws. Costumes of the most various hues presented themselves from the kilted Highlander to the quadruple breeched sons of Holland. From the shirtless sons of the British prison-house to the knuckle ruffles of the haughty Spaniard. From the gaudy tinseled trappings of the dismissed footman to the rags and tatters of the city mendicant. Here, a group of half-starved and squalid wretches, not eating but devouring with rapacity their whole day's provisions at a single meal. There, a gang of sharpers at cards or dice swindling some unsuspecting booby out of his few remaining pence.[34]

Hay was also astonished at all the languages spoken by the numerous foreign recruits: 'To the ear was addressed a hubbub little short of that which occurred at Babel. Irish, Welsh, Dutch, Portuguese, Spanish, French, Swedish, Italian and all the provincial dialects between Landsend and John O'Groats, joined their discordant notes.'[35] The Irishman Henry Walsh and the Scotsmen Daniel Goodall and Robert Hay all spoke English as their first language, but this was not universal since the Irish, Scottish and Welsh languages were the first (and at times only) languages of many. Today, mass communications by radio and television have weakened local dialects, but in Nelson's time even the speech of many English people was virtually incomprehensible to their fellow countrymen from other regions. Nelson himself had a 'true Norfolk drawl'.[36] Captain Rotheram in his survey of the *Bellerophon*'s crew noted details like their manner of speech. Dialects included many 'Scotch', with some being described as 'broad', many Irish, and others from Devon, Somerset, Yorkshire, Newcastle, Northumberland, Welsh and Cockney, as well as men from abroad with a variety of accents, including some described as 'Creole' and a man from Sweden who spoke 'broken English'.[37]

Some foreign seamen spoke next to no English, and in the court martial of Francisco Falso for sodomy, one witness was asked, 'Does Francisco Falso understand English?', to which came the reply, 'He speaks and understands but very little of it. He is a Maltese.'[38] Because the court realised that Falso did not understand the charge – a capital offence – an interpreter was summoned to translate everything. The mixture of foreign accents and languages and the variety of speech of men from different parts of the British Isles were extra obstacles to the attempts by petty officers to impose order and discipline on new recruits. 'The occasional rattle of the boatswain's cane, the harsh voices of his mates blended with the shrill and penetrating sound of their whistles,' Robert Hay remembered, '[all] served [at] once to strike terror into the mind and add confusion to the scene.'[39]

Irrespective of his nationality, it was how a new recruit was rated that determined his duties and level of pay, as Robert Wilson outlined: 'The ratings are thus – able seamen, ordinary seamen, and landsmen; there are also boys, who gradually rise to able seamen according to the length of time they may be on board and as they may deserve.'[40] Wilson himself was twenty years old when taken by the press-gang, and because he had sailed on merchant ships, he was rated as an able seaman, but young Robert Hay had no seafaring experience and was rated as a Boy, being under the age of eighteen. Those under the age of fifteen were Boys Third Class, and those over fifteen were Boys Second Class. Boys First Class, more usually called Volunteers First Class, were literally a class apart, as they were training to be officers and expected to be appointed midshipmen.

Adults with no seagoing experience (of whom many had been pressed) were rated as Landsmen (or Landmen), while expert sailors were rated as Able Seamen. Between these two levels were the Ordinary Seamen, who had been to sea before but were not recognised as skilful sailors. This rating system was based on the level of competence of the crew member, although men could be disrated as a punishment, since it meant a drop in pay and privileges, so it was possible to have a skilled seaman rated as a landsman. The navy really wanted men like Andrew Mouat, on board the *Immortalité* in 1805, who was described as

> thoroughly versed in every branch of a seaman's duty, [but] he had none of the thoughtless, reckless habits and manners, that usually characterize the profession to which he belonged: on the contrary, his were peculiarly quiet, orderly, and sober: whatever duty he was put to perform, or whatever trust was reposed in him, he never left the one until he had finished it, and never disappointed or betrayed the other. And yet Mouat was a pressed man, with a wife and children, from whom he was unwillingly separated. His former situation, too, had been one of respectability, being mate of a vessel that traded between London and one of the north-eastern ports.[41]

The forecastle, in front of the foremast, was where the seamen congregated, and on some ships this was where they ate and slept, and so 'before the mast' meant ordinary seamen as opposed to officers. Similarly, 'men of the lower deck' referred to the seamen, in contrast to the officers who belonged to the quarterdeck.

After being rated, the recruits were told which watch (a naval term for a shift) they would be in, although a few had special duties and were exempt from keeping watch. The period of time when half the crew, including the officers, was on duty was called a 'watch', and the same term was also used for the men who were on duty. Depending on their previous experience, the new crew members were then allotted specific duties, which were largely defined by their place or 'station' in the ship. 'It next follows to station them, and to describe the different employments of every different class of the people, according to their stations,' Wilson recorded. 'The able seamen are stationed on the forecastle, or fore part of the ship, in the tops, and some in the afterguard. The ordinary seamen and landmen compose the afterguard and waisters, except a few of the smartest of the former who are occasionally put among the topmen.'[42] The topmen were stationed aloft, at the top of the mast, and were generally the youngest and most agile sailors, as Wilson acknowledged:

> The duty of the topmen relates to everything above the lower yards, and what relates to the top, whether on deck or aloft; and they occasionally assist at duty on deck when not employed aloft. The topmen are generally smart young men, as the duty imposed on them requires alertness, such as shortening or reducing sails, or canvas, on a ship in a sudden squall, etc. It not only requires alertness but courage, to ascend in a manner sky-high when stormy winds do blow. In short, they must not be slack in stays – *i.e.* indolent – but exert themselves briskly. The youngest of the topmen generally go the highest . . . The fore and maintopmen when at sea look out at their different mastheads,* an hour each – two men, one a foretopman and t'other a main. The mizentopmen do not look out at any of the mastheads.[43]

The biggest problem for such lookouts was coping with boredom and staying alert, and so the masts and woodwork where they stood were 'hacked and scarred and carved with fancy designs and would-be representations of Men-of-War, the handiwork of men aloft on lookout by way of wiling away the time'.[44]

* Mastheads were platforms high up the mast.

The forecastle men handled the sails from the deck towards the bow of the ship, and similar work was done towards the stern by the afterguard. Between these two groups were positioned the waisters, as Wilson detailed: 'The afterguard is composed of able and ordinary seamen and landsmen, and their duty consists in attending about the quarterdeck, trimming sails, etc. The waisters in common are the worst of the landsmen, and are what the seamen call "neither soldiers nor sailors". Their duty is to do all the drudgery work on the main or gun deck and occasionally to assist in working ship.'[45] By contrast, the gunner's crew were able seamen chosen for their skill and experience and were considered to be 'the best seamen in the ship. Their duty is to attend to the main yard and rigging, to the guns and whatever relates to them, so far as they may receive orders from the gunner of the ship. They are allowed 1/- more per month than any other able seamen; what with making of cartridges and wads, etc., they earn it.'[46]

Other workers with special skills like the sailmaker, carpenter and cooper were referred to as 'idlers', because they did not belong to one of the watches and could in theory sleep all night and work by day. Daniel Goodall explained the system:

In all vessels, whether of war or commerce, there are a number of men who keep no watch at all, both officers and crew, and who are known by the somewhat uncomplimentary but misapplied term of 'idlers', seeing they are often the very individuals who work hardest. For instance, the captain, first lieutenant, sailing-master, surgeon, purser, boatswain, gunner, and carpenter – and in all large ships a number of inferior officers – are included in this designation. But it is obvious that, although those officers I have just named are not included in the regular watch of the ship, they are by no means 'idlers' in the ordinary sense of the word. All men who are employed either as mechanics [such as blacksmiths and armourers] or officers' servants during the whole or greater part of the day are also excused from night work, but they are liable to be called up at any moment when the lieutenant of the watch may think their assistance necessary. In all the ships to which I have at any time been attached, there were a few of the crew specially exempted from all duty, save in action with the enemy, such as the captain's steward, the purser's steward, the gun-room steward, and a very few others.[47]

Since a ship had to be a self-sufficient community, as far as was possible, these various specialists were employed primarily for their skills rather than for a direct contribution to the working of the ship. At one end of the scale the ship's surgeon seldom, if ever, helped with the sailing of the ship, although Captain Thomas Cochrane left only his surgeon, James Guthrie, to steer the *Speedy* when he needed every available man to board and capture the *Gamo* in 1801. The surgeon normally concentrated on maintaining the health of the ship's crew, while other specialists, such as the carpenter, cooper and gunner, were also generally exempt from helping to sail the ship. Their assistants or 'mates', though, were frequently called upon to lend a hand, as Wilson noted for the cooper: 'The cooper and his mate are employed in their line [making and dismantling barrels], but seldom having much to do, the cooper generally acts as assistant to the ship's steward and his mate graces the afterguard.'[48]

As well as their rating, station and watch, which governed their pay, duties and the time when they were at work, each man was assigned to a mess. In the short term this could have a much greater impact on a new recruit, as Samuel Leech remembered about his time on board the *Macedonian*:

> The morning after my arrival [in 1810], I was put into a 'mess'. The crew of a man of war is divided into little communities of about eight called 'messes'. These eat and drink together, and are, as it were, so many families. The mess to which I was introduced, was composed of your genuine, weather-beaten, old tars. But for one of its members, it would have suited me very well; this one, a real gruff old 'bull-dog', named Hudson [he probably meant able seaman Richard Hodgson], took into his head to hate me at first sight. He treated me with so much abuse and unkindness, that my messmates soon advised me to change my mess, a privilege which is wisely allowed, and which tends very much to the good fellowship of a ship's crew, for if there are disagreeable men among them, they can in this way be got rid of. It is no unfrequent case

to find a few, who have been spurned from all the messes in the ship, obliged to mess by themselves.[49]

Each mess had its own table, usually with a bench either side, and a variable number of men, as Basil Hall remembered:

The number of men in a mess varies from eight to twelve in a frigate, each mess having a separate table . . . In a line-of-battle ship the tables are larger, and two messes sit at the same table, one on each side. The average number in the mess is the same as in a frigate . . . A petty officer or leading man, who is styled captain of the mess, is at the head of each, and in a well-disciplined ship, he is in some manner responsible for the good conduct and cleanliness of the others.[50]

It was within these messes that the seamen made lasting friendships, which were summed up in the saying about a sailor's loyalty: 'Messmate before a shipmate, shipmate before a stranger, stranger before a dog'.[51] Goodall found that the messes could be quite cosmopolitan: 'The mess to which I was allotted were all seamen, had all served aboard merchant ships, and several of them had been many years in the Royal Navy. They were seven in number before I was added to the mess. Five were Englishmen, one a native of Ireland, and the seventh a Frenchman.'[52]

Most training of newly recruited seamen was centred on the skills necessary to sail the ship. By obeying orders most men learned the job as they went along, but because of the sheer variety of life in the navy, it took time to build up the necessary skills. William Robinson, who volunteered as a landsman in 1805, felt that the routine and discipline helped the learning process: 'By this regular system of duty, I became inured to the roughness and hardships of a sailor's life. I had made up my mind to be obedient, however irksome to my feelings, and . . . I soon began to pick up a knowledge of seamanship.'[53] John Wetherell, an experienced seaman from Whitby taken by the press-gang in 1803, soon realised the difference between being a merchant seaman and one in the navy: 'A little time gave me to understand that I was now entering on my first adventures and must consider myself under the martial laws of my country and must use every means to obey my superiors, attend to my duty, all calls and orders, to be sober, silent and submissive, and above all to curb your tongue and temper was what I soon found a golden rule.'[54]

After his first few weeks at sea, Robert Hay started to learn navy jargon, or, as he put it, 'I had . . . become familiar with a number of those phrases which distinguished the sons of Neptune from those of Terra Firma.'[55] This was a problem for many new recruits, as the very language used at sea was completely different from that on land, and they were also faced with each sail and rope having its own name, reflecting its position in the ship or the purpose for which it was used – for example, stays were part of the standing rigging that braced the masts and helped them stay in position, while braces were used to turn sails to catch the wind. Backstays led from a mast backwards and downwards to both sides of the ship and were large ropes that sometimes supported triangular sails called staysails.

On top of learning all the nautical names for equipment and procedures, recruits also had to come to terms with the sailors' speech, which was full of curious expressions and slang words. Everything was at first strange to the chaplain Edward Mangin, but after a while he became accustomed to the peculiar language and proudly listed his newly acquired vocabulary, including 'the *combings*, or *coamings*, and *shot-lockers*; the *splinter-netting* . . . I knew *bunting* from *spun-yarn*, and *duck* from *canvas*; understood the use of *stanchions*, and *grapnels*, and *grummets*, and *windsails*.'[56] Sailors were notorious for their way of talking, and after Trafalgar, when many letters from sailors were published in newspapers giving details of the battle, a parody of such a letter was published in one magazine, in which the author commented on Nelson's death:

> If it had been the Purser, or the Captain's Clerk, or the Surgeon's Mate, though for my part I like them all well enough, it wo'dn't have mattered the strapping of a topsail-sheet block: but the gallant Nelson to broach to, to start about, to be let go by the run; By the mizen-mast!! I would have given my allowance of grog for six months to come, and have had nothing but banyan days, to have saved his precious life. However, clap

the jigger-tackle on your spirits, honest Bob; for our chaplain says, that the brave Nelson is not dead, but that he liveth; and he must know more about it than we do.[57]

The language used in this parody is exaggerated with meaningless expressions and real sailors' slang used in a odd way, and the fact that it was published as a humorous piece demonstrates that people were accustomed to how sailors spoke, even if they did not always understand every word that they used. In fact, by the end of the Napoleonic Wars in 1815 so many people in Britain had been closely involved with the navy, either serving in ships or shore establishments and ports, or in supplying goods and services to the Admiralty, that many sailors' expressions entered the English language and have survived to the present day. Many do not betray their naval origins, so that it is not obvious that 'to the bitter end' originally referred to the bitts of a ship. These were wooden posts on the deck, to which ropes were secured, so 'the bitter end' was the end of a length of rope that was tied round a bitt. Scuppers were the drains along the sides of the deck that emptied through holes in the ship's side, and to be scuppered was therefore to 'go down the drain'. A 'clean slate' originally referred to changing the watch – any changes in the course, records of occurrences, distances travelled, and so on, were chalked on a slate by an officer of the watch. When the watch changed these records were copied into the logbook, and the new watch started with a clean slate.

If he was lucky a new recruit would find an experienced hand to take pity on him and teach him what he needed to know for any given task, but sometimes this was ordered by the officers, as seems to have been the case with Robert Hay, serving under Vice-Admiral Collingwood, who, he said,

gave each boy in charge to the best seaman of the mess to which he belonged with orders to look carefully after him, to teach him good behaviour, and all the little operations of seamanship. 'I expect,' said the Admiral to these tutors, 'to find, on some future examination, that these boys have been placed in good hands. To you I will look for their improvement, and I expect no remissness will be shewn.' Each of these tutors, strongly desirous that his pupil should not fall behind any of the others, embraced every opportunity of shewing him something; and the boys, on the other hand, resolving that neither they nor their tutors should be disgraced, attended to their lessons with the utmost assiduity and zeal. It was my lot to fall into the hands of Jack Gillies, than whom a handier fellow never left the Emerald Isle. 'Let us have the necessaries first, Robert,' said he, 'and we will attend to other matters afterwards.' Accordingly the cutting out and making of jackets, shirts and trousers, the washing of them when soiled, and the mending of them neatly when they began to fail, took precedence. The making of straw hats and canvas pumps [shoes] came next in order. Then followed various operations in seamanship.[58]

Collingwood was exceptional in being more strict with his officers than with the men, on the grounds that they should set an example to their inferiors. In this he implicitly recognised the class divide between the 'common seamen' and the officers, who were drawn from the middle and upper classes.

The lowest officer rank was midshipman ('mids' or 'middies'). A few years before Robert Hay began to learn the ropes, Jeffrey Raigersfeld was removed from the midshipmen's mess by Collingwood, partly as punishment and partly for the experience. Afterwards, Raigersfeld thought that mixing with the ordinary seamen – the bulk of the crew – was an invaluable lesson:

Another of the midshipmen and myself were put to mess with the common men, where we lived with them three months, performing all the offices of the ships boys such as cooking the victuals, standing the rank [queuing] at the ship's copper for the beef, burgoo and pease soup, and cleaning the mess platters. At first I was indignant at such treatment, but there was no help for it, therefore I quietly resigned myself to my fate, and I am very glad I was so placed, as it gave me a great insight into the character of seamen, and enabled me to govern them as well as their officers . . . during those three months I gained more knowledge of the seaman's character, than in all the other ships I have since served in.[59]

Midshipmen were given some training in navigation, mathematics and astronomy, and sometimes a schoolmaster was appointed for this purpose. However, since the post of schoolmaster was paid the same as that of midshipman, it was hard to fill and often did not attract the best candidates. John Harvey Boteler recalled that 'we youngsters had a schoolmaster, a clever seedy-looking creature, whose besetting sin was the love of grog; with very little trouble it floored him and then, I don't much like to record it, we used to grease his head and flour it'.[60] As well as teaching navigation skills to midshipmen, a schoolmaster often taught the officer boys how to read and write if they were willing to learn. In addition to instruction in religion and morals the chaplain sometimes added to the general education of the midshipmen and boys, but in the absence of a schoolmaster, the teaching of navigation could be rather haphazard, as Abraham Crawford admitted of his time as a midshipman in the *Diamond*: 'As there was no schoolmaster in the ship, one of the elder Midshipmen, a protégé of the Captain, kindly undertook to give me lessons in mathematics and navigation, but I fear I did not profit much by his instruction; nor, indeed, did I ever after show any predilection or much aptitude for figures or abstruse calculations.'[61]

Apart from those subjects that were essential for good seamanship, midshipmen were generally expected to pick up whatever knowledge they needed by their experiences on board ship. Their young age is evident in the instructions to shipboard schoolteachers in a contemporary manual:

> He should never suffer them to come to the mess table, or into the school cabin, without washing their hands and faces; he should insist on their keeping their heads perfectly clean; and, when opportunity serves, make them wash from head to foot ... When the hatchways are open, the youngsters should always be cautioned against playing inadvertently near them; and care should be taken at the same time to tighten a rope round them, to prevent accidents, if possible.[62]

Some captains took more interest in providing training and experience than others, and each had his own particular views. According to Crawford, Captain Edward Griffith of the *Diamond* 'always was in the habit of giving his young gentlemen the opportunity of acquiring as much useful knowledge and accomplishments as the brief time allowed for refitting ships in time of war permitted'.[63] While the ship was in dock,

> an experienced seaman [Matthew Walker] was employed a couple of hours each day in teaching the youngsters every practical part of a seaman's duty. We learned each knot and splice that was known to Matthew Walker himself, and when we were sufficiently instructed in them, we were put to rig a small ship, that stood in the Captain's cabin for the purpose. We were shown how to raise sheers,* and get in the lower masts and bowsprit; then to cut out, mark and serve the lower rigging ... and, in fact, without entering more into particulars, we rigged and unrigged the ship, until we were pronounced perfect by our teacher.[64]

Captain Griffith also provided instruction in 'drawing, French and dancing, and, with a view of not permitting us to forget all early habits, and, from change of element, become "rude and boisterous children of the sea", he invited us [when in port] frequently to his house, and introduced us to several of his friends'.[65] These were useful accomplishments for a future naval officer. Because a large part of the world was still not properly surveyed, many officers sketched profiles of coastal landmarks in difficult waters, as well as the forms of foreign vessels and maps of harbours, shoals and other sea hazards for future reference. French was not only the language of England's principal enemy, but the language of trade and politics in many parts of the world – Nelson tried, unsuccessfully, to master it by spending some weeks in France during the peace in 1783. On some foreign stations the most senior naval officer might also be, by default, British ambassador to the region, and in such cases a knowledge of foreign languages and social graces, such as dancing and

---

* Sheers or sheer-legs comprised two or three wooden posts lashed together at the top and were used like a crane for lifting heavy objects.

dealing with people other than naval officers and seamen, would be advantageous. If a midshipman at sea from the age of twelve or thirteen years was to succeed as a senior captain or admiral in command of a fleet in a remote part of the world, he needed a very broad education.

Midshipmen were often attracted to the navy as young boys by dreams of glory, such as inspired thirteen-year-old James Scott when he received his midshipman's clothes: 'Brightly dawned the auspicious morning that beheld me habited in His Majesty's uniform, and which, in my excited imagination, was at once to make a man and a hero of me.'[66] As many such boys found, though, reality rapidly replaced his hopes:

> I remember well on the following day, when we were receiving our guns, muskets, swords, tomahawks, pikes &c. that my reflections were by no means agreeable. The conviction that they were intended for deadly strife, and that the period might not be far distant when they would be brought into actual use, threw a chill over the enthusiastic ardour that generally governed my feelings respecting the navy. I felt most forcibly that I had not henceforth child's play to encounter, and a feeling allied to fear crept into my mind that I might fail when the moment of trial came.[67]

The young age of midshipmen, who had to give orders to men often old enough to be their grandfathers, seldom gave rise to trouble, because of the rigid navy discipline and the equally rigid class structure in Britain, which kept apart the worlds of the ordinary people and the officers. Along with all the officers, midshipmen were regarded as gentlemen and were even referred to as 'the young gentlemen'. There was a degree of automatic deference from the sailor, but occasionally a midshipman would abuse his authority, as one verse of a contemporary ballad cruelly highlighted:

> There are snotty boys of midshipmen,
> Ha'n't yet done shitting yellow;
> As to their age, some hardly ten

Strike many a brave fellow,
Who dare not prate at any rate,
Nor seem in the least to mumble.
They'll frap you still, do what you will;
It is but folly to grumble.[68]

The Newcastle seaman George Watson, when on board the *Eagle*
in the Mediterranean, detested one midshipman, who, he said,

was haughty, arbitrary, ignorant, vain as a peacock, implacable, revenge-
ful, cowardly, contemptuous and contemptible, hated by all over whom he
had any control; he was one of those creatures that are most useless and
offensive in his Majesty's service, and only calculated to create and nour-
ish sedition and mutiny . . . even seamen, so rude and boisterous in their
manners, expect better things in those that rule them, and never fail to
notice and condemn, the commander that wants them.[69]

William Robinson recalled another midshipman, who was 'a youth
not more than twelve or thirteen years of age; but I have often seen
him get on the carriage of a gun, call a man to him, and kick him
about the thighs and body, and with his fist would beat him about the
head; and these, although prime seamen, at the same time dared not
murmur'.[70] When this particular midshipman was killed in battle,
Robinson noted that 'the general exclamation was "Thank God, we
are rid of the young tyrant!"'[71]

After midshipman, the next rung on the career ladder for officers
was the rank of lieutenant, but several years' experience at sea were
needed before taking the qualifying examination. Some midshipmen
were stuck after continually failing to pass the examination, while
others could be left in the role of midshipman for some time after
passing but not being appointed as lieutenant. The most senior was
the first lieutenant, then the second lieutenant, and so on, with more
lieutenants in larger ships. The first lieutenant was the highest-ranking
officer below the captain, and so one of the most important men in
the ship. He was second-in-command, and took over if the captain
was incapacitated or dead, but he was also responsible for the smooth

day-to-day running of the ship. As the seaman Daniel Goodall commented, 'It was a saying in the navy at the time, amongst the common seamen, that every man's comfort afloat depended upon the kind of man a ship had for its First Lieutenant, for that he was the Prime Minister of the small community over which the Captain ruled as absolute monarch, and, as every measure and arrangement was to be carried out by him, it was better to sail with a bad Captain and a good First Lieutenant than to have the conditions reversed.'[72]

Officers of the rank of lieutenant and above were commissioned officers, and their authority derived from the fact that they each held a commission from the Admiralty. Of all the officers in a ship, it was the first lieutenant who was under constant scrutiny by the crew. They looked first for skill and professionalism, because on many occasions the safety of the ship would rest on his decisions, and after that, leadership and fairness. A first lieutenant who was too harsh or too lax was likely to provoke trouble among the men, who preferred competent but caring leaders, as Goodall observed:

> Mr Thomas Furber [first lieutenant of HMS *Flora*] . . . in 1805 to do him justice, was an officer who well understood his profession, whilst he acted as much as he could up to his conviction that it was better to govern men by fear rather than by love. Very excellent authorities have differed with our noisy First Lieutenant on that particular point – such men, for example, as Nelson, Collingwood, Pellew, Codrington, and a host of others easy to name, having held fast by the opinion that an officer who wins the love of his men will work wonders where a leader of a different stamp will fail.[73]

It was in the post of first lieutenant that an officer gained experience of commanding a ship, and the aim for most officers and probably all first lieutenants was to become a post-captain. The difference between these two ranks was seen as the great hurdle that had to be overcome, either by distinguishing themselves in battle or by the help of friends at the Admiralty. Below the rank of post-captain, promotion was in principle purely on merit, but as Basil Hall was well aware, except 'in cases of extraordinary good fortune, or extraordinary good interest [the help of an influential person], an officer's chance of promotion abroad is very small, unless he either gets actually into the flag-ship, or occupies a place on the Admiral's list of protégés while serving in some other vessel'.[74] Once a first lieutenant 'made post', as it was called, he was a post-captain on the bottom of the seniority list. From then on his promotion was automatic, governed not by merit but purely by the death or removal of the officers ahead of him on the list – hence the toast of officers dining together, 'A bloody war and a sickly season'[75] – events that could kill off officers above them and so lead to promotion. An instance of this was recorded by Aaron Thomas of the *Lapwing* in his journal:

> Saturday 29th Sep'r [1799]. At daylight saw a strange sail; at 7am spoke* her close in under Monserrat. She proved to be an Antigua privateer called the *Scourge* . . . said that Captain Mitford of the *Matilda* was dangerous ill. This is good news for the first lieutenant of the *Prince of Wales*, and also for Masters and Commanders, as should Mitford die, the first Lieutenant of the *Prince of Wales* will be made a Master and Commander, and put into a Sloop of War, and the Captain of that Sloop of War will be put into the *Matilda*, which makes him a Post Captain.[76]

Most captains who commanded ships were post-captains, but some smaller ships were put in the charge of lieutenants or even midshipmen, who then held the temporary rank of commander. They were addressed as 'captain' out of courtesy despite them being of lower rank than a post-captain. Unfortunately for those concerned, Captain Henry Mitford recovered from his illness.

If he survived long enough, any post-captain could eventually become an admiral. The disadvantage of being a post-captain (or other senior officer) was the loneliness. Although officers did not fraternise with the crew, they could socialise with their fellow officers in their own and other ships, but the captain had to remain aloof. He might frequently dine with his officers, but there was always a

---

* To speak, or speak to, a ship was communicating with a vessel at sea.

distance between them. The men in the ship belonged within distinct groups according to their rank, with the captain at their head, which broadly mirrored the class structure of British society at the time. Early in his career, Nelson agreed with a saying common among the seamen – 'Aft the most honour, but forward the better man'.[77] This implied that officers (stationed aft) did not live up to their exalted positions. Later he held the view, not necessarily inconsistent with his earlier thoughts, that 'you must be a Seaman to be an Officer; and also that you cannot be a good Officer without being a Gentleman'.[78] According to Basil Hall, the seamen despised bad-mannered officers who had risen from the ranks – the tarpaulins:

> The sailors, who, from being very quick-sighted to the merits and faults of their officers . . . [and being] critics of great correctness, understand at once the distinction between a well-bred or high-caste officer, and one who, not having been born in a class where good manners are an essential characteristic, has not contrived to adopt them from others. A ship's company like, above all things, to be commanded by gentlemen; while there is nothing they so much hate or despise in an officer as that coarseness of thought and behaviour which marks their own class.[79]

Of course, Hall was himself an officer and a gentleman, which may have led him to overstate the case, but such distinctions were widely held to be essential for good discipline, and Midshipman William Dillon, an inveterate snob, disapproved of his new captain because he brought with him several of his own men: 'Some of the Mids did not cut much of a figure as gentlemen,' he remarked. 'They were rough seamen "from before the mast," as the naval term goes.'[80] A few years later, in 1809, Dillon took temporary command of HMS *Aigle*, so that the ship's captain could appear as a witness at a lengthy court martial, and he found the hierarchy of that ship too lax:

> On the first day that I went on board I had noticed one or two seamen entering the cabin with as much freedom as if in their own homes, and speak to their Captain in the most familiar tones. He seemed to encourage

all that, as he styled them Tom, Jack, Bill etc. My plan of proceeding was diametrically opposed to this, my opinion being that familiarity breeds contempt, and the officer in command ought, by his conduct to all under him, to insure respect. There is a certain deportment which, regulated by firmness and moderation, never fails to produce its object. Upon that principle, I avoided abusive language, but never failed to rebuke the negligent.[81]

This self-imposed isolation on board a cramped and crowded ship took its toll of captains, some of whom went insane. James Scott, who became a captain, summed up the stressful situation:

It strikes me that the difficulties of the position of a captain of a man-of-war are neither fairly nor candidly considered, and that they are too often only abstractedly discussed. It requires no slight command of temper, integrity of purpose, vigour of mind, and abnegation of self, to blend together and harmonise the jarring elements of the different dispositions and habits of the men who may compose his crew. However at variance these may be, he – and he alone – is expected, and exhorted, to bring a set of unruly and discordant beings into a state of perfect discipline and obedience, so that their services in the hour of danger or battle shall be prompt and effective: such as the glory of the country, the credit of the captain, and the safety of the ship may be staked upon.[82]

A rare glimpse of what ordinary seamen thought of this class divide is provided by Aaron Thomas, who was a fairly well-educated man and served as coxswain and steward to his captain. He was in a unique position, being on easy terms with the crew as well as the captain and able to see the situation of both. In one letter to a friend, who appears to have urged him to try for a post as a purser, he cynically wrote:

Now was I a Purser, the moment I became one, I must bid advice [heed advice against] . . . ever *saying* a civil word, or ever giving a *civil* look, to any one of the men before the mast, in presence of a superior officer, for it is held in the Navy to be a proof of something shocking and bad to speak to the men with civility, and if you do do it, your promotion is

damned. Now for my part, I never am more happier than when conversing with my inferiors, for from them I learn more of life than I do by
conversing with officers, whose general talk is to abuse high and low, or
everybody whom they know – besides [this], let my ideas be what they
will, I can never give [them utterance], but on general sentiment [only in
general terms] at the wardroom or gunroom table, and at the Captain's
table I must set [sit] 3 hours to hear him talk of *himself*, and must *never*
contradict a word he utters, but nod *yes* to everything he says – and do not
you think this forced tacitity is paying very dear for a plate of mutton, a
tumbler of porter and six glasses of wine?'[83]

As well as his own officers, the captain also commanded the
marines on board, although they had their own officers and career
structure. Because one of the purposes of the marines was to form a
buffer between the officers and the men in case of mutiny, relations
could become very bad, although if a mutiny did erupt there were
likely to be divided loyalties among the marines as well as among the
seamen, and in well-run ships camaraderie existed between seamen
and marines. Daniel Goodall left the navy in 1802 during the peace,
but joined up as a marine in 1805. Initially, he was put on board a
guardship to await a transfer to Chatham for training, and received
much better treatment than when he volunteered as a seaman: 'My
advent in the guardship as a marine recruit was of a very different
nature to my first experience as a volunteer in the naval service, for all
of the new hands were at once put into the regular messes of the
marines on board, and everything was done that the nature of our
rather limited arrangements would admit of to make us comfortable.'[84]

Training of marines largely consisted of drilling and instruction in
the use and care of weapons. The amount of basic training marines
received on shore, before being assigned to a ship, depended on the
number of vacancies on board the ships. Some marines were sent to
sea with very little training, but however much knowledge of life as a
marine they had acquired, leaving the land could still be a shock, as
Thomas Rees remembered: 'I had never been to sea before, and as the
land began to disappear from my view, and when I could no longer

distinguish it, my heart sunk within me, and it seemed as if I should be distracted by grief; so sad and so dismal were the thoughts which crowded into my mind, of the dear country and home I had left, and beloved relations and friends I might never meet again.'[85] Rees soon recovered from his initial despondency, probably because he was kept busy.

As one of a party of newly recruited marines, Goodall and his companions were first set to slinging (hanging) their hammocks, which proved a more difficult task than he expected:

> There were perhaps as many as nine of the party, certainly not more, who knew how to set about it, but even those of the number who had slung hammocks once-a-fortnight for years, as is the practice in all well-regulated ships, were floored at the very outset by the discovery that the whole of the clews or cords by which the hammocks were to be suspended had first to be made out of rope yarns, and as even the nimblest fingers cannot make a set of passable clews out of such stuff in less than twenty-four hours, the case really began to look desperate.[86]

Fortunately the captain was not a hard taskmaster, Goodall said, and he remarked to the first lieutenant 'that many of us seemed but young hands, with probably little or no experience in such work, and he added that those who knew the duties should aid and instruct those who were ignorant, reasonable time being allowed us'.[87]

Marine captains were equal in rank to a naval lieutenant and tended to be referred to as 'major' to avoid confusion with the ship's captain. It was rare for a marine officer higher in rank than captain to serve on board a ship, and they were only present on board the larger ships that carried fifty guns or more. In smaller ships, such as frigates, marines were usually commanded by a first lieutenant of marines. If a ship was too small to warrant a first lieutenant of marines, they were commanded by a sergeant, even though there was a rank of second lieutenant of marines. Below the rank of sergeant was that of corporal and finally private. Being regarded as somewhere between the army and the navy, the prospect of promotion in the marines was more limited than in the other services. Privates in the marines had little hope of advancement, and even captains of marines were in a difficult position. They received higher pay than a naval lieutenant, and yet had less authority, and when it came to battles the naval first lieutenant was frequently promoted on the death of the captain. In the event of a great victory, every first lieutenant involved was usually promoted, but marine officers were ignored.

Between the naval officers and the seamen were the petty officers. Some were warrant officers, so called because they held a warrant from the Admiralty, and these men were generally specialists in a particular trade. The master (or sailing master) was responsible for the navigation and sailing of the ship and was the most well-paid and senior of the warrant officers. Others included the carpenter, boatswain, gunner, purser and surgeon. The boatswain was in charge of keeping the rigging and sails in good order, in the same way that the carpenter looked after the hull, masts and yards, while the gunner had charge of the cannons and gunpowder, and the purser was responsible for the ship's stores. Even within the group of warrant officers there was a strict hierarchy, which varied slightly according to the size of ship. Some, such as the master, were entitled to walk on the quarterdeck and live in the wardroom, since they were regarded as the equivalent of commissioned officers, while others had the privilege of using the gun room. The lowest level of warrant officer included the ship's cook, sailmaker and armourer. They were regarded as equivalent to those petty officers, like the sailmaker's mate, who held no warrant but were appointed by the captain.

From top to bottom the whole ship's company was highly stratified in a formal hierarchy, with men at each level jealously guarding their privileges, but this hierarchy was due to navy regulations. As Basil Hall put it, 'there is no such thing as a privileged class in the navy. All ranks and orders are alike in respect to the discipline.'[88] A boy might expect to become an able seaman, and then possibly gain promotion to a petty officer rank without a warrant, perhaps as a quarter gunner, which was better paid. In broad terms the hierarchy paralleled British society on land, but within the navy there was definitely more social mobility, although it was midshipmen from the middle classes who had the best chance of improving their wealth and status.

The regulations that governed the ranks and duties of everyone on board even covered religion, as the American Joseph Bates found when he was pressed on board a British warship in 1810: 'When I was asked, "Of what religion are you?" I replied, "A Presbyterian." But I was now given to understand that there was no religious toleration on board the king's war ships. "Only one denomination here – away with you to church!".'[89] His comment was quite literally true, because commissioned officers were subject to the Test Act. On being promoted to lieutenant they were sworn in, as James Gardner, looking back on his career in 1836, commented: 'We can now realise what a very real thing the Test Act of 1673 was, and continued to be, till its repeal in 1828. It required "all persons holding any office of profit or trust, civil or military, under the crown, to take the oaths of allegiance and supremacy, receive the sacrament of the Lord's Supper according to the rites of the Church of England, and subscribe to the declaration against transubstantiation".'[90]

This Act excluded men of other religions, such as Roman Catholics and Jews, from becoming officers unless they gave up their religion. The Act did not apply to the seamen, and non-Protestants were frequently pressed into the navy and then expected to cope with the conditions, such as compulsory attendance at church services aboard ship and the issuing of pork as the meat ration. Captains were required to hold church services, but the frequency of such services depended not only on circumstances such as weather, but also on the religious convictions of the captain or admiral in command – some were evangelical, but most were not. Joseph Bates took a disparaging view of the religious services on board his ship:

> When the weather was pleasant, the quarter-deck was fitted with awnings, flags, benches, &c., for meeting. At 11 a.m. came the order from the officer of the deck . . . 'Boatswain's mate!' 'Sir' 'Call all hands to church! Hurry them up there!' These mates were required to carry a piece of rope in their pocket with which to start [beat] the sailors. Immediately their stentorian voices were heard sounding on the other decks, 'Away up to church there – every soul of you – and take your prayer books with you!' If any one felt disinclined to such a mode of

worship, and attempted to evade the loud call to church, then look out for the men with the rope! . . . The officers, before taking their seats, unbuckled their swords and dirks, and piled them on the head of the capstan in the midst of the worshipping assembly, all ready to grasp them in a moment, if necessary, before the hour's service should close. When the benediction was pronounced, the officers clinched their side arms, and buckled them on for active service. The quarter-deck was immediately cleared, and the floating bethel again became the same old weekly war ship for six days and twenty-three hours more. Respecting the church service, the chaplain, or in his absence, the captain, reads from the prayer book, and the officers and sailors respond . . . King George III not only assumed the right to impress American seamen to man his war ships, and fight his unjust battles, but he also required them to attend his church, and learn to respond to his preachers.[91]

The seaman George Watson, on board the *Fame* warship in 1808, under Captain Richard Bennett, said that while they were refitting at Minorca,

we had divine service every Sunday, by signal from Lord Collingwood, who always maintained that important duty, at sea or in port, when circumstances would permit . . . In our ship Captain B. officiated as Chaplain, as we had not any on board, and performed the duty with a good grace, and was very strict in compelling every man of the vessel to attend, though many would rather excuse themselves, and often did so, by going aloft, or in other parts of the ship, where duty seemed to call them, to avoid being at prayers, and some when they mustered with the rest at church, would, instead of their prayer book, take some old popular history, or perhaps a song book with them, to which they devoted their attention; as for myself I always attended cheerfully enough, though not from proper motives, wishing only to be seen there by the Captain and others, and often instead of directing my thoughts to heaven, they were chiefly fixed . . . on Miss I., our commander's mistress, who generally sat looking at us from the windows under the poop – so much for my piety![92]

Some officers like Captain James Gambier did all they could to convert their crews to religion, though few appreciated such efforts. In 1793 on board the *Defence*, William Dillon thought that Gambier was too fanatical: 'It was the established custom to allow the seamen to go, when at anchor, to see them [other ships] on a Sunday, no work going on on that day: whereas, when seamen came to us on the Sabbath, they were not admitted, being told that we were at prayers . . . By this regulation of Capt. Gambier's we became an exclusive ship in the Fleet, and the seamen styled him "Preaching Jemmy."'[93] Like George Watson, some of Gambier's seamen used the church service to attract his attention: 'Several of the seamen had the tact to place themselves in a conspicuous position at church, and put on the most solemn countenances during the Service. These men were noticed by the Captain, who in due time obtained for them some snug berths.'[94]

At least one ship's chaplain, Edward Mangin, thought the task of converting his crew impossible:

> I perceived that by behaving well, I should probably gain the respect of several, and that the most reprobate among them would not treat me very badly, but I did not see the smallest likelihood of effecting any material change in the morals of such an assemblage. To leave them unreproved and vicious was possible, and I daresay it was equally possible to have transformed them all into Methodists, or madmen and hypocrites of some other kind, but to convert a man-of-war's crew into Christians would be a task to which the courage of Loyola, the philanthropy of Howard, and the eloquence of St. Paul united, would prove inadequate.[95]

The seamen might not be outwardly religious, but Daniel Goodall felt that nearly all of them had religious beliefs that could be broadly thought of as Christian:

> Sailors, it is said, are not the most serious of mortals . . . [but] there is much of fallacy lurking under this assumption – an assumption soon dismissed by those who acquire experience of Jack on service, when he presents a very different phase of social existence to what is witnessed by

those who see him only enjoying a holiday ashore. The comparative soli-
tude of his life on shipboard, and the sublimity of the dangers he is often
called upon to encounter, are not without their effects . . . and hence it
will be found by those who may take the trouble to look beneath the surface of that air of recklessness and dash so generally characteristic of Jack
ashore, that there is underlying it a strong foundation of simple, honest
faith . . . Vice and dissipation I have witnessed in large measure and in
revolting forms amongst the heterogeneous gatherings of humanity with
which our vessels used to be crammed, but I never met an infidel among
seamen – certainly not among those who had been afloat for any length
of time.[96]

Most seamen were also intensely superstitious, as Frederick
Hoffman commented: 'The greater number of the sons of the sea,
although fearless of the enemy and of the weather, however stormy,
are superstitious and have implicit faith in ghost-stories, mermaids,
witches and sea-monsters, as well as in the flying Dutch ship off the
Cape of Good Hope.'[97] This view was shared by William Glascock,
who joined the navy in 1800, seven years after Hoffman:

They implicitly believe in omens, mermaids, the flying Dutchman, evil
spirits, the appearance of the ghosts of the departed, and the pranks of
malicious spirits and goblins. They familiarly talk of frightful sounds and
preternatural noises coming up from the deep, all having an import of
fearful warning, and occasionally portending accidents, or the death of a
messmate. The simple and uneducated mind of the sailor seizes on the
supposition of some preternatural occurrence in all such cases, as the easiest way of accounting for these appearances, which a better-informed
mind would endeavour to unravel by the application of philosophical
principles or a close examination of the facts.[98]

Having been drawn from all over Britain and beyond, the men
brought with them local superstitions to mix with those only associated with the sea. Even in the same ship men would hold different
superstitions and disagree on the best way to invoke good luck and
avoid disasters.

Wind and weather were the source of many superstitions, and the effort to make progress against a wind blowing in completely the wrong direction gave rise to several myths, as on one occasion recorded by William Robinson: 'A headwind is the constant topic, and the boatswain, on coming upon deck, would look about him, to see how the wind was, and, with a great deal of good humour and apparent seriousness, would swear most positively that we should never have a fair wind whilst that holy friar was on board; and all the bad luck on board was set down to his account.'[99] In this instance the boatswain was trying to raise the men's spirits with a joke, as there was no holy man on board, but when people regarded as 'Jonahs', bringers of ill-fortune, were present, such comments could be taken very seriously. On this occasion, Robinson related, the men responded that 'their wives and lasses had not got hold of the tow-rope; a phrase intimating that, from being absent so long, they had taken to themselves other husbands in harbour, and did not want them home yet'.[100] This was even more of an edged joke, since with the men at sea for years at a time they could easily find previous relationships had dissolved. The seaman James Whiting of HMS *Vindictive*, who had been away for several years, received such a reply from his brother after enquiring about his wife: 'You mentioned your wife but I am very sorry to tell you she is not worthy to be called so, for she has had a child by another man, in your absence, and [from] what I can hear, her proceedings is very bad, therefore I did not think [it] proper to deliver the letter you sent her, for she reported you was dead, and more so, that you was flogged to death, which made us very unhappy.'[101]

Frederick Marryat, who became a novelist following his naval career, remembered how they avoided setting sail on Fridays: 'It certainly does savour of superstition, but sailors have an idea that ships have their lucky and their unlucky days; and the lucky day is soon found out. The dislike which sailors have to sail on a Friday is well known.'[102] Glascock agreed: 'Valuable as a fair wind is to a sailor, he would sooner lose it, and run the chance of its chopping about, and detaining him for weeks in harbour, than voluntarily sail on a Friday. Should he be compelled, from circumstances, to sail on that ill-starred day . . . he will not fail to attribute to that circumstance every minutest failure, or most serious accident, which subsequently occurs throughout the voyage.'[103]

Seamen were also superstitious about apparitions and mythical sea creatures. When off the coast of Canada, James Gardner recalled that the seamen mistook a man overboard for something sinister:

> About eight in the evening, with little wind and going two knots, and nothing in sight, a voice was heard astern hailing, 'On board the *Hind*, ahoy!' I must confess I was a little staggered, and some curious remarks were made by the seamen. One fellow said, 'I'll be damned if we were off the Cape but I should think it was the Flying Dutchman.' 'As to that,' says another, 'he has a roving commission and may cruise where he likes.' 'Bad luck to me,' says a marine, 'if it's not a mermaid.' 'And to sum up,' says old Macarthy, the quartermaster, 'it may be the poor fellow that fell overboard the other day.' However, the voice hailed again, saying 'Bear a hand and send the boat, for I'm damned if I can keep up much longer.' The jolly boat was immediately lowered from the stern and sent in the direction of the voice, and will it be believed that the fellows were afraid to take into the boat one of the main topmen (who had fallen overboard out of the main chains, being half asleep) until he had told his name and answered several ridiculous questions?[104]

According to Glascock, the seamen even believed that birds were sent from Satan: 'Their appearance at sea is almost always thought a sinister occurrence. Some are considered the harbingers of a tempest and storm; others, like *"Mother Carey's chickens,"* the active agents of the foul fiend, already bent on their destruction.'[105] After surviving a hurricane in the Indian Ocean in 1809, Robert Hay heard the men of the *Culloden* blaming their misfortunes on various apparitions:

> Some of our seamen gravely affirmed that shortly after the commencement of the gale they had seen the flying Dutchman cross our bows under a very heavy press of sail. This, joined to the circumstance of a large flock of Mother Careys chickens having been recently seen

skiffing along near the surface, and to the knowledge that near the same spot Sir Thomas Troubridge in the *Ramilies* 74 [actually the *Blenheim*] with his whole crew had shortly before perished, augured as they mysteriously hinted no good.[106]

The distinction between religion and superstition could easily be blurred. When the town of St Pierre on Martinique was attacked in 1794, Frederick Hoffman was among the party searching the town after it surrendered:

> The principal church had also suffered, as two sacrilegious shells had penetrated it and fallen near the altar. On entering it we found the models of three frigates. As they had not struck their colours [surrendered], we did them that favour, and made prizes of them. There were also some pictures of grim-looking saints, which one of the sailors was endeavouring to unhook until another called out, 'Let them alone, Jack, they'll only bring you bad luck,' on which he desisted.[107]

The model ships would have been votive offerings, placed in the church by grateful sailors thanking God for a safe journey – a practice that itself would be thought superstitious by many Protestants.

Those who survived to become experienced seamen, and perhaps climb a few steps up the promotion ladder, not only learned the ropes but also the variety, the tedium, the dangers and occasional excitement of life at sea, as well as picking up some vices, and often diseases, on the way. Having spent so long at sea, often from a young and impressionable age, many of them knew no other life, and in Captain James Scott's view,

> Sailors are beings who decidedly differ from the rest of our species. There are many prominent distinctions in their character, but they cannot be fairly judged by the common standard of other men: they enter the service as mere children, before a principle is fixed, or a feeling matured; their studies incomplete, and their minds just in that pliant state, which may be disfigured or beautified, according to the nature and strength of the impressions made upon them.[108]

Such men were the driving force behind the great sailing warships that protected Britain's coastline, took the war to the enemy, and ultimately controlled seaborne commerce. On his way to exile on St Helena, Napoleon acknowledged to his British captors, 'The sea is yours – your seamen are as much superior to ours as the Dutch were once to yours.'[109]

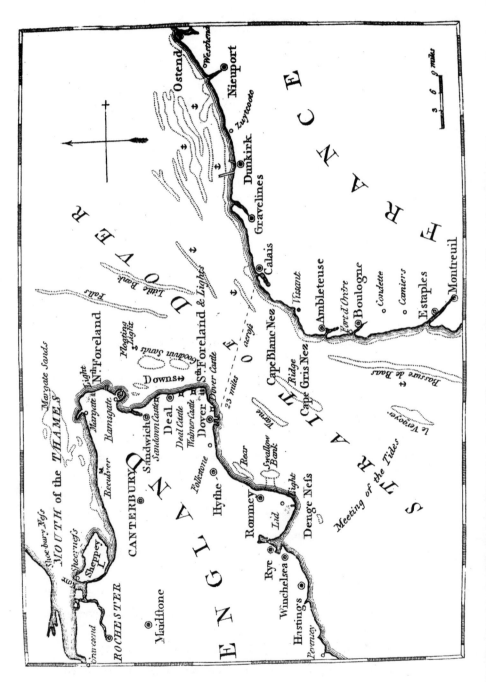

TWO

—·◆·—

PRESSED

On Saturday night there was another hot press on the Thames. Ministry are determined to prepare for the worst. We have now as fine a navy as ever swam on the bosom of the Ocean.

The Times on the press-gang in action in London in 1790 when war was threatening[1]

In April 1810, seventeen-year-old merchant seaman Joseph Bates landed in Liverpool for the first time, hoping to find a ship bound for America. After only a few days at the port, he was shocked and then enraged when 'a "press gang" (an officer and twelve men) entered our boarding house in the evening and asked to what country we belonged. We produced our American protections, which proved us to be citizens of the United States. Protections and arguments would not satisfy them. They seized and dragged us to the "rendezvous", a place of close confinement. In the morning we were examined before a naval lieutenant, and ordered to join the British navy.'[2] Bates had been about to return home to Boston, but instead was forcibly conscripted into the navy:

To prevent our escape, four stout men seized us, and the lieutenant, with his drawn sword, going before, we were conducted through the middle of one of the principal streets of Liverpool like condemned criminals ordered to the gallows. When we reached the river side [the Mersey], a boat well manned with men was in readiness, and conveyed

us on board the *Princess*, of the royal navy. After a rigid scrutiny, we
were confined in the prison room on the lower deck, with about sixty
others.[3]

Such scenes occurred right round the coast of Britain, as well as at
sea and in foreign ports, both in times of peace and war, because
impressment was the most effective method of recruitment. Joseph
Bates was to serve just over two years before being interned as a
prisoner-of-war when hostilities broke out between Britain and
America in 1812. Along with other American sailors, Bates was
eventually taken to Dartmoor prison, from which he was released
on 27 April 1815 – five years to the day after being illegally conscripted at Liverpool.

Impressment was bitterly resented by those men and their families
who were likely to be affected by it, and every trick was employed to
avoid being picked up. In one incident at Cork in Ireland during the
severe winter of 1813–14, John Harvey Boteler, a midshipman aboard
the frigate *Orontes*, was ordered on shore to accompany a press-gang.
'We had intimation of a lot of seamen hid in a small public-house in
the cove,' he said, 'and after a scrimmage secured very prime hands,
such a scene; a wake was got up, women howling over the coffin,
where a corpse was said to be, but our lieutenant would not believe
them, and sure enough out popped a seaman, who laughed himself,
when all was over.'[4]

The Impress Service recruited seamen and was staffed by naval
officers. In each location they operated from a base known by the
French term 'rendezvous', but frequently abbreviated to 'rondy'. This
was often established at a pub, and here volunteers could join the
navy, but regular press-gangs also patrolled along the coast and into
the surrounding countryside, especially along rivers to inland ports.
Press-gangs also acted from warships out at sea or in harbour, at
home and abroad, seizing new hands from coastal settlements and
from merchant ships. Unlike the army, which relied on persuasion
and inducements to recruit soldiers, the navy was allowed to force
men into the service – to impress them. The word 'prest' came from
the French *prêter*, to lend or pay in advance. It was originally a small

sum of money paid to a seaman upon recruitment, who was then said to be 'prest'. It took on a more menacing meaning when conflated with 'press', implying coercion.

By law a press-gang was only allowed to take seafaring men and those who used the river (including bargemen and fishermen), between the ages of eighteen and fifty-five. Experienced seamen were preferred, and they were easily identified, because they tended to wear different types of clothes, their hands were ingrained with tar, and many were bow-legged and walked with a noticeable rolling gait after being at sea for weeks or months at a time. When Lord Eldon met Admiral Collingwood in London, he observed that 'I had not seen him for many years – he had been so long on board ship, that he walked with difficulty.'[5]

Night-time was best for seizing seamen, while they were asleep, and in times of acute shortages of sailors, press-gangs invariably took landsmen, with no sea experience. Even though only seafarers were supposed to be taken, this was not adhered to, and there was obviously corruption, as the *Middlesex Journal* reported in 1771, the year Nelson joined the navy: 'For some time past it has been a common practice for the press-gangs to seize abundance of honest tradesmen indiscriminately, and carry them to the rendezvous houses, where they extort money from them to let them go again.'[6] Bogus press-gangs also duped money from terrified men, as one newspaper reported for London in 1787:

> On Saturday evening a pretended press-gang, consisting of five men, stopped a man in Long-lane as he was going home with his wages, and, under pretence of impressing him for the King's Service, were hauling him away; the man, however, upon producing half a guinea, was permitted to go away. He having watched the party [go] into a public house, went to Horsleydown, and brought a real gang with the proper officer, who surprized the sharpers regaling on their booty, every one of whom were carried on board the tender at the Tower.[7]

A similar story occurred in London during the hot press that began in March 1803: 'On Saturday evening last, a banditti, to the amount of 21, composed of coal-heavers,* &c. formed themselves into two parties, with a view to plunder; and under the pretence of being authorised press-gangs, seized between 40 and 50 labourers coming from their pay-tables, in the neighbourhood of Wapping, from whom they extorted about 20l. [£20] for their liberation.'[8] Unluckily for them, two real press-gangs encountered these fraudsters and forced them into the navy.

Impressment was a royal prerogative, but it was an irony recognised at the time that British freedom, much celebrated in songs like 'Rule, Britannia!', was defended in times of war by a navy totally dependent on conscripting the lower classes into what many regarded as 'legalised slavery'. Captain Thomas Pasley was sympathetic: 'Poor Sailors – you are the only class of beings in our famed Country of Liberty really *Slaves*, devoted and hardly [harshly] used, tho' the very being of the Country depends on you.'[9] Impressment was certainly akin to slavery, as the men were forced to leave their families and employment, with an uncertain future ahead. Their period of service was indefinite – for as long as they were needed – and they were obliged to work every day of the year, with some respite on Sundays, but no entitlement to shore leave and certainly no entitlement to see their families. Consequently, it was constantly feared that these men might desert.

From the time Nelson entered the navy, opposition to impressment began to be linked to other radical campaigns, such as the War of Independence in America and a few years later the revolution in France. The legality of impressment was challenged, and by the end of the war increasing pressure was exerted to reform the system. One letter to a magazine by a London resident was typical in its call for impressment to be abolished: 'This subject demands (if possible) *more* of morality and patriotism than the abolition of the *Slave Trade!* *Pressing* is quite as great a stigma on the country in the eyes of all Europe; and whilst it absolutely makes them doubt our sincerity as to the abolition of the slave trade, it has a dreadful effect on the morals of us all!'[10]

---

* Labourers who unloaded coal from ships in the River Thames.

A system of conscription would have targeted all classes, unlike impressment, as Napoleon commented to his Irish surgeon Barry O'Meara years later when in exile on St Helena:

> You talk of your freedom. Can any thing be more horrible than your pressing of seamen? You send your boats on shore to seize upon every male that can be found, who, if they have the misfortune to belong to the *canaille* [the rabble], if they cannot prove themselves *gentlemen*, are hurried on board of your ships, to serve as seamen in all quarters of the globe. And yet you have the impudence to talk of the conscription in France: it wounds your pride, because it fell *upon all ranks*.[11]

Napoleon's assessment cut right to the heart of the matter, because only the lower classes were affected, and therefore reform would be slow in coming. Working-class men dreaded impressment, and news of an approaching press-gang provoked widespread panic. The campaigner William Lovett was born at Newlyn in Cornwall in 1800, and he wrote of his early years:

> I have . . . deeply engraven on the memory of my boyhood the apprehensions and alarms that were experienced amongst the inhabitants of our town regarding the press-gang during the war. The cry that 'the press-gang was coming' was sufficient to cause all the young and eligible men of the town to flock up to the hills and away to the country as fast as possible, and to hide themselves in all manner of places till the danger was supposed to be over. It was not always, however, that the road to the country was open to them, for the authorities sometimes arranged that a troop of light horse should be at hand to cut off their retreat when the press-gang landed. Then might the soldiers be seen, with drawn cutlasses, riding down the poor fishermen, often through fields of standing corn where they had sought to hide themselves, while the press-gang were engaged in diligently searching every house in order to secure their victims. In this way, as well as out of their boats at sea, were great numbers taken away.[12]

William Richardson spoke of the way impressment ripped

communities apart, as he witnessed with regret in his home town of South Shields in 1795, two years after war had resumed with France:

> From Spithead we sailed away for Shields, to the great joy of my brother and I and other North countrymen in the ship. We anchored off the Bar and my brother and I soon had leave to go on shore, but we soon found Shields altered much from the happy times we had seen it; there was no joy, no merriment as used to be, everything appeared gloomy and the people sad; all the young men nearly were pressed and taken away and moreover we had no parents, brothers or sisters to greet our arrival as formerly, our family had become like a shipwreck and driven to different parts of the coast, but few of our relations here were alive, not a soul knew us as we went along the street, except a woman who had nursed us, and she poor creature was highly pleased to see us again. We called into a Publick house kept by a distant relation and ask'd if they knew where any of Capt Richardson's sons [he and his brother] were, they replied with a sigh that they believed they were pressed into the Navy.[13]

The press-gang trawled the Shetland Isles frequently, and during the American War of Independence the parish minister John Mill wrote in his diary:

> In July [1777], the people being apprised that the Government had sent over a tender, with a demand of an hundred men for their service, they fled from their houses and betook themselves to their hills and skulking places, which made me take notice of this on the Sabbath from the pulpit, saying they made great haste in running away for fear of the Pressgang, who did not want to hang them or put them in prison, but only to serve their King and Country in the suppression of Rebels in America, who had risen up against their lawful superiors without any just grounds, and [they] might be better employed for a year or two than at home; for when the rebellion was over, they might return again with their pockets full of money.[14]

Midshipman George Vernon Jackson, who joined the navy at the age of fourteen in 1801, was in charge of one press-gang at the renewal of war two years later and felt more sympathy:

From [South] Shields we went to Shetland, and I daresay there are people living there yet to whom a remembrance of our visit still clings. We carried off every able-bodied male we could lay our hands upon. I think the number we captured in Shetland alone amounted to 70 fine young fellows. When the ship was on the point of leaving, it was a melancholy sight; for boat-loads of women – wives, mothers, and sisters – came alongside to take leave of their kidnapped relatives . . . [I] often repented having made a capture when I witnessed the misery it occasioned in homes hitherto happy and undisturbed . . . These were strange times when a youngster of my age could lay violent hands upon almost any man he came across and lead him into bondage; but such was the law.[15]

Captain Charles Tyler, based in Pembroke, told the Admiralty about the deep distrust towards press-gangs he experienced when trying to raise a militia force of Sea Fencibles along the South Wales coast that same summer:

The men do not come forward as they ought. Some evil-disposed persons have insinuated that as soon as they are enrolled they will be sent to man the ships. I have taken every pains but cannot quite convince them to the contrary. At Fishguard not a man would enrol, although from the best information there are near two hundred employed in the coasting trade during the summer, and fishing in the winter. Nothing but a strong military force could press them. They bid defiance to any press-gang.[16]

Many men were legally exempt from impressment, such as foreigners, crews of outward-bound merchant ships, apprentices, some fishermen, custom-house employees and militia volunteers, but they had to carry a certificate of protection at all times. Also exempt were those sued and arrested for debt, and it was suspected that many such claims were fictitious in order to evade naval service. The smuggler John Rattenbury from Beer in Devon was taken by the press-gang at Cowes on the Isle of Wight in 1798 and apparently used forged documents relating to a baby boy, German Phillips, who had been baptised at Seaton (near Beer) only a few months earlier: 'When it came to my turn to be examined, I told him I was an apprentice, and that my name was German Phillips, (that being the name of a young man, whose indenture I had for protection.) This stratagem however was of no avail with the keen-eyed lieutenant, and he took me immediately on board the *Royal William*, a guard ship, then lying at Spithead.'[17]

Whenever there was an urgent need to recruit seamen, a frenzied bout of impressment – a hot press – took place when protection certificates were waived, which caused even more panic. The most ruthless started in March 1803 when peace with France was collapsing and an invasion appeared imminent. One of the first targets was Plymouth: 'At Stonehouse, Mutton Cove, North Corner, Morris Town, and in all the receiving and gin-shops at Dock, several hundreds of seamen and landmen were picked up and sent directly on board the flag ships . . . The different press-gangs, with their officers, literally scoured the country on the eastern roads and picked up several fine young fellows.'[18] At Portsmouth on 11 March more chaos was reported: 'The order for impressing seamen is still continued with the greatest vigilance, and not a single vessel of any description, lying in the harbour, but what has been completely searched, and the men, and even boys, taken out. It is with the utmost difficulty that people on the Point can get a boat to take them to Gosport, the terror of a press-gang having made such an impression on the minds of the watermen that ply the passage.'[19] Seamen were brought from all round the coast into the main naval bases, such as Plymouth:

Came in from Liverpool, with impressed men and volunteers, the *Sirius*, of 36 guns, Captain Prowse; also, from Exmouth, the *Eagle* Excise cutter, Captain Ward, with seamen, from Falmouth; the *Active* Excise cutter, Captain Kinsman, with seamen for the fleet. Last night the *Boadicea*, of 44 guns, Captain Maitland boarded, by her boats, the whole flotilla of trawl boats then fishing off the Eddystone light-house, and took two seamen out of each trawl-boat, about forty in number, and sent them on board the flag-ship in Cawsand Bay.[20]

A month later, at the end of April, Rear-Admiral George

Campbell issued a secret order to the captains under his command along the south-west coast of England:

> WHEREAS it is intended that a general impress of seamen should take place at the different ports and places along the adjacent coast, and that preparation should be made with the utmost secrecy and caution to perform that service with promptitude and effect, you will, immediately on receipt of these orders, select from the crew of his Majesty's ship under your command a sufficient number of trusty and well disposed men to man three boats, with as many marines and petty officers as you may judge necessary to send in each, under the orders of a lieutenant, to whom you will deliver a press warrant accordingly; and you are likewise to select sixteen steady marines that may be trusted to go on shore to stop the avenues leading up to the country . . . You will endeavour to have previous communication with one of his Majesty's Justices of the Peace for the district, applying to him to back the warrants, taking especial care to cause as little alarm as possible.[21]

Many requests were made to the Admiralty for the discharge of impressed men and boys, and petitions were even presented when communities felt terrorised. In 1812 the Corporation of Falmouth in Cornwall complained in a petition about Lieutenant Robert Carter, a native of Exeter, saying that they had

> for some time past, viewed with the sincerest regret and heartfelt sorrow, the vexatious and outrageous proceedings of Lieutenant Carter of the Impress Service, at this Port, acting under the orders of James Slade Esq. of the Royal Navy, the Regulating Captain. That said Lieutenant Carter appears to be guided, in such his impressments, by no regard to the authority of the Magistracy, the laws of the land or the welfare of the country; but to consider his own private views and interests paramount to all public considerations. That the said Lieutenant Carter impresses indiscriminately Landsmen, Fishermen, Packetsmen* and Local Militia

---

* The main base for Post Office packet ships was Falmouth, carrying mail and dispatches to naval bases far afield, such as Halifax in Canada and Gibraltar.

Men, dragging them from their houses and quarters at unusual hours of
the night. That the said Lieutenant Carter by firing at and molesting persons not subject to impressment, has interrupted and rendered the passing
of this harbour in boats, dangerous. That said Lieutenant Carter, by
impressing fishermen and others, concerned in supplying the markets
of Falmouth and its neighbourhood with fish, as also with potatoes,
has materially affected the supply of the markets with those, at all times
necessary, but at the present moment of scarcity, indispensible articles
of consumption. That the impressment of a local militia man (and
who we conceive was not liable to impressment) on the second of this
month, whilst the Regiment, in which he is enrolled, was embodied in
this town, occasioned a very great sensation amongst the inhabitants and
others, and was nearly productive of consequences the most alarming.[22]

Foreigners were exempt from impressment, but foreign seamen as
well as prisoners-of-war could volunteer for the navy. Even so, there
were many like Joseph Bates who were picked up by the press-gangs,
often deliberately, resulting in numerous requests for their release.
One example was mentioned to the Admiralty by Captain Edward
Rotheram on board the *Dreadnought* off Ushant in April 1805:

I have the honor to acknowledge the receipt of your Lordship's order of
yesterday's date requiring me to state the cases of John Peterson and Jna.
Neilson on board His Majesty's Ship under my command said to be subjects of Sweden as expressed in your Lordships order. I find that the men
alluded to are both natives of Trondheim in Norway, that they were
pressed the 23rd of April 1803 out of an East India ship, and that neither
of them are married or settled in England or have received the King's
Bounty and as I conclude your Lordship's order means their being discharged, if aliens, I will execute the same the first opportunity.[23]

It had taken these men two years to obtain their release. A decade
earlier, in 1793, the merchant captain Samuel Kelly was at Bristol
where some of his foreign crew were taken:

As soon as we cleared Customs I proceeded with the brig to Pill, to be ready for the first fair wind. Two or three of my crew were Swedes, which were in general secure from the Impress, and always considered so by the Admiralty, but while I was at Bristol the gang boarded the brig and carried off the foreign seamen, knowing them to be such. As soon as I heard of my loss I applied to the two lieutenants for their release, in vain. I then made a humble application to the regulating captain, who heard me with indifference and finally dismissed the petition.[24]

A major source of aggravation between Britain and America was the impressment of American seamen. One problem was deciding who was an American, because there was no especially distinctive American accent and anyone born before the Declaration of Independence in 1776 was formerly a British subject. Certificates of citizenship were issued to many American seamen to prevent their being seized by press-gangs, but bogus protection documents were freely purchased, both in America and in major British seaports, so the Royal Navy tended to treat them all with suspicion. It has been estimated that from the start of the war with France in 1793 to the outbreak of war with America in 1812, between eight and ten thousand American seamen were pressed into the Royal Navy, while others served as volunteers. The British believed that they had the right to board foreign ships to take off British deserters, but frequently removed those of different nationalities on the assertion that they were British. There was great bitterness, and the American Henry Torey,* who became a prisoner-of-war at Dartmoor, angrily complained: 'When the British go on board an American merchant ship to look for English sailors, they adopt one easy rule, viz – they select the stoutest, most hardy and healthy looking men, and swear they are Englishmen. After they have selected one of these fine fellows, it is in vain that he produces his protection, or any other evidence of his American birth and citizenship.'[25]

In practice many naval captains were a law unto themselves, and

---

* His memoirs were written in the first person by Benjamin Waterhouse, but from various records Ira Dye (1987, p. 316) has convincingly shown that it was Torey and not Waterhouse who was the prisoner.

knew very well they would be miles out to sea before some illegally pressed men were even missed by their family and friends. Instances occurred where pressed men just disappeared from their communities, and particularly for those who were illiterate and could not write home, their families might lose contact with them for months or years, sometimes for ever. Even a man like George Price, who could write reasonably well, had trouble making contact with his family, yet he was only based at the Downs off the Kent coast, not in some far-flung location. 'I wrote a letter to you about a fortnight ago and I have received no answer,' he complained to his brother on 25 May 1804, adding, 'in which I concluded the letter miscarried',[26] and again a week later: 'I have wrote four letters to you and cannot get an answer which I think is very strange.'[27] William Lovett said that of those seized in the Newlyn area, 'many of them [were] never more heard of by their relations'.[28] One young boy at Portsmouth who disappeared turned up several years later, in 1812:

> About five years ago, a child of Mr. Sheppard, belonging to one of the coach offices in this town, but who is since dead, was stolen from his parents. Every possible enquiry was made after him, at the time, without success, and he was given up for lost. He has, a few days since, made his appearance in the *Hebe* frigate, just arrived in England. The boy has not the most distant recollection how he was enticed away; but remembers he was put on board the *Royal William*, and afterwards sent to sea in the *Laurel*. He has been 25 months in a French prison.[29]

Built at Bridport in Dorset in 1806, the 22-gun *Laurel* was sent to the Cape of Good Hope. In September 1808 the ship was keeping watch on the harbour of Port Louis in Mauritius, but was forced to surrender after a fierce fight with the much larger French frigate *Canonnière*, which is when the boy was taken prisoner.

Around the shores of Britain, the threat of impressment blighted communities for decade after decade. During most of Nelson's adult life, British forces were fighting in some part of the globe, usually in a war against the French, and so he hardly knew a time when press-gangs did not operate. The press-gang was so prevalent that many traditional folk songs deal with its operations, and one from Tyneside was a typical lament:

> O! the weary cutters – they've ta'en my laddie frae me,
> O! the weary cutters – they've ta'en my laddie frae me;
> They've press'd him far away foreign, with Nelson ayont the salt sea.
> O! the weary cutters – they've ta'en my laddie frae me.[30]

Once the cutter or tender was full, the men were usually taken to a larger receiving vessel, from which they were eventually distributed to the warships that needed them. In 1801, when fourteen-year-old Daniel Goodall was volunteering for the navy, he was treated as badly as the impressed men:

> I was handed over to the tender mercies of a corporal of marines, whose duty it was to conduct me to that purgatory of naval neophytes, the press-room, as the dog-hole in the hold of the '*Tender*' is called, wherein newly-entered volunteers and impressed seamen are confined – for no distinction was made at the first between those who were forcibly deprived of their freedom and those who surrendered of their own will their liberty of action for the time being.[31]

Goodall was sent down a ladder into the hold, which was like a prison:

> The ladder was instantly withdrawn, the grating clapped on again, and then of course, I was in total darkness . . . Such a torrent of oaths and obscenity were immediately poured out upon me from all sides as might well justify of themselves the character of 'floating hells,' only too justly bestowed upon some of those receptions for naval recruits, and before I could stumble to my feet I was again seized and violently shoved forward as before with the same result. This process was again and again repeated, until I was ready to drop between the pain of my bruises and sheer exhaustion. This was called 'hustling', and each time I fell the cry went round, 'Up with him again and hustle him'.[32]

Eventually one man stopped the hustling and found him a place to sleep. Later in life, Goodall bitterly remembered this first encounter with the navy: 'A lapse of more than half a century has not obliterated the vividness of my impressions.'[33]

In May 1805 the seventeen-year-old William Robinson, from Farnham in Surrey, was another volunteer who felt he was treated like a criminal:

> We were ordered down in the hold, and the gratings put over us; as well as a guard of marines placed round the hatch-way, with their muskets loaded and fixed bayonets, as though we had been culprits of the first degree, or capital convicts. In this place we spent the day and following night huddled together, for there was not room to sit or stand separate: indeed, we were in a pitiable plight, for numbers of them were sea-sick, some retching, others were smoking, whilst many were so overcome by the stench, that they fainted for want of air.[34]

Conditions on board the tenders and receiving ships were so bad that they led to the rapid transmission of diseases like typhus in previously healthy men, but calls to improve the system fell on deaf ears. Fifteen years before William Robinson suffered the hell-hole of the tender, *The Times* wrote:

> Instead of a tender to receive the impressed men, and confine them until they are sent on board their respective ships, there should be large roomy houses for them on shore, where the air might have free circulation, and where health could not be forced away by the stench of putrified air. This might be easily accomplished at Tower-hill, Deptford, and Greenwich, and would redound to the humanity of Government, whose duty it is to provide in the most comfortable manner for these men who are torn from their families to do the most dangerous part of the public duty. Deaths and diseases are the consequence of the bad treatment these poor fellows receive before they get on board the fleet. They are crammed together like so many slaves from Africa, and used, not as the men on whose fidelity and courage the existence of this country depends – but as if they were the veriest felons that ever received sentence of transportation.[35]

Probably the most heartless impressment was that of merchant seamen who were returning home after a voyage of one or two years and were taken before they saw their families again. In March 1803, seamen were seized from East India Company ships off Plymouth, having made the long journey from India: 'While the six East Indiamen were lying to off the Eddystone, for the easterly wind, on Monday last the English cruisers in the Channel, manned and armed, boarded them all, and made a fair sweep of nearly 300 prime seamen for the service of the fleets; the crews of the Indiamen, till boarded, had not the most distant idea of an approaching rupture with France.'[36] Even returning prisoners-of-war were liable to be seized. In late 1798, the nineteen-year-old George Mackay managed to flee from France, where he had been held prisoner for four years after HMS *Scout* was captured in the Mediterranean. His escape was through Switzerland and Germany, and at Cuxhaven he boarded a packet boat to Yarmouth:

> After a very boisterous passage of three days, I reached the shores of Albion in perfect safety. How did my heart leap with ecstasy at finding myself once more upon British ground! How exquisite were my antici-pations of a happy interview with an aged father and a beloved sister! Alas! I knew not the luckless fate which awaited me: I knew not, that in the space of a few minutes, every fond and cheering hope would be cru-elly blasted: – I knew not, that such a measure of affliction was awaiting me, as would cause me most deeply to regret having left an enemy's country! But to proceed: I had not been seated long before a cheerful fire, regaling myself with a draught of good English porter, which to me seemed equal, if not superior, to nectar, when a press-gang, who, it would appear, had observed me entering the house, suddenly rushed upon me, and without the least ceremony, dragged me into the presence of their commanding officer. In vain I pleaded my long captivity – In vain I entreated them to suffer me to proceed to London to see an aged father, whom I had not beheld for several years; these sons of Neptune were inexorable; and having securely lodged me on board of a tender, I was from thence carried to the Nore, and put on board a frigate, which in a few days afterwards sailed for the West Indies.[37]

Violent opposition to the press-gangs was inevitable and widespread. A hot press took place at the start of the Revolutionary Wars with France in 1793, but the seamen of one East India Company ship refused to cooperate:

> On Thursday evening a press-gang attempted to get on board the *Camden* East Indiaman, lying at Gravesend; but the crew resolutely opposed their coming into the ship: and appeared with arms in their hands, swearing they would cut them down. A young Irishman, remarkably strong, took up a grindstone lying on the deck, and swore he would throw it upon them if they did not desist, upon which they rowed off, but returned again at four o'clock next morning, and being served as before, were obliged to sheer off.[38]

Sometimes pressed men were successfully rescued, as the merchant captain Samuel Kelly witnessed at Liverpool the following year:

> My lodgings were near one of the naval rendezvous, which gave me an opportunity of witnessing an unpleasant transaction. A carpenter had been impressed and was lodged in the press-hole at the bottom of Water Street. This circumstance being communicated to the shipwrights, a large body of the trade assembled at night with a long spar [of wood] which they used as a battering ram against the prison door, which soon burst asunder and all the men within were liberated. They then proceeded to the rendezvous in Strand Street which they broke open and literally gutted the house, the feathers of the beds were emptied into the streets and the furniture broken to pieces or carried off as booty, in which business a number of women assisted, as well as in drinking the beer and liquors, and even the windows were demolished.[39]

That same year, over two thousand miles away at St John's in Newfoundland, impressed men were also rescued, resulting in the murder of a lieutenant from the frigate HMS *Boston*, as the seaman Aaron Thomas recorded in his journal:

It was deemed necessary for the benefit of His Majesty's Service that a boat should be manned from the *Boston* for the purpose of going ashore a pressing. Lieutenant [Richard] Lawry was sent with the party. They returned with some hands which they had pressed. The next day, Saturday the 25th October [1794], Mr Lawry was sent ashore with two of these men in order to get their cloaths and the wages from the persons whom they had served as fishermen during the season. They landed at the upper end of the harbor, on which Mr Lawry took four of the boat's crew with him, as the men had a few yards to walk. They passed under some fish flakes [frames for drying fish], when suddenly a number of Irishmen, armed with wattles [sticks] surrounded Mr Lawry and three of the boat's crew. They rescued the impressed men, and then beat Mr Lawry in so unmerciful a manner that he *died* the next morning of the wounds he had received in this fray. Two of the boat's crew were beat in a terrible manner, and their lives for some time despaired of. One other got off with a few strokes, and his messmate got off, perhaps with his life, by running for, and gaining the boat.[40]

The logbook for the *Boston* recorded: 'Sunday 26 [October 1794] . . . At half past 1 Lieut. Lawry died of his wounds received from the mob. Carpenters employed making a coffin for him. Sent a party of marines on shore in search of the murderers.'[41] Thomas noted that one of the Irishmen gave evidence against the others, and Richard Power and Garret Farrell were hanged six days later. 'Had this transaction happened in England,' Thomas observed, 'a great scope offered itself for the pleading of counsel. They would a spoke on the *right* and *necessity* of pressing, on volunteers and impressed men . . . The two men that were hanged were natives of Ireland and most deservedly met their deserts.'[42]

Impressment frequently provoked a response from the mob, and nearly four years later in Hull, in July 1798, another incident led to rioting:

On Thursday evening last, as Lieutenant [James] LOTEN of the Impress Service in Hull, was going home from the house of the rendezvous, he met a sailor armed with a large knife, such as is used in

Greenland, with which he instantly struck the Lieutenant and cut him in the hand. Lieutenant L. took him immediately to the rendezvous, and had him sent on board the *Nonsuch* [tender]. A large mob of idle and disorderly persons collected about the house, and broke all the windows of that and some of the adjoining ones. Their disposition to commit further acts of riot was so evident, that it was judged prudent to call out the military and yeomen, who were soon under arms, and continued so for three hours, till the mob had left the streets, and the quiet was restored.[43]

Murders and assaults were also committed by members of the press-gang, who were invariably found not guilty when the cases went before the courts. In 1779 sixteen men from a press-gang under the command of Midshipman William Palmer were tried at Ipswich for the murder of the publican Thomas Nichols at Bury in Suffolk. Because of the sensitivity of the case, it was transferred in June to the Court of King's Bench in London, where it was heard that

> the prisoners [the press-gang] went to a public-house there, with such sticks as press-gangs usually carry, when the door was opened, and they found certain sea faring men there, part of the crew of store ships not paid by government, but contractors: that being told of the purpose for which the prisoners were come, one of them drew a knife, and swore he would stab the man who should prevent him from going to his wife; another with a poker swore he would not be taken alive: that a scuffle ensued, in which the table was thrown down, and candles put out by one of the crews of the storeships: that Thomas Nichols, the deceased, run in amongst them, and told them not to suffer themselves to be pressed: that in the affray Thomas Nichols received a mortal wound from one of the prisoners.[44]

A debate ensued on what constituted murder, during which it was stated that 'the situation of the prisoners would be particularly hard indeed, if, when compelled to a service which they dare not refuse, they are to answer with their lives for consequences which are, if not inevitable, but too probable to follow from the execution of their duty'.[45] It was decided that there was no murderous intention and that it could not be proved who was in the house at the time. The prisoners were therefore discharged.

Captains obviously preferred to have seafaring men, but frequently only landsmen were found, a poor substitute for a proper crew. Among them were vagrants and convicts, who could be forcibly recruited into the navy. In October 1787 *The Times* reported that in London, 'The operations of the press-gangs have made a visible change in the streets – all the idle, vagabonding part, are removed, and an addition thereby made to the safety of the inhabitants. So many poor fellows, without employment, and acting under the combined influence of distress and drink, must be thieves or rogues, if not otherwise provided for.'[46] This system could usefully rid places of troublesome inhabitants, as in Liverpool a few years earlier, where Captain Worth, the regulating officer, said that 'George Wood was impressed at the request of the neighbourhood where he lived, being a common disturber of their peace. I declined taking him at first, but being solicited again and understanding he was a stout fellow, he was taken and carried on board the *Assistance* near three months since; from her he swam away and [was] brought on board the second time by the Wigan gang.'[47] Impressment suited the wealthy – crime was reduced because vagrants and criminals were taken off the streets, wages were held in check for some types of workers, because they were threatened with the press-gang, and the warships were manned so as to protect trade. Another source of recruits was through the Marine Society, which had been founded in 1756 by Jonas Hanway to take young boys off the street and give them clothing and training for the navy.

Especially in times of war, though, the supply of new recruits through impressment was inadequate, and in 1795 two Quota Acts were passed that required every county and numerous ports to supply a specified number of able-bodied men for the navy in return for a bounty. The county of Berkshire, for instance, was required to find 108 men and Staffordshire 245, while the port of Dartmouth was expected to supply 394. This drew in many landsmen and criminals, and when in March 1797 William Hotham was put in charge of

HMS *Adamant*, he thought it was very dangerous to have crews of ships filled up by men of dubious backgrounds. He believed there were seditious elements present – which turned out to be the case, as mutinies at Spithead and the Nore followed soon after. He later commented:

> The scheme of quota men was a new and injudicious one; and threw a mass of population into the fleet, whose habits were altogether strange to the seamen of it, the admixture with whom was unnatural and prejudicial. It was then a common practice with the London Police when they got hold of a confirmed rogue but lacked sufficient evidence to convict him, to send him on board any ship known to be in want of men, in order effectually to dispose of him. Men of this kind, often pronounced demagogues, with a little knowledge of politics and a smattering of education, indignant at their compulsory servitude, were in a frame of mind to excite discontent and defiance in others.[48]

Perhaps surprisingly, many sailors did enlist voluntarily, and their reasons were varied; sometimes lured by the romance of the sea and the chance of adventure, escaping an unhappy situation on land, or quite simply because they wanted to be part of the service. Twenty-five-year-old Irish Catholic Henry Walsh did not dream of a life at sea, but was desperately unhappy at his home near Aghalee, County Antrim, and after an argument with his father in the summer of 1809, he decided to head for Belfast and start afresh. 'I then considered it,' he said, 'the only place of refuge for to ease my troubled mind, as I wished to live in obscurity from all my friends or any that I had ever knew.'[49] He wrote a letter home: 'Dear mother, when these few lines fall in your hands I then will be far from you . . . I hope that my absence will restore happiness in the family. I hope that my father will never frown nor reflect on me for my disobedient and mispent life.'[50]

The majority of recruits who volunteered had limited prospects in jobs on land and so were attracted by the idea of being given meals, accommodation, alcohol, tobacco and medical care, as well as their pay. For many men the harsh and brutal life of a warship was little different from the struggle to survive on land, and the offer of a cash payment or 'bounty' to each volunteer was generally enough to sway them. The hope of prize-money loomed large, and experienced sailors might enlist with ships that had 'lucky' captains who could make them a fortune. A prize was an enemy vessel and its cargo captured at sea, and prize-money was the value of such ships and cargoes paid to the crews involved according to a fixed scale of shares, reflecting the ranks of the officers and the men. Such a system was not far removed from outright piracy and would be alien in today's navy, but it was then a key element of service and could even influence operations.

It is not possible to establish how many men were pressed and how many were volunteers, because the impressed men frequently bowed to the inevitable and agreed to volunteer, which gave them a sum of money. At St John's in Newfoundland in October 1794, on the day he was murdered, Lieutenant Lawry of HMS *Boston* returned to shore with '2 men (who had been preste but had entered) for their cloaths and wages'[51] – the men were deemed as having entered the navy voluntarily. The smuggler John Rattenbury was caught by the press-gang at Cowes on the Isle of Wight in 1798 and taken to the *Royal William* receiving ship at Spithead to await being transferred to his allotted ship: 'I remained there in close confinement for a month, hoping that by some chance or other, I might be able to make my escape; but seeing no prospect of accomplishing my design, I at last volunteered my services for the Royal Navy: if that can be called a voluntary act, which is the effect of necessity, not of inclination.'[52] George Price, rated as a landsman on board HMS *Speedy*, was listed as a volunteer, but was actually impressed at Deptford in November 1803 from an East Indiaman that was on the point of sailing to China. The twenty-three-year-old wrote from a hospital ship to his brother, a publican at Southwark, to inform him of his situation:

I had the misfortune to be prest out of the *Walmer Castle* Indiaman and was very unwell at the time [they] took me on board the *Speedy* brig, and there I got so bad that they was obliged to send me on board the *Sesex* [*Sussex*] hospital ship lying at Sheerness ... After I was on board the

Speedy a few days I got so bad that I did not know where I was, no more than you did, and in that state I lost every article belonging to me, even the shirt of my back. Now I will leave you to guess what miserable state I am now in.[53]

When he was pressed, George Price like numerous others was quick-witted enough to use a false name. In letters to his brother he urged him to reply to his alias of George Green.

Unlike the seamen, no officer was compelled to join the navy, but there was never a shortage of candidates. To be an officer, it was necessary to be a gentleman. Although not impossible, very few officers rose through the ranks from humble social origins, and those who did were sometimes given the disparaging title of 'tarpaulins'. One impediment to success was that few ordinary seamen were sufficiently well educated to pass their lieutenant's examinations, though they might make it to the rank of midshipman.

Thomas Troubridge came from a trade background. Born in London, about three years before Nelson, he was the only son of Richard Troubridge, an Irish baker, and Elizabeth Squinch of Marylebone. He was educated at St Paul's School in London and then possibly joined the merchant navy, before moving to the Royal Navy. With his father's background, Troubridge had no chance of being an army officer, but rose rapidly through the naval ranks. His first naval voyage was on board HMS *Seahorse* to the East Indies as an able seaman, from which he was promoted a few months later to midshipman. This was an eventful time, as he became firm friends with one of the other midshipmen – Horatio Nelson. Troubridge eventually reached the rank of rear-admiral.

Many senior officers disliked the idea of officers rising from the ranks and were all too well aware of a person's origins. Captain George Westcott, from Honiton in Devon, was also the son of a baker. He joined the navy at the age of fifteen, and the *Naval Chronicle* recorded his background:

Young Westcott used frequently to be sent to the mill [at Honiton]. It happened in one of his visits, that by the accidental breaking of a rope, the machine was disordered; and neither the owner nor his men being equal to the task of repairing it, Westcott offered to use his skill in splicing it, although attended with danger and difficulty. The miller complied, and the job was executed with such nicety, that he told him 'he was fit for a Sailor, since he could splice so well; and if he ever should have an inclination to go to sea, he would get him a berth.' Accordingly an opportunity presented itself, of which the lad accepted; and he began his naval career in the humble capacity of a cabin-boy; a situation the most common in the ship, and not much calculated to afford vent to the expansion of genius. But he contrived to exercise his abilities to such good purposes, and discovered such an acuteness of understanding, that he was, in a very short time, introduced among the Midshipmen; in which rank his behaviour was so conciliating and prudent, that further advancement followed.[54]

Thirty years later Westcott was killed at the Battle of the Nile. In January 1801 Nelson went to see Westcott's mother when he was on his way to Plymouth: 'We left Axminster yesterday morning at eight,' he wrote to Emma Hamilton. 'At Honiton, I visited Captain Westcott's mother – poor thing, except from the bounty of Government and Lloyd's, in very low circumstances. The brother is a tailor, but had they been chimney-sweepers it was my duty to show them respect.'[55]

A career in the navy was particularly attractive to younger sons who were not in line to inherit landed estates and titles and also to sons of the respectable middle classes, especially with the lure of prize-money. Unlike the army, where officers' commissions were bought for large sums of money without the need to prove any knowledge of military life and were the preserve of the upper classes, naval officers had to learn to be competent seamen and to demonstrate their skill through years of service and formal examinations by senior officers. All of them (even future kings such as William IV) started their officer career as midshipmen, the lowest officer rank. Such a career structure provided the chance of social advancement and so there was never a shortage of boys and young men wanting to be midshipmen. Despite not buying commissions, most fledgling officers were helped by 'interest' – the coy contemporary term for nepotism. It was crucial for these young men to achieve rapid promotion, because once they reached the rank of captain, they were literally in a line, waiting for the ones ahead of them to die off before they could be promoted. Nelson, for instance, was able to succeed because his maternal uncle Maurice Suckling was a naval captain. While 'interest' was essential for a rapid rise through the ranks, it was no substitute for basic seamanship. Inevitably, a few incompetent officers manipulated the system and rose to a high position, but they could not simply buy their way in, as army officers did.

Before becoming a midshipman, sea experience was needed. A few joined the merchant navy for a while, and others joined as able seamen or as captain's servants. Each captain was allowed four servants for every one hundred men in the crew, though only a handful were domestic servants. The rest were his protégés or apprentices, and in 1794 these servants were classified as Volunteers First Class (or Boys First Class), who had to be at least eleven years old, or thirteen if they were not the son of a naval officer. Their next stage was to be a midshipman, and if they had a minimum of six years' sea service, including two years at midshipman level, then they could take their lieutenant's examination. The rules were constantly broken, as some certainly entered the navy at midshipman level without previous experience, others joined at a much younger age, while several were entered fictitiously on the books when very young to make their sea service appear longer.

The marines were not impressed, but were recruited like soldiers, and posters were printed to induce young men and boys to join. At Portsmouth during the hot press of March 1803, the marines were also trying to obtain extra hands: 'Great encouragement is offered for recruits for the Marines service; bills [posters] have been stuck up this day, offering a bounty of three guineas per man, and a reward offered to any person who will bring a recruit.'[56] During the 1812 war with America, one recruiting poster in Newark proclaimed:

GREAT ENCOURAGEMENT.
AMERICAN WAR.

What a Brilliant Prospect does this Event hold out to every
Lad of Spirit, who is inclined to try his Fortune in that highly
renowned Corps,

The Royal Marines
When every Thing that swims the Seas must be a
PRIZE![57]

The poster enthusiastically announced that marines had plentiful
opportunities to reap prize-money, as well as lots of food and drink
on board, a bounty, generous pay, and the honour of serving king and
country. 'Lose no Time then, my Fine Fellows,' it exhorted, 'in
embracing the glorious Opportunity that awaits you; YOU WILL
RECEIVE **Sixteen Guineas Bounty,** And on your Arrival at *Head
Quarters*, be comfortably and genteely CLOTHED. – And spirited
Young BOYS of a promising Appearance, who are Five Feet high,
WILL RECEIVE TWELVE POUNDS ONE SHILLING AND
SIXPENCE BOUNTY, and equal Advantages of *PROVISIONS*
and *CLOATHING* with the Men.'[58]

One boy who joined up in Norwich on 18 April 1795 was twelve-
year-old William Mallet, not a schoolboy but a labourer, who no
doubt was persuaded that a better future lay open to him in the
marines. Being illiterate, he put his mark X to the statement that:

> I William Mallet do make Oath, That I am a Protestant, and by Trade a
> Labourer and to the best of my Knowledge and Belief was born in the
> Parish of St Andrews in the City of Norwich and that I have no Rupture,
> nor ever was troubled with Fits, that I am no-ways disabled by Lameness
> or otherwise, but have the perfect Use of all my Limbs, and that I have
> voluntarily inlisted myself to serve His Majesty King GEORGE the
> Third, as a Drummer in the First Division of Marine.[59]

This was countersigned by the surgeon: 'THESE are to certify that
the abovesaid William Mallet aged 12 Years, 4 Feet, 6 Inches high,
Fair Complexion, Sandy Hair, Blue Eyes Came before me . . . I have

examined the above-named Man, and find him fit for His Majesty's Service.'[60]

Another volunteer was Thomas Rees, from Carmarthen in Wales. He became bored with being a tailor's apprentice and first joined the militia, then the marines at the age of seventeen in April 1808 because of 'a very great desire to engage in active service, and to be able to visit foreign countries'.[61] Apart from military service or joining the merchant navy, opportunities for visiting foreign countries were virtually non-existent, yet many men were intoxicated with tales of mysterious lands that were spread by sailors, travellers and explorers. Others wanted to join the marines because they had heard about prize-money. John Howe was the second-youngest son of a farming family from Middlezoy in Somerset, but his father died when he was one year of age, leaving his mother in poverty. A few years later she remarried, and John was apprenticed to a clothier in Bradford-upon-Avon, where he was taught to read and write. He began to be treated badly there and so, he recalled, 'at last I thought I would go for a soldier and hearing some Marines had received five hundred pounds a man prize money I determined to go in them. I accordingly enlisted on the seventeenth of June 1779, at this time I was not seventeen years of age being born on the twenty-fourth of July 1761.'[62] His initial plans at joining the marines did not work, as he enlisted as a soldier by mistake:

> The sixteenth of June being Bradford Fair Monday* I enlisted with one of the Queens Light Dragoons but proving too short for him he asked me if I was willing to go in the marines. I said I thought he was one of them for I did not wish to be in any thing else . . . this being Tuesday morning we sauntered about town till meeting with a marine belonging to a party stationed at Froom [Frome] in Somersetshire: he told him he had enlisted a young lad who through a little drink had mistaken him for a marine.[63]

* 16 June 1779 was a Wednesday, so he is mistaken with the dates.

Much misery and tragedy were created with boys and men joining the navy as volunteers or by force and then being denied leave to see their families. When war broke out with France in 1793, thirteen-year-old William Douglas in London volunteered, but five years later, on board the *Lapwing* in the West Indies, he was devastated to receive a letter from his mother giving news of his father's death. His shipmate Aaron Thomas related what happened: 'At the time this Douglas received this letter, containing an account of his Father's death, he was with me, and the very second day afterwards, he got almost as drunk, as a lad could get. This drinking he has learned aboard a man of war . . . He is now 17, was brought up amongst the butchers in Clare Market, but when the war began, he run away from his father and mother, and entered on board the *Enterprize* which is moored [on the Thames] off the Tower Stairs.'[64] Thomas related a tragic incident about another seaman, a landsman from Holborn in London, who had joined around the same time:

> Thursday 26 July 1798 . . . At half past seven PM Peter Bird a seaman aged twenty-three departed this life. He had been ill of a flux about nine days. About three months ago this young man . . . told me, that his mind was fixed upon [a] young woman in London, who he *intended to marry*, when the war was over, adding I am but a young man, and she will forgive me for leaving her as I did . . . His mother lives in London, he was put apprentice to a butcher in Brookes Market, in that city, but on the wars breaking out, he run away from his master, and shortly after entered aboard this ship.[65]

It is hardly surprising that many men deserted or tried to desert. In 1803 Nelson suggested that to prevent desertion, seamen should be given certificates for every five years of wartime service with a bonus of two guineas every New Year's Day and four guineas for eight years' service: 'It may appear, at first sight, for the State to pay, an enormous sum; but when it is considered that the average life of a Seamen is, from *old* age finished, at forty-five years, he cannot many years enjoy the annuity.'[66] Nelson added as a warning that 'whenever a large convoy [of merchant ships] is assembled at Portsmouth, [and] any

[of] our fleet [is] in port, not less than 1000 men desert from the Navy'.[67] Some deserters were killed in the attempt, while others were caught afterwards. Like runaway slaves or apprentices, their descriptions were circulated and rewards for their capture offered. Captain John Clarke Searle on board the *Venerable* at Spithead sent a description of one seaman to Admiral Mark Milbanke in December 1803: 'Charles Lane is aged about 29 years, stout made, 5 Feet Six Inches high; of a dark complexion, short dark hair, inclining to curl. Had on when he made his escape a short blue jacket, with a quantity of small white buttons close together, a blue waiscoat, & Trowsers. He has an aunt & a brother living at Gosport, & is well known both at Portsmouth and Gosport.'[68] It would have been difficult for Charles Lane to hide in a place like Portsmouth, and his only chance would be to move right out of the area, yet he would probably still be easily identifiable as a seaman and in constant danger of being pressed. It was usually excessively harsh treatment or the yearning to see their family that drove men to risk the brutal reprisals and desert. When Samuel Leech was on board the *Macedonian* frigate off Spain at the end of 1810, punishments were so common that many men tried to desert, although, he said, 'many others were kept from running away by the strength of their attachment to their old messmates and by the hope of better days'.[69]

For some, those better days never arrived. In mid-January 1807 William Skill, a former merchant seaman, fell overboard in the Adriatic and was drowned. Robert Wilson, a fellow seaman from the *Unité*, related his tragic story: 'We pressed him out of the India fleet, just on his return from a three-year voyage, pleasing himself with the idea of soon beholding those he held most dear (a mother and sister) for whom he had brought presents many a long mile; and although in his time on board us, he had made away with most of his apparel for grog which he was fond of, yet the presents remained untouched; hoping one day or other to take them home himself.'[70] Everything he had so carefully kept was auctioned off at the end of January, with the ship's log simply stating, 'Sold at the mast the effects of Wm Skill, seaman.'[71]

Map of Europe.

THREE

———— •◆• ————

SALT JUNK AND GROG

A deal of liquor found its way into the ship yesterday, many people were very drunk, and this morning the ship's cook and his mate were so tipsy that neither the one, or the other, could put the fresh water into the copper to boil the fresh beef in.

Journal of Aaron Thomas for 7 July 1798[1]

After a memorable meal on board HMS *Brunswick* in the West Indies in 1802, Lieutenant James Gardner was impelled to record the behaviour of Marine Lieutenant Augustus Field:

Our ship was full of rats, and one morning he caught four which he had baked in a pie with some pork chops. When it came to table he began greedily to eat, saying 'What a treat! I shall dine like an alderman.' One of our lieutenants (Geo. M. Bligh) got up from the table and threw his dinner up, which made Field say, 'I shall not offend such delicate stomachs and shall finish my repast in my cabin,' which he did and we wished the devil would choke him. When he had finished, he said one of the rats was not exactly to his taste as the flesh was black; but whether from a bruise or from disease, he could not say, but he should be more particular in future in the post mortem examination. I never was more sick in my life.[2]

Although seamen, marines and officers were given the same rations, lieutenants and above invariably supplemented their meals by buying better food, and ate rats only out of desperation or experimentation.

Two years earlier in the West Indies, Lieutenant William Dillon was on board a French brig they had just captured: 'The *Diligent* was full of rats. They were so numerous that the French seamen used to kill and cook them . . . But I could not be prevailed upon to taste any.'[3]

Midshipmen were a good deal poorer than the higher-rank officers, and they and many ordinary seamen were less squeamish about eating rats when the basic food was salt meat and hard-baked biscuits. The crew mostly subsisted on a monotonous diet, which Samuel Leech described:

> As our fare was novel and so different from shore living, it was some time before I could get fully reconciled to it: it was composed of hard sea biscuit, fresh beef while in port, but salt pork and salt beef at sea, pea soup and burgoo. Burgoo, or, as it was sportively called, skillagallee, was oatmeal boiled in water to the consistency of hasty pudding. Sometimes we had cocoa instead of burgoo. Once a week we had flour and raisins served out, with which we made 'duff' or pudding. To prepare these articles, each mess had its cook, who drew the provisions, made the duff, washed the mess kids [small wooden tubs], &c.[4]

The food may have been bad by the standards of today, and ignorance prevailed about what food was essential in preventing illness, but at least the seamen were fed, whatever the conditions prevailing on land. At home in Norfolk in 1792, Nelson wrote to the Duke of Clarence (future King William IV) and showed how concerned he was for the plight of the agricultural labourers and their low wages. He listed what a family earned and spent in one year and concluded that they could not make ends meet even if they were 'to drink nothing but water, for beer our poor labourers never taste, unless they are tempted, which is too often the case, to go to the alehouse'.[5] Dreadful weather leading to bad harvests also meant that the poorest starved, especially in times of war.

The uncle of William Wilkinson, writing from Dublin four months after the death of Nelson, thought that service in the navy was preferable to the difficulties of life for everyone else:

One thing is certain. Taxes will increase, necessaries advance in price, and every article of consumption or use grow dearer. These things to you happier beings of the floating region cause little sensation, who have a King for your banker, a King for your butler, brewer and baker, your wine excise free, no house rent, no hearth or window tax, no horse or dog duty to pay, who mounted on the wings of expensive gaiety have no cares, no anxieties other than birds of prey ever on the alert alluring or snaring those we call enemies within your fell grips, who notwithstanding cautious cunning often fall within the influence of your attraction, which like the devouring vortex of a comet, is inevitably fatal to all within its compass.[6]

When Daniel Goodall was a marine in 1805, his ship, HMS *Flora*, was with the North Sea fleet watching the Dutch coast, which was tedious work except when they returned to Yarmouth for supplies. 'When we returned from a provisioning trip,' Goodall related, 'we invariably took with us to the fleet some thirty or forty live bullocks and an abundance of vegetables in bags, so that it was not without good reason that the North Sea station was called by sailors a full belly station.'[7] He added: 'But good rations could not reconcile us to dull and disagreeable work.'[8]

Appetites were never likely to be satisfied when food and alcohol were the high points of many a dull day, but Aaron Thomas writing in 1798 was certainly of the opinion that seamen went hungry: 'How I have heard captains of men of war, boasting ashore, that the provisions allowed to sailors was more than they could eat – yesterday Lynn the armourer begged me to give him something to eat. This day my old servant D. came to me and said he had been hard laboring all day in the boats, and now had nothing to eat, he wished to have a little something to eat, with his dry biscuits.'[9] Over a decade later eighteen-year-old George Watson, serving in the Mediterranean, had similar grievances:

I was now become a proper man of war's man. I could drink, fight, swear, &c. &c. with great eclat, and . . . was perfectly inured to toil. The greatest inconvenience I suffered from was hunger, whether that was

owing to my youth, or to not having supplies equal to the labour we had
to endure, I cannot determine; at any rate I never felt full, nor satisfied.
This may appear strange to those who know the quantity of rations
allowed a sailor on board of a King's ship . . . but it should be recollected,
such allowance has to serve a man, both for night and day, instead of day
only; as a sailor, especially a boatman,* who has to work as much, by night
as by day, and consequently as much inclined to eat.[10]

The biggest complaint was that the purser, responsible for provisions, gave short measure, as he only issued 14 ounces in a pound,
creaming off 2 ounces for himself, a practice that was stopped after
the 1797 mutinies. The type of provisions tended not to be an issue,
since tastes in food were extremely conservative. Every seaman had
a pound of bread and a gallon of beer a day. Each week he was also
given 4 pounds of salt beef, 2 pounds of salt pork, 2 pints of dried
pease, 1½ pints of oatmeal, 6 ounces of sugar, 6 ounces of butter and
12 ounces of cheese. As a daily ration this amounted to a pound of
bread, a gallon of beer, ½ pound salt beef, ¼ pound salt pork, ¼ pint
dried pease, $^1/_{10}$ pint of oatmeal, $^4/_5$ ounce of sugar, $^4/_5$ ounce of butter
and 1½ ounces of cheese. Even assuming that the seamen were
given full measure and that everything was good enough to eat,
this is barely sufficient to sustain a man doing hard physical labour,
often in hostile weather conditions, and working shifts that were
mostly four hours on and four hours off, through a twenty-four-
hour period.

Very often other types of food were substituted, such as fresh vegetables instead of bullet-hard dried pease (nowadays spelled peas),
fresh beef instead of salt beef, flour and raisins to make duff instead
of meat, and grog instead of beer. The physician Gilbert Blane commented on alternative foods for butter: 'There are certain articles
that are the natural produce of the West India islands, which may be
substituted for it with the greatest advantage. These are sugar and
cocoa, which, during the last year of the war [1782], were served in

* Watson was involved with much coastal boat work.

place of butter with great success, and this proved an alteration in diet not only salutary, but agreeable to the seamen.'[11]

The galley (kitchen) was situated under the forecastle on the upper deck in two-decker ships and on the middle deck in three-deckers. A huge cast-iron stove on a brick or flagstone surface burned coal and wood and had a chimney to carry away the smoke. The stove comprised chain-driven spits, coppers with lids for boiling, ovens and hot plates. Cooking was done mainly by boiling in the coppers. The meals of the officers were cooked here as well, mostly by their servants, using more elaborate techniques. The men in each mess took daily or weekly turns as the 'mess cook'. This did not involve actual cooking, but included fetching the day's food from the steward, doing any preparation such as mixing the duff, taking what needed to be cooked to the ship's cook in the galley, fetching the cooked food for his messmates, and keeping clean the mess utensils and equipment. Robert Wilson described the responsibilities of the ship's cook, who did the cooking for the men:

> The ship's cook assisted by his mates dresses the victuals for the ship's company, i.e. for all those under the denomination of officers. The cook's mate does all the drudgery work, the cook inspects him. Every article into which the provisions are put is perfectly clean. The serving out of the provisions out of the boilers or coppers is managed entirely by the cook himself, for if there is any deficiency, he is answerable for it. When he receives the meat from the Ship's Steward he has to count the number of pieces he receives, and to provide himself with a list of thoses messes which have received any raw meat so as to know what quantity of dressed meat to give them. As the cooks in general are not over and above stocked with learning, the manner in which they serve out the provisions by the list is by making a mark with a pin on the paper opposite the number of the messes issued out to.[12]

The post of cook was not a laborious one and was usually given to a disabled seaman:

> The cooks are in most ships men that have lost a precious limb, or other-wise maimed in the defence of their King and Country, so as a

compensation they receive a warrant as cooks. At the same time, the most of them are entitled to pensions, so that with their wages and perquisites, of fat [slush], etc., and their pensions together, they make it out pretty well. They are for the most part of them elderly men who have seen much of seafaring life, and when their work is finished for the day they'll take their pipes, seat themselves in Copper Alley, and spin you a long yard [yarn] . . . about what they have seen and done.[13]

Daniel Goodall became friends with the cook in HMS *Amelia*, a fellow Scot by the name of John Robinson,* usually referred to as Jack, who often entertained the crew:

Jack was a Greenock man, a thorough bred sailor, and had been a petty officer on board the *Temeraire* at Trafalgar, where he lost his left hand. He was a first-rate specimen of the British seaman of the day – a frank, open-hearted, and open-handed fellow, who . . . sang a good song, and sung it well too, his favourites being 'Scots wha hae wi' Wallace bled' and 'Their groves o' sweet myrtles let foreign lands reckon', which he could give with great effect. For these and other reasons Jack was exceedingly popular on board with both officers and men.[14]

All hands were piped to breakfast around eight o'clock, leaving just a few men on duty. Thirty to forty-five minutes were normally allowed for this meal, the first since the previous afternoon. Breakfast was mainly burgoo, which was oatmeal boiled in water with salt, butter and sugar to produce a gruel or porridge, as William Robinson described: 'This meal usually consists of burgoo, made of coarse oatmeal and water; others will have Scotch coffee, which is burnt bread boiled in some water, and sweetened with sugar. This is generally cooked in a hook-pot in the galley, where there is a range.'[15]

At midday they were piped to dinner, the main meal of the day, which was between one and one and a half hours' duration. Basil Hall described the events leading up to the seamen's dinner: 'The ship's

---

* He refers to him as Robertson, but he is Robinson in the Trafalgar crew list of the *Temeraire* and in the *Amelia* crew list.

cook, with his one arm (for he has seldom more; or if he have two arms, he has certainly only one leg), empties the coppers, by means of a monstrous fork . . . He likewise allows the pease-soup to run off by a cock [tap] from another boiler into a huge tub.'[16] The cook actually relied on assistants to do the arduous work, such as removing the cooked salt meat from the boiler. In September 1812 the landsman William Warneck, on board the prison ship *Vengeance*, received 'a severe scald in both eyes, in consequence of hot water having been splashed into them, which has impaired his sight . . . [when] taking up pork from the ships coppers'.[17] Over a year later he was awarded a pension because 'sight of right impaired and left weak'.[18]

The food at dinner was a mixture of bread or ship's biscuit, meat and pease, though Mondays, Wednesdays and Fridays were meatless days (banyan days) when cheese, butter or pease were served with duff, a kind of pudding made from flour, suet and currants or raisins. Lobscouse was the name given to a stew of salt meat, onions, potatoes, any other vegetables and crushed ship's biscuit. The cooked food was fetched from the galley by each mess cook, and Hall noted the state of the containers: 'As the hour of noon approaches, the cooks of the messes may be seen coming up the fore and main hatchways, with their mess-kids in their hands, the hoops of which are kept as bright as silver, and the wood work as neat and as clean as the pail of the most tidy dairy-maid.'[19] He next described the scene as the men were piped to dinner: 'The merry notes are nearly drowned next instant in the rattle of tubs and kettles, the voice of the ship's cook and his mates bawling out the numbers of the messes, as well as by the sound of feet tramping along the decks and down the ladders, with the steaming, ample store of provisions . . . Then comes the joyous grog!'[20]

Supper was about four in the afternoon, sometimes a little later, lasting around 30 to 45 minutes. The galley stove was no longer alight by suppertime, and so this was a cold meal of biscuit with cheese, butter, and anything else that was saved from the midday dinner.

Officers had their meals an hour or two later, and dinner in the afternoon was when they invited guests from other ships or from ashore, taking pride in the entertainment that they offered. Robert

Wilson pointed out that the ship's cook was not the only cook on board, because the officers generally had their own cooks: 'The Captain's cook, and the gunroom ditto, cook for the Captain and lieutenants, etc., are most haughty in their exalted stations. They have not the least connection with the ship's cook.'[21] The ship's cook was a warrant officer while the officers' cooks were personal servants.

Food cooked for the officers was a world apart from that given to the seamen, and Aaron Thomas was highly critical: 'It must be admitted that it is a little irksome to the Seaman to see a train of seventeen or twenty dishes borne in state to the Great Cabin – full of savoury meats and vegetables, with jellys and blomonges [blancmanges], when they themselves have dined off a gob of fat pork or pease and water.'[22] Not that the captain's food was always of the highest quality. Thomas complained that when he dined with the captain, they 'had pease soup, as hot with kian [cayenne pepper] as a Devil. A capon boiled – by its taste I judge the body before it was put into the pot had been used to swab the decks.'[23] Charles Pemberton mentioned that Vice-Admiral Collingwood was also mean with his dinners and was referred to as '*Salt Junk and Sixpenny*, – a soubriquet which his penurious hospitality won. With salt junk, and a wine he was proud of saying "cost him but sixpence per gallon," he regaled his dinner guests.'[24]

The seamen ate in their mess groups, sitting around tables that were set between the cannons – usually wooden boards suspended by ropes from the deck above, which were stowed against the side of the ship when not in use. They sat on benches, chests, casks and any other suitable surface. Only the officers had chairs and proper tables, and they ate in the wardroom, while the midshipmen messed in the gun room, all waited on by servants. The captain ate alone in his cabin, unless he invited others to join him.

For the most part, wooden bowls, plates and tankards were used. An individual sailor might own one or two wooden vessels along with a basic knife and a wooden or horn spoon. Beakers of animal horn and wooden tankards were commonly used for drinking. For easy storage, the wooden plates were frequently square rather than round, giving rise to the phrase 'a square meal'. These plates were flat with a raised rim called a 'fiddle' that stopped food slipping off.

Some seamen acquired earthenware plates and bowls as well as pewter cutlery and tankards, but these were vulnerable. On one occasion Pemberton said that they salvaged everything possible from a captured ship that was sinking: 'Many crates of crockery-ware we thus recovered, which, being much damaged, was distributed, or taken *ad libitum*, among the seamen and marines; and the whole 'tween decks looked like an earthenware warehouse: each mess was furnished with cups, platters, and dishes sufficient for a cruise of half a century to come.'[25]

The officers dined off china, drank from real glasses and even had silver cutlery, but equipment for the midshipmen varied, and the new recruit Jeffrey Raigersfeld recalled that 'our spoons and plates were pewter, a dozen of knives and forks, two cooking kettles, a frying-pan, and a copper tea-kettle, these with a dozen tumbler glasses, two decanters, and a dozen teacups and saucers, of the old blue dragon fashion, with a tin teapot . . . One of the mess took it in turn weekly to wash the crockery ware, lest the boy should break any of it.'[26] The eating utensils might appear clean, but were seldom hygienic by modern standards.

Most food and drink, such as rum, beer, water, butter and salt meat, was stored in the hold in wooden casks, which were hauled up when needed. The marines helped with this heavy labour, which caused many injuries, as with Antonio Bernard, a Viennese private of marines, who had 'a fall from the fore ladder against the armourer's bench which produced hernia on the left side . . . in hoisting up water from the hold'.[27] Once they were empty the casks were often dismantled by the cooper and stored for reuse. Bread and biscuits were kept in sacks in the bread room, along with the cheese. Only towards the end of the Napoleonic Wars were there experiments with canned food, initially with tins of meat.

The salt meat was often years old and so hard that sailors could carve it into fancy goods such as little boxes. Midshipman Robert Barrett in the *Hebrus* frigate off the coast of America in 1814 moaned that 'there was little else in our mess but "salt junk," seven years old, which, of course, was as hard as mahogany'.[28] 'Junk' was a term for worn-out lengths of old rope, and the derogatory term 'salt horse' was

also used. When boiled, salt meat produced a thick salty scum of fat
known as 'slush', half of which was used to waterproof the rigging; the
other half was the cook's official perk, which he sold to tallow merchants, relying on this 'slush fund' to supplement his meagre wages.
According to Archibald Sinclair, who joined the navy that same year,
new recruits when called to dinner were invariably aghast at the
meat:

> In two minutes every man takes his post; but what is the dismay and
> astonishment at the first presentation of what was universally known as a
> piece of mahogany, to which it bore a striking resemblance in hardness,
> dryness, and polish . . . The slightest boiling, or even immersion in hot
> water, melted away anything that had ever borne a resemblance to fat. It
> was now a shapeless mass of hard and dry beef . . . The second day being
> pork day, it is hoped that matters may improve; but alas! we are all
> doomed to disappointment. After a basin of pease-soup, somehow always
> good, the allowance of pork was produced . . . A shrivelled piece of some-
> thing bearing a resemblance to a cut from the hide of a rhinoceros
> appeared.[29]

Although the salt meat was soaked in tubs of water (steep tubs)
before cooking, it evidently remained salty to the taste, and the men
attempted other methods. Basil Hall said that the officer of the watch
had to 'cast his eye along the whole length of the ship's side, to see
if . . . a piece of salt beef or pork, slily tied to a string, be towed
alongside – a practice the men adopt whenever they can, their object
being to wash out some portion of the brine from the meat before
dressing it'.[30]

Live animals were carried in warships for their milk and eggs, as
well as being butchered for their meat, and on board the *Fame* in the
Mediterranean the seaman George Watson related that

> we had live stock on board of every kind, in abundance; bullocks, pigs,
> sheep, goats, geese, ducks, turkeys, chickens, &c.; many of these crea-
> tures becoming domesticated, were spared the general slaughter, and
> had names given to them by the Tars, there was 'Billy, the goat; Jenny, the

cow; Tom, the sheep, Jack, the goose;' and many others, which I shall not
mention; Jenny the cow, after being two years on board, ran dry, and
therefore, was killed . . . poor Tom, the sheep, was killed by lightning.[31]

Livestock such as bullocks had to be hoisted individually from boats
up into the ship, and Captain Griffiths advised that cattle should be
treated carefully and that 'if they do not like the water, &c. it arises
from FEAR, and beating them, or any violent measures, will only add
to it, while conciliation will overcome it. Always sling them to hoist
them in. By the horns is a bad way.'[32] When at St Kitts Aaron
Thomas of the *Lapwing* watched one such transfer: 'A canoe brought
a very large American ox alongside, a rope was put about his head
and horns, to hoist him in by, as usual. When he was just suspended
over the boat, the animal being in a laxative state, he let fly with violence his excrement, which went with great force against the breast
and face of one of the black men in the boat; to the high entertainment of the people leaning over the side.'[33]

Except for the bullocks, the animals were usually private property,
and it was mainly a privilege of the officers to bring them aboard,
though sometimes one or more seamen were allowed their own animals if they had enough money. Captain Thomas Fremantle and
other officers did this at Cork just before their ship, the *Ganges*, set
sail to Bantry Bay in October 1803. 'We have three dozen of turkeys
on board,' Fremantle told his wife Betsey, 'which cost us only two
shillings a piece, fowls half a guinea a dozen. I have got a nice cow for
ten pounds and we begin to bake very tolerable bread.'[34] In March
1780, after leaving the Cape Verde Islands, Captain Thomas Pasley of
the *Sybil* wrote: 'Ship absolutely full of hogs and goats: the first I must
order to be killed – goats make little dirt',[35] but two days later he was
in a rage: 'My steward, John . . . acquainted me this morning that my
coops under the forecastle were in the night robbed of seven fowls;
turned all hands up, talked to them, and pictured in the strongest
possible terms the infamy and disgrace of such a conduct. There are
many good and honest on board, but intermixed with a set of
damned Irish villains, especially among the marines.'[36]

On board the *Crescent* at Jamaica in 1800, William Dillon

remarked: 'In our last cruize we had not much sickness. The Captain had allowed the seamen to supply themselves with pigs. These were left to run about on the Main Deck, and I one day counted more than one hundred of them. They were washed every morning and regularly fed by their owners. That indulgence contributed essentially to keep off the scurvy.'[37] The environment of a warship was not good for animals, and when he was captain of the *Neptune* off Ushant in June 1805, Fremantle told Betsey about an accident to their goat: 'Malheur, the only poor goat that was in the ship fell down the hatchway yesterday and I am obliged to drink my breakfast without a drop of milk.'[38]

A few days before the Battle of Trafalgar, Fremantle was blockading Cadiz and lamented that 'We are now plentifully supplied with all sort of fresh provisions, eleven bullock we got today but such miserable devils you can scarcely imagine, they are however much better than salt meat.'[39] The quality of live animals purchased was a frequent complaint. William Richardson, a gunner in the *Tromp* at Martinique in 1800, said that 'Our little crew were now victualled from the shore daily – every morning the jolly boat was sent to the Beef Wharf and brought off the day's allowance of fresh beef, bread and a turn of water. The beef was like carrion and a man could bring up the side [of the ship] a whole quarter in his hand, they were so small.'[40] Midshipman Barrett, stationed near the American coast in 1814, also complained that 'The fresh beef, for which the Navy Board paid three shillings and fourpence per pound, was scarcely eatable, disguise it as you would, and in England would have been regarded as mere offal.'[41]

Off Sicily a decade earlier, Midshipman Gardner of the *Berwick* disapproved of the men objecting to their rations:

> A mutiny took place among the ship's company, in consequence of some bullocks that were anything but fat being sent for the use of the people . . . A survey was then held, and the report stated that as no other meat could be obtained, double allowance of this lean kine should be served out to make up the deficiency; but all to no purpose; and John Bull, forgetting his duty and only thinking of his maw, broke out into open rebellion. Some of the scoundrels were put in irons.[42]

At the start of a voyage, a ship sounded and smelled like a farm-yard, with animals stowed in odd corners of the decks and their fodder crammed in every available space. In the West Indies in 1798, Aaron Thomas recorded that 'we have now on board [the *Lapwing*] six live sheep, five goats and six kids. They eat under the half deck, the smell of their excrement, breath etc is that of nature . . . this morning when I came first on deck, the smell from the live stock, under the half deck, was almost as fragrant as a cow yard.'[43] In 1801 Dr Thomas Trotter, physician of the fleet, expressed his opinion about pigs: 'Nothing has been so offensive on the decks of our ships as pig-styes. I am glad to find that Lord St. Vincent has ordered them to be moved into the waist [from the forecastle], to make room for the sick berth. Our opinion has been long at war with these nuisances: officers ought cheerfully to give up a few messes of fresh pork to their stomachs, to let their lungs have the full benefit of pure air in their sleeping and waking hours.'[44]

Animals had to be looked after and fed, and Aaron Thomas spoke of making hay wherever possible, as at one island off Newfoundland in 1794: 'Being in want of hay for our livestock on board we cut a quantity of grass, made the hay on shore, stowed it in the ship. It was a serviceable and very useful article.'[45] This was fine for animals that were for the common good, but Thomas thought it outrageous that cows should be looked after at public expense for the benefit of the captain and officers only: 'Captains of 74 [guns] and larger ships of the line generally have a cow on board at sea, which they take for the sake of her milk. This is a practice I mean to find fault with. Although the expense comes from the Captain's private purse, yet the Public may be said to have a property in one of her caretakers, he being paid by them.'[46] Thomas also thought it unacceptable that the seamen were not allowed to waste water, yet the cow was allowed huge amounts so that the captain could have milk, something the men never had except occasionally if they were ill:

When a Sailor, in the morning, is sitting on a gun eating dry biscuit or oatmeal and water, and sees a bowl of new milk carrying [being carried] to the captain's table, I wonder what he thinks of it – particularly if he is

on a long voyage and that morning had carried his flour and plumbs
[raisins] on the quarter deck, and there mixed his pudding before the officer of the watch, in order to prevent him embezzling of water. A cow will
drink seven gallons of water a day if given to her, and I need not comment
by asking how useful this seven gallons would be to seven messes, when
under the vertical sun. Cheesecakes, custards, cream etc. which are produced by the new milk are desirable delicacies, but the Sailor and the
Admiral are born with the same appetites.[47]

The bullocks were slaughtered whenever required and cut up by a
butcher on board. After the landsman George Price was impressed,
he was employed as a butcher, because he had previously worked in
that trade. 'I am a butcher in the ship [*Speedy*],' he told his brother,
'but at the same time I must lend a hand in every part of the ship,
both below and aloft where the ship's duty is required.'[48] Of slaughtered carcasses, Dr Trotter commented that 'There is another very
filthy practice in ships when in port, of hanging their fresh beef
under the half-deck, or under the booms in the waist. It is in these
places exposed to the breath of the whole ship's company, and is
often brushed by them as they pass. The sight is extremely disgust-
ing.'[49]

Among their rations, the men were given small quantities of butter
and cheese, but these supplies soon became rancid. Anything unfit
for eating had to be officially condemned and was usually returned to
the victuallers, who were the contractors responsible for supplying the
ships. Instead of butter and cheese, the men received alternative food
such as cocoa. In warmer climates, Jeffrey Raigersfeld noted, the midshipmen were allowed to purchase butter and cheese from the purser
before it deteriorated:

Our mess got a firkin of butter, and when it was half out, the butter,
which was at that time one may say oil, was so full of small hairs, that
however often we washed it we could not separate the hairs from the
butter, so we swallowed both butter and hairs, and every day as the
butter got lower in the firkin the hairs became more numerous until we
got to the bottom, where was found a mouse with all its hairs off . . . the

poor animal, as we supposed, fell in after the butter had melted, and sunk to the bottom.[50]

The stench of decaying cheese was thought to endanger health, and according to Dr Trotter,

> The provisions which afford the most disagreeable exhalations are cheese and butter when they grow rancid. Cheese is very much disposed to putrefaction, which is greatly increased by the heat of the bread-room, where it is usually kept. Plain as this observation is, yet . . . there is scarcely a ship that does not condemn a quantity of cheese three or four times a year.[51]

If feasible, mammals and fish were caught and cooked, and on one occasion in the West Indies, Aaron Thomas noted that 'At 4 P.M. catched a shark, measured 7 feet, cut her open and found 7 young sharks all alive, each measuring 10 inches. Our people eat the mother and all the young ones, except one which was thrown overboard.'[52] Sailors relished turtles as a source of fresh food, and the best place to catch them was at Ascension Island, where ships often stopped during Atlantic voyages. Landsman Robert Hay, travelling back from the East Indies in 1809 in the *Culloden*, the flagship of Vice-Admiral Sir Edward Pellew, went on a turtle raid, as he related:

> Shortly after leaving St. Helena we touched at the small barren island of Ascension, where we got an abundant supply of turtle. The method of catching these is as follows: On the arrival of the boat ashore the crew conceal themselves behind the rocks as near the beach as possible, and watch for the turtle coming ashore. As soon as it is a little way from the water, one or two men rush from the hiding places, seize it by the side of its shell and turn it on its back. They do not wait to convey it to the boat because they would be seen, and would prevent any more coming ashore. They just leave it in that position from which it cannot recover itself* and

---

* The origin of the term 'to turn turtle'.

when they have as many turned as they want they carry them at leisure to the boat. Our men in a few hours succeeded in taking 16, the greater part of which would weigh between 2 and 4 cwt.[53]

Turtles were easy to keep throughout a journey, Hay explained: 'In our water tank, and in a couple of large tubs, purposely constructed, we kept a few of them constantly in salt water, which was renewed daily. The others lay on their backs at random about the decks, their eyes were washed every morning, a wet swab was kept under their heads, and in this state they lived until made use of and some of them even till we arrived in England.'[54] Gunner William Richardson said that on one voyage they lived on turtle soup:

> Every evening for near six weeks a turtle was hung up to the skids by its two hind fins, the head was then cut off to let it bleed and although each one was large enough to serve our crew of three hundred men a day, little more than half a pint of blood came from each. Next morning it was cut up and put into coppers, then well boiled and served out to all hands, every part of it is good to eat, but the eggs – perhaps two or three buckets full out of one turtle – taste rather fishy.[55]

Soup made from turtles was an expensive delicacy, and in Britain a cheaper alternative, made primarily from the heads, hoofs and tails of calves, was becoming popular.* On board Robert Hay's ship, the sailors were not keen on the genuine version: 'On one occasion, turtle soup, that distinguished dish on the table of the voluptuary, was made for the whole ships crew, but as it wanted all its usual accompaniments it was but a very sorry dish. The seamen turned it into ridicule, remarking in a phrase in common use among them, that God sends meat, but the Devil sends cooks.'[56]

Fish were not caught and eaten as much as might be expected, which Dr Trotter regretted: 'Sir Edward Pellew encourages his

---

* Later, Lewis Carroll satirised its popularity by including a character called the Mock Turtle in his book *Alice's Adventures in Wonderland*: this beast had the body of a turtle, but the head, hoofs and tail of a calf.

squadron off Rochefort to employ every method for catching fish, which has much retarded the appearance of scurvy in his own ship, and others. What a pity that this excellent practice is not general in the fleet, when there is nothing else for employment. Lord Duncan, in the North Sea, has always been remarkable for his indulgence in this duty.'[57]

At times fish were more than plentiful, as at the Newfoundland Banks in July 1779, where the marine John Howe described being stuck for a fortnight in dense fog: 'We were served fishing lines and hooks and a man or two from each mess had leave to fish. A great deal was caught, so much that the People could not use it all, and [it] was left hanging about in different parts of the ship till it stunk. This very much displeased our captain.'[58]

Fresh bread only survived the first few days of a voyage, after which there was just ship's biscuit, which was also called bread. The circular or hexagonal biscuits were made in victualling yards and stamped with an iron biscuit press that included the government's broad arrow and the yard's initial. These biscuits deteriorated quickly and became prey to insects. Writing some years after the end of the war, Basil Hall said that the methods of storing biscuit were misguided, as they should have been in airtight containers, not exposed to the air: 'I remember once falling in with a ship, and buying some American biscuit which had been more than a year from home. It was enclosed in a new wine puncheon [cask], which was, of course, perfectly air-tight. When we opened it, the biscuit smelled as fresh and new as if it had been taken from the oven only the day before. Even its flavour and crispness were preserved so entire, that I thought we should never have done crunching it.'[59]

By contrast, Robert Barrett could not forget the 'biscuit that had traversed more than half the globe, each piece of which was filled with numerous insects called weevils, – and, when struck against the table, (a most necessary preparation before putting it in your mouth,) these maggots would be scattered about in every direction. But as no better could be procured on the station, it was, of course, of no use to condemn what we had.'[60] Midshipman Raigersfeld, on board the *Mediator* frigate in the 1780s under Captain Collingwood, also remembered the dreadful supplies: 'The biscuit that was served to the ship's company was so light, that when you tapped it upon the table, it fell almost to dust, and thereout numerous insects, called weevils, crawled; they were bitter to the taste . . . if, instead of these weevils, large white maggots with black heads made their appearance, then the biscuit was considered to be only in its first state of decay; these maggots were fat and cold to the taste, but not bitter'.[61] Like Barrett, he confessed that these biscuits would have been condemned and thrown overboard 'had it not been known no better were to be had'.[62]

According to George Watson, 'The first things sailors generally buy, when they come into port, are soft bread and butter; which are considered and they truly are, a great treat to teeth, long inured to the uniform resistance of flinty biscuit.'[63] Many of the men would have found hard biscuit painful to eat without soaking it, as most would have had poor dental hygiene or suffered from scurvy, with missing and decaying teeth, like the purser of Raigersfeld's ship, with his 'toothless jaws'.[64] Henry John Whick, a musician in the marines, wrote to his sister Margaret at Wolverhampton from the *Victory* in June 1810, saying that he was 'greatly at a loss for teeth. For on Friday last I sat down and had seven double teeth took out in less than half an hour, so I shall soon become an old man if I follow that for half a dozen times.'[65] With or without teeth, the physician Gilbert Blane observed that seamen aged far quicker than those on land:

for, in consequence of what they undergo, they are in general short lived, and have their constitutions worn out ten years before the rest of the laborious part of mankind [manual workers]. A seaman at the age of forty-five, if shewn to be a person not accustomed to be among them, would be taken by his looks to be fifty-five, or even on the borders of sixty.[66]

Soft bread was also a treat for the chaplain Edward Mangin, on board the *Gloucester* in 1812. When he went ashore at Hollesley Bay, on the Suffolk coast, with three others, he admitted that 'we touched at a public house, for the avowed purpose of eating soft-tommy (fresh bread and butter)'.[67] Having sampled both, he said that 'I preferred *soft-tommy* to *Purser's nuts* (ship's biscuit)'.[68] He also said that the midshipmen often played tricks by making false announcements, such as declaring that a boat was in sight, carrying all manner of desirable goods such as 'fresh beef, soft-tommy, Dutch herrings, new laid eggs, clean shirts, lavender-water, scented soap, snuff, onions, Chili vinegar and London-Porter'.[69] To Abraham Crawford, the sight of the Essex coast in the summer of 1804 was frustrating, as they were not allowed on shore, which denied them 'some of the good things that it produces – such as *soft tommy*, milk, butter, &c'.[70]

As they approached Batavia on Java in August 1811, just after the island had been captured from the Dutch, the sailors eagerly spotted areas of cultivation, with the prospect of fresh fruit and vegetables, and the surgeon James Prior reckoned that 'after having been several weeks at sea, these are luxuries more grateful to the eye of a sailor, than the bones of a favourite saint to the most orthodox Catholic'.[71] On long voyages the most common vegetable comprised dried pease, which were boiled so long that they turned into soup, but there are instances of vegetables and salads being grown on board, as Fremantle of the *Neptune* explained to his wife Betsey: 'I have got a garden on my poop and the weather is so mild the salads grow prodigiously'[72] – this was in the month of January while they were blockading Cadiz. On board HMS *Jupiter* in 1782, Captain Thomas Pasley had many men dying of scurvy. Because of a mistaken belief that they could be cured by being buried in soil, Pasley decided to dispense with his large garden beds: 'To day my garden (which it has been my practice to raise daily salad in) I have given up, and buried as many men in it as possible.'[73] The next day they had by chance improved so much that Pasley said 'I have dismantled my third tray of earth likewise . . . How fortunate my having a garden! Little did I think of its answering so valuable a purpose – it affords comfort to my heart, the first and best of salads.'[74]

'The greater part of the food of a ship's company is necessarily salted meat,' the physician Gilbert Blane wrote in 1789. 'Biscuit and pease, though of a vegetable nature are hard of digestion, and though they qualify the animal food, they do not answer the purpose of fresh vegetables.'[75] A few years later, in 1795, lemon juice was issued daily to prevent scurvy, with a gradual realisation that fresh produce such as vegetables, lemons and limes was essential for health. In the Mediterranean in 1804 Nelson mentioned that he was always on the lookout for fresh produce, and he was especially fond of onions, 'which I find the best thing that can be given to seamen; having always good mutton for the sick, cattle when we can get them, and plenty of fresh water . . . but shut very nearly out from Spain, and only getting refreshment by stealth from other places, my command has been an arduous one.'[76]

British warships that were blockading French ports were at times supplied with fresh produce from England. When the Basque Roads anchorage was being blockaded, one of those on board HMS *Gibraltar* was surprised that 'Bum boats frequently come from Torbay or Plymouth to supply our ships with vegetables, porter, fruit &c, and notwithstanding the many risks they run, continue to make a profitable market. They seldom have more than 3 or 4 hands, and no arms.'[77]

The food stored on board was at constant risk of being spoiled and eaten by vermin such as rats, mice, weevils and cockroaches. The surgeon James Prior gave some idea of how rats came on board, considering that warships were not moored too close to land:

> They are first introduced on-board, in the various packages of provisions and stores; neither is it possible for any vigilance to exclude them . . . To ships they are a great nuisance, destroying not only stores and provisions, but, urged by the continual noise of the water, will sometimes eat their way through the timbers, thus causing leaks, which it is supposed have proved fatal to many vessels. It is remarkable, that they always swim off to shipping when the distance is not considerable, and ascend by means of the cables; in case of a rope being made fast to the shore, they may be distinguished in the night, crawling off in numbers.[78]

In some ships there was fishing for rats, as Aaron Thomas noted on board the *Lapwing* in the West Indies: 'So plentiful are the rats in the ship, that every night I see the boys are sitting on the combings* of the twix't decks main hatchway, a-fishing for rats, with the same philosophy as I [might] see an angler angling on the banks of a river. The boys have a line with a bait, and some oakum twirled about the bait, which when the rat gets [it] in his mouth, is entangled in his teeth, by which they draw him up.'[79]

——•——

When Archibald Sinclair, a Scottish schoolboy in Edinburgh, learned in April 1814 that he was to enter the navy, he immediately began to prepare all his clothes and other equipment. Of these, one item was considered essential – 'pounds of tobacco, in half-pounds and quarters, to give to the sailors for doing odd jobs'.[80] Tobacco could be bought by the men from the purser at a set price deducted from their wages, although from 1806 they were given an allowance of 2 pounds per month in the form of dried leaves complete with stalk. They usually prepared the leaves by soaking them in rum and then tightly rolling them in canvas. This package was wound with a length of wet cord, producing a cigar-shaped object about a foot long, called a 'perique' or 'prick'. As the cord dried, it tightened the package and compressed the rolled tobacco, which matured while stored in this way.

Tobacco was much more commonly chewed than smoked because the only place below decks where smoking was permitted was the galley. The records of a court martial showed that on board the *Prince Frederick*, late at night in August 1798, a few men were sitting in the dark galley, even though the main fire of the stove was extinguished. One witness testified that 'The Sergeant of Marines was smoking a pipe on the other side of the galley',[81] while another related that 'the Maltese [the accused] came into the galley where there was a little fire and lighted his pipe'.[82] Opportunities to smoke on deck were infrequent, particularly during bad weather, but some did smoke there, as in another court-martial testimony when the marine Edmund Riley said that: 'Between four and five bells in the afternoon

* Coamings – raised lips around hatchways to prevent water on the deck from pouring down the opening.

watch as near as I can guess, I was near the sick bay on the starboard side of the main deck smoking my pipe.'[83] Most smoking of tobacco was with white or off-white clay pipes, and Midshipman George Jackson long remembered his visit to Diamond Rock, off Martinique, because it was there that he first tried smoking a pipe:

> One of the Lieutenants at the Rock insisted on trying to make me a disciple of the 'fragrant weed', and failed most disastrously in his kind intentions. I became so horribly ill, and took such a dislike to him, and tobacco, and the place in consequences, that I never think of them without a qualm. Perhaps I lacked energy to persevere and conquer, but I have never touched tobacco since, and perhaps am all the better for it.* From being considered a filthy indulgence, it has reached the character of a gentlemanly habit, so I must not abuse 'what all the world approves.' A long way off, and in the open air, I do not mind it much, and even this is a great admission to make. There are some young fellows I know who, when they come to see me, are sure to have a stale pipe in their pockets, and I can scent them from afar off; but they assure me the more beastly a pipe looks and smells, the nicer it is to smoke. So much for taste.[84]

Cigars were also smoked and snuff taken by some officers, both of which Thomas Fremantle admitted to his wife: 'I find I don't take so much snuff as I used to, but I have got perhaps a much worse habit which is smoking Segars [cigars], – which does not agree with me, notwithstanding which I continue to do so like a child and deserve whipping.'[85] A few weeks after Trafalgar, when he was blockading Cadiz, Fremantle mentioned to Betsey that 'my snuff is just out and I shall be obliged to manufacture more from the Ships Tobacco, I don't take more than I did, but full enough'.[86]

It was far easier to chew tobacco, and a quid of tobacco would last all day, could be kept overnight and was usually good for a second day's chewing. Those men who chewed tobacco would have been

---

* He died at the age of eighty-eight.

more likely than most to spit, but random spitting was unacceptable. Captain Robert Barlow of the *Phoebe* frigate ordered that 'It is forbid to spit about the decks. Spitting boxes to be put in different parts of the ship to be filled with sand by men appointed.'[87]

—————•—————

While food could at least be disguised by cooking, the water was more difficult to stomach, though much of it was used for diluting rum or cooking. The men were allowed to drink water from a cask placed on deck known as a scuttle butt, which had a square hole or scuttle cut in it. Sometimes a marine was posted by the scuttle butt to prevent wastage, because obtaining fresh supplies for hundreds or thousands of men in a squadron was a constant challenge. Water was generally collected from rivers, which meant loading empty wooden casks into the ship's small boats, going on shore, filling them and hauling them back into the boats, before returning to the ships. The casks were stored in layers or tiers in the hold, the bottom layer resting on the shingle ballast. Fresh water was pumped up from the hold or else the casks were hauled up on deck.

Watering was regarded as one of the hardest jobs of all, causing ruptures and leading to the men contracting malaria in mosquito-ridden areas. Yet it provided a welcome opportunity to go ashore. Rear-Admiral Sir Charles Pole, in September 1799, ordered boats to stop watering at Torquay, on account of

Complaint having been made to the Commander in Chief that the boats sent on the watering service to Tor Quay have robbed and destroyed the gardens and orchards and otherwise done considerable damage to the neighbourhood, to the great disgrace of those who have been guilty of such riotous and improper conduct.[88]

When Nelson's squadron was desperately looking for the French fleet that had escaped from Toulon, a few months before Trafalgar, they paused near Cagliari in Sardinia to obtain water, and Thomas Marmaduke Wybourn, a twenty-nine-year-old marine lieutenant, described the operation:

Everything being in readiness to receive the water, all the boats proceeded on shore with casks etc., and in a short time tents were pitched, guards stationed, triangles [lifting tackle] erected . . . Never was a place better adapted for watering a fleet: the boldness of the shore admits the ships to approach within a few hundred yards, and about a dozen paces from the sea shore is a delightful river, divided only by a bank from the sea, and empties itself into it; it is a running serpentine stream from the interior, of course very clear. The boats are ranged along close to shore, the casks rolled over to the river, and when filled by one party, are returned to the boats, hoisted in by the triangles and rowed to the ships, and so return. The tents pitched on shore are for the guards who attend these proceedings . . . In this manner is a fleet of 15 ships completed with water for 12,000 men for 4 months and in the space of 2 days and some hours.[89]

A different method of watering was described by Jeffrey Raigersfeld on the island of Dominica in the West Indies: 'The process of filling was as follows: The casks were landed from the boats and rolled to a deep part of the river, filled and bunged up; they were then rolled down again into the salt water, when the men floated them, and fastening them one to the other, they were towed on board, and as the wind blew off shore, the boats were soon alongside the ship, which was at anchor between two and three miles off shore.'[90] A good supply was not always easy to find, though, and on the island of Diego Garcia in the Indian Ocean, William Richardson spoke of their desperate search for water:

As we were in want of fresh water, the people were sent about to see if there was any . . . As we could find no watering place here we had recourse to digging holes in the ground for each empty cask and generally in the course of a night they would be filled by the morning, by the water rising up to the bung holes, but this was a tedious method, moreover the water was brackish perhaps by being too near the sea shore, further inland it might have been better, however we made it answer for cooking.[91]

The worst water was from the River Thames, and when he was a merchant seaman, the American Joseph Bates said that at London they left the dock and then 'commenced filling our water-casks for our homeward journey with the river water that was passing us, finding its way to the great ocean; I thought, how could a person drink such filthy water. Streaks of green, yellow, and red muddy water, mixed up with the filth of thousands of shipping, and scum and filth of a great portion of the city of London. After a few days it becomes settled and clear, unless it is stirred up from the bottom of the water-casks.'[92] Bates was subsequently pressed and served on board HMS *Rodney* in the Mediterranean, where, he said,

> we were emptying out all our old stock of fresh water; the ground tier [bottom layer of barrels] was full of the same river water from the Thames, only a little further down from London, and had been bunged up tight for about two years. On starting the bung and applying our lighted candle, it would blaze up a foot high, like the burning of strong brandy. Before stirring it up from the bottom, some of the clear [water] was exhibited among the officers in glass tumblers, and pronounced to be the purest and best of water.[93]

The wooden casks were reused again and again, and a few weeks of storage made even the cleanest water stagnant and slimy. Sailing back to England from Gibraltar, Marine Lieutenant Wybourn told his sisters that the passage was terrible, with insufficient provisions, 'but the greatest misfortune was want of water: we were allowed only *one* pint a day for these last five weeks, and this was so bad sometimes, as to oblige us to hold our *noses* while drinking'.[94] During his very first voyage in the English Channel, on board the *Phaeton*, Midshipman James Scott was recovering from seasickness and decided to try something to eat and drink, but 'the liberal portion of salt junk and stinking water brought within hail of my olfactory nerves threw me on my back again'.[95] Edward Mangin thought that a lot of the men's illnesses were caused 'by the foul water they are obliged to drink'.[96]

Iron tanks for water in the hold began to replace wooden casks towards the end of the war, but Archibald Sinclair could never forget the old methods: 'Before iron tanks were invented, the water on board ships was generally almost indescribably bad. The stench was abominable, long flakes of green grassy looking substances floated about, and if left alone for a time in a tumbler, the sediment was frightful to look at.'[97] Attempts were made to purify the water and the casks, mostly by adding lime. Rainwater was also collected, and sea water was distilled using apparatus fixed to the galley stove. On board the *Favourite* in October 1805, the surgeon Francis Spilsbury mentioned their charcoal purification system: 'The machine for purifying our water was by some means stopt. The cooper was therefore ordered to open it: the principle was by conveying the water through charcoal, by which method, the most putrid water becomes immediately sweet; but it was insufficient to supply the whole ship's company.'[98]

Water frequently ran short, as when HMS *Boston* was accompanying a convoy of merchant ships from England to Newfoundland in 1794 in poor weather. Aaron Thomas noted the captain's attempts to economise: 'As we made no very great progress on our voyage, Captain Morris found it necessary to be careful of our expenditure of water, and as on this day [10 May] flour and plumbs were served to the ship's company to make puddings of, orders were given that the men must go to the scuttle butt on the quarter deck for water, and there mix their puddings to prevent a waste of water.'[99]

Alcohol was safer and more palatable to drink than water, and certainly more acceptable. In 1789 Gilbert Blane commented:

'As the solid part of sea diet is very dry and hard, and as the salt it contains is apt to excite thirst, a freer use of liquids than at land is necessary, particularly in a hot climate. It has been the custom, as far back as we know, to allow seamen the use of some sort of fermented liquor. We need hardly inquire if this is salutary or not, for it would be impossible at any rate to withhold it, since it is an article of luxury, and a gratification which the men would claim as their right. There is a great propensity in seamen to intoxicating liquors, which is probably owing to the hardships they undergo, and to the variety and irregularity of a sea life.[100]

It was certainly true that the twice-daily issues of grog were the highlights of a sailor's day, served with their dinner and supper. The seaman Robert Wilson explained the ration: 'In our naval service, each man is allowed a quart [two pints] of grog a day if grog is served out twice in the course of the day; if not, ½ pint of wine and one pint of grog. Now it is mixed thus: – 3 gills of water to one of rum or brandy, which is called 3-water grog and is very good, but when a fourth gill of water is added, it is insipid.'[101]

Grog was originally one part rum to four parts water with the addition of lemon juice and brown sugar, a drink devised by Admiral Edward Vernon in 1740 in an effort to reduce drunkenness, with lemon juice being added to help prevent scurvy. Rum was most readily available in the West Indies. Because Vernon's nickname was 'Old Grogram', from the grogram* that he habitually wore, the name 'grog' transferred to the drink. In Nelson's navy, the rum allowance was a quarter of a pint at a time (a total of half a pint a day), but this was in 'wine measure', roughly one-fifth less than an imperial half-pint and equivalent to the modern US half-pint. Each serving was usually topped up with three-quarters of a pint of water to make a full pint, but as a punishment might be watered down further or even withheld.

Everyone was given the same allowance, even the boys, but payment could be received instead of taking the full amount. Boys unaccustomed to drinking alcohol quickly adopted the habit, as George Jackson found when he first went on board the *Trent* as a young midshipman. He was invited to dine by the captain, Edward Hamilton:

Sir Edward turned sharply to me and said, 'Take a glass of wine, sir.' 'No, sir, thank you,' I replied timidly, but was electrified by his shouting out savagely, 'What, sir. Devil take it! Take one directly.' I mechanically filled a glass and gulped down the contents, which might have been physic [medicine] for all I knew at the moment. 'Now, sir,' rejoined my tormentor, 'do you ever drink grog?' 'No, sir, never,' I gasped out faintly, expecting an order forthwith to drink a hogshead on the spot; but I was

* A waterproof cloak made of grogram fabric – a mixture of mohair, wool and silk, often stiffened with gum.

spared so much by his adding, 'Then I shall give orders that you are to have some every day; you look as if you needed it.'[102]

Grog was actually only given when the beer ran out. The official beer allowance was a 'wine measure' gallon a day, equivalent to a modern US gallon, or four-fifths of an imperial gallon. Beer was much more commonly drunk by the seamen and was usually fairly weak small beer brewed by the Admiralty. Because beer did not keep well, it was drunk during the initial stage of a long voyage and then replaced by grog. According to Gilbert Blane, 'The common quantity of small beer allowed daily is so liberal that few men make use of their whole allowance.'[103] Spruce-beer was brewed by the ship's crew wherever possible. Aaron Thomas said that when in Newfoundland they brewed this beer on shore, as spruce trees were widespread. One place was 'called Brewing Cove, so called because Men of War, who come to anchor in this bay, brew their spruce beer in this cove. Here is a small hut erected to shelter the men from the rain . . . The spruce beer, when brewed, is laid on the ground in casks to work. The ship's boats then take it on board for use.'[104] Captain Fremantle, while enduring tedious blockade work off Cadiz in September 1805, only a short time before Trafalgar, wrote to his wife: 'I have just got some spruce given me by Sir Robert Calder, and am brewing spruce beer, this will amuse me for some days, one is really glad to catch at anything for variety.'[105]

In the Mediterranean especially, wine was often given out in the ratio of one pint of wine in place of one gallon of beer, but sailors preferred beer or grog. Red wine had the derogatory nickname 'blackstrap' and was of poor quality, full of sediment and unpopular. According to George Watson, 'The wine generally drank by seafaring people at Gibraltar, is Malaga, a sweet port-coloured liquor, and another species by the tars called "black strap" rough unpalatable heady stuff; these cost about fourpence a quart, and the best not more than a shilling.'[106] To be stationed in the Mediterranean, where this wine was commonly given to seamen, was known as being blackstrapped. The fiery white Spanish Mistela wine was more acceptable, although Basil Hall reckoned it was 'a most insidious tipple, called

Mistela in Spanish, but very naturally "transmogrified" by the Jacks into Miss Taylor'.[107]

According to Archibald Sinclair, grog was also a form of currency:

The standard of value, the medium of circulation on board a man-of-war, was a 'glass of grog.' If any one had propounded the question, 'What is a glass of grog?' sailors would have been as much puzzled to define what constituted the exact quantity or quality as the financiers to determine the value of a pound sterling. On Saturday night, each sailor that looked after a midshipman's hammock was considered entitled, by the usages of the service . . . to a glass of grog . . . the climax as to the uncertainty of the currency question was, when an old salt, who had really been attentive, smoothed your pillow, and made your bed without once failing during the week. As you presented him with an empty measure, and began to pour into it the much coveted spirit, 'Say when,' is all that passes; but an air of abstraction comes over his old weatherbeaten face; no notice is taken till it comes to be within a thimbleful of running over – 'Stop, sir, a little water.' The thimbleful of water is added, which converts it from a dram into a glass of grog, and the currency question is settled for a week.[108]

Sailors were frequently 'groggy' – in some state of drunkenness, and George Watson described a drunken shipmate as 'rather more sail than ballast, that is, groggy'.[109] Many of them lived only for the next issue of grog and drank to excess if possible. According to Samuel Leech, 'One of the greatest enemies to order and happiness in ships of war is drunkenness. To be drunk is considered by almost every sailor as the *acme* of sensual bliss; while many fancy that swearing and drinking are necessary accomplishments in a genuine man-of-war's-man. Hence it almost universally prevails.'[110] A good number were undoubtedly alcoholics, doing everything they could to obtain more to drink, including selling their own clothes. Robert Wilson of the *Unité* off the island of Tenedos in 1806 said that – bizarrely – the men sold their buttons to buy wine there:

For a few horn buttons the boat's-crew could get as much wine as they could drink; it was laughable to see them on their return on board with scarcely a button on their clothes. So fond are seamen in general to liquor that I have heard them declare sooner than lose half a pint of liquor they would rather lose so much of their blood; yet it is odd to see how willingly they will part with their grog as payment for favours received, for sailors with all their faults are not void of the sense of gratitude.[111]

Wilson's captain punished the crew by introducing weaker 4-water grog, because 'he was really tired and annoyed by continually flogging of men, only for that beastly habit of drunkenness, so ill becoming an Englishman'.[112] In vain, because a week later, Wilson recorded, 'Two men were punished for intoxication. Captain Campbell ordered the men that messed with them to have their grog extra watered for not reporting them when intoxicated, but the sailors in general would rather screen than report a brother sailor in his cups.'[113]

Daniel Goodall explained how they were able to get so drunk:

It may be a matter of wonder to the reader, who knows that each man has a limited allowance, to guess where the liquor came from to produce intoxication, seeing there was no source from which it could be procured save from one another. Some of the hardest drinkers, however, would at times take what might be called a sober fit, and would then save their allowance day by day for weeks together in bottles, when they would either sell it to those who could purchase of them or assemble their chosen friends for a carouse – too frequently ending with confinement in irons and a parade at the ship's grating [a flogging] afterwards. Of course, such practices were very strictly prohibited in the navy, but were still very common on board even the best of ships, all efforts to the contrary notwithstanding.[114]

In February 1809 George King was at Spithead in the *Melpomene* and after a drunken spree on shore, he was paid prize-money which he immediately spent on liquor:

As the ships boats usually went on shore on the impress service, I gave a pound note to one of my messmates to bring me off a gallon of rum which he accordingly did, about twelve at night, I being fast asleep in my hammock, my messmate Frederick Thomas brought me a quart basin full of rum and washed me. I sat up in my hammock and took a hearty drink and laid down; in a short time I began to feel it and immediately jumped out of my hammock and commenced drinking more but mixed with a little water. The morning following I was completely stupid with grog.[115]

At that stage King was a marine, as was his messmate Thomas. The seamen and marines often smuggled spirits on board, and George Price believed that 'a man of war is more like a gin shop than anything else'.[116] In his general orders Captain Barlow of the *Phoebe* insisted that 'It is strictly forbid to buy or sell grog . . . The boat keepers are to be accountable for any liquor smuggled into the ship in the boats.'[117] However, sailors were ingenious smugglers and usually managed to bring liquor on board. While the *Minerva* was being repaired at Bombay, the crew were held in the *Alexander* hulk, and William Richardson said that they went frequently on shore and constantly smuggled drink on board by passing bladders and bottles from the boats into the lower deck through a porthole:

> Here the greatest indulgence was given to the ships company with plenty of liberty on shore and as they had received several sums of prize money previous to my joining the ship, plenty of hollands gin soon found its way on board from the shore. As the proper officers always attended at the gangway to see there was no spiritous liquors smuggled in when liberty men returned on board, they were greatly at a loss to find out how it was got into the ship. Little did they think of a scuttle hole on the orlop, abaft the main chains, for whenever liberty men came off they were sure to not let the boat reach the gangway, but only near the scuttle hole, then they passed in their bottles and bladders in a twinkling, where their messmates were waiting to receive them, then the boat was hauled up to the gangway and they went on board as innocent as if they had been doing nothing and this continued the whole time we were hulked on board her.[118]

In 1801 Dr Trotter described some of the smuggling methods he had witnessed: 'Singular strategems had lately been devised for carrying liquor into ships; for, in proportion to the vigilance of officers, cunning and invention are set to work. Vessels [containing alcohol] in the form and dress of a sugar loaf, and other articles, the small guts of animals, and bladders formed into the most fantastical shapes, and covered with silk or cotton, to be concealed in different parts of the female dress, have been all detected.'[119] This smuggling of liquor was also recorded by Samuel Leech of the *Macedonian*:

> Were it not for the moral and physical ruin which follows its [alcohol's] use, one might laugh at the various contrivances adopted to elude the vigilance of officers in their efforts to procure rum. Some of our men who belonged to the boat's crews provided themselves with bladders; if left ashore by their officers for a few moments, they would slip into the first grocery, fill their bladders, and return with the spoil. Once by the ship's side, the favorable moment was seized to pass the interdicted bladders into the port-holes, to some watchful shipmate, by whom it was carefully secreted, to be drunk at the first opportunity. The liberty to go on shore . . . was sure to be abused for drunken purposes.[120]

It was not just the seamen who drank to excess, but also petty and commissioned officers, especially when they were at places where alcohol was plentiful and cheap. Writing to his wife Elizabeth from his ship the *Saint George* in March 1802, Lieutenant John Yule informed her that 'We are at present cruising off the island of Saint Domingo [West Indies] merely to keep the ship's company in health. If continually in harbour it is probable many might suffer from intoxication. The officers say the sailors die from drinking new rum; the sailors say the officers die from drinking old rum.'[121] The West Indies were a major producer of rum, and while the *Lapwing* was there in 1798 the hard-drinking boatswain, John Dixon, and his wife took full advantage of it. Aaron Thomas constantly referred to their antics, and in early July he wrote:

> Our Boatswain and his wife went ashore on Anguilla on Friday last, on

leave. They are a pair, whose principal failings are, that they will get drunk, whenever they can *get* the liquor. They both got drunk this last night, the woman was taken care of by a black girl, but the boatswain laid himself down in a boat which was hauled ashore under a manganeel tree. It rained in the night, which dropped off this poisonous tree on the Boatswain; the consequence is that now his hands are swollen, blistered and enflamed.[122]

Jeffrey Raigersfeld noted that 'Your Johnny Newcomes, who arrive fresh to the West Indies, when a shower of rain falls, are very apt to seek shelter under the fine spreading trees that grow by the roadside, some of which are poisonous, particularly the Machineel, so that if the rain which runs off drops upon your skin, a blister rises.'[123] In mid-July Thomas recorded yet another incident: 'The Boatswain's wife was ashore, tipsey as usual. But as she had drunk porter, her speech was quite gone.'[124]

Thomas's journal presents a succession of drunken sprees on board the *Lapwing*, particularly by Robert Ridgway, the surgeon, Alexander Craer, the surgeon's mate, William Dunn, a quarter gunner, John Dixon, the boatswain and the boatswain's wife. At the end of July, he noted: 'before 11 oClock this day, the doctor and gunner got drunk, the captain sent for the gunner into his cabin about the guns being loose. The Gunner came in, and fell against the tail of the foremost gun. Captain gave him a long, a piercing look, and then left him to get out of the cabin as well as he could.'[125] Six months later things had become so serious that 'our Boatswain and Surgeon in confinement for drunkenness, and both will have court martials'.[126] In April 1799 the *Lapwing* chased and captured a French schooner, and the next day Thomas commented: 'Our Gunner was so drunk last night, during the business of the chase, that he was speechless. Captain sent for him this day, stopped his grog, and threatened to put him in irons; however, he was drunk again this evening. Craer pissed under the halfdeck against the capstan, he being stupefyed drunk.'[127]

The following month the boatswain was court-martialled: 'At 7 A M the *Vengeance* fired a gun, and made a signal for a court martial. At 8 all our officers and several men went on board the *Vengeance* as witnesses for and against Dixon, the Boatswain of the *Lapwing*. He was tried by a court martial and sentenced to be broke,* for drunkenness and neglect of duty. He was left on board the *Vengeance*, and in her I suppose he will go to England.'[128] Thomas claimed that Craer was given a certificate of service by the captain, in which it was stated that 'he conducted himself with sobriety, and always obedient to command'.[129] Thomas thought this was a huge joke, adding: 'Craer was drunk 10 months, out of the 12, during the time he was with us, but the Captain signed this *Sober* certificate.'[130] Even when the surgeon and his mates were not drunkards, seamen were reluctant to report sick, because they were not allowed grog or tobacco in the sick-bay.

Too much alcohol was also the root of countless arguments and fights. The court martial of the *Lapwing*'s boatswain had little effect on others, and in August Thomas related another incident: 'The Surgeon, Gunner, Captain's Clerk, and Mr. Tildersley [Midshipman Thomas Tildesley] were all drinking grog together this evening in the clerk's cabin. After they were strongly grogged, a general quarrel issued, which ended in the surgeon kicking the bum of the gunner, and the rest of the party shoving him across to his own cabin.'[131] Drunkenness caused so many accidents that seamen often ended up in the care of the surgeon, or were even killed. During the winter of 1808–9 the *Superb* warship was iced up near Gothenburg until the spring, and the marine Thomas Rees, who was on board the *Temeraire* in the Baltic, heard what happened:

> What a dreadful description they gave to us of the time they had passed there, whilst blockading the port . . . The *Superb* had lost a great number of men, as they would frequently slide over the ice to the shore, and getting intoxicated, fall asleep, never to wake again in this world. What a sorrowful sight it must have been, when their companions went to look for them, to find them in that shocking state, and their bodies sometimes cut in two by the keenness of the ice![132]

---

* To deprive an officer of his commission as a sentence of a court martial.

On special occasions, the seamen attempted to have a celebration despite their meagre rations, and Samuel Leech recorded the Christmas festivities at Lisbon in 1810 on board the *Macedonian*:

> The Sabbath was also a day of sensuality. True, we sometimes had the semblance of religious services . . . but usually it was observed more as a day of revelry than of worship. But at Christmas our ship presented a scene such as I had never imagined. The men were permitted to have their 'full swing.' Drunkenness ruled the ship. Nearly every man, with most of the officers, were in a state of beastly intoxication at night. Here, some were fighting, but were so insensibly drunk, they hardly knew whether they struck the guns or their opponents; yonder, a party were singing libidinous or bacchanalian songs, while all were laughing, cursing, swearing or hallooing; confusion reigned in glorious triumph; it was the very chaos of humanity.[133]

From Malta, George Watson's ship, the *Fame*, returned to England, but instead of being allowed to return home, he was transferred to the *Eagle*. While waiting for that ship to arrive, he and many others were detained on board the *Trident* guardship, where they spent Christmas:

> Christmas day arrived, a day kept with great festivity in a man of war, owing to there being generally on that day, a double allowance of grog, &c. given to the sailors; besides, they also provide themselves with many indulgencies for that memorable occasion, such as wine, plums for puddings, &c. &c. In the year that I am speaking of [1808], it fell upon a Sunday, and on that account, we ought to have set some limit to our carousals, but we did not; towards evening, the major part of us (the *Fame*'s) were half seas over, or better, and to a late hour kept up loud singing, (or rather roaring,) and many other demonstrations of infatuated joy. The officers and crew of the *Trident*, not accustomed to witness such extraordinary uproar and profligacy on so sacred a day, sent some of the marines to request us to moderate our outrageous festivity, and cease to shout in the manner we had done. This request was made with the greatest calmness and good nature,

but answered very differently by us – We replied, 'they might go to hell'.[134]

On New Year's Day 1814, the *Orlando* was off Smyrna in Turkey, and the seaman George King (who had by now changed ships several times) related that 'The ships company had a week to ourselves . . . The whole ships company being at liberty to drink their fill and not forgetting [they did not forget] to pour the wine down the throats of sheep, goats, pigs, fowls &c. but no man in the ship attempted to run.'[135]

Map of the Baltic

FOUR

FACING THE ELEMENTS

The lightning was awfully grand, but at the same time dreadful to behold, flashing blue flame every moment in our faces, and making the darkness darker, while the hoarse thunders grumbled over us in terrible succession, loud enough to make the stoutest heart tremble.

The seaman George Watson at the masthead of the *Eagle* during a Mediterranean storm[1]

Enduring storms at sea was more perilous than facing the enemy, yet immense acts of bravery during such weather attracted no official gratitude. In a letter to his brother William after the fierce storm that followed the Battle of Trafalgar, Captain Edward Codrington summed up the challenge of such everyday hazards: 'It is not fighting . . . which is the severest part of *our* life, it is the having to contend with the sudden changes of season, the war of elements, the dangers of a lee shore,* and so forth, which produce *no food for honour or glory* beyond the internal satisfaction of doing a duty *we* know to be most important, although passed by others unknown and unnoticed.'[2]

Because they journeyed to every part of the globe rather than keeping to established trade routes, sailors in the navy faced extreme conditions more often than most. Nevertheless, James Prior, an Irish

---

* A lee shore is downwind of a ship and could be treacherous because of the likelihood of being driven on to the shore and wrecked.

surgeon from County Antrim on board the *Nisus* frigate, had great faith in his ship's ability to weather a storm:

> A frigate is the perfection of ship-building; her compactness, equip-ments, number of men, guns, and stores of every description, render her fit to carry the British flag to any part of the world, amid the conflicts either of elements or enemies. It is annoyance, more than danger, that makes a storm irksome: we cannot walk, stand, or sit, nor can we scarcely lye, at least with any prospect of repose, in this wooden castle. If there be any purgatory in this world, it is in the sufferings of a gale of wind. It is quite a season of lamentation and low spirits.[3]

Barely a year old, the *Nisus* was in a good condition to cope with par-ticularly bad weather off Madagascar:

> On the 19th of March [1811], about noon, we experienced a tremendous storm, exceeding, in violence, any I have felt during my naval career. During the evening and night, it increased so much in violence, that every rag of canvas was obliged to be taken in, to prevent being blown away. Daylight, next morning, found us lying-to under bare poles [the masts], the ship rolling violently, the sea breaking, occasionally, over the weather gang-way, the hatches battened down,* and the wind, in gusts, bursting upon us with incredible fury . . . I hurried on-deck to gain a mouthful of fresh air, supporting myself by clinging to the ropes of the weather bulwark. Here the scene, to any unwary landman, would have been truly awful.[4]

In severe storms the only thing to be done was to keep the ship's stern to the wind to prevent being rolled sideways and capsizing, but sometimes the huge waves whipped up by the wind would catch up with the ship. Off Toulon in November 1807, the four-year-old warship

---

* Hatches or hatchways were the openings with ladders that led down to each deck and to the hold. Tarpaulins were spread over wooden gratings and were fastened around the edges by strips of wood called battens, to prevent sea water pouring into the ship in heavy seas.

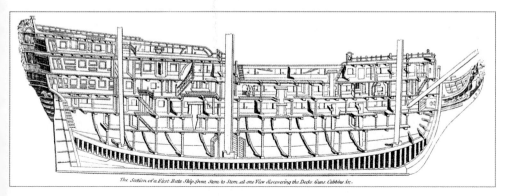

Section through a first-rate warship, 1790

The press-gang at work seizing landsmen at Tower Hill, London, with an informant
on the right awaiting payment

A 1782 caricature of the press-gang seizing a woman's husband. The seamen are
dressed in typical loose trousers and round hats, while the officer in front wears
a bicorn hat and long coat

Rear-Admiral Lord Nelson wearing full dress uniform, including bicorn hat, distinctive epaulettes on his coat and all his decorations and honours

Cuthbert Collingwood in the full dress uniform of a vice-admiral, including long blue coat with gold epaulettes and other trimmings, waistcoat, breeches and sword. Under his arm is a telescope. This engraving by William Holl shows him looking younger than the original oil portrait

Marine privates around 1802–10 wearing red coats, white cross-belt,
white breeches, gaiters and round hats with a feather plume

A seaman wearing short jacket, loose trousers, neckerchief and glazed hat. He is heaving the lead – throwing into the sea a line with a large piece of lead attached in order to measure the depth of water

Caricature of 1799 showing seamen 'on a cruise' in Portsmouth, spending all their money, after being given a rare period of liberty on shore

A romanticised view of leisure time below decks when in port. Many men are shown smoking clay pipes, which would not have been permitted

'Jack and his Money', a 1785 caricature of a seaman counting his prize-money and dressed in a wig and long coat for special occasions

Portraits of the 1801 mutineers of HMS *Temeraire*

The lower gun deck of HMS *Victory*

The Battle of the Nile after intense fighting and the explosion of the French flagship *Orient*

Repulse was hit by an enormous wave at the stern, which shattered the glass windows that lit the officers' wardroom. Marine Captain Marmaduke Wybourn witnessed the terrifying scene:

> The galley fire was put out by it, and everything displaced everywhere; the men said the ship trembled *fore* and *aft* and everyone thought a thunder bolt had struck us . . . the wave burst in all our windows, window frames, woodwork etc. and rushing into our cabin, our mess room and every place at once, filled us all with consternation and we really thought we were going down, the crash was so great, which with the loud thunder, and all confusion, that no one had power to get away till washed in a heap together: tables, chairs, musical instruments, backgammon boxes etc., etc., all swimming about, the water above our knees before it got vent, when it rushed impetuously out between decks and half drowned all the sailors.[5]

For once, the officers suffered most from the storm. 'It afforded some mirth,' Wybourn acknowledged, 'the ludicrous figures we all cut when the Seamen came in to put all to rights, and see the extent of our mischief. We were of course wet thro' and thro'.'[6] The next day he added: 'The ship exhibits a pretty scene – a perfect wreck at our end, and no glass to mend our windows . . . The sailors are no doubt enjoying the thoughts of *all* the *officers* suffering *only* . . . It is considered by seamen to be the most dangerous of any accident at sea, as the ship is of course broadest at the stern, and the weight of a large wave generally presses her so much that she cannot right again and goes to the bottom, stern foremost.'[7]

Aaron Thomas described another incident in May 1794 while on board HMS *Boston* accompanying a convoy to Newfoundland: 'The sea this day may with truth be said to run mountains high, the long tremendous swells, formed into mountains, broke over the *Boston*'s gangway, while the gunwhale on the larboard side lay under water. Some vessels of our convoy not half a mile from us buried some minutes from our sight.'[8] Like Wybourn, he gave some idea of the damage that could occur:

I have often wondered that artists do not exercise their talents in picturing a Captain's cabin after a gale of wind. I can only account for it by supposing that few men of abilities make long voyages at sea. Quadrants, chairs, compasses, tables, quoins, guns, tackle, ports, maps, pistols, tomahawks, lanthorns, windows and quarter galleries – split, cracked, stoved, rended, dashed and broke all to pieces, would form a good subject for a humorous limner. Possibly such a picture may be in existence but it has never fell my way.[9]

A few days later, the *Boston* reached the Newfoundland Banks, with its notorious fogs:

Our ship was enveloped in one of those fogs which eternally hover over the Banks. Fog guns were constantly fired, and a horn continually kept sounding to warn other vessels of our situation. A European, who has never been in this part of America, can have but a faint idea of these fogs. You frequently can see but a few yards before you, and by getting on deck for two hours you will get wet to the skin. The ship's rigging and yard collect great quantities of these particles, which fall on deck in drops which would cover a half crown piece.[10]

Some hours later Thomas was startled by the sight of an iceberg:

For the first time in my life, I saw one of these awful and massive bulks, an island of ice. The fog was very thick and it was not more than half a mile from us. The *Boston* was going at the rate of six knots an hour, it passed us on the larboard side. I could not but look at it with horror and amazement, to see such an enormous mass floating in the midst of the Ocean . . . part of this frightful structure, had the *Boston* struck on it, would a been sufficient to a consigned her to a watery tomb.[11]

The Newfoundland Banks were as treacherous as storms, and John Howe, a marine, who sailed from Torbay to America on board the *Defiance* in June 1779, considered that 'every thing went on very well three or four weeks; by this time we were got on the banks of

Newfoundland; here we was becalmed and as it were buried in a thick fog for a fortnight'.[12] Luckily, they reached their destination in safety, but later victims included HMS *Scout*, which is remembered by a plaque in a Dorset church that commemorates Henry Roberts Carpenter, eldest son of Thomas and Charlotte Carpenter, 'aged about 14 years, a midshipman on board H.M.S. *Scout* sloop of war, which foundered at sea in November 1801 on the Banks of Newfoundland in her voyage to Halifax in Nova Scotia when all hands perished'.[13]

The worst of conditions could strike close to home ports, something Lieutenant James Gardner of the *Blonde* frigate experienced when sailing from Portsmouth to Guernsey:

> After going through the Needles in the evening, it came on thick weather in the first watch; and about eleven the wind, at SE, began to blow a hurricane, with snow so thick that we could not see half the length of the ship. We sent topgallant yards and topgallant masts upon the deck, and hove the ship to under storm staysails. The topsails and courses [lower sails] were frozen as hard as board, and being short of complement it took nearly the whole of the middle watch before they could be furled. One of our main topmen was frozen and died soon after. The officers were also aloft, and all hands suffered most dreadfully. I was speaking to the man at the wheel when a sheet of ice fell out of the mizen top and knocked both of us down. It gave me a severe blow on the shoulder and the other a staggering thump on the back. I was so benumbed when I got below that I had hardly life in me.[14]

Some of the bad weather hit vessels when they were sailing from one climatic zone to another. In a letter to his wife Betsey, written on 17 March 1801, Thomas Fremantle described the snowstorms they encountered as they approached Copenhagen, before Nelson's bombardment of the city: 'We have since we sailed experienced a second winter; it has snowed every day since, and the ship's company are hacking from morning to night with coughs.'[15] A few days later Midshipman William Salter Millard said that they 'reefed the courses in the midst of a storm of hail, snow, and rain, assisted by large pieces of half-frozen ice from the rigging'.[16] The seaman Henry Walsh, on board the *Ulysses* in 1813, was also in the Baltic in March and pointed out that 'the frost and snow is so excessive in this country in the winter seasons that ships is generally froze up and is then obliged to stop there all winter . . . I have also known the armourers or smiths forge to be placed on the ice convenient to the ship and there work all winter.'[17]

Of all the weather conditions, lightning strikes were probably the most dangerous and terrifying because they could occur with little warning, and the damage was unpredictable. Even in the Mediterranean storms could be savage, as George Watson discovered:

> We steered toward Zante, off which place we experienced a most dreadful thunder storm; it came on about 8 P.M. and increased until midnight, when it was at its height; when it first commenced, the hands were aloft taking in sail, and before they could get that duty performed, the lightning burst upon the main mast, and by it the men on the main top gallant yard, were all knocked off, and scorched in a pitiable manner, and tumbling into the top, and crosstrees, some of them were maimed for life.[18]

It was not just the sailors exposed on the masts who were at risk, because lightning endangered everyone on board. While returning from Jamaica in 1801, Alexander Scott, who was Nelson's chaplain at Trafalgar, was asleep in a cabin when lightning struck:

> The electric fluid rent the mizenmast, killing and wounding fourteen men, and descending into the Captain's cabin, in which Mr. Scott was sleeping, communicated with some spare cartridges and powder horns, which lay on a shelf immediately over his head. By this means he sustained a double shock, the electric fluid struck his hand and arm, passing along the bell wire, with which they were in contact, and the gunpowder exploding at the same time knocked out some of his front teeth, and dreadfully lacerated his mouth and jaw. The lightning also melted the hooks to which the hammock was slung, and he fell to the ground, receiving a violent concussion of the brain. His cabin was found in flames, himself in a sheet of fire, and he was taken up senseless and apparently not likely to live.[19]

Lightning conductors, though not properly understood, were effective, as Henry Walsh witnessed when sailing in April 1815 in the *Ulysses* from Cape Coast in Ghana:

> There was nothing very remarkable on our passage excepting most dreadful thunder and lightning, greater than I had ever seen before. There was balls of fire struck our lightning conductors which happily conveyed them down our rigging and fell overboard without any damage either to our ship or men. Those lightning conductors above mentioned is made of brass or copper links or chains, which goes over the ship's royal mast heads down the rigging, and hangs over the ship's side. This chain attracts the lightning or fire, if it comes over the ship, and so conducts it overboard into the water and by this means preserves both ship and men from ruin.[20]

Too often, though, lightning conductors were only rigged to the masts after a storm had begun or else were set up incorrectly, or not at all, so that there were frequent, alarming strikes. In these incidents, with all the gunpowder on board, ships were lucky if they did not catch fire and even blow up. In the East Indies in 1798, the *Resistance* frigate was destroyed by such an explosion after a lightning strike. Two crew members were fortunate to be rescued, and they revealed what had happened, otherwise the *Resistance* would have been added to the long list of ships that mysteriously disappeared at sea, with all hands lost.

Particularly during storms, sea water and rainwater poured into the ships, even if the hatchways were battened down. The men were then ordered to pump out the water, which was the most exhausting work they ever had to do. The pumps were chain pumps, unsophisticated, theoretically simple to repair, but inefficient, working on the same principle as hauling up water from a well in a bucket. A chain of scoops inside a pipe acted like a series of buckets, raising the water from the lowest part of the ship and dumping it in a cistern at the top, from where it drained overboard. The chain passed over a sprocket wheel, and the pump was powered by men turning a handle attached to the axle of this wheel. Even with extensions to the handle, a considerable effort was needed to turn the wheel and raise the whole weight of water in the pipe. It was gruelling work that left men with strained muscles, torn ligaments and hernias, and in dire emergencies men would die of exhaustion.

Marmaduke Wybourn described the pumps to his sister Emily when sailing from Egypt to Malta in HMS *Madras*: 'We sprung a dangerous leak, which however did not alarm us much until we were overtaken by a storm, the most tremendous. It lasted many days, and our leak increased from one to four feet of water in an hour with all the pumps going, and I must tell you that the pumps of this ship are calculated to throw out three tuns of water a minute.'[21] In February 1811, at Plymouth, the *Amethyst* frigate was blown on to rocks in a violent gale, which Robert Hay recounted:

> One part of the carpenter's duty who keeps watch is to try hourly how much water is in the ship and make a report of the same to the officer commanding the watch that the pumps may be set agoing when need requires. Being a carpenter of the watch I accordingly sounded a few minutes after she first struck and found 3 feet water in the hold. I reported this to the captain who had assumed the command and the chain pumps were set a going. By the time she got broadside on the water had increased to 5 feet. It was therefore considered in vain to labour any longer and the pumps were accordingly abandoned.[22]

On abandoning ship, Hay took the chance to desert.

Unless the leak was massive, the pumps usually had a good chance of holding their own until the weather improved. The marine Thomas Rees, on board the *Temeraire*, described another storm at Plymouth some two years earlier: 'By eight at night it blew a perfect hurricane. We had then three feet water in our lower decks, and two in the middle: it had entered through the hawse-holes,* and through the bow-ports also. The sea kept rolling in so fast, that we expected every moment either to go to the bottom, or to be driven on shore.

---

* Holes at the bow for the anchor cable.

All hands were at the pump: every exertion was made to save our ship and our lives.'[23] They continued to pump until the storm abated at five the next morning, Christmas Day.

Another Christmas Day storm, in 1781, was experienced by the marine corporal John Howe in the West Indies on board the *Robust*: 'We sprung a leak under the starboard chesstree which the carpenter could not get at to stop so that the ship made water very fast, and one half of the ship's company obliged to keep constantly pumping and with hard labour could hardly keep her from gaining on us. We had 4 feet of water in the hold for five days, and the gale continued with very little alteration.'[24] They obtained a spare sail from a passing merchant ship to place over the leak and made their way to Antigua, meeting up in English Harbour with HMS *Janus*, which had fared even worse, as Howe learned:

> She having sprung a leak also and hove part of her guns overboard to prevent her from sinking, they as well as us were continually pumping with all their pumps. Six men died at their pumps with hard work, and we had one died. 16 days and nights we were constantly at it, and not a man could go to bed all this time, or be from the pumps more than twenty minutes at a time every other 4 hours when it was his watch below, and the other 4 hours was his watch on deck, and we must be there to work the ship.[25]

The *Janus* had left New York in early December, accompanying a convoy of ships, and the weather deteriorated all month. On the 18th the master's log recorded: 'two foot 10 inches [water] in the well, both chain pumps at work, two hand pumps at work'.[26] The next day they hove overboard several cannons, and from the 20th the pumps were in constant use. On 8 January they reached English Harbour, four days before the *Robust*, but still kept the pumps going. On the 15th 'came on board thirty men from the *Royal Oak* to assist pumping, also twenty-nine negroes'.[27] While the pumping continued, the remaining guns, casks and shingle ballast were removed, but on the 29th they were 'employed in getting on shore shingle ballast, at 7 A.M., found the ship to make so much water that the Blackmen could not keep her; got twenty men from the *Robust* and twenty from *La Nymph*, to assist in pumping in the night.'[28] In February, the ship was cleared of the last stores and ballast, enabling the caulkers and carpenters to make the ship watertight, and pumping finally ceased in April.

While lightning strikes and accidents sometimes caused ships to disappear without trace, vessels also sank rapidly in storms if they struck rocks or icebergs, if they were overwhelmed by waves, or if water broke through a leaky hull. Captain John Nicholson Inglefield was a survivor of one such tragedy, and therefore a rare eyewitness. In September 1782 his ship, the 74-gun HMS *Centaur*, was accompanying a convoy from Jamaica to Britain when they were struck by a terrific storm off the Newfoundland Banks. About two in the morning conditions abated when suddenly, Inglefield related,

> A gust of wind, exceeding in violence every thing of the kind I had ever seen, or had any conception of, laid the ship upon her beam ends. The water forsook the hold, and appeared between decks, so as to fill the mens hammocks to leeward: the ship lay motionless, and, to all appearance, irrecoverably overset. The water increasing fast, forced through the cells of the ports, and scuttles in the ports . . . I gave immediate directions to cut away the main and mizen-masts.[29]

To his dismay, the foremast and bowsprit went overboard as well: 'The ship upon this immediately righted, but with great violence; and the motion was so quick, that it was difficult for the people to work the pumps. Three guns broke loose upon the main deck, and it was some time before they were secured . . . The officers who had left their beds (when the ship overset) naked, in the morning, had not an article of clothes to put on, nor could their friends supply them.'[30] After daybreak, several merchant ships offered assistance, but Inglefield refused as he expected his distress signals to be heeded by HMS *Ville de Paris*, which was in sight, but tragically no help came. Their situation looked bleak – guns and gun-carriages were thrown overboard, and the men were constantly pumping. The next morning Inglefield was informed that there was 7 feet of water in the hold, the pumps were wearing out, and all the food, rum and water were ruined. In desperation, they tried bailing out the water with canvas buckets:

> The water by noon had considerably diminished by working the buckets; but there appeared no prospect of saving the ship if the gale continued. The labour was too great to hold out without [drinking] water; yet the people worked without a murmur, and indeed with cheerfulness . . . but as the evening came on, the gale again increased . . . The *Centaur* laboured so much, that I had scarce a hope she could swim 'till morning. However, by great exertion of the chain-pumps and bailing we held our own, but our sufferings for want of water were very great, and many of the people could not be restrained from drinking salt-water.[31]

Just as their situation was improving, the weather deteriorated once more, and water came pouring in. It was obvious to Inglefield that the ship was beginning to sink: 'The people, who till this period had laboured as determined to conquer their difficulties without a murmur or without a fear, seeing their efforts useless, many of them burst into tears and wept like children . . . Some appeared perfectly resigned, went to their hammocks, and desired their messmates to lash them in; others were lashing themselves to gratings and small rafts; but the most predominant idea was, that of putting on their best and cleanest clothes.'[32] The crew numbered nearly six hundred, and there were passengers as well, including Captain George Augustus Keppel. There was no concept of lifeboats, but Inglefield ordered their three working boats to be lowered over the side and rafts to be made: 'While these preparations were making, the ship was gradually sinking, the orlop decks having been blown up by the water in the hold, and the cables [thick ropes] floated to the gun-deck. The men had for some time quitted their employment of bailing, and the ship was left to her fate.'[33] In the bad weather one boat was smashed, and there was little time left: 'As the evening approached, the ship appeared little more than suspended in the water . . . It was impossible indeed for any man to deceive himself with a hope of being saved upon a raft in such a sea; besides that the ship in sinking, it was probable would carry every thing down with her in a vortex.'[34]

Having placed armed guards in the two remaining boats, Captain Inglefield decided that this was the time for him to leave the sinking ship. Many jumped into the sea to try to get into the boats, but he managed to escape with just a dozen men on board, and they never saw the final moments of the warship in which everyone else perished. They were at the mercy of the prevailing winds 'in nearly the middle of the Western Ocean, without compass, without quadrant, without sail, without greatcoat or cloak; all very thinly cloathed, in a gale of wind, with a great sea running!'[35] After a fortnight Thomas Mathews the quartermaster died, and Inglefield admitted that the rest of them were convinced they would soon follow, though 'it was somewhat comfortable to reflect, that dying of hunger was not so dreadful as our imaginations had represented. Others had complained of the symptoms in their throats; some had drank their own urine; and all, but myself, had drank salt-water.'[36] Shortly afterwards, land was spotted – they had reached the Azores.

HMS *Ville de Paris* and the nearby *Glorieux* warship did not come to the assistance of the *Centaur*, because those ships also perished in the hurricane, as the *Annual Register* reported:

> A Danish merchant ship from the West Indies took a man off a fragment of wreck quite insensible, and for some time motionless. The Dane carried him to the hospital at Havre de Grasse, where he recovered, and was sent in a Russian ship to the English Admiralty. His name was Wilson; he had been on board the *Ville de Paris*, and when she was going to pieces clung to a piece of the wreck. He perfectly recollected that the *Glorieux* had foundered: he saw her go down, the day preceding that on which the *Ville de Paris* sunk.[37]

Over one thousand lives were lost in a single storm, far more than in any battle.

Apart from storms, a whole range of weather conditions threatened the lives and health of seamen, who were constantly exposed to the elements. Modern technology has produced myriad man-made, lightweight fabrics that can cope with the most difficult conditions, but all that a sailor of Nelson's navy had to protect him were materials like cotton, wool, linen, leather, straw and silk. No uniform existed for seamen until 1857, but on land they stood out because of the sort of garb they chose to wear. People on land at the time wore 'long clothes' – long coats or jackets with long tails, knee- or calf-length breeches and stockings. When Robert Hay deserted his ship at Plymouth, he took with him his best clothes, but reluctantly sold them and instead 'purchased a long coat, breeches and other corresponding vestments, and assumed as much as possible the looks and gait of a landsman'.[38] A typical seaman's garb was described by Charles Pemberton: he was persuaded to join the navy by 'two well-dressed sailors, that is to say, two clean white-trowsered, neat blue abundant-button jacketed, glazed-hatted, long pigtailed, mahogany-wainscot-faced quid-cheeked men'.[39]

Seamen preferred short jackets, usually blue in colour, with sleeves that could be rolled up, and wide, loose long trousers, often white, that could also be rolled up. Also favoured were short waistcoats, checked shirts and neckerchiefs. The traditional petticoat breeches – very wide breeches down to the knee – were gradually going out of use. The physician Thomas Trotter was critical of the men's ability to dress appropriately: 'They are too indolent to suit their dress to circumstances, unless they are forced to do it, nor is anything more common than to see them with a pair of thin linen trowsers on in the severity of winter, and a pair of greasy woollen ones in the hottest weather.'[40]

For those who had not purchased their gear ashore or needed to replace something beyond repair, the purser had lengths of cloth or ready-made garments for sale that were referred to as 'slops', a term of uncertain derivation dating back to Chaucer. Dead men's clothing was also sold off, though the regulations specified that 'No seamen shall be permitted to bid for deceased officers clothes that are above their wear [rank]',[41] because at sea as well as on land clothing was an indication of status. Clothes and shoes, mostly second-hand, were available from slop-sellers who came out in boats to the warships, as on one unfortunate occasion in March 1808: 'Thursday the *Mars*, of 74 guns, Capt. Lukin, was paid wages at Portsmouth, and there being a number of Jews and other slop-sellers round the ship, as usual, endeavouring to obtain admission to vend their commodities, they were ordered to keep off from the ship, but one boat persisted in coming alongside, when the marine on the gangway fired into her, and shot a young man of the name of Abrahams, dead on the spot.'[42] The marine, Joseph Jones, was tried for murder at Winchester, but was instead convicted of manslaughter as he was under orders at the time. He was fined 6 shillings and 8 pence, which was paid by the Admiralty. As a result of this incident, the regulations were tightened, and marines were issued with blank cartridges for similar occasions in future.

Seamen were not averse to selling their own clothes for other goods, usually grog. At Madras in India in 1804 on board the *Culloden*, Robert Hay recounted one fraudulent transaction:

> It was a standing rule aboard that no seamen were permitted to exchange articles of clothing for any of the commodities that came alongside for sale. The natives knew this, so that when any bartering took place it was all performed in an underhanded way. On this occasion none of the articles of barter could be examined narrowly lest the officers should discover what was going on, but as soon as the exchange was made the parties secreted their wares in the best manner possible. One of our seamen had a red flannel shirt, an article to which the natives are very partial. Resolving to make the most of it he cut it into 4 pieces, back, front and two sleeves. He enclosed in each piece as much rubbish as made it into the size of a full shirt, and sold each piece into different boats as a full shirt.[43]

When Samuel Leech joined the navy at the age of twelve with the reluctant support of his mother, after his father died a decade earlier, he was lucky that she bought him some basic items, including

> a complete suit of sailor apparel; a tarpaulin hat, round blue jacket and wide pantaloons. Never did a young knight swell with loftier emotion

when donning for the first time his iron dress, than I did when in sea dress I trod the streets of Gravesend . . . That I should not lack the means of comfort, my good mother purchased me a chest of clothing, and, as her last token of maternal care, presented me with a Bible, prayer book, and, strangely inconsistent companions, a pack of cards![44]

Many sailors had to make their own clothes, especially those who were pressed and only had what they stood up in, like William Richardson who was seized by the press-gang at Calcutta in 1793 to serve on board the *Minerva* frigate: 'As there were no slop cloaths on board, the Purser soon after served out so many yards of dungaree to each man with needles and thread to make shirts, jackets and trowsers of it, and my messmates being a good set of fellows and accustomed to the work soon taught me to cut out and make, and soon after I got decently rigged with some to spare. With a new straw hat I made by their instructions, I was not badly off.'[45] Some captains listed the clothes that the men should have, like Captain Barlow of the *Phoebe*, who specified '3 jackets, 2 p[air] shoes, 4 shirts, 4 p[air] stockings, 4 p[air] trowsers, 1 hat or cap, 2 inside jackets, 2 pair of drawers, 1 pair blue trowsers, 1 frock'.[46] He added: 'The men are positively forbid to wear dirty or ragged cloaths.'[47] Captain Edward Riou of the *Amazon* in 1799 gave a similarly detailed list 'in order to produce uniformity and neatness of dress'.[48] He also directed that 'officers are to observe that each man has some sort of mark upon his linen so that thefts may not only be discovered but prevented, and mistakes avoided'.[49]

The seamen went for practicality, but they relished fine clothes for their rare trips ashore, as Robert Wilson related:

It's curious to see a tar lay hold of a piece of fine white linen (to make himself a go-ashore shirt, as he terms it) and a black cinder and mark where he wishes to cut the linen. Then, after he has cut out the body, sleeves, cuffs, gussets, collar, etc., to see him take into his hand, that's like unto a shoulder of mutton, a fine small needle and sew away, and that not slow. I say it is in a manner surprising, and you could not but give credit to him when he has finished his shirt.[50]

After deserting at Plymouth, Robert Hay went into hiding, and watched from a window the swaggering seamen on shore leave dressed in their best: 'The jolly tar himself was seen with his white demity trowsers fringed at the bottom, his fine scarlet waistcoat bound with black ribbon, his dark broadcloth jacket studded with pearl buttons, his black silk neckcloth thrown carelessly about his sunburnt neck. An elegant hat of straw, indicative of his recent return from a foreign station, cocked on one side; A head of hair reaching to his waistband.'[51]

Unlike seamen, even the lowliest marines had a uniform, which they wore when on duty. Each marine received annually a set of clothes from the Navy Board, and this uniform was similar to that of infantry soldiers: 'A red cloth coat, white cloth waistcoat and breeches. One shirt, with one black stock [neckband]. One pair of stockings, to sergeants only. One pair of shoes. A hat.'[52] Their red coats had a white border or lapel and long tails, though by the early 1800s the jackets became short at the front and were lined in blue. Marines also sported gaiters and a cross-belt – two leather straps whitened with pipeclay for suspending their bayonet and cartridge-pouch. Rather than breeches, they often opted for white or blue trousers.

While helping out with everyday chores and in battle, marines did not wear their full uniform, but preferred casual seamen's clothes, and men of the Marine Artillery were allowed to wear blue coats with a red collar and cuffs when involved in gun practice or if working ashore. During the Battle of Trafalgar Marine Lieutenant Lewis Rotely noticed his men's casual appearance: 'In the excitement of action, the Marines had thrown off their Red Jackets and appeared in their check shirts and blue trowsers. There was no distinguishing Marine from Seaman, all were working like horses.'[53] The regulations distinguished between the official uniform for marines and their unofficial clothes: 'When any marine belonging to the Ship dies, his clothing and effects (except his uniform marine clothing) are to be sold at the mast, by auction.'[54] Like seamen, marines also sold their clothes for alcohol, as John Howe did at Halifax in Nova Scotia in 1779, when he was fit enough to leave the hospital there:

Being quite destitute of money I had recourse to selling my clothes to raise drink. This I done several times until all my spare clothes was sold. I stayed here near a month and went again to the ship which was repairing alongside the King's wharf. My clothes was examined according to custom by the sergeant and found deficient and he reported it to the Captn. of Marines who said I should be well flogged for it if I didn't tell who I sold them to, which I wouldn't do knowing the people would be fined for buying them. He accordingly brought me before the Captain of the ship and requested him to punish me for selling my necessaries. But as the things were my own that I had sold he wouldn't flog me as he allowed the men to get things from the purser to sell, they having no other way to get money. I was now sadly distressed for clothes as our Captain would not allow me to get any from the purser. I was now obliged to buy things and give my grog for them to the other men in order to keep free from vermin.[55]

Marine officers were expected to set an example with their uniform, as Rotely told his father in Swansea, when asking him to send more clothes: 'I am the first [in line] here for sea duty [so] you will see the necessity of my having my shirts as soon as possible. Please to lock them up in my large black trunk, you need not send the key as I have got one with me that will open it. You may put in the old red coat – I shall find it useful on board ship as we are not allowed to wear any thing else but uniform.'[56] The uniforms of marine officers were made for them by tailors, and their rank was distinguished by epaulettes on the shoulders of their coat, as well as other trimmings such as sashes round their waist.

Uniforms also had to be worn by naval officers, though they were only stipulated for warrant officers from 1787, and surgeons were not included until 1805. A full dress uniform was for formal occasions and an undress (or frock) uniform for everyday purposes, and like the marine officers, these uniforms were made at great expense by tailors. The uniform varied according to rank, and as the regulations did not specify the cut, they also varied from officer to officer, according to his tastes. Everyday uniforms had more scope for interpretation, but most comprised long blue coats that were lined in white and had sloping fronts, though it became fashionable to have coats that were short in front. From 1795 gold epaulettes adorned the coats of lieutenants and above, though they had been unofficially worn before then.

Most officers removed their epaulettes before a battle, because they were a distinctive item of their uniform and so could attract the attention of snipers. At Trafalgar Nelson wore his uniform as usual, and the Londonderry-born surgeon William Beatty recorded that when Nelson was shot, 'The ball struck the epaulette on his left shoulder'.[57] When doing the autopsy, Beatty noted that 'A very considerable portion of the gold-lace, pad, and lining of the epaulette, with a piece of the coat, was found attached to the ball.'[58] The irony is that before they became part of the official uniform, Nelson disparaged the wearing of epaulettes. In France in 1783, during a brief period of peace, Nelson met two British naval captains and sarcastically commented that 'they are very fine gentlemen with epaulettes: you may suppose I hold them a little *cheap* for putting on any part of a Frenchman's uniform'.[59]

Other aspects of uniform such as the design of buttons, type of collar, gold braid and lace trimmings also denoted rank, but for everyday use officers wore white waistcoats and shirts, black neckcloths or stocks, breeches in white, blue or grey that fastened below the knee with buttons or buckles, and stockings that resembled what would now be called long socks, but which were held in place well above the knee by a garter. Instead of breeches, many opted for long tight pantaloons or loose-fitting trousers of various colours. Neckcloths were often wound relatively tightly round the neck, while stocks, which were leather or velvet neckbands with a buckle at the back, had an even greater tendency to restrict head movements and tilt the head backwards. These were middle- and upper-class garments, worn by military and civilians, that literally made the wearers 'stiff-necked' and forced them to 'look down their noses' at other people.

On board the *Pegasus* in 1788, the captain – Prince William, the future king – issued orders about what his officers should wear:

It is my positive orders and directions that the officers . . . never go out of the ship upon duty but in their full [dress] uniforms. On board they may wear their frock uniform, except mustering on Sundays, and on other occasions when directed. The rest of the officers, under the denomination of warrant officers, are to comply with the late regulations adopted by His Majesty for the Royal Navy. The officers and gentlemen belonging to His Majesty's ship under my command are not to wear any other waistcoats and breeches than the established uniform, except brown at sea, or long blue cloth trowsers, with or without boots as they like best; in the West Indies, linen breeches and trowsers.[60]

When on duty in poor weather, officers had greatcoats, but Nelson apparently never bothered much about the cold or wet, and Beatty noticed that 'he took no pains to protect himself from the effects of wet, or the night-air; wearing only a thin great coat: and he has frequently, after having his clothes wet through with rain, refused to have them changed, saying that the leather waistcoat which he wore over his flannel one would secure him from complaint'.[61]

Everyone wore hats, which were used as a mark of respect, and Captain Barlow had to issue an instruction that 'The People are to be particular in taking off their hats when they come on the quarter deck.'[62] When Lieutenant Robert Young was tried for drunkenness and contempt towards Captain Lake on the quarterdeck in September 1809, one witness was asked by the court martial: 'In what manner did the prisoner pull his hat off and put it on again', to which came the reply 'He took his hat quite off in the normal way.'[63] For those on land, cocked and broad-rimmed hats were normal, but at sea these would have blown away or been constantly dislodged, and so the seamen devised more practical styles, including ones of leather, canvas or straw that they frequently wove themselves, then painted with varnish or tar to waterproof them. The name of their ship was commonly added as well, and Samuel Leech said that on Sundays, they all dressed up with 'our black, glossy hats, ornamented with black ribbons, and with the name of our ship painted on them'.[64] These hats, being coated with tar, were called tarpaulins, and seamen also wore knitted caps, often referred to as Monmouth caps, a style worn by seafarers since medieval times and traditionally made in the Monmouth area.

There were few regulations for officers regarding hats. Bicorn or tricorn cocked hats were round hats with two or three brims permanently turned up – cocked. They were made from beaver fur, dyed black, and sometimes adorned with lace. Bicorn hats were most fashionable by 1800 and were originally worn with the two pointed ends over each shoulder, but by 1805 most officers wore flatter bicorns in a 'fore-and-aft' position, at right-angles to their shoulders, though admirals still wore them in the old style. For everyday use, many officers chose to wear low top hats of lacquered felt, glazed leather or beaver, which they called round hats. Most midshipmen and warrant officers wore these round hats, and they were also introduced for marines, replacing the bicorn. Not everybody liked the new-fangled way of dressing, and as a midshipman on board the *Barfleur* in 1790, James Gardner found that 'Captain Calder was a . . . very strict disciplinarian. We dared not appear on deck without our full uniform, and a round hat was never allowed.'[65] Similarly at Lisbon seven years later, Earl St Vincent issued an order to his captains: 'The Commander-in-chief having seen several Officers of the fleet on shore dressed like shop-keepers, in coloured clothes, and others wearing round hats with their uniforms, in violation of the late order from . . . the Admiralty, does positively direct, that any officer offending against this wholesome and necessary regulation in future, is put under arrest and reported to the Admiral.'[66]

It was impossible for regulations to cover footwear, because shoes for men at this time were limited to black leather ones fastened at the front by a single large buckle, though leather boots were worn by the marines and were becoming popular with navy officers. Marine Lieutenant Rotely wrote to his father, saying: 'I shall want my . . . boot hooks [and] blacking brushes . . . I'll thank [you] to send my old boots and shoes – shoes are 12 shillings a pair here'.[67] The only alternative for the men was to make their own shoes from materials like canvas, and one of the first things that Robert Hay learned as a boy in the navy was how to make 'canvas pumps'.[68] Officers increasingly wore knee-high or calf-length black leather army-style Hessian boots (introduced originally by troops from Hesse in Germany) into which they tucked their pantaloons or trousers. At Trafalgar, Collingwood's servant recalled that the admiral 'dressed himself that morning with peculiar care; and soon after, meeting Lieutenant Clavell, advised him to pull off his boots. "You had better," he said, "put on silk stockings, as I have done: for if one should get a shot in the leg, they would be so much more manageable for the surgeon."'[69] Captain Hardy was wearing shoes at the same battle, and Dr Beatty recorded that 'a shot struck the fore-brace bits on the quarter-deck, and passed between Lord NELSON and Captain HARDY; a splinter from the bits bruising Captain Hardy's foot, and tearing the buckle from his shoe'.[70]

According to Beatty, Nelson mainly wore shoes, even in bad weather:

> He seldom wore boots, and was consequently very liable to have his feet wet. When this occurred he has often been known to go down to his cabin, throw off his shoes, and walk on the carpet in his stockings for the purpose of drying the feet of them. He chose rather to adopt this uncomfortable expedient, than to give his servants the trouble of assisting him to put on fresh stockings; which, from his having only one hand, he could not himself conveniently effect.[71]

It was probably the tying of garters round his stockings that Nelson found most difficult, but the seamen never experienced the luxury of drying their stockings on carpet, and many preferred to go barefoot rather than get shoes and stockings sodden. At times even the officers went barefoot, like Vice-Admiral Pellew when the *Culloden* was caught in a hurricane in the Indian Ocean in 1809. 'Dressed in a short jacket, a pair of trowsers, a small hunting cap and without shoes or stockings,' Robert Hay observed, 'he went about infusing courage and fortitude into all.'[72] When in India, William Richardson said that 'As for shoes and stockings they were not worn by common sailors in this hot country'.[73] They were dispensed with in other climates as well – after the *Repulse* was hit by the huge wave and all the glass windows shattered, Marine Captain Wybourn wrote with concern in his diary: '34 panes of glass was precipitated about the ship in thousands of pieces and it will be a providence if the men, who will go barefoot, do not lame themselves'.[74]

There were worries that the sores on their bare feet were harmful to the men's health, yet at other times the officers had difficulty parting them from their footwear. Captain Barlow of the *Phoebe* ordered that 'People washing decks to take their shoes and stockings off',[75] while the physician Thomas Trotter lamented:

Seamen are naturally indolent and filthy, and are merely infants as to discretion in everything that regards their health. They will assist in washing decks, and sit the whole day afterwards, though wet thereby, half way up the legs, without shifting themselves, to the great injury of their health. They should therefore be compelled to put off their shoes and stockings, and roll up their trowsers on those occasions, which will not only cause their feet to be dry and comfortable the rest of the day, but necessarily cause a degree of cleanliness which otherwise would be disregarded.[76]

The seamen were not supposed to sleep in their clothes, and Barlow warned that 'If any of the ships company are discovered making a practice of sleeping in their clothes and tending by that means to breed or harbour vermin, he shall be severely punished.'[77] They were expected to keep their own clothes clean, even though on land this was regarded as women's work. There was no laundry room and no efficient way of washing and drying clothes, which proved a constant struggle for the men. Just after he was seized by the press-gang at Belfast in June 1809 and taken on board the tender, Henry Walsh was shocked to witness men do this work. He only possessed the clothes he was wearing, and grew increasingly worried about his laundry, after 'seeing the sailors washing their clothes. I was very much alarmed on my own part how I should wash my own clothing when they were dirty.'[78] At the time it was acceptable practice for a shirt to last several days, and the surgeon of HMS *Pompée* in 1811, Guy Alexander Acheson, ordered that 'Every man in the Sick List is to have on a clean shirt every Sunday and Thursday, and on those days a clean tablecloth will be provided for the sick mess.'[79] It was only after a week that Walsh became anxious about obtaining a clean shirt for Sunday: 'As I [had] seen no woman on board that I might fee [pay] for washing them, these thoughts continuously affected my mind.'[80] Another pressed man, William Caslet, asked him how he would get his shirt clean for Sunday:

> I answered him very plain and told him that I was as rich as Job and that I had nothing but what was on me and that it was time these was with the washerwoman if I knew where she lived. He let me know that his situation was the same and that he was then going to strive to wash them and told me he would wash mine if I pleased. I thanked him for his kind offer, so sought for a convenient place to take off my shirt but to my unspeakable grief I had none for to put on while it was washing . . . I had plenty of clothing at home, but I leaving my father's house so suddenly I brought nothing with me but what was on my back. But however in some short time necessity soon made me find the use of my hands, so I once thought that man's hands was never made to wash linens. But now I see that they have now to wash, make and mend or soon know the want of all.[81]

Sea water was commonly used for laundry – fresh water was too valuable to waste, though at times they were given hot water from the galley. Washing clothes was one way that the wives of sailors, accompanying their husbands unofficially and therefore without any entitlement to rations, could earn a little money. These women often illicitly used fresh water as it left the clothes cleaner and less prone to damp. On several occasions Rear-Admiral Sir John Jervis,* who kept a sharp watch over expenditure on supplies within his fleet, felt compelled to issue a warning:

---

* Soon to become Lord St Vincent as a reward for his success at the Battle of Cape St Vincent.

There being reason to apprehend that a number of women have been clandestinely brought from England in several ships, more particularly in those which have arrived in the Mediterranean in the last and present year, the respective Captains are required by the Admiral to admonish those ladies upon the waste of water and other disorders committed by them, and to make known to all, that on the first proof of water being obtained for washing from the scuttle-butt or otherwise under false pretences in any ship, every woman in the fleet who has not been admitted under the authority of the Admiralty or commander in chief will be shipped for England by the first convoy, and the officers of the fleet are strictly enjoined to watch vigilently their behaviour, and to see that no waste or improper consumption of water happens in future.[82]

The physician Thomas Trotter, with his customary disapproval of the men's habits, felt that they were not keen to keep their clothes clean:

Seamen have a custom of dressing themselves to undergo inspection at stated periods, while at other times they are covered with rags and nastiness. They should be compelled to keep their trowsers and other cloaths clean, how much soever they may be worn . . . Whenever any payment is made on board, the officers of divisions should take care that their men do lay in a sufficient stock of clothes, with soap, and such other articles as may be necessary for them, before they are allowed to squander any of their money in dissipation.[83]

As the rigging was coated with tar, the men and their clothes would have become impregnated with the stuff, which would be almost impossible to remove. On board the *Defence* in 1794, under the evangelical Captain Gambier, everyone was obliged to attend a church service on Sundays and kneel on the tarry deck, and Midshipman Dillon watched how one lieutenant took precautions:

In the winter, Lieut. Twysden would attend wrapped up in a great coat, and would make his servant place a folded piece of canvas over the pitchy seams, that his smalls might not be injured. This act of the Lieutenant's annoyed the Captain exceedingly; but, in making his excuses, he complained of being cold, and, as to the pitch, he stated that his trowsers were more than once spoiled from kneeling on the seams of the deck, as well as those of many others.[84]

Traditionally, household laundry was cleansed by soaking in an alkaline solution – lye or ley – of vegetable ashes mixed with water or urine, which lifted the dirt and grease. Clothes were also bleached by soaking them in urine. The wood ash from the galley fire would have been suitable, and urine that was collected in tubs could also have been used for laundry. Soap for laundry began to be issued to seamen from 1796, though Gilbert Blane was pleased that over a decade earlier every seaman on the sick list in the fleet off America was given half a pound of soap weekly, because 'the supply of soap was a thing entirely new in the service'.[85] In Britain the most common method of manufacturing soap was to boil a solution of wood or plant ashes with waste animal fat (tallow) or occasionally with olive oil dregs. The water evaporated and the fatty acids reacted with the alkali carbonates to form soap, a process known as saponification.

Around 1790 the French chemist Nicolas Leblanc developed a way of making soda ash from brine that advanced soap production. Most soap was coarse and could retain an offensive smell, but the initial jelly-like substance could be scented before pouring into moulds to form hard blocks. Soap suitable for laundry done in sea water was much sought after, and in September 1806 an advertisement appeared in *The Times*, saying that 'His Majesty hath been graciously pleased to grant his Royal Letters Patent to WILLIAM EVERARD BARON VON DOORNIK, for his Invention of an Improved Method of Manufacturing SOAP, whereby Linens, &c may be as effectively cleansed with Sea or Hard Water with as much facility as is done by the common Soap when used with soft water.'[86] There followed several testimonials from naval officers, including one signed by captains of warships anchored at the Nore, who claimed that 'This is to certify, that we whose names are hereunto annexed, have caused the Patent Soap, invented for the purpose of washing linen, &c. with salt water, to be tried in various instances, and find it to possess all the qualities, and to answer its intended purpose equally well as the common yellow or mottled soap does with fresh water.'[87]

The men had to wash clothes at times appointed by the captain, which varied from ship to ship, and despite the difficulties of drying clothing, the appearance of the warship came first, with strict rules about where wet laundry could be hung to dry. Captain Barlow of the *Phoebe* instructed that 'Mondays and Fridays are the days appointed for washing or drying and it is expected that in case of a muster of clothes on Monday every thing will be clean but those taken off that morning.'[88] He insisted that 'It is forbid hanging clothes about the bowsprit, heads chains, or running rigging – anchors or tops &c . . . Nobody is permitted to wash clothes at any time or any where except when and where it is particularly allowed by order.'[89] The American seaman Joseph Bates remembered with bitterness the difficulties on board his own ship, HMS *Rodney*:

> The discipline was to muster all hands at nine o'clock in the morning, and if our dress was reported soiled or unclean, then all such were doomed to have their names put on the 'black list' . . . If sufficient changes of dress had been allowed us, and sufficient time to wash and dry the same, it would have been a great pleasure, and also a benefit to us, to have appeared daily with unsoiled white dresses on, notwithstanding the dirty work we had to perform. I do not remember of ever being allowed . . . only one day in the week to cleanse them, viz., about two hours before daylight once a week, all hands (about 700) called on the upper decks to wash and scrub clothes. Not more than three-quarters of these could be accommodated to do this work for themselves at a time; but no matter, when daylight came at the expiration of the two hours, all washed clothes were ordered to be hung on the clothes-line immediately . . . Orders were most strict, that whoever should be found drying his clothes at any other but this time in the wash-day, should be punished.[90]

He unsuccessfully tried to circumvent the regulations: 'To avoid detection and punishment, I have scrubbed my trowsers early in the morning, and put them on and dried them. Not liking this method,

I ventured at one time to hang up my wet trowsers in a concealed place behind the maintop-sail: but the sail was ordered to be furled in a hurry, and the lieutenant discovered them.[91]

On board HMS *Indefatigable* in 1812, Captain John Fyffe gave orders that

> No person is upon any pretence whatever to hang up clothes or lay them in the boats or on the booms without permission from the commanding officer. On the washing days, if in harbour and in fine weather at sea, lines will be got up between the masts for the purpose and on no account are clothes to be hung up anywhere else except when no lines are got up then in the rigging. Whenever clothes are wet, either from casuality of weather or clearing hawse etc, on application to the commanding officer leave will be given for their being hung up to dry. Wet clothes are on no account to be left between decks when the weather will permit their being hung up.[92]

Clothing was just as much a problem for the officers since they were expected to keep up appearances, which could be difficult, as William Lovell remembered as a midshipman: 'Soap was almost – indeed, I might say, quite – as scarce an article as clean shirts and stockings. It was a common thing in those days of real hard service to turn shirts and stockings inside out, and make them do a little more duty. Sometimes we used to search the clothes-bag to see "if one good turn deserved another".'[93] Turning clothes inside out implied that the smell of dirty clothes was not deemed offensive – only their appearance. Officers usually had servants to take care of their laundry, which was often taken on shore. William Wilkinson, master of the *Minotaur* off Spithead in November 1807, wrote to his wife: 'At present no officer is allowed to go on shore from any of the ships here and I have not had my things washed since you were at Yarmouth, nor do I know whether I shall be able to get any washed or not.'[94] Four days later, he complained to her again: 'I have had no opportunity of sending my linen to wash, but last night on examining my trunks, I was surprised to find that I had not a clean shirt left, and thinking that I must have one in a day or two, looked over the bags and picked out two of the cleanest, paying most attention to the collars. I have given six of those without frills to be washed by a woman on board, which I do not expect to have done very well.'[95]

Aaron Thomas often sent his washing on shore, including one time at Antigua: 'I was finding fault with my washerwoman for not washing my linen clean. Sir, says she, some of them were so dirty, that I was obliged to wash them in *hot water* which gave me a fever.'[96] The surgeon Francis Spilsbury at Goree, on the West African coast, recorded that 'Washing on the island is charged at the rate of a dollar for a dozen pieces, counting a handkerchief etc as a shirt. They are beaten on stones and then rinsed. This is the only kind of washing in use, notwithstanding which, the articles are bleached very white.'[97] Lieutenant John Yule off Saint Domingo in the West Indies wrote to his wife Eliza about the same pricing structure there: 'Washing is 10 shillings for one dozen pieces whether they consist of pocket hand-kerchiefs, sheets or blankets.'[98] The seamen at times paid for their washing to be done on shore, and in a petition written at Plymouth by the men of the *Royal Sovereign*, not long after Trafalgar, they complained that they 'would not even be allowed to send their dirty cloths out of the ship to be washed, not having time for the duty of the ship to wash them on board'.[99]

Laundry washed and dried on land could have been ironed with flat irons, but on board flat irons heated on the galley stove were probably only feasible for the clothing of the officers. Most of the men were lucky if their clothes were cleaned and dried properly, let alone ironed, but they had the option of resorting to any smooth object like glass linen smoothers, bottles or large pebbles. When Lieutenant William Dillon and several seamen were marooned in a boat in a dead calm sea, he noted that 'My first annoyance was the want of clean linen. One of the seamen, Driscoll, a paddy, offered to wash my shirt. I gave it to him. He managed uncommonly well, then smoothed it with a glass bottle, till it approached very near to having been ironed.'[100]

The same standards of cleanliness applied to the men's hammocks, which did not remain constantly suspended ('slung') on board a ship, but each morning were rolled up with the bedding, lengthwise like a sausage, put in a numbered bag and taken to the upper deck. Captain Barlow of the *Phoebe* ordered that 'In fine weather the hammocks to be got up at 7 o'clock in harbour, and ½ past 7 at sea and got down again at sunset. The bedding to be occasionally aired . . . Men to be appointed to bring up the hammocks of the mates and midshipmen.'[101] He added: 'The centinels are to keep their posts clear [and] not to suffer any person to lean on the hammocks'.[102] Each man had two hammocks, and Barlow emphasised that 'Every man being allowed two hammocks that he may keep them clean and in good order, he is charged to take particular care of them and if any are lost without a satisfactory reason they will be charged against his wages.'[103]

Those who encountered ships and seamen of other nations often commented on the lack of cleanliness, highlighting how much better the British were. Major-General George Cockburn greatly approved of the high standards of the frigate *Lively*: 'Our ship is so clean that seasickness (which, I think, in nine cases out of ten, arises from the dirt and bad smells) is out of the question.'[104] He was even more impressed when at Cadiz he saw a foreign warship: 'In our way to shore this morning, we called on board a Spanish 70-gun ship: such dirt, filth, and misery I could not conceive.'[105] Similarly, when the Irish surgeon James Lowry was captured on board the *Swiftsure* in 1801 in the Mediterranean, he observed that 'The French have very bad discipline amongst their men: hence the superiority of our fleet at sea. The men are very dirty, the smell not of the most fragrant kind.'[106]

Washing of the men themselves on board Royal Navy ships was irregular, and no purpose-built washing facilities were provided. The physician Thomas Trotter recommended that 'Great pains should be constantly taken that the men are cleanly in their persons, and that they are furnished with all necessary cloathing',[107] but unlike on other issues, he made no further remarks. The Admiralty regulations stated that 'The captain is to be particularly attentive to the cleanliness of the men, who are to be directed to wash themselves frequently, and to change their linen twice every week.'[108] Soap was occasionally used, probably mainly the coarse soap intended for laundry. Some finer soaps such as pure white Castile soap from Spain were used on the skin, and from 1789 Andrew Pears in London developed a refined, translucent soap, still known today as Pears soap. These could only be afforded by a few since soap was heavily taxed. Towels for drying were probably the preserve of the officers, and in a letter to his father, Marine Lieutenant Rotely asked him to send 'a few towels'.[109] The seamen would have doused themselves with water in buckets or a tub, and some ships provided larger tubs in which the men could immerse themselves. Some did bathe in the sea, but not all could swim.

Everybody shaved, as beards were not tolerated. Shaving was done for the men by somebody who acted as a barber, using a cut-throat razor, and the majority of men were shaved once a week so as to look smart for Sundays. Most mentions of shaving are associated with 'crossing the line', when those who had never before crossed the Tropic of Cancer or the Equator were subjected to all sorts of ceremonies, such as being ducked in sea water. One common practice was to threaten to shave the novices using noxious substances like tar instead of soap and grotesque implements instead of razors, unless they paid a fine. The soldier John Spencer Cooper observed one incident when his regiment was being transported to the West Indies:

> A bucket and an iron hoop, instead of a razor, were also in readiness for the shaving. The bucket, or lather box, was half filled with a compound of tar, grease, and something I shall not name. The razor was about a yard long, rusty and jagged at its edges. Then a seaman, who was not willing to pay the usual fine, viz. – half a gallon of rum, was . . . blindfolded. An old tar then proceeded to lather the poor fellow most outrageously, at the same time asking sundry questions, in order that he might have an opportunity of thrusting his brush into the patient's mouth. Having satisfied himself with lathering or daubing the sufferer, the barber began with the hoop to scrape off the lather and a little skin from the man's jaws.[110]

As an officer, Lieutenant William Dillon was accustomed to shaving himself daily, and so when he was marooned on a boat he complained that after dirty clothing, 'My next annoyance was the length of my beard. Pat tried shaving me, but the razor was so blunt that I could not endure the pain.'[111] Marine Captain Wybourn was luckier – when on shore in May 1813 attacking the American town of Havre de Grace, they went into some hotels, whose guests had fled: 'A most welcome prize fell to my lot – a gentleman's portmanteau stood open, in which clean white shirts were exhibited and a case of razors, neither of which I had seen since I left the ship, and when we embarked I instantly began my toilette in the boat. There were 5 shirts, those razors, a pair of nankeen pantaloons and waistcoats and neck handkerchiefs. I shared everything out, except two shirts and my razors: these were too great a luxury to part with.'[112]

Teeth were inevitably neglected, resulting in gum disease, which for many seamen would have meant losing many or most of their teeth. When describing Davy Reed, master of the *Edgar* in 1787, James Gardner said that he

> had the misfortune, like many others, to lose his teeth. I was at dinner in the wardroom when a small parcel was handed in directed for Mr. Reed. 'What the hell can this be?' says Davy (who did not like to have sixpence to pay the waterman), 'and who gave it to you?' continued he. 'Sir,' says the waterman, 'it was a young lady who sent it off from Common Hard [at Portsmouth].' As several tricks had been played with Davy before, he was afraid to open the parcel, and begged of one of the officers at the table to do so for him, but when opened, what was his amazement to find a set of sheep's teeth for David Reed, Esq., with directions for fixing, and a box of tooth powder that, by the smell, appeared to be a mixture of everything abominable. Poor Davy was in a dreadful rage.[113]

Toothbrushes and tooth powder were used by officers, such as the product advertised as a new Asiatic tooth powder by one London chemist on the front page of *The Times* newspaper in 1785: 'This Tooth Powder derives its Name from being prepared of a soft earthy Substance, the Produce of Borneo and Sumatra, in the East

Indies . . . The Preparation of it as a Tooth-Powder has hitherto been kept a Secret from the Europeans.'[114] The same chemist was also selling 'India Tooth Brushes, 1s. each. English ditto, 6d. each'.[115] During the blockade of Ferrol on board the *Ganges* in May 1804, Captain Thomas Fremantle wrote to his wife: 'If there is one thing that I feel distressed about, it is the want of tooth powder and brushes for my teeth. I beg you will promise me a pretty large assortment well packed up, and send them directed for me at Mr. Glencross's Plymouth Dock.'[116] When Midshipman Robert James was a prisoner-of-war at Sarrelibre in France, he was horrified at having to share accommodation with ordinary merchant seamen: 'Judge of manners when I caught one of them using my tooth brush. I broke it and threw it out of the window – he said I was *vary fulish* to fling it away as he would have returned it to my drawer nicely rinsed – but however it would serve. He went and picked it up and used it on Sundays.'[117]

Sanitary arrangements were as sparse as washing facilities. The toilets were called heads and were located right up in the bow of the ship in an area called the beakhead, on either side of the bowsprit. The toilets consisted of adjacent seats with holes ('seats of ease') over a clear drop to the sea, completely exposed to the weather and at times dangerous. The name 'head' was probably taken from the beakhead, the figurehead beneath and the nearby catheads,* and 'going to the heads' meant going to the toilet. It was burdensome for the men to have to make their way to the bows of the ship, and George King related that in port one Christmas Day, the 'yeoman had drank too much grog and whisky that on his coming up from the cockpit to go to the head as was supposed, he crawled out of one of the main deck ports and fell overboard . . . when he was hoisted on board he was quite dead'.[118]

There were very few seats, only six in the *Victory* for hundreds of men, though to some extent this reflected the constipation caused by the diet. Nor did everyone at the heads sit down on toilets to defe-

---

* Catheads were wooden beams projecting on each side of the bow, from which ropes were used to heave up and secure the anchor once the anchor cable had been hauled in.

cate, but some crouched over the side of the ship supported by ropes. Even so, there were complaints about the poor facilities, and a petition from the seamen of the *Nereide* at Bombay in 1808 declared bitterly that 'we are more like a prison ship, than a man of war. From gunfire in the morning until sunset the gangway is attended by the Master at Arms to prevent more than two [men] at a time going to the privy, so that the pains we labour under is insupportable, some discommode their trowsers thro' a griping.'[119]

Near the seats of ease were two semicylindrical cubicles called roundhouses with similar facilities, one for the midshipmen and warrant officers, and one reserved for men in the sick-bay. These roundhouses gave a degree of privacy and were sheltered from the weather. The surgeon of the *Pompee*, Guy Acheson, ordered that each day the attendant of the sick-bay was 'to throw a bucket of salt water down the round house'.[120] In larger ships the captain had his own private toilet in a small cubicle at one end of the stern gallery that ran across the width of the stern, with a row of windows giving light into the captain's cabin. This cubicle was known as a quarter gallery, and on the decks below similar quarter galleries were provided for the officers. Although private, these toilets still only consisted of a seat with a hole over a vertical waste pipe or over an open drop to the sea. In smaller ships, with no room for such facilities at the stern, the officers probably used chamber pots or buckets, which their servants emptied. On board the *Malta* warship off Cartagena in Spain in 1813, during the Peninsular War, the officers entertained some Spanish women, and Lieutenant Abraham Crawford was amused by the reaction to their quarter galleries:

> Every part of the ship was then shown to them . . . when the elderly ladies, in their desire to examine everything within view, peeped into certain little boudoirs fitted on the quarters, their ecstasy and delight at the discovery knew no bounds. They actually shouted with admiration, calling to each other . . . 'Johanna! Maria! Come here, come here, for the love of God! Look what cleanliness! What convenience! In my life I never saw anything so pretty, so elegant! Certainly the English are the neatest and cleverest people in the world.'[121]

Toilet paper was not invented in Britain until the later nineteenth century, but newspapers and other scrap paper were utilised by the officers, as exemplified in one contemporary novel: 'Here some person knocked at the [captain's] cabin-door, and the steward going to it, returned to the table with a bundle of papers. "The gentlemen [midshipmen], sir," said he, have sent you their day's work." "Very well," replied the captain; "put them in the quarter-gallery."'[122] The seamen made use of scrap fibrous materials such as tow (unwashed, uncombed wool or flax that was a general-purpose cleaning and packing material), oakum (rope fibres) or a natural sponge that they shared and rinsed in a bucket of sea water.

Men would often not have bothered using the heads simply to urinate. One method was to urinate while hanging from the shrouds at the points where they were secured to the sides of the ship. In these places, wooden ledges known as the chain-wales, channels or, more commonly, chains provided footholds, and the lee (downwind) side of the ship was chosen, because the wind tilted the ship over in this direction, giving a clear drop to the sea. Depending on the discipline in the ship, this practice was often not tolerated on board warships. Tubs for urine were strategically placed, even in the galley, as Richard Cunningham, a boatswain's mate from the *Prince Frederick*, described: 'The galley was wet; the people go into the galley to piss, where tubs are placed for them'.[123] Elsewhere in the ship – on the decks well above the water-line – were a number of pissdales ('dale' being an old word for 'drain'). These were simple basins or trough-like urinals made of lead, copper or sometimes wood, mounted on a bulkhead (an internal wooden partition), with lead drainage pipes that took the waste water to the side of the ship and emptied out through openings known as scuppers.

Perennial problems occurred with the men and officers relieving themselves in inappropriate places, but there were few complaints about the smell, implying that it was all-pervasive. Aaron Thomas related numerous stories on board the *Lapwing* frigate, which must have been mirrored on board many other ships. Men obviously urinated against the inside of the ship and into the scuppers at night, and the *Lapwing*'s captain, Thomas Harvey, 'ordered, that for the future, two men should keep watch, during the night, in the waist, to keep people from water-ing against the ship's sides'.[124] Two months later Aaron Thomas reported that 'Last night Mr Tripe [Midshipman William Dunning Tripe] sent for 5 bottles of porter and drank it all himself; by it, he got very tipsy, and in the night he shit upon the skylight which overlooks the captain's cabin.'[125] Soon after, another incident occurred: 'One of our surgeon's mates eased himself in a tank, where the men get fresh water from'[126] – this was Mr Craer, who had been drunk the night before. Thomas also heard about one unnamed lieutenant's method: '[I] asked the cause of the speaking trumpet smelling so strong, said [was told] it was caused by reason that Lieutenant —— had been using it as a piss-ing machine to carry his urine from his body, off the quarter deck, through one of the ports, into the sea.'[127]

Particular problems with sanitary arrangements arose during pro-longed bad weather, when the hatches were battened down for days at a time. Buckets ('necessary buckets') were used as toilets, but could not be emptied until conditions improved, and the situation was exacerbated by increased seasickness in such weather. Talking partic-ularly of those ill with dysentery, the surgeon Robert Robertson on board the *Rainbow* in the West Indies in 1777 gave a graphic idea of what happened in storms:

> They [the poor conditions] are undoubtedly much increased when the weather is so bad as not to admit the lower deck ports to be up in large ships, or the hatchways in small ships to be unlayed. The foul air then being much more confined around the sick, and where the well people lie, is consequently drawn into the lungs again and again by respiration, and soon becomes more foul and noxious, which renders it unfit for the salu-tary purposes of both the sick and the healthy. This circumstance is perhaps a much more powerful agent in enfeebling the seamen; in depressing their spirits during bad weather; and in rendering the dysen-tery epidemic in the ship, than the inclemency of the weather to which they are exposed upon deck in their watches. It is very pleasing to observe the immediate alteration which appears in the countenances of the men, when the ship is well washed and aired, and when they have cleaned themselves after bad weather.[128]

It was not uncommon for a marine to be posted at the gratings above the hold to prevent the sailors relieving themselves there. Any waste water eventually got into the lowest part of the ship, the bilge, and the smell of this bilge water could be overpowering, as it seeped into the ballast in the hold where all the stores were kept. The physician Gilbert Blane thought that life was more healthy on board a frigate than a larger ship: 'a small ship is more easily ventilated, and the mass of foul air issuing from the hold, from the victuals, water, and other stores, as well as the effluvia exhaling from the men's bodies, is less than in a large ship'.[129]

———•———

As there was no heating, the men were frequently cold and wet, and they tended to congregate round the galley stove. The officers had small portable stoves, but the surgeon Barry O'Meara thought these were useless when compared with the galley stove. In the Dardanelles in March 1807 Marine Captain Wybourn wrote to his sisters of the terrible weather, saying that 'we are perished with cold and wet, the climate here is as bad as in England'.[130] In mid-November 1805, after returning to England after the Battle of Trafalgar, Lieutenant John Yule grumbled to his wife that 'It is dreadfully cold to us who have been so long in warm climates. I can hardly hold my pen.'[131] When O'Meara was Napoleon's surgeon in exile on St Helena, he talked to him about being on board Royal Navy warships in winter: 'I remarked, that the seamen were better off in point of being able to warm themselves at a fire than the officers. "Why so?" said Napoleon. I replied, "Because they have the advantage of the galley fire, where they can warm and dry themselves." "And why not the officers?" I said, that it would not be exactly decorous for the officers to mix in that familiar way with the men.'[132]

Much of the time the men were unable to keep dry and warm, and Dr Trotter urged that 'When their watches expire in rainy weather, they should be obliged to take off their wet shirts before they get into their hammocks, which, from laziness as well as fatigue, they will not do but by compulsion. Nothing can be more pernicious than going to sleep wrapped up in wet linen, and it causes also their bedding to be damp and unwholesome for some time afterwards.'[133] Writing in

1801, he observed that 'The practice which has lately been adopted of having stoves with fires placed occasionally in those parts of the ship where the men reside, and in others subject to humidity, is of the utmost importance to the health of the people and should never be omitted in damp weather.'[134]

Keeping dry was certainly not just a problem of winter weather, as Major-General Cockburn on board the *Lively* discovered when they encountered very high humidity in the Mediterranean off the North African coast:

> The damp, considering the latitude we are in, and the season of the year [July], is extraordinary; there is a constant thorough air in the cabin; ports and doors open all day, and yet, leave a pair of boots three days in a corner, and they will be quite damp and mouldy. We have also had frequent fogs, and though the weather is so hot, our clothes and every thing in the ship feels clammy, and our linen is as damp as in Ireland during winter . . . many complain of slight rheumatism.[135]

In March 1811 the *Nisus* frigate quitted the harbour of Port Louis in Mauritius (the island having been captured in December), and the surgeon James Prior said that he was not sorry to leave as it had become very unpleasant walking the streets where conditions were excessively humid, yet he found the ship no better: 'On-board we were scarcely more comfortable; for, in excluding the showers, we were likewise obliged to shut out a large portion of air. This, added to the close atmosphere of a ship, and external moisture, produced an oppressive sultriness that was not merely heat, but the heavy, thick, overpowering sense of being steamed.'[136]

Different weather conditions favoured different groups of vermin on board ship, and particularly in hot climates vermin were a problem, causing damage to clothing, provisions and the men themselves. As the fuel for the stoves was both coal and wood, the men were frequently sent on shore to forage for wood, and Jeffrey Raigersfeld described the unwanted wildlife they encountered when he was a servant to Captain Collingwood on board the *Mediator* in 1783: 'In the West Indies, the fuel made use of on board a ship is wood, among which varieties of insects are brought, such as scorpions, centipedes, and tarantulas, with now and then a few snakes; these soon begin to crawl all up and down a ship, even into the hammocks, and the men frequently got stung and bit by them.'[137] Robert Hay on board the *Culloden* in Madras in 1804 described the vermin at length. After talking about mosquitoes, he then wrote about other pests:

> The next is the tarantula, an insect resembling a spider, but considerably larger and hairy like a mouse. The centipede, an insect eight or ten inches long, scarcely as thick as the little finger and having about 20 feet on each side. The scorpion, an unsightly reptile 2 or 3 inches long with a tail nearly of the same length. The two former of these bite . . . These reptiles, as also snakes of a small size generally are brought aboard in the hollow parts of firewood and are very dangerous. Though death has been known to follow their sting, no such fatal instance occurred with us, but I have known their stings and bites prove very painful and often long in heal-ing.[138]

The surgeon James Prior graphically portrayed the conditions on board the *Nisus* off Mauritius:

> At all seasons, at all hours, and in all places, they attacked us in every pos-sible manner. Rats, mice, mosquitoes, locusts, flies, bugs, moths, cockroaches, fleas, scorpions, centipedes, and others, infest the shipping more than the shore, for, having numberless places of concealment in the holds, in the interstices of the beams and timbers, and in the provision-casks, it becomes impossible to eject the enemy after his having once made good a lodgement. Besides being pestered in the day, we have been frightened in our beds by the prowling of rats, blistered by mosquitoes, bitten by fleas, driven out of bed by bugs, and in danger of being fairly carried off by thousands of cockroaches.[139]

The cockroaches were an especial nuisance:

> They fly about confusedly in the night, continually dart on our faces, sometimes extinguish the candles, and lay eggs in which the young in

embryo present the same appearance and numbers as the roes of herrings. My cabin is frequently covered by clouds of these creatures, which give it the semblance of being daubed with animated brown varnish; and my only remedy is a furious assault, right and left, with a weighty towel, which stuns a few of the enemy, and drives the remainder to their covert abodes . . . raw Europeans make a delicate food, as well as a species of fair game to all of them. Our juices form a perfect living larder to every thing than can either bite or puncture.[140]

Two years later, Prior recorded that the rat infestation on board the *Nisus* was even worse: 'these animals had so much increased that they ran about the lower deck almost without dread. It likewise became an amusement among the boys to fish for them down the hatchways with hook and line; during the first few days, the bait was no sooner down than it was eagerly seized, and many were thus caught.'[141] Rats were a problem on board the *Culloden* as well, which Robert Hay recounted:

Rats and bandecouts [the name given to Indian rats], animals nearly alike, are from their surprising numbers very troublesome. I have known them to leave the marks of their teeth in the thick skin of men's toes when asleep and on one occasion to draw blood. In order to keep down the number of these vermin, it was prescribed as a daily task to each of the boys to produce either a rat, a bandecout, a scorpion, a tarantula, a centipede, 20 cockroaches, or 20 eggs of the last-named fly. Though this doubtless kept down their number considerably, still they abounded greatly and proved very troublesome.[142]

Once they were further out to sea, the problem with insects diminished. 'Thanks, however, to the cooler air of the sea, many have retired to their fastnesses,' Prior noted with relief, 'to be again drawn forth by the quiescence and warmth of the harbour.'[143]

Despite the constant presence of vermin in the ships, army Major-General Cockburn appeared envious of the Royal Navy, but he was critical of the risk of fire:

The principal thing I see in the navy, requiring improvement, is the galleys, or fire-places; considering their formation and the motion at sea, I am astonished that half our ships are not burned; to be sure the facts are against this, it does not happen: so many [people] are at all times about the fire during the day, and it is so carefully put out at night, that no doubt the probability is against it; but why leave it a possibility, when security might be had at very trifling expence? To observe the fire, and the number of grates, boilers, ovens, &c. and the combustible material all around, it is astonishing more accidents do not happen: I should be alarmed with a kitchen fire so constructed in my house. I am confident ship kitchens might be improved, and made secure from the danger to which they expose the ship.[144]

What Cockburn did not consider was the risk of fire from candles. Captains were advised 'to be extremely attentive in taking every possible precaution to prevent accidents by fire'.[145] It was very dark below decks, pitch black in places, and unless there was moonlight, darkness reigned at night on the upper deck as well. Light from lanterns and candles was dim and did not extend any distance. Beeswax and tallow (animal fat) candles were placed inside lanterns of tin and translucent horn, or else oil was used as a fuel, and these lanterns were suspended from beams or carried around at night by those on duty, as Robert Wilson described: 'The sergeants and corporals [of marines] in their watches at night time have to go round all the decks with a lantern and candle every half-hour to see if all is well; and when they have done so, they are to report to the Officer of the Watch accordingly.'[146]

Only lanterns were allowed in the lower part of the ship, and naked candles were not supposed to be used by seamen because of the danger of fire. The captain was urged 'strictly to forbid the sticking of candles against the beams, the sides or any other part of the ship. He is strictly to enjoin the officers not to read in bed by the light of either lamps or candles; nor to leave any light in their cabins without having some person to attend it.'[147] Captain Cumby of the *Hyperion* emphasised this warning in his own orders: 'no lights, whether at sea or in harbour, are to be allowed to remain unattended in any berth or cabin; and none to be allowed in the tiers except in lanthorns'.[148]

The court martial of Francisco Falso and John Lambert demonstrated the degree of darkness. These two seamen were accused of committing sodomy in August 1798 in the galley of the *Prince Frederick*, at about eleven-thirty at night. Thomas King, a waister, said that 'I heard a bustling on the bench, but did not know what it was, being so dark. I walked up to it, and touched a man's naked flesh with my hand.'[149] The boatswain's mate, Richard Cunningham, was summoned, and he sent King for a light: 'I brought the lanthorn and held the light to Cunningham and saw both prisoners, they were laying down and both their trowsers down.'[150] Cunningham was then cross-examined: 'Q. Was there a sufficient light for you to see anything by the Master at Arms lanthorn? A. It was a moonlight night and the light shone thro' the gratings but was not so light as for me to determine who the persons were.'[151] Thomas Ellis, a seaman, was in the galley at that time, dozing nearby, and he too was cross-examined: 'Q. As you were sitting so near the prisoners, if they had been in the Act of Sodomy, with which they are charged, must you not have seen them? A. It was dark and I could not see them. Besides I had no suspicion of anything of the kind.'[152] The two men were eventually acquitted because the galley was far too dark for those present to have seen the offence take place.

Candles were always in short supply, and in another court martial one witness said that 'the prisoner came with one of the lanthorns in his hand holding it up to me. I thought there was something amiss, and so I asked him what was the matter. He said he wanted a fresh candle as that was burnt out; I said it is impossible that the candle is already burnt out, it is hardly 10 minutes since I lighted it, and they will burn two hours and longer.'[153] Wax and tallow candles were also burned in candleholders, but Captain Thomas Fremantle complained to his wife Betsey that his cabins were so large 'that two wax candles are not perceived in them'.[154] The chaplain Edward Mangin was forced to compose his sermons in his cabin, with only a small window for light. 'I read and wrote by what, at best, could scarcely be called twilight;' he complained, 'and very frequently, even in the noon-tide of a summer-day, carried on these operations by candle light, or by what seamen facetiously termed, a Purser's moon.'[155] The purser was responsible for providing candles, and years later Basil Hall remarked: 'Even at this distance of time, I have a most painfully distinct recollection of these dirty tallow candles in the midshipmen's berth; dips, I think they were called, smelling of mutton fat, and throwing up a column of smoke like that from a steamboat's chimney. These "glims" yielded but little light.'[156]

When performing operations down in the cockpit during battle, the surgeons struggled to see, and what happened to the surgeon Forbes Chivers on board the *Tonnant* at the Battle of Trafalgar demonstrated the lack of light: 'The place was utterly dark, half of its depth being below the water-line. C. did all his amputations by the light of tallow candles, held torch-like by two assistants, to whom he said, "If you look straight into the wound, and see that I do, I shall see perfectly" . . . A consequence was that, when he washed his face at the first opportunity, he found that his eyebrows had been burnt off.'[157]

In the deepest recesses of the ship, the darkness was such that a man could – literally – live undetected. This happened with one Irish seaman who survived for weeks in the hold of the *Nisus* frigate anchored off Port Louis in Mauritius in early 1811:

John Herring, a youth of eighteen, was discovered by the master-at-arms crawling into one of the tiers; he being supposed to have jumped overboard and been drowned, on the 4th of November last. For five months he had secreted himself in the main hold, unseen by any person whatever; during all which time he subsisted upon what he could nightly steal out of the mess kids and bread-bags between decks. His supply was, of course, precarious, and he says he was once five days without eating, though he could generally procure water. When detected diving to his hiding-place, he had two bags in his hand, one full of biscuit, and the other of onions, which he had just stolen. He could crawl pretty well, but stood with difficulty; he was unable to walk, and being very weak and emaciated, would not probably have lived many days longer.[158]

Even in good weather, with ports and hatches open, little light penetrated as far as the lower decks, but when bad weather set in the problems of coping with the elements were compounded by the lack of light within the ship. Aaron Thomas, who wrote his journals in his cabin by candlelight, found the shadowy darkness could conjure up strange fantasies: 'I am sitting below in my cabin, with the Purser's dull rush light before me. Its horrible glance gives so deadly a hue to all around that I sometimes fancy myself in the regions below, amongst my ancestors in our family vault. So dismal is the light of my candle, and so black is the table on which I write, that the other day I thought I was using my pen on the lid of my Great Grandfather's coffin.'[159]

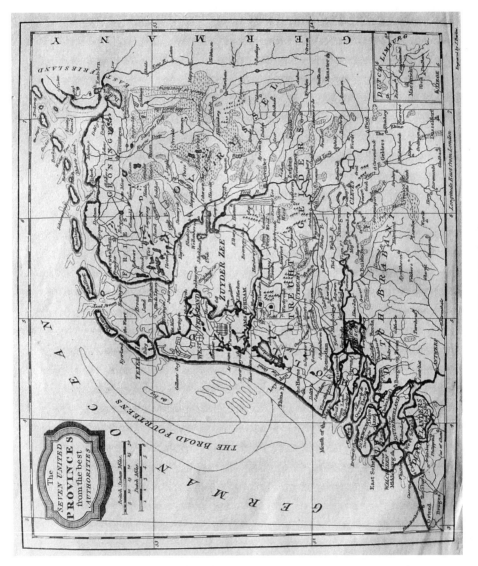

Map of the Netherlands

FIVE

A WIFE IN EVERY PORT

> I can say little about Cephalonia, having been but once on shore to my recollection, however I heard that there were plenty of fruit, wine and 'bonny lasses', which are the principal things sailors look for in any port.
>
> Able Seaman George Watson[1]

When 'in' a port, warships seldom moored alongside or close to a quay or jetty, as the water was not always deep enough, and it was sometimes difficult to manoeuvre a ship in a confined area, but the overriding reason was to stop the seamen deserting. Most warships anchored in the roads, sometimes called roadsteads, which were anchorages outside the ports or harbours that were as safe and sheltered from the prevailing winds as possible. In Britain, probably the best-known and certainly the busiest of such anchorages was Spithead, lying between the great naval base at Portsmouth and the Isle of Wight. With the mainland to the north, the island to the south and a series of sandbanks to the east, it provided good protection combined with easy access. Here ships could be positioned well over a mile from the nearest land – far enough to deter all but the most confident swimmer.

Other measures could be taken to prevent anyone escaping, such as posting a boat on guard duty during the night, which would be rowed round and round the ship. On top of such precautions, many captains rarely allowed shore leave to prevent desertion, and this only added to the men's frustration. As Captain Anselm Griffiths admitted in 1811, 'by far the larger portion of a ship's company are there against their consent. Many are impressed and forcibly brought; others enter because if they do not, they will be impressed, and although they are cheerful and apparently contented, still there is that difference between them and the officers: the latter are there by choice.'[2]

Because so few men could enjoy the benefits of going ashore, with no entitlement to days off or to holidays, it was customary for bumboats to carry traders out to the ships to sell all manner of goods from fresh food to clothes, cheap watches and trinkets, but an even larger number of boats carried prostitutes. When Edward Mangin joined the *Gloucester* warship at Gravesend as chaplain in 1812, it was his first time at sea, and the presence of prostitutes on board was explained to him as necessary for the welfare of the seamen, even those who were married:

> According to custom while in harbour, and before the ship was paid, there were multitudes of women in her; some quartered with the midshipmen in the cable-tier and cockpit; the rest with the common men. This arrangement is asserted to be a necessary evil, and better than allowing the seamen to go and visit their friends and acquaintances on shore; and with reference to the interests of the Naval Service, this licence may be necessary; but, it was productive of considerable embarrassment to one in my situation on board.[3]

The idea that sexual frustration would lead the men of the lower decks to 'unclean acts' of homosexuality was one reason why prostitutes were permitted on board when the ships were in port. While a first-time navy chaplain might be taken aback, even the seamen were sometimes shocked at the sheer numbers of women at the main naval bases. In the summer of 1809 the Irish seaman Henry Walsh in HMS *Alfred* arrived at Portsmouth, which in his view was 'the capital naval seaport in England and consequently in the world'.[4] The sight of the prostitutes was less agreeable:

I was astonished in beholding the crowd of those women of pleasure that daily surround those ships of war and there remains until the man goes down into these boats and there chooses one. And then he asks the waterman what is the price of his wife. It is generally a shilling or more according to the state of the weather. When in harbour this is the way the sailors generally spends their time, in the arms of these infamous prostitutes, which indeed is a disgrace to womankind when on board. I have seen above four hundred of these ladies on board at one time, and they are not very particular about the convenience of sleeping in private, as that is impossible to find among so many men. Their expressions in conversation is quite beyond the limits of prudence or modesty.[5]

The main ports had large populations of prostitutes awaiting the arrival of warships – at least one thousand in Portsmouth alone according to the 1801 census figures – and out of all the potential clients, naval seamen were likely to provide rich pickings, as this contemporary song demonstrates:

> Don't you see the ships a-coming?
> Don't you see them in full sail?
> Don't you see the ships a-coming
> With the prizes at their tail?
> Oh! My little rolling sailor
> Oh! My little rolling he;
> I do love a jolly sailor,
> Blithe and merry might he be.
>
> Sailors, they get all the money,
> Soldiers, they get none but brass;
> I do love a jolly sailor,
> Soldiers they may kiss my arse.
> Oh! My little rolling sailor,
> Oh! My little rolling he;
> I do love a jolly sailor,
> Soldiers may be damned for me.[6]

Major-General René-Martin Pillet, who was a prisoner-of-war in England for six years, provided an embittered French perspective:

Some English sailors have been in the service twenty-five years; they have sailed to every part of the known world, and these sailors have never set foot on land for six hours . . . To deprive the sailor of a wish to visit the land, and to prevent the spirit of revolt . . . the vessel is opened to all the girls of a dissolute life, who offer themselves. Sometimes moreover, for form's sake, a hypocritical captain requires the female visitors to take the title of the sister, niece, cousin or relation of the sailor they designate, according to the list sent ashore; it is to them a real lottery of age, form and money. These women never fail to bring with them a great abundance of provisions of the dearest kinds; some spiritous liquors, but not without some contrivance and secrecy.[7]

Whenever a warship appeared, a rush of women tried to get on board, with only a few being genuine wives, as Daniel Goodall found:

No sooner had the 'Temeraire' cast anchor off Plymouth than she was surrounded by shore boats, for the fact that a ship's company was coming in to receive pay spread somehow with a rapidity and certainty that would have seemed marvellous to those who did not know how numerous were the harpies that preyed upon poor Jack, and how keen was their scent when plunder was in prospect. The first arrivals were, of course, the fair sex, who set up the most clamorous demands for admission on board, each claiming to have a husband amongst the crew. Some of them, it is true, really were the wives of men belonging to the ship, but, if all had been admitted who set up the claim of connubial right, it would have been a clear case of polygamy, for there could not have been less than a proportion of three or four to every man of marriageable age and position on board. As it was, three days sufficed to see fully more than two hundred of the Delilahs of Plymouth settled amongst the crew, not ten per cent. of whom could have made out a feasible claim to marital connection with any of the men.[8]

Marine Lieutenant Robert Steele related one verse sung by these women:

> Come, ferryman, ferry me over,
> To a ship that's call'd the *Fame*
> For there I've got a husband,
> But hang me, if I know his name.[9]

Some captains, particularly those regarded as devout or even fanatical Christians, insisted that the women should prove they were married before being allowed on board. Writing to his wife Sally in February 1809, thirty-year-old William Wilkinson assured her:

> In regard to your wishing to know if there are any bad ladies onboard, I am very happy to be able to give you an answer that will be very satisfactory. Two days after the *Christian* joined the fleet under Admiral Lord Gambier (who is a very good and strict religious man) he gave a written order that none should be permitted to come onboard any of the ships of the fleet, saying that it was to the great annoyance of married men, and against all decency and morality, and if any officer disgraced himself so much as to break this order his name was immediately to be given by the first lieutenant to the captain and sent to the Admiral, that he might be severely punished. And I have no doubt but the person so offending would be broke ... You may be sure that I was much pleased to see it. For the longer I live I feel the more disgusted with those creatures who do not deserve the name of woman.[10]

When younger, Wilkinson had presumably resorted to prostitutes, because he was treated in the hospital at Plymouth for 'venereal'[11] at the end of 1803.

Prostitutes were at times allowed to stay on board ships sailing between British ports, but a few years earlier, when Gambier took command of the *Defence*, Midshipman Dillon said he became instantly unpopular by insisting that the men only have wives on board when they sailed from the Nore anchorage to the Downs:

In character and disposition he was, it seems, a strictly devout, religious man, bordering upon the Methodist principles. The first act was to ascertain whether all the women on board were married. All their certificates were demanded – those that had any produced them; those that had not contrived to manufacture a few. This measure created a very unpleasant feeling among the tars. It was the custom on board the ships of war to allow the seamen to take their wives as passengers when sailing from one port to another – but they did not go to sea. A few of the seamen were married, the others had nominal wives – an indulgence winked at generally in the Navy. Consequently, when our Captain began this inspection you may easily comprehend the impression it caused upon the crew.[12]

The artist and diarist Joseph Farington noted a similar situation with his nephew William, who was commander of the *Clio*:

On board the *Clio* [at Leith in May 1813] Captain Farington allows the wives of seamen to abide with their husbands both in harbour and when cruising, and there were 10 or 12 wives now in the ship. He does not permit admission to the ship *to any loose women*. To the unmarried men he gives leave for them to go on shore occasionally, a certain number at a time. Thus he takes care that the married women shall not be offended by the society of loose women and the good effect is felt in the order which prevails.[13]

Establishing who were genuine wives could be difficult, though. The seaman John Martindale Powell described the forging of marriage certificates in a letter to his mother in London:

I have been ready always to write for the men but I have had an escape, for I have been requested by one of the women on board to write out a certificate of marriage between her and one of the men, she telling me she had forgot to bring the right one with her on board and that she might perhaps have occasion for it, she should be glad if I would make one out and she would direct me how to draw it up but this I absolutely refused to do, well knowing the consequence of forgery, so by this you may see how soon any unexperienced person may be taken in by a set of abominable wretches like them. When the men received their money they were ready to tear them to pieces to buy them new things. One man belonging to another ship had received one hundred pounds and getting drunk the next morning he lost it all, every farthing.[14]

Once the women were on board, the resulting revelry was chaotic and deafening, as Daniel Goodall described:

This addition to our company made a noise more than proportionate to their number, and, I am bound to add, they displayed such a reckless disregard of every claim of decency and morality as Jack, even at his worst, could ever hope or would ever attempt to equal. A ship-of-war at that period was often enough compared to a portion of the 'lower kingdom' set afloat, and truly the comparison was not undeserved when applied to the period that a ship was in harbour during pay. The brawling and uproar never ceased the whole day long, and sometimes continued during the greater part of the night also. As long as the ladies could contrive to obtain drink – and it astonished me to see how very successful they were in getting it – they solaced themselves with libations stinted only by the extent of the supply. Smoking was quite a prevalent fashion amongst the dear creatures, and, as for swearing, they seemed to take quite a peculiar delight in uttering the 'oldest oaths the newest kind of ways,' and those ways the most revolting it is possible for even the vilest to imagine. The coarsest seamen on board were far outdone by those damsels.[15]

Little could be done, Goodall acknowledged, to control these women:

The officers, of course, did all they could to keep the sisterhood within bounds, but, as there was no other means of coercion save the threat of sending them ashore, and as they were well aware that this threat was never carried out except in extreme cases, remonstrances produced little effect beyond the moment. Some there were, even amongst the degraded class I am treating of, who seemed sickened by the outrage to womanhood of which their viler sisters were guilty, but the poor creatures who thus paid homage to virtue amid their degradation were held in but small account by the majority of their companions. There were, too, some few – alas, how very few! – really virtuous females amongst them, wives of seamen on board, whose modesty and worth was unsullied amid all the vice and pollution by which they were surrounded.[16]

In 1821 Captain Edward Hawker, who was deeply concerned about the morals of the seamen, anonymously published a pamphlet deploring the continued tradition of allowing prostitutes on board. He was particularly concerned for the genuine wives and children:

> The tendency of this practice is to render a ship of war, while in port, a continual scene of riot and disorder, of obscenity and blasphemy, of drunkenness, lewdness, and debauchery. During this time, the married seamen are frequently joined by their wives and families (sometimes comprising daughters from ten to fifteen years of age), who are forced to submit to the alternative of mixing with these abandoned women, whose language and behaviour are usually of the most polluting description, or of foregoing altogether the society of their husbands and parents.[17]

Others were concerned with more practical issues than the moral health of the seamen, and attempted to prevent the spread of sexually transmitted diseases. One officer commented anonymously: 'The next step which, in many ships, is insisted upon, before the seaman is allowed to take his prostitute on the lower deck, is to get her examined by the assistant surgeon, to ascertain whether she is infected with the venereal disease; in which case she is sent out of the ship. It must however, be mentioned, to the honour of the assistant surgeons in the navy, that some have resisted this order of their captains.'[18]

Another practical concern was overcrowding, since the arrival of women could more than double the number of people on board, especially if one officer was correct in asserting that 'it is frequently the case that men take two prostitutes on board at a time, so that it sometimes happens that there are more women than men on board'.[19]

The seaman John Wetherell described the scene in June 1803 when his ship HMS *Hussar* moored at Plymouth:

> In the course of an hour the ship was surrounded with shore boats. First the married men had liberty to take their wives on board then the young men had their girls come off* and took them on board, a curious sight to see boats crowded with blooming young girls all for sale. Our crew were mostly young men and caused the boatmen to have a quick dispatch or as we usually term it a ready market; this business over, nothing particular occurred that day. Next morning it was found that there was two more women than men on board . . . a mighty jovial crew [of] 616 souls.[20]

Such overcrowding could have lethal consequences and was undoubtedly a contributing factor to the *Royal George* disaster on 29 August 1782. That summer the twenty-six-year-old 100-gun warship was anchored at Spithead and was full of visitors – a mixture of prostitutes, wives, children, workmen and some traders. An officer from a nearby ship noted the situation: 'There was unfortunately more than even her own complement of men as a first-rate on board – a large number of artisans and workmen from the yard to expedite her repairs – some 200 or 300 women and children come to see husbands and fathers – and 100 or 200 ladies from the Point [at Portsmouth], who, though seeking neither husbands nor fathers, yet visit our newly-arrived ships of war – and also a due proportion of the Jewish tribe with their various tempting baubles.'[21] To carry out repairs below the water-line, the ship had been heeled over at an angle by the customary procedure of moving the cannons from one side to the other until their weight tilted the vessel. Because the decks were at a steep angle, the visitors had difficulty keeping their footing, to the amusement of the sailors – until water began to wash in at the lowest gunports on the underside of the ship, which were still open and through which a lighter was transferring barrels of rum. To keep the

---

* To 'come off' means here 'to come from the shore to the ship'.

ship heeled over and the gunports open was an error of judgement by the officers in charge, and an order had just been given to bring the *Royal George* upright when the huge warship passed the point of no return. Saved from capsizing at once by the lighter, which was pushed under the waves by the weight of the mast, the *Royal George* lay on one side, filled up with water and sank.

One survivor, twenty-four-year-old James Ingram, an ordinary seaman, told how he struggled clear of the wreck:

> I caught hold of the best bower-anchor, which was just above me, to prevent falling back again into the port-hole, and seized hold of a woman who was trying to get out at that same port-hole, – I dragged her out. The ship was full of Jews, women, and people selling all sorts of things. I threw the woman from me, and saw all the heads drop back again in at the port-hole, for the ship had got so much on her larboard side, that the starboard port-holes were as upright as if the men had tried to get out of the top of a chimney with nothing for their legs and feet to act upon . . . When I got on the main topsail halyard block I saw the admiral's baker in the shrouds of the mizen-topmast, and directly after that the woman whom I had pulled out of the port-hole came rolling by.[22]

Ingram shouted for assistance:

> I said to the baker, who was an Irishman named Robert Cleary [actually Robert McClary], 'Bob, reach out your hand and catch hold of that woman; – that is the woman I pulled out at the port-hole. I dare say she is not dead.' He said 'I dare say she is dead enough; it is of no use to catch hold of her.' I replied, 'I dare say she is not dead.' He caught hold of the woman and hung her head over one of the ratlins of the mizen shrouds, and there she hung by her chin . . . but a surf came and knocked her backwards, and away she went rolling over and over. The captain of a frigate which was lying at Spithead came up in a boat as fast as he could. I dashed out my left hand in a direction towards the woman as a sign to him. He saw it, and saw the woman. His men left off rowing, and they pulled the woman aboard their boat . . . The captain of the frigate then got all the men that were in the different parts of the rigging, including

myself and the baker, into his boat and took us on board the *Victory*, where the doctors recovered the woman, but she was very ill for three or four days.[23]

The *Royal George* crew numbered 867, though some may have been on shore that day. Because no record was kept of any visitors, the exact number of people on board was not known, but probably around 1200. Two hundred and fifty-five people survived, among whom were only eleven women and one child. A court martial concluded that the hull of the ship was decayed and had given way, despite witnesses testifying that the cause was the deliberate tilting of an overloaded ship. Newspapers all over the country reported the scenes:

> There was on board nearly the full complement of 850 seamen. The marines, of which the whole was on board, and many of the officers, went off for Portsmouth the preceding evening. There was also a body of carpenters from the dock, to assist in careening the ship; and, as usual on board all ships of war in the harbour, a very large number of women, probably near 400. Of these the bulk were the lowest order of prostitutes; but not a few of the wives of the warrant and petty officers. A most poignant scene of anguish and distress was exhibited by a respectable-looking old woman, whose daughter and five children had gone on board the same morning to see their father.[24]

A fund was set up at Lloyd's Coffee House in London to help the widows and children of the sailors who lost their lives, marking the start of the Lloyd's Patriotic Fund that has, over the centuries, provided assistance to the families of sailors and continues to help ex-servicemen and ex-servicewomen and their dependants. However, nothing was done for the prostitutes and other civilians who were victims of the disaster.

The prostitutes at Portsmouth, where they were frequently called 'Portsmouth Polls' or 'Spithead Nymphs', were depicted in a colourful passage by the surgeon George Pinckard:

Imagine a something of more than Amazonian stature, having a crimson countenance, emblazoned with all the effrontery of Cyprian confidence, and broad Bacchanalian folly: give to her bold countenance the warlike features of two wounded cheeks, a tumid nose, scarred and battered brows, and a pair of blackened eyes, with balls of red; then add to her sides a pair of brawny arms, fit to encounter a Colossus, and set her upon two ankles like the fixed supports of a gate. Afterwards, by way of apparel, put upon her a loose flying cap, a man's black hat, a torn neckerchief, stone rings on her fingers, and a dirty white, or tawdry flowered gown, with short apron and a pink petticoat; and thus, will you have something very like the figure of a 'Portsmouth Poll.'[25]

It may not have taken long for a prostitute to come to resemble the hard-bitten caricature figure that Pinckard presented. They were of all ages and most had become prostitutes through necessity, with no other means of supporting themselves apart from turning to crime. There were few ways that a single woman could earn a living, and it was customary for a woman to be supported by her family until she was married. If she became a social outcast, often by giving birth to a child whose father had abandoned her, she was left with barely any choice. The common view at the time, expressed by the seaman George Watson about the prostitutes at Portsmouth, was that they had all been seduced and abandoned:

Notoriously wicked young women flock here from all corners of our island, and some from Ireland, and live by prostitution. I mean women that are previously seduced, and cast upon the world, abandoned by the villains that caused their ruin: it would be absurd to suppose any truly modest girl, though brought to the greatest extremity of penury and want, would deliberately come hither to join herself to such an unblushing set of wretches as pervade the Point at Portsmouth, where a modest woman would be as hard to find as a Mermaid.[26]

The situation in British ports was mirrored in all the major foreign ports frequented by naval vessels of different nations. At Palermo in Sicily, Watson described the way prostitutes gathered as warships arrived:

When we anchored, in less than half an hour, we were entirely surrounded by boats containing those wretches, seeking admittance on
board. Almost every boat had a fiddler, or some other inspirer of mirth in
it, to whose melody the wanton ladies capered away in every posture of
lascivious incitement speaking, as it were, unutterable things and were
they as happy, and in reality as beautiful as they appear, you would think
it the height of bliss to be in their society, and to be a partaker of that
felicity they pretend so abundantly to possess.[27]

These prostitutes, Watson was amazed to find, were devout
Roman Catholics:

> They are all religious harlots these, in their way, they go on shore uniformly
> every morning to confess their sins, and get absolution of the Priest! What
> a delightful task he must have, to hear all their amorous relations, and to be
> able, after such a night's work, to speak peace to the minds of so many guilty
> Magdalenes! It seems strange that women under such circumstances . . . can
> sin cheerfully all the hours of darkness, and without any compunction on
> their part, inherit the joy of the righteous in the morning, and at it again at
> night as fresh as ever, falsely believing that one stroke from the magic wand
> of a confessor, grey in iniquity himself, can entirely remove all their guilt, and
> leave them in quiet possession of all their iniquitous delights.[28]

Watson emphasised that he was speaking the truth, having accosted
one woman and 'asked her one morning, why she did not stay on
board all day. She told me, she must go on shore to confess, and be
made clean by the Father, but she would come off again in the
evening.'[29] He was also struck by the beggars who accompanied the
prostitutes: 'In several boats there were some of the most pitiful
looking beings, halt, maimed, blind, exhibiting their imperfections,
asking for charity, and exclaiming, "much-a miserable, John!" at the
same time holding up arms without hands, legs without feet, or
some other portion of deformity, to excite our commiseration.
These scenes are quite common, and whenever you see a group of
whores come off, you are to expect a party of "miserables" in the
train.'[30]

In some parts of the world the prostitutes were slaves. This in itself did not seem to bother the seamen unduly, but cruelty towards slaves quickly roused them to anger, as John Nicol recalled:

> While we lay at any of the West India islands, our decks used to be crowded by the female slaves, who brought us fruit and remained on board all Sunday until Monday morning – poor things! and all to obtain a bellyful of victuals. On Monday morning, the Jolly Jumper, as we called him, was on board with his whip; and, if all were not gone, did not spare it upon their backs. One cruel rascal was flogging one on our deck, who was not very well in her health; he had struck her once as if she had been a post – the poor creature gave a shriek. Some of our men, I knew not which, there were a good many near him, knocked him overboard; he sunk like a stone – the men gave a hurra! One of the female slaves leaped from the boat alongside into the water, and saved the tyrant, who, I have no doubt, often enough beat her cruelly.[31]

Those seamen given shore leave in the West Indies found the same easy access to female slaves, as Aaron Thomas observed:

> What a dissolute life does man lead in the West Indies. The Blacks never marry. But have intercourse one with another promiscuously. All the white men, planters as well as merchants, have connection with their female negroes. As to the black girls themselves, any white or creole man may have commerce with them, so very little difficulty is there on this head, that it is as easy to lie with them, as it is to convey a glass of wine to your mouth . . . A white sailor may go amongst the huts upon an estate, where there is 70 female negroes and he will not find the smallest opposition to his will, but will be courted to stop amongst them. All the seamen at the Naval Hospital generally have a black girl.[32]

Thomas was outraged by the rules of property that governed slaves, and while at Antigua, he recorded the plight of the ship's surgeon:

> Doctor Ridgeway asked me this morning to lend him 12 Joes, until the ship went down to St. Kitts. His reason for being in want of money was

rather curious. He says that he was here in the *Lapwing* fifteen months ago, and that a woman *now* daily brings him a child and says that he is the *father* of it. That [claim] he himself believes; that he had the greatest hand in making the pudding . . . therefore being convinced of this great and uncertain truth, he wishes to buy the infant's freedom . . . I did not lend him the money, but he got it this evening from Captain Harvey. Wretched slavery. What a disgrace it is to all Christian countries to traffic in human flesh. Here is an instance of its infamy. A surgeon of an English Man of War has a child by a black woman, but has no more property in the infant than he has claim to the Throne of England, because the woman he had the child by is not free, unless he buys the child, of the owner of the girl, and then the buying of his own son or daughter will cost him 20 or 30 pounds.[33]

White prostitutes were at a premium here, and when anchored at Nevis, Thomas noted in his journal that 'several of our officers stopped ashore last night. Canes and Lash met in a baudy house, and had a quarrel about a white girl. Lash got her, by throwing six dollars at her: Canes could only muster 2 dollars.'[34] Among the slaves, many children must have been fathered by visiting seamen, and on Antigua in 1799 Thomas had a long conversation with an old lady, part of which he wrote down:

Was at Mrs Ramseys [who] said Admiral Nelson was an old friend of hers, when he was here 17 years ago in the *Boreas* frigate . . . [she also talked about] James Pitt [who is thought to be] son of James Pitt, brother to the Hon'ble William Pitt: this mulatto boy is said by his mother, a black woman, to be begotten by Captain Pitt in 1783 when here in the *Hornet*. [Also there is] a son of Admiral Parker, begotten by him on a Creole woman, and is called Parker. [There are] plenty of mustee and free Creole peoples about English Harbour, which by length of time, have been begotten by sailors, whose ships have been refitting here.[35]

While working-class people in Britain recognised the necessity for girls and women to earn a living, others frowned upon it, and especially on those engaged in work more commonly done by men. A gentleman traveller visiting Plymouth in 1806 wrote to his sister about crossing to Mount Edgecombe: 'We were ferried over by women, who seem as dextrous in the use of the oar, as if they had been intended by nature for this vocation. I mention this, my dear Louisa, because it disgusted me: I hate to see females following masculine employments; when they do "all the winning softness of the sex is lost."'[36] Class prejudice was rife through all layers of society, and Marine Lieutenant Henry Hole, carrying dispatches to the East on board HMS *Dedaigneuse* in 1802, included in one letter to his father a story about a midshipman who asked a young woman at Gosport to dance with him: 'She replied that his question could not be resolved, till she knew whether he was rated, as her Mama had forbidden her to dance with any that were not. Such a strange charge induced him to enquire of her who her friends were, to which she answered with the utmost unconcern that her Papa was cook of the *Royal William* and her Mama went a bumbing.'[37] Hole added an explanation for his father:

> You will know that the former is one of the lowest situations as an officer in the ship, but the latter may perhaps require a little elucidation, familiar as you are both with Plymouth and Portsmouth. Every man of war has a small boat to attend it every morning with bread, milk, vegetables etc for the use of the sailors, and is called a bumboat, from whence the occupation of those employed in them is taken. The officer of course on hearing this walked off in disgust.[38]

A handful of women were employed as nurses in the hospitals, and at Plymouth George Watson commented that while his fellow sailors had a wife in every port, the nurses had a husband in every ship:

> The nurses of the hospital were chiefly of the frail sisterhood, some of them had several husbands, or men they called by that name, all living at once, on board of different ships, and as there was seldom more than one of them in port at a time, they equally enjoyed the caresses of their pliable spouses, in happy ignorance of their dishonour. Being accustomed to the manners, and association of sailors, those ladies are exceedingly

bold and audacious, and without concern make use of the most indecent observations, and actions in their common conversation.[39]

Most of the men who were married left their wives at home, but by 1795 all of them could choose to have part of their wages deducted at source and paid to their wife, children or mother, collected by these dependants from a pre-arranged location. The seamen were paid irregularly, at least six months in arrears (nominally to deter desertion), and generally only when the ship returned to a port in Britain. In September 1804 John Booth, yeoman of the sheets* on board the frigate *Amazon*, filled out a form so that his beloved wife Sarah would receive half his wages (the maximum allowed for a petty officer), to be sent to the Collector of Customs at Hull where she lived. A year later, the *Amazon* was at Spithead, after taking part in a fruitless chase, led by Nelson, of the French fleet in the West Indies, and on 21 September 1805, Booth wrote Sarah a puzzled letter: 'Dear Wife, I received 4 letters this day, 1 dated May, 1 July, 1 Aug, and Sep . . . You told me my half wages is stopt since July but there is no reason on board the ship for it. It must be some mistake of yours or the Custom House . . . If there is any dispute of paying you now, let them see this letter for there is no stoppage ordered from the ship.'[40] At the end of the letter he added: 'Don't forget the particulars about the half pay. So no more at present from your affectionate husband till death.'[41] Less than three years later he was dead – from the beginning of 1808 he had been second master's mate, and the crew list recorded that he died on 29 June 'by the visitation of God, off Corunna'.[42] He was thirty-one years old. For a long period afterwards Sarah Booth was still trying to obtain his prize-money.

Thomas England allotted half his wages to his mother, and each time she went to the custom house at Deptford to collect her money, she had to produce a certificate which stated that 'Thomas England, now serving as an *Ordinary Seaman* on board His Majesty's ship *Indus* having declared that he has a mother living at Deptford in the

---

* In charge of some of the ropes called sheets used to adjust the sails.

County of Kent . . . WE do hereby direct you to pay or cause to be paid to Ann England living in the place and county aforesaid, at the end of every twenty-eight days from the 1st day of May one thousand eight hundred and 13 the sum of eleven shillings and eight pence, being at the rate of fivepence per day.'[43]

At the end of 1797, when pay rates were revised after the mutinies of that year, a landsman (the lowest-paid man in the crew) earned £1 1s 6d for a month of 28 days, while an able seaman received £1 9s 6d and a sailmaker's mate £1 13s 6d. A midshipman earned between £1 15s 6d and £2 10s 6d, the exact amount depending on the type of ship in which he served – the larger the ship, the higher the pay rate. Lieutenants were paid £7 a month, with expenses for the employment of a servant. By 1807 a lieutenant's pay had risen to £8 8s 0d for a 28-day month, with those in a flagship earning £9 2s 0d. Midshipmen now earned between £2 0s 6d and £2 15s 6d, a sailmaker's mate was paid £1 18s 6d, an able seaman £1 13s 6d and a landsman only £1 2s 6d.

Those women whose husbands and sons had not made arrangements about their pay only received money when they met them. A wife who wanted to see her husband had first to find out when and where his ship was returning to Britain, and she could have a long and expensive journey from one side of the country to the other. When he was at Spithead in 1805, John Booth was very reluctant for his wife to visit him on board, even though he had not seen her for so long:

> We are let out of quarantine yesterday, but when we go into the harbour I cannot tell . . . My Dear as you wish to come to me, if only you knew the disagreeableness of our situation, you [would] wish yourself at home again. I should be as happy of a sight of you as you would of me but our ship is going into dock to be repaired and whether we shall be kept or sent on board another I cannot tell. If we are, we shall be at sea again shortly . . . I shall endeavour to get liberty home if I can and if not perhaps I shall send for you to Portsmouth but not to come on board the ship.[44]

At times the effort to visit their husbands and obtain their pay went unrewarded, something the seamen of the *Adamant* recorded in a petition to the Admiralty in 1798: '[We were] deprived of every indulgence, which every other ships get after coming from sea. Our wives and children turned out three days before the ship was paid, which was very piercing, as they had no money to subsist on.'[45] Finding out where a ship would arrive was as much a problem for wives of officers as for the men – summed up by Captain Rotheram in one of his 'Growls of a Naval Life':

> Your ship arrives in Torbay. Your affectionate wife hurries round from Plymouth twenty-one Devonshire miles and shocking roads, when finding no person is allowed to land, she takes a sailing vessel and in spite of opposing elements comes off to the ship, but just in time to see her under weigh, for in the squall which wets her to the skin the wind shifted and the fleet instantly weighed. Your attention to the ship prevents your even thanking her for her kindness and you only see her wipe the tear of anguish and disappointment from her eyes as the two vessels separate.[46]

Captain Griffiths, in his textbook on seamanship, advised against keeping the men's wives waiting in boats alongside the ship before letting them on board because, unlike the prostitutes, they had to pay the boatmen and such delays increased the cost and caused ill feeling:

> Few things are more teasing to the men than to have their wives, etc. plying off on their oars, as they are sometimes kept, even for a long while, and that too at times when it rained or blew so as to wet them. Independent to the distress thus occasioned to them, I think those ladies should not, even on the score of policy, be unnecessarily annoyed; their influence over the men is well known, and at least it would be judicious not to stimulate them to exert it. Although there are times when duty renders it improper they should be admitted at the moment, yet in general that is not the case, and if it be necessary it is better to tell them to come at a given hour than to keep them hanging on. Waterage is an heavy expense to them, and it must be augmented by these delays of getting on board.[47]

After the Battle of Trafalgar, Lieutenant John Yule in the badly damaged *Victory* was desperate to see his wife and children. He wrote her a letter expressing his wishes, very mindful of the long and difficult journey from Seaton in south Devon to Portsmouth:

> I embrace the possibility of sending this by the *Belleisle* before she parts from us as she is bound to Plymouth and we are going to Portsmouth. I think it is probable you may receive this before we arrive . . . how can I be in England and not be with my Eliza? And yet I know it is cruel to ask her to travel at this inclement season . . . you are sensible how much I should wish to see my dearest children; you also know the inconvenience of bringing them so long a journey considering the inclemency of the season and the distance, but if you think John able to bear the fatigue he might be shoved in among you. I am afraid poor Tom is too young . . . Such are the precarious situations we are placed in in a sea life that altho' I expected to have been with you a week since, the weather has been so bad we have not been able to get into any port . . . they are endeavouring to tow us into some harbour. The elements are against us, for tho' I am at this instant directly opposite the hallowed spot on which my dearest family reside, and not more than 30 miles from her, the wind blows so directly from the south that it is impossible to get near England or its shores in any place, and we may yet be a week at sea.[48]

The *Victory* did not anchor near Portsmouth until almost three weeks later, when Yule discovered that Eliza was not at their home but staying with her sister at Hatherleigh in mid-Devon. 'I am glad you did not come,' he wrote, 'as we sail from this place tomorrow to go to the Downs and from thence to the Nore where the body of the departed Hero [Nelson] will be put into one of the King's yachts and be lodged in Greenwich hospital . . . I think it would be better you remain there [in Devon] until you hear again from me as I know not to what port we may be bound or when we shall be there.'[49] Before posting this letter, he received a note from her and rapidly added a postscript to try to stop her leaving for Portsmouth: 'this note may reach you I hope before you take your place [in the coach]. If not you had better proceed to London or else remain. We shall have sailed before you can possibly have reached Portsmouth.'[50]

Whether a seaman's wife was sent an allowance, or relied on meeting him on pay day, she usually led a harsh and impoverished existence. The only method of social support was the workhouse, organised locally and grudgingly paid for through local taxes. Consequently, it was cheaper to take a destitute sailor's wife back to her parish of origin than support her in a port until her husband returned. This was especially true of places like Portsmouth and Plymouth that were continually overcrowded with seamen's wives from all parts of the country, since the burden of supporting them would have crippled the local economy. A workhouse was, in any case, an absolute last resort: deliberately made uninviting, they were also frequently badly run and had a high mortality rate, because the sick and the destitute were housed together with hardly any medical help.

Particularly in the ports, where countless women congregated, there was little work available for them and begging was seldom an option as so many beggars filled the streets already. Sailors' wives were frequently faced with the choice of accompanying their husbands on board ship, if this could be arranged, or else turning to prostitution or starving. Wives and girlfriends certainly did accompany their men, though this was usually regarded as a special favour or mark of privilege for the seaman concerned. Some wives were smuggled on board as stowaways, without the knowledge or permission of the officers. Many others were the wives of warrant officers, such as the gunner, carpenter and purser, who had a higher status than the ratings. When William Richardson was about to sail to Martinique in early 1800 he found his wife was determined to join him. Since the West Indies were notorious for fevers that could decimate ships' crews, he thought she was mad:

I went to bid my wife and family adieu [at Portsea] but found she had fixed her mind to go with me as there was some hopes that the ship would return to England after delivering her stores, so after some entreaties I consented, especially because the Captain's the Master's and

Purser's wives were going, the Armourer, the Boatswain, the Serjeant of
Marines and six other men's wives likewise got leave to go; one would
have thought they were all insane in wanting twelve of them to go to such
a sickly country. As there was no time to be lost we took a hasty leave of
our friends, my wife was so affected that she nearly fainted and I was so
moved I hardly knew what to do; however it was soon over and we got on
board with our linen all wet from the washerwoman from her not having
time to dry it . . . we got under way next morning . . . little thinking how
few of us would return again.[51]

Although Richardson and his wife survived, many others died of
fevers in the West Indies. Wherever a ship was headed, sailors could
be torn by the desire to take their loved ones with them and fears for
their safety. George Watson became attached to a woman at Minorca
and considered taking her to sea with him on board the *Fame*, but
then thought better of it:

What could I have done with her, or she with me? It might have been
[that] she would have had to wipe my languid face, or tie up my bleeding
head with her napkin, or, peradventure, I might have had to do the same
office for her, and afterwards to have consigned her to the briny wave, for
who is safe in battle – the cannon ball pays no more respect to the petticoat, or powerful charms of a lovely damsel, than to the rugged cheek and
coarse tarpawling jacket, of a sturdy tar, so it is better as it is. I often cast
my tearful eye to the place where she dwelt, and with lingering looks,
watched to get another and another more distant view, till at last, I was
reluctantly forced to forego the pleasing, but melancholy scene, and sadly
sigh, farewell![52]

Watson would have obtained permission because his captain,
Richard Bennett, allowed some of the crew to have their wives and
partners on board at sea, and he also had his own female companion:

He loved the society of women, as most men do, and nearly all the time
he was with us, had one in the ship with him, and at the period which I am
speaking of, there was a Miss Jen—gs on board as his mistress, and had left

England with him. She was a lovely looking woman, and modest in a great degree, compared with the majority of her sex who plough the seas on the same footing, and while she was much respected by the captain, she was also held in estimation both by the officers and men.[53]

Some months later the *Fame* sailed to Minorca again, and Watson recorded that Miss Jennings was replaced: 'Our Captain previous to our coming to Minorca this time sent his English Lady home . . . and at this port got another, a beautiful dark Spanish girl. She was about eighteen or nineteen years of age, of a genteel and handsome figure, and had large black and brilliant eyes. She dressed gaily and lightly, and appeared always at ease and full of pleasure.'[54]

Despite their unofficial status, women on board warships were expected to conform to navy regulations, and sometimes specific commands were given concerning their conduct, such as one that appeared in Captain John Fyffe's orders for HMS *Indefatigable* in 1812: 'The women belonging to the ship are to be permitted to go on shore twice a week on market days. Should they go on any other day, or in any respect act contrary to the regulations of the ship, they are not to be suffered to come on board again.'[55] It is doubtful if attempts at controlling the women were ever very successful, though Rear-Admiral Sir John Jervis tried more than once to curb their fresh water consumption, and in June 1797 he issued another threat:

Observing, as I do with the deepest concern, the great deficiency of water in several ships of the squadron, which cannot have happened without waste by collusion, and the service of our King and Country requiring that the blockade of Cadiz, on which depends a speedy and honourable peace, should be continued, an event impracticable without the strictest economy in the expenditure of water, it will become my indispensable duty to land all the women in the squadron at Gibraltar, unless this alarming evil is immediately corrected.[56]

Nelson, who was then serving in the fleet under Jervis, responded: 'My dear Sir, The history of women was brought forward I remember in the Channel Fleet last war. I know not if your ship was an exception, but I will venture to say, not an Honourable [captain] but had plenty of them, and they always will do as they please. Orders are not for them – at least, I never yet knew one who obeyed.'[57]

Because of their unofficial status, specific women who accompanied their husbands to sea in navy ships are rarely mentioned, and we only know the names of a handful. At the Battle of the Nile in 1798 Ann Hopping (known as Nancy Perriam after she remarried) was on board the *Orion*, while Ann Taylor, Elizabeth Moore, Sarah Bates and Mary French were in the *Goliath*. Four were wives of seamen, and Mary French was the wife a marine. Edward Hopping survived, but the husbands of the other four women were killed, and the captain of the *Goliath*, Thomas Foley, entered the women in the muster book as 'being the widows of men slain in fight on the 1st Aug[t] 1798 victualled at ²/₃ds allowance by Captains order, in consideration of their assistance in dressing and attending on the wounded'.[58] These women were provided with victuals from the ship's stores until 30 November, when, it was noted, 'their further assistance not being required'.[59] Also at the Nile was another woman, Christiann White, who later wrote to Nelson for help: 'Your petitioner Christiann White has taken the liberty to lay her case before your Lordship, that I lost my husband in your glorious action of the 1st of August 1798 at the Nile, and . . . where we lost the Honourable Captain Westcott, and as for myself was left a widow and with 2 children to the mercy of God. Your petitioner humbly hopes that your Lordship will consider her worthy of your notice.'[60]

At the same battle the seaman John Nicol was stationed in the gunpowder magazine of the *Goliath* and afterwards acknowledged that he 'was much indebted to the gunner's wife, who gave her husband and me a drink of wine every now and then, which lessened our fatigue much. There were some of the women wounded, and one woman belonging to Leith [in Scotland] died of her wounds, and was buried on a small island in the bay. One woman bore a son in the heat of the action; she belonged to Edinburgh.'[61] It was not unusual for women to give birth during a battle, as the noise and stress of the situation tended to induce labour. Nor was it unusual for the women to have their children with them. Mary Campbell, whose parents were

Thomas Watson and Mary Buek, was born at sea on board the *Ardent* during the Battle of Copenhagen in 1801 and spent her early years with her mother aboard navy ships.

Young children are much less frequently recorded than women. In newspaper coverage of shipwrecks, there are occasional glimpses of children being saved or having tragically drowned, with scattered mentions elsewhere, as on Thursday 12 July 1798 when Aaron Thomas jotted in his journal: 'A girl called Peg Robinson who lives with [William] Woodcock a gunners mate, had a premature birth this day',[62] while two months later in the Mediterranean Robert Bailey noted in his journal that 'Sept 4th The wife of Wm White a midshipman was delivered of a girl at 4 o'clock in the morning.'[63] In the frigate *Macedonian* in 1812 Samuel Leech talked about two more births:

> Sailing from Madeira, we next made St. Michael's. At this place we had an increase to our crew, in the person of a fine, plump boy – born to the wife of one of our men. The captain christened the new comer, Michael, naming him after the island. This birth was followed by another. Whether the captain did not like the idea of such interesting episodes in sea life, or whether any other motive inspired him, I cannot tell; but when, shortly after, we returned to Lisbon, he ordered all the women home to England, by a ship just returning thither. Before this, however, one of our little Tritons had died, and found a grave under the billows, leaving its disconsolate mother in a state little short of distraction. A man of war is no place for a woman.[64]

Children occasionally appear in other incidents that were considered noteworthy, such as the action on 16 June 1812 between the sloop *Swallow* and two more heavily armed French ships off Fréjus. In this case, the story about twenty-six-year-old Joseph Phelan from Waterford, his wife and their baby Tommy was related by an unnamed officer and published in the *Annual Register*:

> In the gallant and sanguinary action . . . there was a seaman named Phelan, who had his wife on board; she was stationed (as is usual when

women are on board in time of battle) to assist the surgeon in the care of the wounded. From the close manner in which the *Swallow* engaged the enemy, yard-arm and yard-arm, the wounded, as may be expected, were brought below very fast; amongst the rest a messmate of her husband's . . . who had received a musket ball through the side. Her exertions were used to console the poor fellow, who was in great agonies and nearly breathing his last: when, by some chance, she heard her husband was wounded, on the deck . . . she rushed instantly on deck, and received the wounded tar in her arms; he faintly raised his head to kiss her – she burst into a flood of tears, and told him to take courage, 'all would yet be well,' but had scarcely pronounced the last syllable, when an ill-directed shot took her head off. The poor tar, who was closely wrapt in her arms, opened his eyes once more – then shut them for ever.[65]

The seamen were particularly affected because a child was involved:

The poor creature had been only three weeks delivered of a fine boy, who was thus in a moment deprived of a father and a mother. As soon as the action subsided . . . the tars were all interested for poor Tommy (for so he was called); many said, and all feared, he must die; they all agreed he should have an hundred fathers, but what could be the substitute of a nurse and a mother! However, the mind of humanity soon discovered there was a Maltese goat on board, belonging to the officers, which gave an abundance of milk; and as there was no better expedient, she was resorted to, for the purpose of suckling the child, who, singular to say, is thriving and getting one of the finest little fellows in the world . . . Phelan and his wife were sewed up in one hammock, and it is needless to say, buried in one grave.[66]

The ship's log merely stated: 'found the killed to be as follows – Mr William Jackson (clerk), Joseph Phelan (S), John Beckford (S), Nicholas Defons (S), Richard Millington (S) and Thomas Millard (marine) and seventeen wounded',[67] with no mention of Phelan's wife because technically she did not exist.

Several women claimed to have been at the Battle of Trafalgar, including Mary Sperring and Sarah Pitt on board the *Victory* and Jane Townsend in the *Defiance*. When, in 1847, it was decided that Queen Victoria would award a Naval General Service Medal to those survivors of the major battles fought between 1793 and 1840 who were still living, Jane Townsend applied. Sir Thomas Byam Martin was one of the men deciding about eligibility for the medal, and he wrote:

> The Queen, in the *Gazette* of the 1st of June, directs that all who were *present* in this action shall have a medal, without any reservation as to sex, and as this woman [Jane Townsend] produces from the Captain of the *Defiance* strong and highly satisfactory certificates of her useful services during the action, she is fully entitled to a medal. Upon further consideration this cannot be allowed. There were many women in the fleet equally useful, and it will leave the Army exposed to *innumerable* applications of the same nature.[68]

There was certainly a fear that hundreds of women might apply, because large numbers of wives and other camp followers had accompanied the army regiments abroad. This fear led to discrimination against the wives of seamen and soldiers, while the medal was awarded to a few male civilian passengers caught up in various battles. Ann Hopping and Mary Ann Riley also applied for the medal, and were similarly refused.

While the awarding or refusal of medals was dictated by a concern for maintaining appearances, the authorities could occasionally be persuaded to acknowledge the contribution of the women aboard navy ships in a less public manner. In 1780 Eleanor Moor was awarded an annual pension of £4 for a fractured skull sustained on board the *Apollo* earlier that year, after the administrators wrote to the Admiralty for permission:

> We beg leave to acquaint you that at our last sitting we were applied to by Eleanor Moor, having a certificate that she was wounded on board His Majesty's Ship *Apollo*, when in action with a French frigate on the 15th June 1780, by receiving a gun shot wound on the head, being then

actually on service carrying powder to the gun at which her husband was quartered. And though we have no precedent of any persons being relieved who have not been born on the ships books, yet we hope their lordships will approve of our giving this woman the allowance that would have been given to a man under the same circumstance.[69]

Many women during battle, like Eleanor Moor, acted as powder monkeys, carrying gunpowder cartridges from the magazine to the guns on the decks above. Other women helped the surgeon, but there is some evidence that they also played a more active role in battles. At the Battle of the Saintes in April 1782, the quarter gunner John Peace noted that 'the damage on board the *Prince George* was severe, we had nine men killed and 24 wounded, amongst the wounded was a woman which stood at her gun till she had a musquet shot through her arm some[what] dangerously'.[70] Most women who sailed in navy ships received no official recognition, although in later life a few made capital from their experiences. One woman, arrested as a vagrant in 1807, claimed she had served in the navy for many years, disguised as a man:

> At the Public Office, Queen Square, an old woman, generally known by the name of Tom Bowling, was lately brought before the Magistrate, for sleeping all night in the street; and was committed as a rogue and vagabond, and passed to her parish. She served as Boatswain's Mate on board a man of war for upwards of 20 years, and has a pension from Chatham Chest. When waked at midnight by the watchman in the street, covered with snow, she cried '*Where the devil would you have me sleep?*' She has generally slept in this way, and dresses like a man; and is so hardy at a very advanced age, that she never catches cold.[71]

Bowling was a name derived from the rope known as the bowline, and 'Tom Bowling' was a common name for fictional sailors in songs and plays, so if her story about a pension from Admiralty funds (the Chatham Chest) was true, it was probably not the name she actually used when claiming her pension.

While some might doubt Tom Bowling's story, there were other well-documented instances of women disguised as men, such as Mary Anne Talbot. The story of her life was written by a London publisher, Robert Kirby, for whom she worked as a servant. Published in 1804, the book sold so well that Kirby brought out an enlarged edition in 1809, a year after her early death at the age of thirty. Although the first book brought Mary Anne temporary fame, she may not have seen much of the profit, because she subsequently fell into debt and spent some time in Newgate prison. Perhaps inevitably with such a sensational celebrity biography, subsequent research[72] into her life has suggested that much of the book was embellishment, if not total fabrication.

This, and other books telling similar stories, were part of a long tradition that went back at least to 1750 when an account was published of the experiences of Hannah Snell, who served as a soldier and marine disguised as a man and later built a stage act on this impersonation. More widespread than the books were popular songs that often had the theme of a woman disguised as a man. Examples of these ballads have survived as traditional folk songs, such as 'Susan's Adventures in a Man-of-War', 'William Taylor' and 'The Female Tar'. This romanticisation may have inspired some young girls to follow suit, as in one incident at London:

> This day [probably 6 May 1809] two females, who, disguised in seamen's clothes, had entered a few days since on board the tender, in the River, underwent an examination at the Thames Police Office. A respectable tradesman from Holborn claimed the younger, who is only 18 years of age, as his daughter; and stated that the other had been his servant; but that they had without any known cause, eloped together a fortnight ago. The Magistrate dismissed them with a severe reprimand.[73]

Other stories appeared of women who maintained the deception for longer:

> Amongst the crew of the *Queen Charlotte*, 110 guns, recently paid off, it is now discovered, was a female African, who has served as a seaman in the Royal Navy for upwards of 11 years, several of which she has been

rated able on the books of the above ship by the name of William Brown, and has served for some time as the captain of the fore-top, highly to the satisfaction of the officers. She is a smart well formed figure, about five feet four inches in height, possessed of considerable strength and great activity; her features are rather handsome for a *black*, and she appears to be about 26 years of age. Her share of prize money is said to be considerable, respecting which she has been several times within the last few days at Somerset-place. In her manner she exhibits all the traits of a British tar and takes her grog with her late messmates with the greatest gaiety. She says she is a married woman, and went to sea in consequence of a quarrel with her husband, who, it is said, has entered a caveat against her receiving her prize money. She declares her intention of again entering the service as a volunteer.[74]

Despite being a contemporary account in *The Times*, the woman's story was probably taken at face value and the facts were not checked. Recent research has shown that the service careers of three William Browns, seamen aboard the *Queen Charlotte*, were conflated.[75] The female William Brown only served for a few weeks before being discovered and discharged, and the ship was in port the entire time.

A song that has proved particularly durable is 'The Female Cabin Boy', and there are various documented instances of young women passing themselves off as boys on both merchant and naval ships. One girl was persuaded by the steward of Captain Philip Beaver to dress as a cabin boy so that she could come on board the *Nisus* frigate, but Beaver found out her true identity:

Before sailing [from Plymouth in 1810], I wanted a lad as an under servant, and my steward, George, recommended me one. Last night this youth was discovered to be a buxom girl, dressed in boy's clothes, a wench of the rascally steward's, who . . . has a respectable wife. I have ordered her to dress 'en femme' again, and never to appear in my presence. I shall send her home by the first opportunity; but I am thus deprived of one servant, and have lost all confidence in the other by this abominable deception.[76]

In another case it proved fatal for a first lieutenant when a girl disguised as a boy was a key witness at his court martial. Elizabeth Bowden, born at Truro in Cornwall, was fourteen years old and had been on board for six weeks before it was discovered that she was a girl: 'Her father and mother being dead, she had walked from Truro to Plymouth to her sister; but not being able to gain any knowledge of her abode, was obliged, through want, to disguise herself, and volunteer into his majesty's service. Since she made known her sex, the captain and officers have paid every attention to her; they gave her an apartment to sleep in and she still remains on board the *Hazard* as an attendant on the officers of the ship.'[77]

The *Morning Chronicle* of 6 October 1807 reported the trial at which she was a witness:

On the 2nd instant a Court Martial was held on board the *Salvador del Mundo*, in Hamoaze, Plymouth, on charges exhibited by Captain [Charles] Dilkes, of his Majesty's ship *Hazard*, against William Berry, First Lieutenant of the said ship, for a breach of the 2d and 29th articles; the former respecting uncleanness, and the latter the horrid and abominable crime which delicacy forbids us to name. THOMAS GIBBS, a boy belonging to the ship, proved the offence, as charged to have been committed on the 23d August, 1807. Several other witnesses were called in corroboration, among whom was ELIZABETH BOWDEN, a little female, who has been on board the *Hazard* these eight months; curiosity had prompted her to look through the key hole of the cabin door, and it was thus she became possessed of the evidence which she gave. She appeared in Court dressed in a long jacket and blue trowsers . . . . . . The unfortunate prisoner [William Berry] is above six feet high, remarkably well made, and as fine and handsome a man as is in the British navy. He was to have been married on his return to port.[78]

At that time the term homosexuality was not used, and despite the reputation of sailors for cursing and blaspheming, 'buggery' and 'sodomy' were taboo words. In 1786, the captain of the *Pegasus* – Prince William, the future king – included in his orders that 'As it is but the too frequent practice on board His Majesty's ships to make use of that horrid expression Bugger, so disgraceful to a British seaman; if any person shall be heard using this expression they may be assured they will be severely punished.'[79] Homosexuality between consenting adults, homosexual rape, paedophilia and bestiality were all covered by a euphemistic form of words such as 'unclean and unnatural acts' and were regarded with horror and severely punished. In this case Thomas Gibbs, being under fourteen years of age, was considered blameless – if older, he would also have been convicted of the crime, despite the evidence that he had been forced against his will. He was probably fortunate in escaping punishment, since the crew list of the *Hazard* showed him to be at least sixteen years old. The background of Elizabeth Bowden remains uncertain, and the court martial simply stated her to be 'Elizabeth alias John Bowden (a Girl) borne on the *Hazard* books as a Boy 3rd Class'.[80] She was subject to a cross-examination:

> Prosecutor: Did you ever, during the time you have been on board the *Hazard*, look through the keyhole of Mr. Berry's cabin door and see the boy Thomas Gibbs in any way in an indecent manner employed with his hands with the prisoner.
> Answer. Yes, once, a little before we came in. I looked through the keyhole and I saw Thomas Gibbs playing with the prisoner's privates . . .
> Court. Are you sure that it was the prisoner's private parts that you saw Thomas Gibbs have hold of.
> A. Yes.
> Court. What light was there in the Cabin at the time.
> A. One candle.[81]

Although Elizabeth Bowden was the only eyewitness of sexual relations between Berry and Gibbs, the boy had complained of abuse for some time, and there was plenty of circumstantial evidence to back up his story. Berry was found guilty and sentenced to death – he was hanged a few days later, and *The Times* noted that 'He was a native of Lancaster, and only 22 years of age. For the last week he seemed very penitent, and perfectly resigned.'[82]

Many men were court-martialled for similar crimes, with terrible penalties for those found guilty. It was very difficult for the seamen to engage in illicit homosexual acts, as there was so little privacy, but being an officer, Lieutenant Berry had his own cabin and would not have expected to be discovered. Some men were caught in acts of bestiality, as happened to William Bouch, an ordinary seaman of HMS *Hotspur*, who was court-martialled for the offence. On the night of 28 June 1812, in the Bay of Biscay, Lieutenant Charles Kirkwood related,

> I was in the first watch between the hours of eleven and twelve o'clock. I was going forward in the galley with a lanthorn and lighted candle in it, when I got forward near the manger. I perceived the prisoner Wm Bouch laying over a sow pig on his belly on top of her, and she was laying on her side. I immediately on perceiving him to be certain of it, took the candle out of the lanthorn, and held it close to the prisoner, I was so shocked at the moment conceiving the action he was about, that it took me about two seconds to articulate when I recovered. The first thing I said was 'you beast'.[83]

Kirkwood told the court that he had then called for witnesses and also for the surgeon to examine the man. The cross-examination continued:

Q. Did the surgeon examine the pig as well as the man?
A. No.
Q. Are you certain that the man had entered the pig's body?
A. I cannot say.
Q. When he drew from the pig and you saw the state of his penis, did you observe whether it came from the pig's body or not?
A. I could not see if he was entered into the pig as he was laying upon her belly, but I conceive from the way he drew back, the pig's grunting at the time, and his remaining perfectly quiet, that he was in the pig.
Q. What was done with the pig?
A. Hove overboard next day.
Q. Do you know if the prisoner is a foreigner or a British subject?
A. By his description in the ships books, he is from Whitehaven in the west of England.[84]

Bouch was found guilty and sentenced to 300 lashes, to forfeit all his pay and to be imprisoned in solitary confinement for a year in Marshalsea Prison in Southwark.

The women who lived with their husbands certainly had next to no privacy, though the exact conditions they lived in reflected their husbands' status. Commissioned officers and some warrant officers had cabins at the stern of the ship, and others at the bow end. The captain's cabins were spacious, but most other cabins were small and formed by flimsy partitions that could be removed to provide more space when the ship went into battle. Such accommodation was not luxurious, as the chaplain Edward Mangin found when he joined the *Gloucester* in 1812:

> My accommodation, for the double purpose of repose and study, was all that could be expected; a short description of my transom cabin will show whether or not it was calculated to answer the end proposed. This apartment was formed into what appeared to be a room of about 8 feet broad and long; and nearly 6 feet in height: one end and one side being composed of the ship's timbers; the other end, and the external side, of canvas strained in wooden framework; with a door of the same materials, and a small window in each, opening on hinges, and intended to admit as much light as could enter from the stern-port-hole; and the after-port on the ship's starboard side: which latter was occupied by a 32-pounder, and open only in fair weather. The stern-port was still more frequently closed to prevent the sea, when heavy, from rushing in.[85]

This was about the best Mangin found to say about his temporary home, and his description continued:

> I have said that this tenement appeared to be eight feet long, and as many wide: inside, however, it was not quite 5 feet broad at one end; and less than 2 at the other: the ship's timbers projecting in the form of a shelf, on which my cot rested, when taken off the hooks in the day-time: and then the interior of this retirement was, in shape precisely, and in size, nearly the same as a grand-piano-forte: for it should be observed, that, when the cot was slung, as it is termed, the entire space was occupied.[86]

Like Mangin, officers usually slept in wooden cots, with a mattress, which were suspended from the deck beams, while the men slept in hammocks. Lack of space, though, was not the only factor that made Mangin's cabin uncomfortable:

> At midnight, and at 4 o'clock in the morning, the watch is called, and in a voice designedly of most alarming loudness. This order to turn out, as may be conjectured, is not obeyed without considerable noise. Another inconvenience, which affected me somewhat, arose from the hot and foul air of the region allotted to me; for on the same deck with me, when the crew was complete, slept between five and six hundred men; and the ports being necessarily closed from evening to morning, the heat, in this cavern of only 6 feet high, and so entirely filled with human bodies, was overpowering.[87]

The wives of warrant officers at least had a few comforts in such cabins, but not the wives of the lower-ranking sailors, who shared their husband's hammock. For these women, there was little space and less privacy, as seen in the court martial at Hamoaze in December 1794 of able seaman William Read of HMS *Marlborough*. Thomas Roach, of the gunner's crew, related what he observed: 'I was in the best bower tier and I turned out when I heard the noise, which happened with his, the Pris[r], Girl, she being down in Mr. Cenyllins cabin and the Prisoner could not get her to come to bed, and he fetched her out by force and got her down to his berth in the sheet tier. He then wanted her to go to bed and she would not go, without his beating of her. She began to make a noise, and Mr Pardoe said he would not have such noise there.'[88]

Midshipman William Pardoe confirmed what happened: 'On the 24th Dece[r] about eleven o'clock at night the Prisoner was going to bed and making a noise in the tier when I order'd him to go to bed quietly.'[89] He was asked what was meant by the prisoner making a noise, to which he replied: 'He was beating his wife and ordering her to go to bed.'[90] Midshipman John Wilson was also called as a witness: 'On Wednesday night the 24th Dec. the prisoner and his wife were going to their hammock and were quarrelling. Mr Pardoe desired them to be silent. They continued still making a noise, he threatened to turn them out of the tier, and sent for the Master at Arms, and the first time he quieted them; after which they began to make a noise again.'[91] William Read was not being tried for beating his wife, but for mutinous expressions and contempt for his superior officer, of which he was acquitted.

This incident highlights the crowded sleeping arrangements for the ordinary seamen and marines, where any disturbance affected a great number of people. The scheme for placing hammocks varied a little between ships, but with limited room there was not much scope for variation. Hammocks were the only viable method of providing somewhere to sleep for so many men in a confined space, with the added benefit that they could be rolled up and stored during the day. The upper deck, exposed to the weather, could obviously not be used, and so in a three-decker warship like the *Victory*, the middle and lower gun decks were for sleeping. The orlop deck below, regarded as a more desirable berth, was usually given to midshipmen and some petty officers, who also slept in hammocks. The men could not sleep where they wanted. They were allocated a precise spot, whose size and position reflected their rating and their watch. Where they slung their hammock was not necessarily where they ate and relaxed with their messmates and where they kept their personal possessions in a ditty bag or sea chest. As Samuel Leech remarked, 'every hammock has its appropriate place . . . the beams are all marked; each hammock is marked with a corresponding number, and in the darkest night, a sailor will go unhesitatingly to his own hammock'.[92]

Hammocks (also known then as hammacoes) were made of canvas into which was placed a thin mattress – the bed – and a blanket. The length of hammocks was reduced over time, reflecting the seamen's habit of shortening them to make sleeping more comfortable. From 7 feet long in the late eighteenth century, their length was gradually reduced by the end of the war to 5 feet 6 inches, about the average height of the men. The width for a hammock space was 14 inches, but midshipmen might have 20 inches and a petty officer, such as the master-at-arms, 28 inches. Petty officers were also placed near the sides of the ship, which gave them slightly more room. Surviving plans of hammock arrangements show that they were squashed together in rows, but as most warships worked on a two-watch system, half the seamen would be on watch at any one time. The hammock spaces of men from each watch were alternated in each row, so that when the ship was at sea each man had an empty hammock space on either side, giving him the equivalent of 28 inches, rather than his allotted 14 inches. In port there was seldom any need to continue working in shifts or watches, which meant that sleeping arrangements were very cramped, especially with prostitutes added to the throng. The marines were frequently allotted an area between the seamen and the officers.

The hammocks themselves were not the most comfortable of beds, but the weariness of the men made any sleeping place attractive, as Basil Hall remarked of his experience as a midshipman:

> Most people, I presume, know what sort of a thing a hammock is. It consists of a piece of canvas, five feet long by two wide, suspended to the deck overhead by means of two sets of small lines, called clews, made fast to grummets, or rings of rope, which again are attached by a lanyard to the battens stretching along the beams. In this sacking are placed a small mattress, a pillow and a couple of blankets, to which a pair of sheets may or may not be added . . . the whole of the apparatus just described occupies less than a foot and a half in width, and . . . the hammocks touch one another. Nevertheless, I can honestly say, that the soundest sleep by far, that I have ever known, has been found in these apparently uncomfortable places of repose; and though the recollection of many a slumber broken up, and the bitter pang experienced on making the first move to exchange so cozy a nest, for the snarling of a piercing north-west gale on the coast of America, will never leave my memory, yet I look back to those days and nights with a sort of evergreen freshness of interest.[93]

The hammock that Hall described was slung in the cockpit of HMS *Leander*, his first ship on entering the navy in 1802. In a letter to his father he explained that it took him some time to get used to his new sleeping arrangements:

I went to my hammock, which was not my own, as mine was not ready, there not being enough of clues [clews] at it, but I will have it tonight. I got in at last. It was very queer to find myself swinging about in this uncouth manner, for there was only about a foot of space between my face and the roof; so, of course, I broke my head a great many times on the different posts in the cockpit, where all the midshipmen sleep. After having got in, you may be sure I did not sleep very well, when all the people were making such a noise going to bed in the dark, and the ship in such confusion. I fell asleep at last, but was always disturbed by the quarter-master coming down to awake the midshipmen who were to be on guard during the night. He comes up to their bed-sides and calls them; so I, not being accustomed to it, was always awaked too. I had some sleep, however, but early in the morning, was again roused up by the men beginning to work.[94]

Accidents and injuries could occur with hammocks, particularly when they were close to open hatchways between decks. The surgeon of the *Canopus* recorded that 'Richard Cronan, boy ... received a wound of the scalp upwards of nine inches in length in consequence of a fall from his hammock on the main deck down the main hatchway to the orlop.'[95] Sleep could also be disturbed by the wind, rain and even waves breaking over the ship and coming down through the open hatchways. In 1799 in his standing orders for HMS *Amazon*, Edward Riou specified when canvas screens could be used:

Screens are never to be admitted except where women sleep, and then only during the night, and to be taken down (not rolled up) during the day. Any man or men who sleep near hatchways or scuttles who feel any draught of wind or who are subject to be wet in their hammacoes from seas or rain, are to acquaint the first lieutenant, [so] that painted canvas screens may be neatly nailed up to make their berths as comfortable as possible. If they are not neatly furled during the day and fine weather, but hanging down, and preventing the free circulation of air, they will be taken away.[96]

The main idea behind the circulation of air below decks was prevention of disease, which was thought to be a result of bad air or 'miasmas', but with no effective heating in much of the ship there was a delicate balance between too little ventilation and letting in too much wind and weather. Usually the areas where the hammocks were slung rapidly became hot and airless, as Edward Mangin had found. In the day, the hammocks were taken down and the lower decks were aired as much as possible with a canvas construction called a windsail, which Basil Hall recorded in another letter home:

> All the men's hammocks are brought upon deck, and laid in places at the side for the purpose, both to give room for the men to work under the decks, and to give them air. All the decks are washed and well scrubbed every morning, which is very right, as they are often dirtied. There is a sort of cylinder of sail-cloth, about two feet in diameter, which is hung above the deck, and is continued down through the decks to the cockpit. The wind gets in at the top, and so runs down and airs the cock-pit, which is a very pleasant thing, down here, at the bottom of the ship.[97]

The thickness of the atmosphere below decks was not helped by the livestock, which were stowed in any odd place where they would not obstruct the day-to-day running of the ship. Some places, though, proved unsuitable and Admiral Lord St Vincent issued an order about the stowage of pigs to his Mediterranean fleet in 1798: 'It having been ascertained by recent experience that the hogsties under the forecastle are a nuisance and extremely injurious to the sick berths, they are immediately to be removed and the place where they stand to be purified.'[98] This followed on from a previous order to move the sick-bay to beneath the forecastle to improve the air for the sick.

In some ships the men were allowed to sleep on the deck itself, if they wished, rather than in hammocks, but generally only in special circumstances, such as sailing in tropical waters. They might then be allowed to set up hammocks on parts of the open deck, or sleep on the deck itself, when it became too stifling below. Even in relatively benign Mediterranean waters life could be very unpleasant, as Midshipman George Allen described in a letter home from Malta in 1808:

Our crew at this place are very sickly owing I believe to the scarcity of wind and the unwholesomeness of the water, which together with the intolerable heat is sufficient to put any person out of order – I have as yet escaped nor indeed do I think it will reach me at all. I constantly bath every morning before sunrise and again in the evening after sunset, eating scarcely any fruit and keeping as much out of the sun as possible, so that (as you may perceive), I am grown quite a Surgeon.[99]

In general, though, Allen liked warm climates and the opportunity to see new places, as he had written in a letter to his family from Gibraltar two years earlier: 'I can suppose you sitting round a fire as big as our *Galley*, shivering and shaking like so many frozen *Bears*, whilst I am perspiring up to the eyes, eating delicious grapes a half-penny a tub full, "Do not *you* envy me" You may judge that I am not very melancholy at the thought of leaving England, I assure you [I] am quite the contrary, as I shall now have the opportunity of seeing the World.'[100]

For the families, and especially the wives, who were left behind, their feelings were not of envy as George Allen had joked, but of worry. William Wilkinson's wife Sarah was in a state of constant anxiety, and she poured out her emotions in a letter to him in mid-December 1809:

It is now a fortnight since I heard from you and then your letter was dated a week back. I cannot tell what to attribute it to, as I see by the papers there have been several actions from off Rockfort [Rochefort], and that you have sent in a small French prize. I am not willing to think my dear husband would let an opportunity slip that could afford me the pleasure of hearing from him and knowing he was well. I have a thousand fears for your safety, first your being surrounded by the French land and this dreadful stormy weather you have had makes me fearful it may have blown you on rocks off the French shores, then again I think you may be pursuing some of the enemy ships. Hearing there is so many of the French ships nearby, and some ready for sea, I think perhaps they may all come out some of these dark nights, and that you might be forced to engage them. God forbid that any of these should be the case, or that any harm should happen to you; my dear husband is and ever will be my prayer. I am afraid you will have had a bad night again tonight as the wind is getting up dreadfully. There has been dreadful work among the shipping in the Downs in particular. Whether it is the sad accounts I have heard and my being unhappy not hearing from you I know not. But I have no peace sleeping or awaking, for every night I have such unpleasant dreams. I often think if it should please the Almighty to spare us both to meet again I never would suffer you to leave me if, by my persuasions, it could be done.[101]

Map of France

SIX

———•◆•———

BELLS AND WHISTLES

> Having at the beginning of every week some twenty or thirty
> petty offences to enquire into and punish consisting of all the
> lower classes of vice such as drunkenness, lewdness, theft,
> gambling, quarrelling, neglect, mutiny, disobedience,
> equivocation, lying &c. – militating not only immediately
> against the health and good order of the ship but against her
> safety also.
>
> One of Captain Rotheram's 'Growls of a Naval Life'[1]

'A vessel of war contains a little community of human beings,' Samuel
Leech remarked, while summarising the daily round of life aboard a
warship:

> This community is governed by laws peculiar to itself; it is arranged and
> divided in a manner suitable to its circumstances. Hence, when its mem-
> bers first come together, each one is assigned his respective station and
> duty. For every task, from getting up the anchor to unbending the sails,
> aloft and below, at the mess-tub or in the hammock, each task has its
> man, and each man his place. A ship contains a set of *human* machinery,
> in which every man is a wheel, a band, or a crank, all moving with won-
> derful regularity and precision to the *will* of its machinist – the
> all-powerful captain.[2]

The details of the day-to-day running of a ship were set down by
most captains in what were termed his standing orders – fixed orders

that all the captain's officers had to follow, in addition to the official printed Admiralty rules known as *Regulations and Instructions Relating to His Majesty's Service at Sea*, to which there was a major revision in 1806 and slight amendments two years later. The standing orders varied from ship to ship, yet much similarity existed because captains had themselves experienced such orders while serving as midshipmen and lieutenants. Junior officers commonly made their own copy of these orders, so by the time they were promoted to captain they might have accumulated a mass of orders as a basis for their own regime.

The standing orders were prominently posted, for those who could read, but the men who were illiterate became acquainted with the routine through experience, especially if they contravened the orders. When on board the *Unité*, Robert Wilson noted that 'There are, to be sure, printed directions for to be observed by all King's Ships, but then, generally speaking, most officers have plans of their own, which the crews over which they command do follow; and it's a common saying, "different ships, different rules," for it must be considered that every commanding officer of a vessel of war is like unto a prince in his own state and his crew may be considered as his subjects, for his word is law.'[3] In William Dillon's view, 'one of the most unpleasant duties of a captain is to train the crew of a vessel which has been disciplined by another commander. If his regulations differ from what they have previously been used to, it occasions unpleasant occurrences, murmurs, and sometimes even mutiny.'[4]

Captains generally divided the crew (except for the idlers) into two watches, and they worked in alternating shifts. 'The ship's company,' Robert Wilson said, 'are equally divided, not only in numbers but also in a fair manner (so that one half has as good men as the other) into two separate watches, called the starboard and larboard'[5] – larboard being the old term for port side. The alternating watches worked for four hours and then had four hours off, seven days a week, so that the men never had a lengthy period of sleep. Two shorter shifts, from 4 p.m. to 6 p.m. and 6 p.m. to 8 p.m., were called the dog watches and broke this daily pattern to ensure that men were not constantly on duty during the same periods. Daniel Goodall complained about this routine because they had so little sleep:

> The common system of watch adopted even now [he was writing in the early 1850s] in small vessels is that which divides the whole of the crew into two watches only . . . The result of this arrangement was that the half of all those who kept watch were on deck night and day, and that one watch during each alternate night had not more than three and a-half hours in their hammocks and six and a-half on the night following – that is, supposing the exigencies of weather or other causes did not necessitate a call for all hands, in which case every one of the crew liable for duty in reefing and furling, &c., was obliged to turn out. This system of watch is indeed the only one available in small vessels, where a third of the crew would certainly be found inadequate to the necessary safety and working of the ship.[6]

In a few of the larger ships, particularly in the last years of the war against Napoleon, a three-watch system was used, which Goodall much preferred: 'Where the crew, as in a vessel of the first class like the *Temeraire*, is numerous enough to allow of subdivision, no better plan for the comfort and consequent efficiency of the men could be devised than that adopted by Captain Marsh [the *Temeraire*'s captain when Goodall joined in 1801] – namely, of dividing the ship's crew into three watches.'[7] To Goodall, the benefit of the three-watch system was that they worked fewer hours and could sleep much longer:

> Only a third of them were required to be on deck night and day, and consequently every person who kept watch had at least six hours rest during the night, under ordinary circumstances. This is a subject of deep interest to seamen . . . it is a subject I have often heard discussed in the course of my service, both by officers and men, and the general opinion I found was, that it could be made quite practicable in all ships of seventy-four guns and upwards which were properly manned according to the full complement allowed by the rules of the navy.[8]

Time on board was measured according to the number of bells and the watch, rather than by hours and minutes. Regulated by sandglasses, time was announced every half-hour by a number of strokes on the ship's bell. Using this system, one bell was half an hour and two bells was one hour into a watch, three bells was one and a half hours, four bells was two hours, five bells was two and a half hours, six bells was three hours, seven bells was three and a half hours, and finally eight bells was four hours – the end of the watch. Being able to tell the time depended not only on counting the number of bells but also knowing which watch it was. A further complication to telling the time by bells and watches was the two consecutive two-hour dog watches, during which four bells indicated the end of the first dog watch, but instead of five bells being struck half an hour later, the sequence was one bell, two bells, three bells, and lastly eight bells to mark the end of the second dog watch.

The first watch started in the evening, at 8 p.m., so six bells in the first watch was 11 p.m. This watch ended at midnight, and the middle watch began, until 4 a.m. From then until 8 a.m. was the morning watch, followed by the forenoon watch from 8 a.m. to midday. From midday to 4 p.m. was the afternoon watch, and the two dog watches then followed, from 4 p.m. to 6 p.m. and 6 p.m. to 8 p.m. Despite the fact that the first watch started at 8 p.m., the ship's official day began at noon rather than midnight, although this was changed in 1805. The probable reason for this start of the calendar day was that whenever possible the ship's position was measured at noon by observing the angle of the sun with the horizon at its highest point. The observance of noon was something of a ceremony, as Basil Hall recounted:

> In one way or another the latitude is computed as soon as the master
> is satisfied the sun has reached his highest altitude in the heavens. He
> then walks aft to the officer of the watch, and reports 12 o'clock, com-
> municating also the degrees and minutes of the latitude observed. The
> lieutenant proceeds to the captain, wherever he may be, and repeats that
> it is 12, and that so-and-so is the latitude. The same formal round of
> reports is gone through, even if the captain be on deck, and has heard
> every word spoken by the master, or even if he himself assisted in making

the observation. The captain now says to the officer of the watch 'Make it 12!'. The officer calls out to the mate of the watch, 'Make it 12!'. The mate, ready primed, sings out to the quarter-master, 'Strike 8 bells!'. And lastly, the hard-a-weather old quartermaster, stepping down the ladder, grunts out to the sentry at the cabin-door, 'Turn the glass, and strike the bell!'.[9]

This noon observation produced an accurate point in time during most twenty-four-hour periods, from which the sand-glasses and any clocks and pocket watches on board (usually less accurate than the sand-glasses) could be checked. Although seamen did buy pocket watches, officers were more likely to afford such timepieces and to opt for a more accurate mechanism rather than an expensive-looking case. John Peace, a Scottish gunner, recorded in a notebook around 1782: 'This is the number and maker's name of my watch: James Hinton maker London number 6584',[10] a watchmaker known to have been working in London then. In surviving manuscripts, it is notice-able that officers usually recorded time as on land, whereas a seaman referred to bells and watches, so he might talk of 'between one and two bells in the first watch', while an officer would say 'at a quarter to nine at night'. Since pocket watches were unreliable, an officer might actually be less accurate than the sailor who was referring merely to a half-hour period notified to all by the ringing of the bell. With this system of marking the hours, ship's time was always behind Greenwich time, but the number of hours and minutes it was behind depended on where the ship was in the world. Until 1805, the calen-dar date was also half a day behind, which made no difference to the seamen, but is more of a problem for historians today – in the morn-ing the date on board ship would be recorded in official logs and correspondence as the previous day's date, though afternoon dates would be the same.

Just as the passing of time was marked by the sound of bells, orders given to the seamen were punctuated by whistles. The boatswain and his mates each had a whistle (also called a 'pipe' or 'call'), which was capable of several different notes. Such pipes had already been in use for many decades and were not just a tool but also a mark of the boatswain's authority, who was often known as 'Tom Pipes' or just 'Pipes'. To carry out any task, the boatswain would blow his pipe and shout an order, which was echoed throughout the ship by means of the boatswain's mates blowing their pipes and repeating the order. Different sequences of notes on the whistle prefaced different orders, so the seamen would in most cases know what order to expect from the sound of the whistle. Some sequences had become ceremonial, such as that used in 'piping the side' – three drawn-out low-high-low notes were sounded to herald the arrival on board of naval officers, royalty and foreign dignitaries. Other calls gave rise to popular sayings, such as 'pipe down'. In the evening, the call for the seamen to go down to their hammocks and go to sleep, in silence, was called 'piping down' and so to tell someone to 'pipe down' became another way of telling them to be quiet.

The day started off by waking the men of the watch who were asleep in their hammocks. 'The first sound that breaks the stillness of the night,' Robert Hay recalled, 'is uttered at five o'clock in the morning. It consists of a "whe–e–e–ugh all hands wash decks a ho–o–o–y".'[11] Samuel Leech was rather more prosaic in his description:

> The boatswain is a petty officer of considerable importance in his way; he and his mates carry a small silver whistle or pipe, suspended from the neck by a small cord. He receives word from the officer of the watch to call the hands up. You immediately hear a sharp shrill whistle. This is succeeded by another and another from his mates. Then follows his hoarse cry of 'All hands ahoy!' which is forthwith repeated by his mates. Scarcely has this sound died upon the ear, before the cry of 'Up all hammocks ahoy!' succeeds it, to be repeated in like manner. As the first tones of the whistle penetrate between the decks, signs of life make their appearance.[12]

As Hay explained, this was followed soon after by the boatswain's mates moving through the lower deck to rouse those men not yet awake:

The clearing of the men out of the hammocks is not so easy, but it must be done. They press their shoulders against every one of them, roaring out with a voice of thunder, 'A sharp knife, a clear conscience, and out or down is the word.' If the weight of a hammock indicates an inmate, the sharp knife and the head lanyard come into immediate contact and down comes the occupant head foremost. He has no time to dress, but snatching his jacket and trousers in hand, flies off.[13]

The hammocks, Leech related, were stored away in the daytime:

With a rapidity that would surprise a landsman, the crew dress themselves, lash their hammocks and carry them on deck, where they are stowed for the day. There is a system even in this arrangement; every hammock has its appropriate place ... They are also kept exceedingly clean. Every man is provided with two, so that while he is scrubbing and cleaning one, he may have another to use. Nothing but such precautions could enable so many men to live in so small a space.[14]

The first task was not breakfast, but cleaning the decks, a constant necessity with the dirt generated by so many people on board, the excess tar, as well as all the animals. Pets such as dogs and monkeys often roamed freely, and some of the livestock, particularly goats and occasionally sheep and even pigs, wandered about. Others might be tethered or penned on the deck, which at least kept their dung within a small area, but bedding and fodder were easily scattered by the wind, and the animals – like some of the crew – suffered from seasickness. Captain Pasley of the *Sybil*, infuriated by the lax cleaning, wrote in his journal on 21 February 1780: 'Found great fault this morning with cleaning the ship. Written orders [are that] every watching officer has to move every arm chest, hencoop &c. abaft daily; yet this morning I had only too incontestable a proof that my orders were not complied with. [It is] Above ten days since we sailed; yet I discovered lodged between the coops the whole dirt made by the stock since the day of taking them on board. Bushels of it – horrid.'[15]

The cleaning, Leech explained, was done by holystoning and washing down:

By holy-stoning, I mean cleaning them with stones, which are used for this purpose in men of war. These stones are, some of them, large, with a ring at each end with a rope attached, by which it is pulled backwards and forwards on the wet decks. These large stones are called holy bibles; the smaller hand ones are also called holy-stones, or prayer-books, their shape being something like a book. After the decks are well rubbed with these stones, they are wiped dry with swabs made of rope-yarns. By this means the utmost cleanliness is preserved in the ship.[16]

The holystones used for cleaning were generally blocks of a suitable sandstone, and at Port Mahon in Minorca, Joseph Bates saw a 'rocky mountain'[17] and remarked that 'the stone of this mountain is a kind of sandstone, much harder than chalk, called "*holy-stone*", which is abundant on the island, and made use of by the British squadron to scour or holy-stone the decks with every morning to make them white and clean'.[18] Cleaning the decks in this way was harsh labour because, William Robinson pointed out, 'the men suffer from being obliged to kneel down on the wetted deck, and a gravelly sort of sand strewed over it. To perform this work they kneel with their bare knees, rubbing the deck with a stone and the sand, the grit of which is often very injurious.'[19]

The never-ending cleaning also involved sweeping, often with besom brooms, and whenever going on shore to obtain water, they went 'brooming' as well and fetched twigs to make brooms, as the marine John Howe mentioned at New York at the end of 1779: 'I was sent on board a brig to go to Straton [Staten] Island for water and brooms.'[20] Brooms would have worn out rapidly when sweeping up the dust from dry holystoning, something that Captain Griffiths abhorred because of the men's health:

Dry holystoning is a practice on which so much admiration has been bestowed, from the beautiful appearance it gives to the decks, and it has been so generally adopted; that to oppose it is treading on slippery ground. Under impressions that it was injurious to health, it did not prevail in the ships I commanded. The decks, therefore, looked brown, though they were in *reality* not less clean. The objection to it was this. The sand is made quite hot, and if you go between decks while the process is in operation; you will find yourself in a constant dust, which the men employed must inhale. If a black handkerchief be tied over their mouths, a crust of this dust will be formed, where the breath moistens it; and which without this precaution would be inhaled.[21]

There is no doubt that some captains insisted on excessive holystoning and washing of the decks by the men of each watch in order to keep them occupied, and crews bitterly resented such treatment. The crews of warships were significantly larger than those of merchant ships, not because warships were more difficult to sail, but because many hands were needed to fire the guns during battles. George Watson praised Captain Bennett of the *Fame* for treating the crew fairly and not giving them work merely to keep everyone occupied, a practice that Watson railed against:

The Captain, R.H.A. [Richard Henry Alexander] Bennett was a good man, and did everything in his power to make his crew comfortable . . . nor did he ever oppress them with unnecessary exercises, to '*keep them at it*', as some call it. 'Keep them at it!' I dislike that expression – do those who use it think men under them no better than brutes, and fit only to drudge continually as if insensible to toil, and unworthy of rest from their labour that they like to keep them at it? If they do, let them learn that such treatment generally creates, in the oppressed, a dislike to their masters, and a reluctance to lawful and proper employment.[22]

Such sentiments were as accurate on some navy ships as on land – there were some officers, as there were many employers ashore, who did indeed consider that those they commanded were 'no better than brutes'. Another task commonly given to the men to occupy their time was 'working up junk' – picking to shreds worn-out pieces of tar-covered rope, and the resulting oakum was useful for anything from caulking to toilet paper.

After holystoning, it was time for breakfast. From then until noon the watch on duty kept the ship sailing, the cleaning of the decks continued, and new recruits were trained. The specialist craftsmen such as the cooper, carpenter and armourer and their mates carried on their work as normal. Sundays were generally treated as special, and the almost idyllic picture painted by Basil Hall demonstrated, by contrast, a warship's activity during the rest of the week:

> The circumstance which most distinctly marks the afternoon of Sunday on board a man-of-war, even more than on land, is the absence of all the usual stir caused by the multifarious occupations of the artificers and crew. The fire in the armourer's forge, abreast of the fore-hatchway being extinguished, the rattle of his hammer, and the gritting of his rasp, are no more heard. The wearing and tearing of the adzes and axes, planes and saws of the carpenter, cease to torment the ear. The spunyarn-reel of the forecastlemen is stopped in its revolutions, and stowed away till Monday. The noisy thump-thumping of the cocoa-pounder is laid asleep. The bayonets of the marines, the cutlasses and boarding-pikes of the sailors, and all other weapons of offence, have some respite given to their points and edges. The tailors close their shears, and bundle up their remnants; while the sail-makers draw off their palms, and thrust their stools on one side.[23]

Apart from the noise generated by their toil, in most ships strict silence was maintained when at work – hard labour was not aided by the rhythm of sea shanties in the Royal Navy. James Gardner recounted that on board the *Barfleur* in 1790, 'in working the ship no one was allowed to speak but himself [Captain Calder], and I have seen the *Barfleur* brought to an anchor and the sails furled like magic, without a voice being heard except his own'.[24] Gardner thought such silence was exceptional, but Aaron Thomas showed that at least some tasks were done in silence:

> When a ship is under sail in hazy weather, has land in sight on both boards, is within soundings, has rocks and sandbanks laid down on the charts near where she supposes herself and is entering a harbour or bay, all hands are on deck. Silence is ordered. The sails full of wind, the sea dashing against her bows, the waves in contest against her sides, and she in motion, gliding on the liquid fluid with immense impetuosity – All

yet is silence! The Captain speaks, he gives his commands, they are all executed in quiet alertness. All, all are mute but one – the man heaving the lead [for measuring the depth of water].[25]

The captain of the *Pegasus* in 1786 insisted that

> The officers are to use every means in their power to prevent that but too common and absurd practice of seamen in making a noise on every occasion, when the duty of the ship is carrying on, by *huzzaing, hallowing*, etc, when boats etc are hoisting in or out, working at the capstan, hoisting the sails, etc. They are to be acquainted that no such custom will be allowed, and if they dare to persist, they will be severely punished.[26]

He added: 'The strictest silence to be observed whenever the men are at their quarters, and the officers are particularly ordered to prevent any noise or confusion.'[27]

Gunnery practice was carried out up to noon, but otherwise the off-watch seamen had some time to themselves, which they frequently spent in catching up on their sleep in a quiet corner on a lower deck. Typical days rarely occurred, because even if there were no enemies to encounter or potential prizes to chase, changes in weather conditions ensured that the sailing of the ship needed constant attention. Basil Hall spelled out the variety of shipboard life:

> In many other professions, it is possible to calculate beforehand, with more or less precision, the degree and kind of work which a young man is likely to be called upon to perform, but there is a peculiar difficulty in coming to any just conclusion upon these points, even in a vague way, in the life of a sailor. His range of duties includes the whole world; he may be lost in the wilderness of a three-decker, or be wedged into a cock-boat of a cutter; he may be half fried in Jamaica, or wholly frozen in Spitzbergen; he may be cruising six days of the week in the midst of a fleet of a hundred sail, and flounder in solitude on the seventh; he may be peacably riding at anchor in the morning, and in hot action before sunset. He may waste his years in idleness, the most fatal contingency of all to subordination; or he may be worn out by sheer fatigue. If employed

on the home station, he may hear from his friends every day; or if serving abroad he may be fifteen months (as I have been) at a time, without receiving a single letter or a newspaper. He may serve under a soft or easy-going commander, which is a great evil; or be ground down by one of those tight hands, who, to use the slang of the cockpit, keep everyone on board 'under the fear of the Lord and a broomstick'. In short, a man may go to sea for twenty years, and find no two commanding-officers, and hardly two days, alike.[28]

On the other hand, much of the work was repetitive, and when blockading a port or escorting a convoy it could easily become tedious.

Daily life for the marines on board was more predictable than that of the sailors, because their main role was in battle, either between ships or attacking shore installations. When not needed for fighting, which was for the vast majority of their time, marines were used as unskilled labour and as sentries. They acted as a buffer between the officers and the men and guarded key parts of the ship, like the gun-powder magazines, to keep order or to prevent men gaining access. 'Their duties are various, such as circumstances require,' Robert Wilson elaborated. 'In harbour, the one half of them, or one division, mount guard three days in the week and are exempt from ship's duty – *i.e.* in the working line – while the other division that is off guard work in common with the ship's crew and are called the working part of marines. At sea, they do their duty with the afterguard, except those that are on sentry.'[29] Samuel Leech said that 'there are from thirty to forty marines to be disposed of. These do duty as sentries at the captain's cabin, the ward-room, and at the galley during the time of cooking. They are also stationed at the large guns at night, as far as their numbers run.'[30] Wilson gave more details about their sentry duties:

Concerning the different posts of the sentries, there are [always] four . . . at sea or in harbour, *viz.* the fore cockpit, down where the gunner's, boatswain's and carpenter's store-rooms are, and the fore magazine of powder; the gunroom door, by the after cockpit, where the captain's and lieutenants' store-rooms for wine, etc., are, also the purser's steward's store-room and the after magazine for powder; the captain's cabin door; the scuttle butt, where fresh water is kept, also when the captain's and officers' dinners are dressing, attendance at the galley fire is another post. In harbour, in addition, the posts are the gangways and forecastle, with the poop at night time only. The posts mentioned are the regular ones. One marine only has to remain four or two hours according to his watch.[31]

The marines also spent their time in weapons practice, drilling and cleaning their kit. A manual on the training of marines, published by Lieutenant Terence O'Loghlen in 1766, recommended the type of exercise to be used at sea:

> The best method, in my opinion, to exercise marines on board a ship is, first to draw up the soldiers in a single rank round the deck, facing inwards, and make them go through the Manual and Platoon Exercise in that position. The officer stands in the centre to give the words of command, and to see that every man is attentive as if he had been ashore in battalion. So soon as the Platoon Exercise is ended, the detachment must be formed into three ranks, at either side of the deck, facing outwards, and subdivided into small platoons as you have room. The soldiers are then to get their cartridges, and prime and load . . . When the detachment fires [has fired] six rounds, the general beats [on a drum]. The officer must then form his detachment two deep . . . and perform Parapet Firing in that order.[32]

O'Loghlen's view of training marines on board ship was to keep exercises simple and repetitive, and he also recommended that 'no other firing or evolution should be attempted at sea. It can answer no purpose whatever to puzzle men with impracticalities. Soldiers kept in constant practice in the manner prescribed, cannot forget more than they will be able to recover in two or three days on shore. Marines should be accustomed to fire frequently with ball* on

---

* The bullets fired by muskets were spherical lead balls.

board ship at a mark hung for the purpose at the extremity of the
fore-yard arm.'[33]

The marines occupied an ambivalent position in the general running of the ship, for while they often worked and fought alongside
the seamen, they were regarded as a defence of last resort for the officers if the crew mutinied. One of the duties of marines was to stand
guard while men were punished. A serious crime such as mutiny
could well result in hanging, but crimes of a less serious nature were
invariably punished by floggings, which all hands were called to witness around eleven o'clock. Afterwards, dinner was served at midday,
along with the first issue of grog, while just enough men were left to
keep the ship sailing. These were the seven-bell men who ate half an
hour earlier. Following their dinner men not on watch might be
allowed leisure time, or else they undertook training and exercises,
while the idlers continued with their work. In the next watch, the first
dog watch, it was time for supper along with the second issue of
grog, after which was the daily routine of 'beating to quarters' when
the men were assembled at their battle stations. Sometimes this was
followed by gunnery practice, or the men might be given leisure time
again. At 8 p.m., the end of the second dog watch, all the hammocks
were piped down, and the idlers and the watch that had just come off
duty went below to sleep. After this the master-at-arms, whose role
was that of a policeman, keeping law and order, and his assistants
known as corporals (who were all seamen) went through the ship to
check that fires and lights were extinguished.

———•———

The seamen, marines and petty officers could be accused of all manner
of misdemeanours and more serious offences, but the type of punishment
depended very much on the attitude and tolerance of the captain. Royal
Navy law was embodied in an Act of Parliament of the mid-seventeenth
century, which was revised in 1749 with subsequent amendments and
comprised thirty-six Articles of War. These had to be read aloud
to the seamen each month – some captains read them out instead of
holding a religious service on Sundays. Most of the articles were
concerned with various offences and the types of punishment available.

For less serious offences, grog could be stopped or watered down, and skilled seamen and petty officers could be disrated (demoted) so that they were reduced in rank and their pay was decreased, or they could be flogged – referred to frequently as flogging at the gangway, or simply being punished at the gangway. This was by far the most common form of punishment, though in theory only a dozen lashes were allowed without a court martial – something captains frequently ignored or circumvented. The 1806 regulations merely reminded the captain that he alone could order punishments 'which he is never to do without sufficient cause, nor ever with the greater severity than the offence shall really deserve'.[34] It was not until the war was almost over that an effective check on the power of captains was introduced, as Basil Hall noted: 'Antecedent to June 1811, the date of the order by which officers in command of ships were required to send quarterly returns of punishments to the Admiralty, there was little or no restraint upon the despotic authority of the captain, as far, at least, as corporal punishments were concerned.'[35]

What happened when the men were called to witness a flogging was revealed by Samuel Leech:

The hoarse, dreaded cry of 'All hands ahoy to witness punishment!' from the lips of the boatswain, peals along the ship as mournfully as the notes of a funeral knell. At this signal the officers muster on the spar deck, the men on the main deck. Next came the prisoner; guarded by a marine on one side and the master at arms on the other, he was marched up to the [wooden] grating. His back was made bare and his shirt laid loosely upon his back; the two quartermasters proceeded to seize him up; that is, they tied his hands and feet with spun-yarns, called the seizings, to the grating. The boatswain's mates, whose office it is to flog on board a man of war, stood ready with their dreadful weapon of punishment, the cat-o'-nine-tails.[36]

Leech described the legendary cat: 'This instrument of torture was composed of nine cords, a quarter of an inch round and about two feet long, the ends whipt with fine twine. To these cords was affixed a stock, two feet in length, covered with red baize . . . it is a most formidable instrument in the hands of a strong, skilful man.'[37]

Next, Leech related the painful scenes that they had to watch:

> The boatswain's mate is ready, with coat off and whip in hand. The captain gives the word. Carefully spreading the cords with the fingers of his left hand, the executioner throws the cat over his right shoulder; it is brought down upon the now uncovered herculean shoulders of the man. His flesh creeps – it reddens as if blushing at the indignity; the sufferer groans; lash follows lash, until the first mate, wearied with the cruel employment, gives place to a second. Now two dozen of these dreadful lashes have been inflicted: the lacerated back looks inhuman; it resembles roasted meat burnt nearly black before a scorching fire; yet still the lashes fall . . .Vain are the cries and prayers of the wretched man . . . four dozen strokes have cut up his flesh and robbed him of all self-respect; there he hangs, a pitied, self-despised, groaning, bleeding wretch; and now the captain cries, forbear! His shirt is thrown over his shoulders; the seizings are loosed; he is led away, staining his path with red drops of blood, and the hands, 'piped down' by the boatswain, sullenly return to their duties.[38]

The vast majority of punishments were either for drunkenness, or for crimes committed under the influence of drink, as Daniel Goodall observed:

> In all the ships I ever served in, the Captains made continual but, I am sorry to add, generally the most unavailing efforts to check this vice. The punishments were of the old stock kind where flogging was not resorted to, such as stopping the grog of all convicted of drunkenness for a month or six weeks at a time, or putting an extra quantity of water into it, and compelling the culprits to drink it in the presence of officers – a most unpalatable punishment to many offenders. Sometimes a trial was made of the infliction of extra duty, generally of the most disagreeable kind, and in many instances these modes of meeting the evil were far more efficacious than flogging. But on board every ship afloat there were some characters, often the very best of the seamen too, who seemed to take a

special pride in getting drunk, notwithstanding the risks they ran in indulging their whim or propensity.[39]

The frequency with which men were punished depended partly on how strict the captain was and partly on how prone the men were to break the rules. Aaron Thomas of HMS *Lapwing* commented in his journal that 'Upon an average we flog two men in 3 weeks, but we have had many heavy squalls amongst the officers we have at this time, our boatswain and surgeon in confinement for drunkenness, and both will have court martials.'[40] George Vernon Jackson's first ship in 1801 was HMS *Trent*, under Captain Edward Hamilton. Jackson thought the ship was well disciplined and efficient, 'but these qualities had all been promoted at no small sacrifice of humanity. No sailor was allowed to walk from one place to another on deck, and woe betide the unfortunate fellow who halted in his run aloft, unless expressly bidden to do so for some particular purpose. The "cat" was incessantly at work.'[41] One passenger's view on board HMS *Gibraltar* in 1811 was somewhat different, since he thought punishments were fairly meted out and to only a few men:

I could not but observe how very seldom the men were punished; and that they never were disgraced at the gangway but for some wilful fault. The captain does not choose to flog a man for an error which is excusable, and the only crimes for which punishment was inflicted were drunkenness, insolence and quarrelling, or a wilful neglect of duty where it was plain to everybody that the culprit deserved the correction he received. It generally happened that the same men were constant offenders; nothing could keep some of them sober, or quiet, which convinces me that a ship's company could not be kept in order unless the fear of corporal punishment deterred some of the notorious bad characters, who too often disgrace a Man of War . . . I have known a boy at school receive more lashes at one time, than ever the captain of the *Gibraltar* inflicted upon the most incorrigible of his people. Sir Francis Burdett [radical reformer] and co may talk, but I wish they could point out any other means than that of occasional flogging by which 600 men confined in a ship could be restrained from faults which would lead to more serious consequences . . . There are always a very great proportion of a ship's company who never felt it [flogging]. Generally speaking, not one 20th out of 600 or 700 men ever allow themselves to be thus disgraced.[42]

The degree to which different men felt and reacted to flogging varied considerably, and this, apart from the brutality of the punishment, was what made it unjust. George Watson spoke of how he was flogged: 'I was seized to the grating, and there received a dozen lashes, from the cat o' nine tails, whose claws I believe are worse than theirs which are said to have nine lives, and I felt them so keenly, being the first and the last time they scratched my back, that I thought I would rather let the rogue that caused what I endured kick me overboard another time, than have those unnatural devil-cats at my shoulders.'[43] The seaman George King, however, made light of the frequent floggings that he received, usually for being drunk. On one occasion he recorded that 'at ten the hands was turned up, thirteen of us being in the Master at Arms report. When my name was called I received my batty [punishment] which was two dozen right and left. It was a piercing cold morning but I was warmed for that day.'[44]

What irked the men was the inconsistency of punishment, and Aaron Thomas noted the apparent injustice or at least illogicality of sentences, as on Monday 13 August 1798:

Punished William Dun, the quarter gunner, for striking Peg Roberts (Woodcock's whore) on Friday night with one dozen lashes. Punished Michael Byrne the marine with 9 lashes for finding fault with the Doctor's physic &c. Punished the boy [Richard] Skipper on his backside with 12 lashes for giving half a gill of rum to Gater the marine for washing his clothes. There is something particular in this case. The boys are allowed their rum, and if they drink it, they often get drunk with it, therefore it is understood they may give it to persons who wash and mind for them. And many boys in some ships sell their liquor. But this particular boy was flogged for giving his liquor away to a marine who had done work for him. So that by flogging this lad, it is the same as giving out orders for all boys to drink their own allowance, and thereby get drunk with it. The best that can be said of it is that it will encourage intoxication.[45]

What was regarded as a crime in one ship might be tolerated in another, such as swearing. On board the *Minerva* in 1793, William Richardson observed the ill feeling when they were forbidden to swear:

> No one was to swear on any account, but as there were so many new hands lately pressed from the Indiamen, it was almost impossible to prevent it at first and when any one was heard, his name was taken down on a list and at seven next morning were called and punished, it was not severe tho' galling, being a new crime and few got more than half a dozen lashes, how I escaped God only knows, as my name had been taken down more than once . . . Tho' the punishment was light, it displeased the old seamen, who had not had time to divest themselves of a crime they had been so long accustomed to in the merchant service.[46]

He noted in his journal that 'it's a thousand pities that Sailors should be so fond of strong liquors, that is the only thing that disgraces them', but later added: 'and swearing'.[47] The evangelical Captain Gambier would not tolerate swearing, as Midshipman Dillon related:

> Swearing was strictly forbidden, and the fine of one shilling was imposed for every oath uttered: but the collection of the money was not insisted upon from the officers. For the seamen there was a different plan adopted. When they were brought aft for committing that offence, a large heavy wooden collar, with two 32 lb. of shot in it, was secured upon the shoulders by a lock and key. The culprit would be ordered upon the poop, and kept there for hours, walking to and fro. These regulations caused much discontent and murmuring among the ship's company, who deserted when they could.[48]

Archibald Sinclair certainly believed that everyone cursed:

Swearing in the navy, and among all classes of seamen, was at this time carried to a great excess. It had become habitual with almost every one, and was expected. No great harm was meant. A fearful anathema against one's own eyes or limbs, or, to draw it more mildly, in the phraseology of the day, a good round oath, but scarcely an expletive, either before or after an order had been given, made it more emphatic, and was considered merely as the proper emphasis, without which promptitude and alacrity might be dispensed with.[49]

Some captains did their best to be lenient, which Daniel Goodall appreciated:

On board the *Temeraire* the Captain was always disposed to give the delinquent the benefit of his character, if good, on his first appearance for punishment, and in such cases dismissed him with an admonition only. The first time I ever saw all hands turned up for punishment, under Captain [Edward] Marsh's orders, there were four men charged with the crime of drunkenness, all of whom had been before paraded for the same offence. On this occasion, very fortunately for them, news of the victory of Copenhagen [1801] had just arrived in the fleet, and the Captain, after reading them a very severe lecture, told them, to their own great pleasure and the contentment of their mates, that he should overlook their offence for that time, so as not to mar the rejoicings for the success just announced, but that he should consider himself bound to inflict a double allowance if he ever found them before him again charged with the same or any other offence. A month had barely elapsed before one of them was called up for punishment on the same charge, and the Captain certainly did not quite forget the promise he made on the former occasion.[50]

Not all seamen who were sentenced to be flogged actually suffered the punishment, according to James Scott: 'The fact is that thorough-bred good seamen, or respectable men, seldom place themselves in a situation to call for corporal punishment, and if unfortunately they should inadvertently at any time break through the rigid rules of a man-of-war, it is generally so arranged that some officer steps forward, and by pleading in their behalf, obtains a remission of the punishment, unless the offence is of a very deep dye.'[51] Robert Wilson was reprieved in this way: 'I was called upon to be punished for some fault, but through Lieutenant Wilson [no relation] giving me a good character, and speaking in my favour, I was forgiven. I had been seized up, and made (as sailors called it) a spread eagle of, by having my arms extended to their full extent. By my having been forgiven, it gave rise to a report that I was a Freemason, nor could I ever after persuade them to the contrary.'[52]

What made seamen rebellious was the injustice and bullying that could result from a harsh regime rather than the brutality of punishments. 'Starting' was the informal beating of seamen with a rope's end or cane ('starter') and could be more common than flogging, but was rarely noted in official records. Daniel Goodall was critical of the *Prince George*:

> The *Prince George* was one of those ships mismanaged on the driving principle. All the boatswain's mates carried canes, or pieces of rope's ends, in their hands, and an indiscriminate shower of blows, accompanied by a volley of the most revolting oaths, was the usual mode of enforcing any order, however simple. It followed as a natural consequence that the vessel was one of the worst handled of the whole fleet, the duties being infinitely better performed on board those ships where driving was rare and rope's-ending not allowed.[53]

This punishment was frequently done to drive the men harder but could easily lead to bullying by the petty officers and resentment by the men, and in 1809 it was prohibited.

Another punishment was running the gauntlet, which was usually reserved for crimes like theft that did not just break regulations but affected other members of the crew. On board the *Lapwing* in October 1798, Aaron Thomas witnessed a scene of running the gauntlet when a man by the name of Thomson, who was formerly the captain's cook but had been punished and demoted for stealing pieces of meat, was caught thieving money from other seamen:

> At 10am Thomson's arms was lashed; the ship's company formed a lane all around the waist of the ship, every man being provided with a nettle

[length of knotted cord], 2 marines faced him with each a bayonet point at the thief, a cord was thrown over the prisoner's body, the ends of which were held behind by two quartermasters. Things being thus ordered, he run the gauntlet, every man striking him as he passed, the noise of which I thought at the time resembled reapers at work, when cutting corn. After passing once round, he fainted and dropped down. The surgeon threw some hartshorn in his face, and he was ordered into irons, to receive more punishment when his back recovers.[54]

Running the gauntlet was abolished by an Admiralty order in 1806.

A few captains put some thought into making the punishment fit the crime, so that 'John Watson (seaman) was ordered to clean out the head [toilet] for the space of one month for heaving a bone out of one of the ports on the main deck'.[55] Refuse such as animal bones was supposed to be emptied down the heads, not thrown randomly overboard, as stipulated in the orders for HMS *Superb* in 1803: 'it is strictly forbidden to thrown bones, dirt, or dirty water out of them [the gunports], but dirt of all sorts is to be taken to the head and lowered well down'.[56] In the *Temeraire*, which was preparing to sail from Plymouth in 1801, Daniel Goodall related how an attempted deserter received a relatively light punishment, though he could have been flogged through the fleet or hanged:

The women were all ordered out of the ship, and in making the clearance it was discovered that one of the seamen had got into a shore-boat amongst a party of the damsels, disguised in a female dress, his object being to desert. Before the boat could shove off, he was, however, detected by the keen eyes of the Master-at-Arms, brought on board, and immediately placed in irons. His detection was no matter of surprise to anyone, for his 'make-up' seemed as if it were expressly meant to challenge notice, and gave rise to a suspicion that the ladies who had aided his toilette meant him to be discovered. He was kept in irons for a week, still wearing his 'masquerade habit' as some of the men called his female dress, and at the end of that time he was brought up in the same guise and received three dozen lashes.[57]

That was not the end of the matter, Goodall recounted:

After this infliction, he was told that he had got only half of his punishment, and that he should be compelled to do duty in his adopted suit until it was judged proper time to give him his other instalment of the 'cat'. This degradation, however, it was evident, was never intended, for after a few days confinement he was ordered to do duty in his proper dress, and nothing further was said of the balance of punishment owing to him – the officers judging rightly that he would suffer far more from the ridicule of his shipmates than from the infliction of any severity they might inflict. The poor fellow, during the remainder of his stay on board was known by no other name than 'Polly'.[58]

Women on board ship were often regarded as troublesome by the officers because they were not officially subject to navy discipline, and some were at least as prone to drunkenness as the men, but as a last resort a captain could always put a woman ashore. In the *Lapwing* in 1798 the boatswain John Dixon and his wife had a long history of drunkenness and troublemaking, and on 15 July Aaron Thomas recorded in his journal: 'At 10 a.m. the Boatswain's wife came aboard very drunk, her husband got her below, and began thumping her so, that in a few minutes he came up under the half deck, for raw fresh beef, to apply to her black eyes.'[59] The next day, Thomas recorded, 'The Boatswain's wife turned ashore for drunkenness. At 5 p.m. left Basseterre . . . for Martinico.'[60] On 18 August the ship returned to Basseterre Roads, St Kitts, and the boatswain's wife returned on board, but within twenty-four hours Thomas was writing, 'The Boatswain's wife sent ashore, after gun fire, for being drunk – long bother with the Boatswain and the officers about his wife.'[61] The ship sailed the next day, but just as they were leaving 'the Boatswain's wife came alongside to beg to have her cloaths with her'.[62]

In one respect navy regulations might appear more lenient than the harsh laws that prevailed on land, where the law came to be known as 'The Bloody Code'. In a frantic attempt to protect property from an underclass of people who were unable to make a living in a time of soaring food prices, and were rapidly becoming hardened criminals, more and more capital offences were incorporated into law. By 1815 there were approximately 225 crimes for which someone could be hanged. A Devon newspaper in August 1813 recorded:

> Devonshire Assizes [Exeter] *Jane Dannatt* alias *Anne Williams*, charged with feloniously personating Sarah Gander, wife of James Gander a seaman of his majesty's ship *Rota*, and thereby receiving money from Mr. Smith, clerk of the cheque, at Plymouth – *Guilty* . . . The trials at the Crown-bar having closed on Thursday morning, the several prisoners whose sentences had not been passed at the close of their trials, were brought up . . . The Judge (Sir Vicary Gibbs) then put on his black cap (the sign of condemnation) and an awful shudder shook every heart, when the following prisoners were brought forward altogether, to receive the dreadful sentence of the law: – *John Kidwell, Jane Dannatt.*[63]

Disagreements and petty crimes might be settled and punished unofficially by other members of the crew, although such actions might themselves be subject to punishment if they came to light. Midshipmen in particular maintained their own code of conduct, and James Scott recalled how they were treated on board the *Achille* if they fell asleep on duty:

> All being duly prepared [with buckets of water], one dashes the contents of his bucket full in the face of the delinquent, loudly bawling in his ear at the same moment 'A man overboard!' and before the poor devil can recover the scaring effects of the first dose, he is almost suffocated by the repeated shocks that assail him from all parts, and so bewildered and mystified that he is led to believe he is the identical fellow who is overboard. Arms and legs are seen striking out in every direction, and 'Sa–sa–save me!' plaintively uttered, till the streams cease flowing, and permit the affrighted culprit to recall his scattered senses.[64]

Maintaining their own code of conduct could easily lead to bullying, as Scott himself experienced:

> I have often been surprised that the difficulties and mortifications encountered by youngsters on their entrance into the service . . . did not disgust a

larger proportion of aspirants than was actually the case . . . in a few months
the tormented became the tormentors, so rapid was their initiation in the
art of quizzing and bullying their younger brethren, the greenhorns as they
were termed, and who were too generally considered as fair game; the practical jokes passed upon them were often dangerous in their tendency and
issue . . . if the poor boys complained, or expressed regret at the step they
had taken in entering His Majesty's Navy, the only comfort they received
was the old question echoed from all sides, 'Why did you [en]'list then?'.[65]

Scott admitted that if he could have 'honourably' left the navy he would have
done so, 'but pride . . . left me to make or mar my fortunes, as it might be'.[66]

Midshipmen were rarely flogged but were often punished by 'mast-
heading', when they were sent up to the platform on the mast known as
the masthead. Midshipman Dillon suffered such treatment when he was
late taking over the watch from his messmate at four in the morning:

I made my appearance on the Quarter Deck just at the moment when he
was making a complaint to Lieut. Twysden of my not being up to relieve
him. 'Here I am,' I called out. 'It is only a ¼ of an hour past 4.' However,
Mr. Twysden thought proper to be very severe, and, not choosing to
listen to what I had to say, ordered me up to the Mast Head. It was a cold
morning, with a damp mist. Away I mounted the rigging, and remained
aloft till 8 o'clock, then the Lieutenant called me down.[67]

More injurious to the midshipman's dignity was the punishment of
being tied to the shrouds for a period of time. The midshipman John
Courtney Bluett considered punishments meted out to his rank
counter-productive, particularly with so many bullying officers:

That strict discipline and subordination are essentially necessary . . . is a
truth that no one . . . would attempt to deny. But that it should be carried
on in the extent it is towards Midshipmen of the Navy is unnecessary,
injudicious and unjust. It depresses the spirit of emulation which ought
to be nourished and encouraged, it cramps their exertions and completely
damps their ardor for the services. A young man entering the Navy must be
prepared for every rebuff, must almost stifle every feeling, must be prepared

to put up with everything he meets with, even though it should appear to him oppression and injustice.[68]

If warrant and commissioned officers incurred the displeasure of the captain, they were tried before a court martial – they were not subjected to the punishments of the lower deck. Depending on an officer's crime, punishments could be harsh, but alternative methods were used to punish them, such as being demoted in rank, reduced in seniority, or dismissed from the service. The death penalty was also used, though officers were normally shot and not hanged. Writing in 1805, the purser John Delafons thought it very fair that punishments for seamen and for officers, who were gentlemen, should differ:

> Habits and education create essential differences in the minds and manners of men. To dismiss an officer from His Majesty's service, would be esteemed a heavy punishment; whereas a common sailor would look upon it, in many cases, as a favour conferred upon him. Corporal punishment, which seldom operates on the feelings of a common seaman or soldier, must affect a petty officer (such as a midshipman) &c. so sensibly, if he has the sentiments of a gentleman, as to render his future life a burden to him.[69]

At times the seamen became so resentful of particular issues that they sent petitions to the Admiralty. Their complaints included tyrannical captains, harsh punishments, no shore leave and poor food, but rarely excessive workloads. In 1795, though, the men of the *Blanche* frigate were moved to complain:

> To the Right Honourable Lords of Admiralty. A humble petition on account of ill usage. In the first place, we are employed from morning to two or three of clock in the afternoon washing and scrubbing the decks, and every day our chest and bags is ordered on deck, and not down till night; nor ourselves neither even so particular as to wash the decks with fresh water, and if we get wet at any time and hang or spread our clothes to dry, our captain throws them overboard; by which we beg the favour of another commander or another ship. We still remain your most worthy subjects. *Blanche's* Crew.[70]

Petitions were not written lightly, as they were of doubtful legality, and might cause those who signed them to be tried for mutiny, a term used for anything from aggressive language towards an officer to armed insurrections. Many officers sympathised with Captain Thomas Troubridge's opinion that 'whenever I see a fellow look as if he was thinking, I say that's mutiny'.[71] It was doubtless fear of reprisals that prevented individual seamen of the *Blanche* from signing the petition. William Robinson, who volunteered in 1805 and immediately regretted it, commented that the new recruit 'may *think*, but he must confine his thoughts to the *hold* of his mind, and never suffer them to escape the *hatchway* of utterance'.[72] Some petitions were written as round robins, with the men's names arranged in a circle to disguise the order of writing and prevent the organiser being identified. William Dillon encountered one example when he joined HMS *Glenmore* at Cork in 1798, during a time of unrest in Ireland. He thought such round robins were sinister:

> On the afternoon that I joined the frigate, a round robin was found under one of the quarter deck guns. That is the term for a threatening letter from the crew: the names are signed in a circle, from which you cannot select the leader, there being no first or last. This letter informed the officers that, if they did not change their conduct, they had a chance of swinging at the foreyard arm . . . This was to me a most unpleasant beginning in my new ship: still more so because it was the first letter of the kind I had ever seen.[73]

Considering the number of warships in service, the number of pressed men, and the fact that conditions for them were frequently harsh, it is perhaps surprising that relatively few protests or outright mutinies occurred. The most famous was that on the *Bounty* in 1789 when Captain Bligh and eighteen men were set adrift in the ship's launch by the mutineers near Tonga. After an epic voyage of 3600 miles, Bligh's boat reached Timor, while the mutineers sailed to Pitcairn Island. Fourteen of the mutineers were later captured at Tahiti, but the rest lived out their lives on Pitcairn Island.

In 1797 large-scale mutinies took place in the fleets anchored at Spithead and the Nore. Smaller mutinies also occurred from time to time, usually confined to individual ships, and were generally nipped in the bud by astute captains before they officially became mutinies. Otherwise they tended to be vigorously suppressed. One mutiny occurred in late 1801 on board the *Temeraire*. Everyone was expecting peace with France, and the warship was withdrawn from the blockade of Brest and ordered to Ireland's Bantry Bay. Instead of being decommissioned as the sailors were hoping, the *Temeraire* was ordered to the West Indies, but the crew were not told. The seaman Daniel Goodall remembered the event:

> Rumour whispered that we were destined for the West Indies – a most unhealthy and consequently unpopular station. This was a fatal blow to all the fond hopes so many of us had been but recently nourishing in fancied security, and as it was quite evident from the preparations that were going forward, that our ship and three others were destined for a foreign station, a spirit of discontent became rapidly prevalent on board the *Temeraire*, and it was soon only too evident that something very like mutiny was in contemplation by no inconsiderable portion of the ship's company.[74]

The protesters were confronted by the admiral, who calmed the men, but the *Temeraire* remained at anchor, leading to more frustration, as Goodall related:

> How they thought to carry out their mad resolutions without avoiding collision with the authorities is among the mysteries of infatuation. The most ignorant amongst them could not but be aware that, were a collision once to take place, they must inevitably be crushed, either by superior power in the course of their resistance or by the strong hand of the law after they were overpowered. It is strange, but not more strange than melancholy, how often men are blinded to the consequences of a rash course upon which some of them so heedlessly enter, but it is the same sad story, as old as the world itself, of passion obscuring every gleam of reason.[75]

When some of the men did rise up, Goodall witnessed, they were overpowered by the marines, and then the entire crew was called on deck:

When all were mustered, the Captain and other officers went deliberately amongst the mutineers and picked out fourteen of the number known to be ringleaders in the unfortunate affair, and placed them as prisoners under charge of a party of marines ... the ringleaders were ironed [put in irons] and sent on board of Admiral Mitchell's ship, the *Windsor Castle* ... In the course of a few days, six more of the crew were picked out and sent on board the *Windsor Castle*, making the whole number of prisoners twenty. All these men were able seamen, with the exception of two, one of them the ship's butcher, the other belonging to the carpenter's crew. Some of the delinquents were petty officers, and all of them, previous to this painful affair, were considered well-behaved men.[76]

For the most serious crimes like mutiny, murder, desertion or homosexual acts, a man might be flogged through the fleet or hanged, but both these sentences required a court martial to judge the case. The accused was held in irons until he could be tried. Officers were suspended from duty and confined to their cabin until the court martial if their crime was serious. Between five and thirteen post-captains or admirals were required for a court martial, and the procedure was started by a captain applying to the commander-in-chief of the station in which they were operating. Because he convened the court martial, this commander-in-chief could not take part and usually his second-in-command presided over the court. In the absence of a commander-in-chief, other arrangements were made, and ultimately the senior officers from any five ships could make up a court martial, but even so a prisoner might be held in irons for weeks or months before the required number of captains could be assembled in one spot. A court martial automatically took place of any captain who lost his ship, for whatever reason, such as by shipwreck or capture. Officers were of course tried by their peers, but for accused seamen there was always the gulf of rank and class between themselves and the judges. The accused was allowed a defence counsel, however, and in most cases there seems to have been at least an attempt at fairness.

John Wardocks, a twenty-three-year-old ordinary seaman from HMS *Warspite*, evidently believed in the court, as he chose not to be flogged but opted for a court martial at Plymouth after being accused of striking forty-three-year-old Philip Buckhawson, a ship's corporal, in January 1814, causing him bruising and bleeding. Wardocks was one of several seamen ordered to do cleaning in the dark cockpit, and Buckhawson was in charge of lanterns, but refused to give Wardocks a new candle, accusing him instead of thieving. In his evidence the corporal testified that Wardocks 'said in a loud voice to the people, here this old fellow of a liar says I cut the candle, upon which I took my hand and struck him upon his mouth saying you d—d "rascal" hold your tongue, at the same time I received a blow upon my face from the prisoner'.[77] Wardock's evidence, corroborated by another seaman, was that he struck him in self-defence: 'The Ship's Corporal . . . accused me with stealing . . . He then took me by the handkerchief [round his neck] and dragged me along the wing and in a state of nearly suffocation I struck him to disengage myself. I hope your Lordships will consider the embarrassment I labour under, struggling with a man endeavouring to strangle me, and pardon the offence I committed in striking him to extricate myself.'[78]

If a court martial gave a sentence of flogging round the fleet, this involved the prisoner being rowed in a boat from one warship to another where he was flogged each time, watched by all. A surgeon accompanied the procession and would call a halt if the man was unable to endure any more – though the punishment would be continued on another day. Seamen were flogged round the fleet for crimes that on land might lose them their life, but having witnessed the landsman Peter Richieu flogged in such a way in 1812, the chaplain Edward Mangin was not sure which was the lesser evil:

This day, a man of the *Valiant's* crew *went round the Fleet*, a very serious and ceremonious mode of inflicting punishment. The delinquent, who was a foreigner, had quarrelled with another seaman, and drawing a long knife, endeavoured to stab him in the breast, but the object of his vengeance falling backwards over a cask, received the weapon through his kneepan. For this act, which in England is capital, and would have sent the perpetrator to the gallows, the criminal was sentenced by court-martial to get one hundred and fifty lashes . . . When he arrived at the *Gloucester*, he was very faint and bloody, and before he returned to the *Valiant*, must have endured what, to me, appeared worse than death.[79]

The seaman Henry Walsh was outraged by this form of punishment:

Any crimes such as robberies, desertion or any such depredations committed in a manawar, contrary to what is specified in the articles of war, they punish them through the fleet in the manner following. They rig a triangle in a large boat and then, having seven or eight marines well armed and a drummer in the boat, so they beat the rogue's march through the whole fleet giving him a certain number of lashes on the bare back long side of each ship in the fleet. This is done to keep good order among the men.[80]

Many men never fully recovered from such punishment, which could be up to one thousand lashes, and according to Daniel Goodall it was not much of a deterrent. To him it was

a heart-sickening exhibition of barbarity, the sight of which I would gladly have been spared . . . I have often heard the question of corporeal punishment discussed by both officers and men, and many of the very best and bravest in command have I repeatedly heard declare against it. Speaking as a seaman who knows something of the sort of reasoning prevalent amongst his class, I have no hesitation in saying that it is the least effective check that could be devised for degraded minds, and that men of sensitive feeling are but too certain to be sunk to the degraded class by its infliction, thus inflicting an irreparable evil on the service.[81]

The ultimate punishment, reserved for the worst crimes, was hanging. A yellow flag was flown from the ship where an execution was to be carried out – usually the condemned man's own ship. All the ships' companies near by were ordered to witness the ceremony, which began with the crime and punishment being read out to the condemned man. A gun was fired and the prisoner was hanged from the fore yardarm, where he remained suspended for an hour or more as a deterrent to others. Hanging evolved into a rather theatrical ceremony, which George Watson described:

> Directly below the platform, which is projected from the ship's side, right under the fore yard arm, a gun is loaded, and when the signal is given for the execution, it is fired and the unhappy culprit is run up amidst the smoke, by a number of men, who man the yard rope, and when the cloud from the cannon clears away, you see the sufferer suspended at the yard arm, lifeless, whom a moment before, you saw standing alive upon the stage, but never saw ascend.[82]

John Wardocks was adamant that he should not be flogged for a crime that he had committed in self-defence, but his decision to rely on a court martial had tragic consequences, as no mercy was shown:

> The Court having very maturely and deliberately weighed and considered the evidence in support of the charge as well as what the prisoner had offered in his behalf was of opinion that the charge had been proved against the prisoner John Wardocks and the Court did in consequence adjudge him to be hanged by the neck until he was dead at the yard arm of such one of His Majesty's Ships or Vessels and at such time, as the Commissioners for executing the Office of Lord High Admiral of the United Kingdom of Great Britain and Ireland should direct.[83]

All too often, instead of being a deterrent, a hanging evoked sympathy among the seamen. In February 1809 Marine Sergeant John Chapman of HMS *Carnation* was court-martialled at Martinique on board HMS *Pompée* for cowardice. During a battle a few months earlier with a smaller French ship, the *Palinure*, Chapman fled below, followed by many others, just when he should have led a boarding party to capture the French ship. As a result, the French rallied, and boarded and captured the *Carnation*. The court martial took place after an exchange of prisoners, and James Scott recorded that 'the unhappy sergeant was condemned to be hung, and thirty-two of his cowardly followers to run him up to the yard-arm, and to be afterwards transported for fourteen years to Botany Bay'.[84] Scott described the scene of the execution:

> The signal gun was fired from the Admiral's ship for the boats of the fleet to attend punishment, and repeated by the *Pompée*. The unhappy man was engaged with the chaplain in deep prayer . . . From the period of his condemnation his conduct was edifying and devout: he expected no mercy – he sued for none. To have judged him by his behaviour after sentence, it would have been difficult to believe that he could have ever failed in courage or fortitude. The boats assembled around, marines were stationed in the bows and stern-sheets, the hands were turned up, the rigging of the different ships of the squadron filled with their respective crews dressed in their best and uncovered. All was ready, and the sergeant walked from the cabin on to the quarter-deck, attended by the clergyman. An awful stillness pervaded the ship; the sentence of the court, and the order for the execution, were read. His demeanour was so correct, so firm, and yet so submissively resigned, that the feelings of the bystanders were strongly, painfully excited in his favour: the fault for which he was about to suffer was forgotten in the admiration of the Christian fortitude with which he encountered his fate.[85]

As was often the case, the condemned man made a final speech to the ship's company, which Scott reported:

> He spoke to them in an impressive and collected manner; he acknowledged the justice of his sentence; called upon all those who were about to witness his ignominious death to remember they owed their lives to the service of their country – that by having yielded to unmanly fears he had led others astray, and that he felt he had fairly forfeited his life to the offended laws of his country, adding, that he hoped his fate would be considered a sufficient atonement for his offence. The address was delivered in a tone of deep humility, and he concluded by returning thanks for the kindness he had received.[86]

Everyone watching was affected by Chapman's bravery:

> The silent tears might be seen coursing each other down the furrowed
> and bronzed cheek of many a hardy veteran. The scene became over-
> poweringly distressing as the signal was given to move forward to the
> scaffold. As he passed the main rigging, a suppressed groan, and 'God
> bless you!' might be plainly heard to issue from the overcharged hearts of
> the crew . . . Arrived on the forecastle, he again thanked the clergyman,
> and with a resolute step mounted the scaffold. He continued absorbed in
> prayer until the cap was drawn over his eyes. In a few seconds he dropped
> the handkerchief; the gun exploded under his feet, and in the smoke of
> the discharge his luckless and condemned shipmates ran him up to the
> yard-arm. Death must have been instantaneous, for the body never
> moved. It was an awful, heart-rending ceremony, such as might shake a
> man with iron nerves.[87]

A similar fate awaited the mutineers of the *Temeraire*, as Goodall
recorded: 'A court-martial soon assembled on board the *Gladiator*,
harbour flagship [at Portsmouth], for the trial of the unfortunate
men, and after what was considered by all who read the minutes of
evidence a fair and impartial inquiry, the whole twenty were found
guilty. Eighteen of them were condemned to death, and two were
sentenced to one hundred and twenty lashes each round the fleet.'[88]
It is not clear if all these sentences were carried out. At least six men
were hanged, but according to Goodall twelve men were hanged, and
the rest had their sentences commuted to transportation. Some of
the men were executed on board the *Temeraire*, after which Goodall
wrote:

> This lamentable affair having terminated, we now proceeded with all
> possible dispatch to get ready for sea, and . . . we sailed for the West Indies.
> Most of the men considered it likely that we should have to submit to a
> stricter discipline and a greater degree of rigour in consequence of the late
> revolt and the anticipations on board prior to our sailing were therefore
> not of the liveliest description imaginable. In these anticipations we were,
> however, mistaken, for the Admiral, the Captain, and indeed every officer

on board, seemed desirous of doing their utmost to efface the painful impressions of our late melancholy experience, and were sedulous to show the men that they were as much trusted as if nothing had occurred. Every effort was made to raise the spirits of the crew, and every encouragement given to amusement on board, but it was no easy matter to shake off our gloom.[89]

SEVEN

CONVOY AND CAPTURE

Having captured a Spanish ship after a long chase of many
shot, on removing the prisoners to your ship you are
informed [of] . . . much treasure which, as you are joyously
sending your boats for, she sinks from the perforations you
have made.

One of Captain Rotheram's 'Growls of a Naval Life'
on losing a prize ship[1]

The war at sea was one of attrition, with the navy of each side prey-
ing on merchant shipping to starve the enemy of supplies, reduce
prosperity and thereby limit the capacity to wage war. From the
seaman's point of view the attraction of this strategy was prize-money
from captured ships and the chance of loot. Inevitably, the constant
search for prizes was carried on by enemy warships as well, so that
one responsibility of Royal Navy warships was to ensure the safety of
convoys of British merchant ships, including those involved in the
slave trade until this became illegal in 1807. Looking after a convoy
of ships was monotonous work, with only rare chances to capture
prizes and make money. Lieutenant John Malcolm of the Royal
Highland 42nd regiment explained one reason for the tedium: 'In a
voyage under convoy, it is no avail that you happen to be in a fast sailing vessel: nay, it is rather a circumstance of annoyance; for no sooner
has she shot a-head of the rest a few miles, than she must lie-to
during the finest breeze, in order to wait the slow approach of the
heaviest lugger in the fleet.'[2]

Warships also escorted transport ships that were carrying troops and supplies to arenas of war, and accompanied convoys of convict ships – to the American colonies when Nelson first joined the navy, and later to New South Wales after the American War of Independence. John Malcolm was on board a transport ship in a convoy that left Spithead in June 1813 on a voyage to Portugal and the Peninsular War. He wrote down his impression of what it was like to be afloat and leaving England for the first time:

> Signal being made for sailing, our convoy, consisting of three ships of war, led the way . . . The coast of England began to fade at the night-fall; but the wind had almost died away, and the low and indistinct hum of the shore came floating over the waters. I remained upon deck the greater part of the night, listening to the distant and dying sounds, which seemed like farewell voices from the land, until they gradually sank into silence, and nothing was heard but the low ripple of the waves around the prow of our ship, as she glided almost imperceptibly onwards. Next morning, we had lost sight of land – and the world of waters was around us.[3]

This month-long voyage was, Malcolm believed,

> a sufficient time to give one some idea of the sameness of a sea life. During the greater part of that period, its varieties consisted of contrary winds, light airs, dead calms, and two or three smart gales from the wrong quarters . . . The first part of our voyage, however, was the most unpleasant, as we were for about three weeks without sight of land in the Bay of Biscay. During the calm summer evenings, I used to sit upon deck for hours together, watching the long array of ships spreading their white wings over the ocean.[4]

In 1807 Seaman George Watson likewise commented on the monotony of a convoy when he was on a three-month voyage in a transport ship with troops sailing from Spithead to attempt to rescue the disastrous military expedition to South America:

in the fleet were about 10,000 men, there were about fifty sail of us in all ... Little occurred the first two or three weeks of our voyage worth relating, as there is so much sameness at sea in a fleet, the same ships appear every day, and seem so stationary around you, that if you did not feel the change by your approach to the sun, or the want of some useful commodity you would imagine yourself still where you were when you started.[5]

In February 1812 Seaman Henry Walsh was with HMS *Ulysses* when they received orders to accompany a merchant convoy from the Downs to the Baltic, a potentially dangerous destination owing to the changeable weather and narrow sea channels. They remained in the Baltic so as to escort convoys into and out of the narrow waterway called the Belt. Although the Danish fleet was destroyed at Copenhagen in 1807, smaller vessels still posed a threat, and so British warships were needed to maintain trade to and from Britain. By July Walsh was at Rostock in northern Germany, where, he said,

our admiral immediately ordered us to unmast and sail with the convoy through the Belt and protect them from Danish gun boats and privateers which is very numerous in this place. This is a very difficult place to preserve a convoy in calm weather from these privateers and gun boats for they can row those large gun boats and privateers any place they wish, and our large ships cannot get at them. This Belt is only 4 miles in breadth and narrower in many places and the enemy's shore on each side, as the belt runs right through Denmark. They made many attempts to take some of our convoy but never could complete the design.[6]

It was not always enemy ships but weather that played havoc with convoys. Walsh related that towards the end of October they were at Carlscrona, where

our admiral ordered our captain to take charge of 120 sail of merchant ships in company with H.M. ship *Antelope*, along with other manawar

brigs, and sail immediately for Gothenburg . . . The weather became very
stormy and daily increased, which gave us wonderful trouble with our
convoy, but after repeated trouble we brought them safe through the
Belt. After we got clear of the Belt we stood our course for Gothenburg.
But the tempest increased almost beyond expression so we were unable to
carry any sail whatever. Our convoy was greatly scattered and all appeared
to be in great distress. Many had suffered very much on their masts and
sails . . . We were obliged to make more sail and haul our wind so as to lay
into Wingo Sound. I then saw many merchant ships in great distress, and
particularly one which drove upon a rock and was instantly dashed to
pieces and all her crew perished before my eyes. I was informed that 12 sail
of merchant ships was wrecked in this cruel harbour the day before we
came in.[7]

It was much more popular among the crew for a ship to be sent
on a cruise to intercept enemy shipping, particularly to places where
many merchant ships might be captured, thereby earning large
amounts of prize-money. Nowadays the term 'patrol' would be
employed, as 'cruising' has become associated with the holiday
trade. For naval officers a tension existed between their desire for
promotion, honour and glory and their need for spoils of war – a
tension that, in most cases, was not shared by the seamen and
marines who they commanded. Although merchant ships, privateers and naval ships were legitimate targets, sailors hoped above all
to capture merchant vessels with expensive cargoes that offered the
prospect of reasonable prize-money, preferably in return for mini-
mal risk and few casualties. In various parts of the world, because of
the volume of traffic, this was easily achieved, and the seas around
the West Indian islands were renowned for the opportunity of capturing prizes. In April 1799 the frigate *Lapwing*, off the coast of
Barbuda, saw a ship and gave chase, as Aaron Thomas recorded in
his journal:

Continued the chase until night, and then lost sight of the chase. At
a ¼ past 10pm saw the chase about a mile distant, on our lee bow.
Set all sail and at 11pm found ourselves alongside the chase. Hailed

her; said she was a French Letter of Marque [privateer] schooner from St Bartholomews, bound to Guadaloupe. Out boats, and got prisoners on board. Sent Mr Tildersley and ten men into the prize, which is laden with flour, rice, hams, hats, ten tons of salt fish, dry goods, ladies shoes, beef, pork and sundry other articles. The name of the schooner is *La Amiable*, and had 30 men in her when we took her.[8]

Ultimately, everyone dreamed of fabulously rich treasure ships en route from South America to Spain, and sometimes their wildest dreams came true. The output of the silver mines in Peru was vast, and to save transport costs much of it was refined and turned into coins before being transported to Spain. To spread the risk, these coins were carried in both warships and merchant vessels, in convoy and sometimes alone, so that in the periods when Spain was at war with Britain the interception of any homeward-bound Spanish ship inevitably raised the seamen's hopes. In 1799 the frigates *Naiad*, *Ethalion*, *Triton* and *Alcmene* captured the *Thetis* and *Santa Brigida* in the Bay of Biscay, and these two Spanish prize ships were taken to Plymouth. Because they were carrying coins and valuable merchandise, their capture was newsworthy, as one Plymouth historian chronicled:

The arrival of the *Thetis* and the *San Brigida* [in Plymouth], after their reduction in a running fight, created exceptional interest. Sixty-three waggons were required to transport the treasure from the Dockyard for temporary deposit in the Citadel dungeons; and, when it was removed to the Bank of England, it was escorted through the Pig Market 'in great style' . . . Great was the delight that 'so much treasure, once the property of the enemy, was soon to be in the pockets of our jolly tars.' As the ladies waved their handkerchiefs, the 'honest seamen' reciprocated by cheering. One gentleman, who wanted to know how the dollars were packed, was asked if he would like to smell them; and, upon his naive retort that he would rather taste them, the ready-witted salt pulled a small Spanish coin and a quid of tobacco from his mouth, and, placing both in the civilian's palm, exclaimed: 'By Davy Jones, tasting is better than smelling, so your honour's welcome.'[9]

The treasure was sold to the Bank of England for just over £661,000 – the modern value would exceed £120 million. Even the lowest-ranking seaman's share was more money than he would normally see in a lifetime.

Legally, a prize belonged to the Crown, which allowed it to be sold once it had been judged to be a legitimate ('condemned') prize in a prize court, with the proceeds distributed as a gift to the captors. Ships taken as prizes were supposed to be sent into a friendly port with their cargoes intact, where the value of the prize was officially determined and, eventually, prize-money distributed among the officers and men of the ship, or ships, involved in the capture. Inevitably, in such a system there was plenty of scope for fraud and delayed payments – because of the delays, naval officers frequently employed prize agents to handle the legalities on commission, which of course encouraged more delays and more fraud. Short cuts were often taken, and writing several decades later, Basil Hall looked back wistfully to the time when prizes were not always dealt with strictly according to regulations:

> At some stages of the late war, and under particular circumstances, I believe many enemy's vessels were taken, condemned, and their cargoes shared out, all in the same breath. If there happened to be money on board, it was straightway parcelled out on the capstan-head, and each officer and man got his whack, as they called it, without the tedious intervention of unintelligible legal forms, interminable proctor's bills, and the doubly-cursed agent's percentage.[10]

Such informal proceedings were very familiar to Aaron Thomas. A few days after a prize was sent into port to be valued, he noted that 'This day served out to the ship's company a great quantity of cutlery, such as knives, needles, scissors, buttons, spoons, snuff boxes &c., all of which came out of *La Revanche*, our prize schooner.'[11] Such informality was certainly the experience of William Richardson when cruising off Cuba on board HMS *Prompte* in 1799. He mentioned that they spotted a recently wrecked Spanish merchant ship, whose crew had evidently escaped in panic, leaving behind valuable cargo. The *Prompte's* boats were rowed to the wreck:

We continued all the afternoon in sending away to our ship cordage, canvas etc and even unbent some of her best sails and sent [them], and when that was done liberty was given to plunder. In the Captain's cabin we found a bag with a thousand dollars in it, several boxes of sugars, solid silver spoons and forks etc, with many other valuables, all of which were taken out and placed on the quarter [deck] as they were found, and left under charge until sent to our ship. The men who were searching below no doubt found many valuables in the officers' cabins and people's chests, but little was brought by them to the heap on the quarter deck; cocked hats and laced cloaths were laying about in all directions.[12]

After setting the ship alight, they returned to the *Prompte*, and Richardson was amused at the scene: 'Nothing could exceed the fun and laughs that there was when we got alongside, by the boats' crew being dressed so fantastically; some had on a Spanish officer's laced coat, some large cocked hats, some laced jackets and white frilled shirts and some booted and were metamorphosed that their own messmates hardly knew them.'[13] Despite being able to share in the looting, he complained that they were cheated of their prize-money: 'The plate was sold and with the dollars gave me seventeen for my share, but the sails and cordage were left with the agents for a public market and I never got a penny for them.'[14]

For many officers and men it was mainly the dream of capturing a very rich prize that made life bearable, and the letters of seamen and officers alike are littered with mentions of prize-money paid, or calculations of prize-money expected from recent captures. Few if any of the men saw a clash between the constant search for prizes and the need to maintain a warship as an effective fighting machine. When Midshipman George Allen first joined the navy, his ship HMS *Imogene* was cruising the North Sea, and from the outset he was absorbed by the prospect of prizes. Writing to his mother in August 1806 he informed her that 'We have detained a Galliott under Danish colours, with Dutch papers on board, and the trial is now going on whether or no she will be condemned; we have great expectations that she will be a lawful prize – if she is I will get about £30 for her as my share.'[15]

In another letter written from the Mediterranean at the end of 1808, Allen happily reported that 'we are destined I believe for a cruize off Corfu, a small island in the entrance of the Adriatic Ocean with a very good harbour, and the rendezvous of a vast number of French privateers and merchant vessels, so that we have every prospect of making prize money'.[16] Two years later he expressed his concern to his brother William that he had not been allowed home for more than four years – during which time his father had died. A few months passed, and then on 3 July 1811 Captain William Stephens had the painful task of writing to Allen's mother with news of the loss of her son:

> On the 8th of Feby last we captured an enemy's vessel, sixty tons laden with grain from Barletta to the Island of Corfu, in which he was sent a prize master with 5 good men and two prisoners to conduct to Malta. The vessel was in perfect condition in every respect. They kept company with another vessel which had been taken by one of the squadron three days; when a gale of wind coming on, they separated, from which time, sorry am I to say, we have never heard of them . . . There is prize money due to him, which you can recover from Greenwich Hospital, *should you not be blessed by his return.*[17]

Stephens did say there was a faint chance that George had been captured and made a prisoner-of-war – but it was not to be. Like so many others, his vessel had been overwhelmed by the weather and disappeared.

Apart from capturing or destroying enemy shipping, another vital function for the Royal Navy was to deny access to the sea by blockade – literally, the shutting up of an enemy's harbour or line of coast. The purpose was to keep enemy naval and merchant shipping confined to port and also to employ economic warfare by preventing imports and exports. This was probably the most important work of the war that the Royal Navy did, yet it was generally hated, because it was usually more tiresome than convoy work, with even less chance of capturing rich prizes. Before the Battle of Trafalgar in October 1805, when the British were blockading the Spanish port of Cadiz,

Captain Thomas Fremantle of HMS *Neptune* told his wife that 'here we have no news of any kind, and the very sad sameness makes all days like one day, and as the song says, only for prayer day we never know Sunday, the fact is a sea life under present circumstances, is really a life of misery and ennui'.[18]

Blockade work was also more dangerous than being in a battle, because always sailing close to shore, they were liable to be driven on to rocks in adverse weather. Midshipman Robert Bastard James explained that, 'In former wars, the naval service used to follow the military system of retiring into winter quarters, but the skill of our modern commanders in chief have shown that in the winter season and the most dreadful weather, the blockade was strictly kept up, and braved the elements as well as the weather.'[19]

When Napoleon was exiled to St Helena at the end of the war, his surgeon Barry O'Meara talked to him about the blockades: 'I ventured to say that I thought the French would never make good seamen on account of their impatience and volatility of temper. That especially they would never submit without complaining, as we had done at Toulon, to blockade ports for years together, suffering from the combined effects of bad weather, and of privations of every kind.'[20] Napoleon inevitably disagreed, but had to admit that British seamen were better than French ones.

Rather than sit idly by doing blockade duty, attempts were periodically made to go right into ports and harbours to capture and destroy shipping, as well as coastal defences. Such 'cutting out' operations were usually done at night in the ship's boats in order to approach undetected, in shallow water, using both sails and oars, so they were not reliant solely on wind power. To midshipmen, though, as Archibald Sinclair revealed, the term 'cutting out' had two meanings, 'one of which is a dashing, gallant attack by ships' boats upon anything – forts, ships, nothing came amiss. The other meaning, if not so honorable, was more profitable.'[21] This, he said, involved the two midshipmen's messes relieving each other of special food such as hams, on the grounds that they should have taken better care of it.

True cutting-out operations using ships' boats were risky and mainly relied on volunteers. In July 1809 the British fleet cruising in the Baltic spotted several Russian gunboats and merchant vessels at anchor off the coast of Finland, with guns mounted on the nearby cliffs. Because these gunboats were causing such a nuisance to British shipping, it was decided to undertake a daring night raid using boats from the *Bellerophon*, *Implacable*, *Melpomene* and *Prometheus*. There were seventeen in all, and George King was one of the volunteers from HMS *Melpomene*. He remembered that they had several miles to row before reaching the harbour, where the action began:

> The commodore ordered every boat to lay upon their oars and every man received one gill of rum and a biscuit. At the same time we were cautioned not to hurrah until we saw the first gun boat fire and then five boats immediately to rush upon her. When we had finished our biscuits the commodore pulled into the mouth followed up close by the other boats. After passing about a mile we were hailed by a sentinel on shore but he received no answer. He immediately fired a musket to apprise the gun boats when they instantly fired a thirty two pounder, but not in the direction of the boats as they could not discern us in the dark. We then commenced hurrahing and boarded the firing gun boat and in less than ten minutes some [were] jumping overboard and the others slaughtered. Having no time to lose she was quickly manned and we thence proceeded towards the second.[22]

Unfortunately, boats became entangled in the darkness when approaching the second gunboat, with devastating results:

> When pretty near to her our black cutter in the confusion of boats got jammed between the *Melpomene*'s launch and one of the *Implacable*'s boats right in front of the muzzle of the enemy's gun about ten yards distant, when they let fly. Our loss by this fire was ten killed and wounded . . . The captain's coxswain was close alongside of me. His head was blown clean off his shoulders, part of his head took my hat, and his brains flew all over me. At this boat the commodore was killed. We soon took possession of the second boat whilst the *Bellerophon*'s boat was on the opposite side of the harbour capturing two more boats, and by half past one we had six in our possession. Having sunk one we now got them out in the

middle of the harbour . . . we took as many dead and wounded as we could stow and was ordered to pull out of the harbour while the rest of the boats secured the gun boats and manned the merchants which were laden with pork and brandy.[23]

In this operation, over fifty seamen and officers were killed on the British side, out of 270 volunteers. They then started to row out of the harbour and back to the ships, as King related:

Arriving outside the harbour we met with three gigs with the surgeons in them. They commenced using their tourniquets where it [was] required and dispatched us off to the *Prometheus* sloop of war, which ship we reached about seven o'clock [in the morning], but before we reached her one of the *Implacable*'s men having both his legs off close to his knees was laying down in the bottom of the boat. Being in such misery [he] had got his knife out of his pocket and opened it and was going to cut his belly right athwart but we took the knife from him. He then begged that we would heave him overboard. However, before we reached the sloop he had drawn his last [breath], and when coming alongside, the captain was looking overside and he directly ordered some of his crew to relieve the boat's crew and began to hoist in the dead and wounded. He then called us aft, that was left, and ordered us down below to rest ourselves, sent for the purser's steward, and ordered him to give us immediately, each man, half a pint of rum and as much bread and cheese as we could eat. When we soon commenced upon the grog and in less than an hour some of our chaps were singing one of Dibdin's songs.[24]

Charles Dibdin (1745–1814) was a prolific dramatist and composer of popular songs, many of which were about the men of the navy. The song that King's friends were singing was likely to be something like 'Jack in His Element', the first verse of which ran,

> Bold Jack, the sailor, here I come;
> Pray how d'ye like my nib,
> My trowsers wide, my trampers rum,
> My nab, and flowing jib?

> I sails the sea from end to end,
> And leads a joyous life;
> In ev'ry mess I finds a friend,
> In ev'ry port a wife.[25]

About ten o'clock, King's boat crew returned to the *Melpomene*:

The captain asked us if we could guess at our loss. We said no. He then ordered us a glass of grog each and the purser took us all down to his cabin and gave each of us a tumbler of Hollands gin. I drank it off and went and laid down in my berth under the table and was soon fast asleep and never woke until the hammocks were piped up the following morning, not having been disturbed or called upon to keep any watch the ensuing night.[26]

In coastal waters gunboats, each carrying at least one cannon, were as much a threat to British shipping as the enemy's warships. This was particularly the case when there was little or no wind, so that a stationary warship presented an easy target for boats propelled and manoeuvred by oars. To counter this threat, the boats from British warships often patrolled up and down enemy coasts, looking for anything worth attacking. In late 1812 George Watson was part of the crew of HMS *Eagle* who were involved in boat operations in the Adriatic, and, as he said, 'We had no particular object in view, on leaving the ship, our design was merely to reconnoitre the coast in the morning, and intercept the vessels if we found any trading between Venice and Ancona.'[27] He considered this work much more dangerous than full-scale battles, though his view was probably coloured by being severely injured in one such boat operation: 'I have no hesitation in saying that individual valour is more conspicious in, and more necessary to sustain, such a conflict, which is also severer while it lasts, than any general action . . . I had a boatmate who was in the *Victory* at Trafalgar, and no coward either, who said, (in his way of speaking) he would rather be "in twenty Trafalgars," than in one such combat, as we sustained often in the green barge.'[28]

Some enemy vessels were better armed than anticipated, as in one incident in mid-May 1807 off the south coast of France, near Nice. The *Spartan* frigate under the command of Jahleel Brenton was chasing what seemed to be an unarmed poleacre (merchant ship). When both ships were becalmed, boats from the *Spartan* were rowed the 5-mile distance to capture the vessel. James Bodie recounted what happened:

> I, James Bodie, Quartermaster belonging to H.M. Ship *Spartan* under the command of Capt. Brenton, was sent from the said ship on the 13 May under the command of Lieutenant [Benjamin] Weir, after a large ship inshore. Which, at 10 a.m., we went alongside of her, and when seeing the boat the enemy called to all hands, the same as a British man of war. Which, Mr Weir ordered me to stop for the rest of the boats. Accordingly I did so. The jolly boat and cutter was in sight but a good way off then. The launch came up, and it was agreed among the officers to board her . . . At a distance of pistol shot of her, the fire begun. Which, I steered the boat that Mr Weir was in, and laid him on the starboard quarter, according to his orders. Which, we was under a very hot fire for a considerable time.[29]

Another report described the ensuing disaster:

> The boats of the *Spartan* with the two senior lieutenants, Weir and Williams, and 70 of the best men, pulled alongside in two divisions, and attempted to board her on the bow and quarter with the usual determination and valour of British seamen; but the vessel was defended by a numerous and equally gallant crew . . . The first discharge from their great-guns and musketry laid 63 of our brave fellows low, the first and second lieutenants and 26 men being killed or mortally wounded; seven men only remained unhurt. The few remaining hands conducted the boats back to the ship.[30]

Bodie never made it back to the *Spartan*, because he had already boarded the merchant vessel, as he recounted:

> I jumped in the mizzen chains and went forward without being discovered by anyone. I spiked 4 of the guns on the starboard side with the

ramrod of my pistol. The boats shifting off, I was discovered by a small boy that was coming up the fore hatchway, who called out, *Engles, Engles* [English, English]. Upon which, I was directly attacked by the Capt. and one of the seamen. After some time, I was surrounded by the whole ship's company and being wounded in the back and legs, and seeing my shipmates flee from me, I thought it was best to make them understand that I was a prisoner of war. She proved to be the ship *L'Orient*, Letter of Marque. Mounted 22 guns and had 36 for the crew.[31]

Only when the boats returned to the *Spartan* was it discovered that Bodie was missing, presumed dead:

The deceased men were all laid out on the main deck; the wife of Bodie, a beautiful young woman, flew with a lantern from one to the other in search of her husband, but in vain: all the survivors declared that he had undoubtedly perished; they saw him wounded, and fall between the ship and the boat. The poor woman became delirious, got into the barge on the booms, and taking the place lately occupied by Bodie, could with difficulty be moved from it. A few days, with the soothing kindness of the officers and crew, produced a calm, but settled grief. At Malta a subscription of 80 guineas was made for her, and she was sent to her parents in Ireland. Some weeks elapsed when the *Spartan* spoke a neutral vessel from Nice, and learnt that a poleacre had arrived there, after a severe action with the boats of a frigate; that she had beaten them off, and that when they had left her, a wounded Englishman was discovered holding by the rudder chain; he was instantly taken on board, and after being cured of his wounds, sent off to Verdun.[32]

Until Napoleon completely overturned the rules regarding prisoners-of-war, it was normal for the officers and men to be officially exchanged. The process was fairly rapid for officers, since they did not need to wait for several hundred of them to be exchanged simultaneously, as happened with the seamen. Being gentlemen, they simply gave their word of honour not to serve in the navy until they were deemed officially exchanged. Ordinary seamen were judged unsuitable people for keeping their word of honour, even in revolutionary

France, so they were held prisoner until they could be physically exchanged for the equivalent number of prisoners, a process that could drag on.

George Mackay was taken prisoner when he was a fifteen-year-old servant on board the *Scout* sloop. He was rated as a first-class boy and had been at sea for two years. In August 1794 the *Scout* was accompanying a convoy off Algeria when they were taken by two French frigates. Mackay thought that the *Scout*'s seamen were too intent on trying to hide their prize-money to put up a fight, 'with the exception of a few who, like true British tars, finding they were in the hands of the enemy, broke open the spirit-room and in a few minutes totally forgot the situation'.[33] The ships took several days to reach Toulon, from where the captured men began a march of over a hundred miles northwards to their prison, or depot, at Gap, but Mackay said that after a few days, 'my feet, unaccustomed to a series of travelling, were severely blistered'.[34] At the town of Gap they were allowed to roam at will until dark, and money was sent to them by the prize agent at Leghorn (now Livorno) in Italy. Mackay was fortunate in being able to speak French, and after being a prisoner-of-war for nearly a year, he tried twice to escape but was caught both times.

'In the following year, (1796),' Mackay related, 'finding that we were not likely to be soon exchanged, I prepared myself for another effort to regain my liberty.'[35] This time he travelled as far as Paris, before he was again apprehended, taken back to Gap and thrown into prison for thirty days, 'and to my further mortification, I learned that the crew of the *Scout* had been exchanged by cartel, during my absence'.[36] Having missed his opportunity to be exchanged, Mackay instead obtained a passport to return to Toulon, 'where it was supposed I would embark on board of a cartel. On my arrival . . . I was given to understand that there was no cartel appointed, and that I must await the recovery of some other prisoners in order to embark with them at a future period.'[37] Mackay subsequently fell in love with a French girl of fourteen, but she died soon after of smallpox, and he himself became very ill and depressed. He remained in hospital until spring 1798, when 'despairing of ever obtaining my freedom by exchange, I petitioned the Commissary at War to allow me to return

to the Interior, where I would enjoy a greater extent of liberty'.[38]
Eventually, Mackay escaped via Switzerland and Germany, and at
Cuxhaven he boarded the packet boat to Yarmouth – where he fell
straight into the arms of the press-gang, was forced back into the
navy and sent to the West Indies.

The year Mackay escaped, 1798, a parliamentary report was published on the treatment of French prisoners-of-war confined in
England and of British captives held in French prisons following
the outbreak of war five years before. This was a time of heightened
emotions because two years earlier Captain Sir Sidney Smith had
been captured and kept in the Temple prison in Paris, instead of
being released as an officer – in April 1798 he made a dramatic escape
back to England. The report complained that the British had released
many French prisoners-of-war, but that the French were behaving
dishonourably and not fulfilling their side of the agreement – they
owed 2995 men. Further treachery was uncovered, because

> every effort was made to induce the British seamen to go on board the
> French fleet, particularly at the times of the expedition against Ireland . . .
> All efforts were used to inveigle them; they were frequently threatened to
> be starved, and at other times, liquor was given to them, and advantage
> was taken of them when in a state of intoxication . . . Three or four hun-
> dred were debauched into the scheme, under the expectation of being sent
> home for exchange.[39]

James Colnett was captain of the *Hussar* frigate that was wrecked
on the north coast of Brittany on 24 December 1796. He and his crew
became prisoners-of-war, and although Colnett as an officer was
eventually exchanged, in his evidence to the parliamentary commit-
tee he was critical of his treatment:

> After we escaped from the wreck, and surrendered ourselves to the mil-
> itary, we were pillaged by them of everything but what was on our
> backs. We were five days on our march to Brest, on foot, during which
> time we had only a small quantity of bread given us one day, no other
> lodging than wet straw in a church was procured for us, unless we could

pay for it. After our arrival at Brest, we were confined in the Common Gaol at Pontanezan; for the first two days fed with nothing but the common prisoners rations, which were parts of a bullock cut up by the lump, liver, lights, offal, and part of the horn with the jaw. After being let out of the gaol, a larger quantity of provisions was allowed the officers, but of the same quality. After remaining some time at Pontanezan, where a very small part of my effects was returned to me, we were forced to go on parole a hundred miles from Brest to Pontavie, and were obliged to pay our own expences, as well as those of the soldier who had the care of us. The whole time of our stay at Pontavie, we had no more than the French common soldier's rations, and even the worst part of the meat, and no wood to cook the victuals. When our release was ordered, we were marched back in the same way, paying our own expences; but finally some wood was procured, for which we signed receipts.[40]

On being asked if he knew of any steps to entice the British seamen to join the French Navy, he replied: 'Not personally, but from my own crew, of whose veracity I had no doubt. Several of them applied to me for my consent, rather than be starved in prison, as they were threatened to be, which I positively refused.'[41]

Once war resumed in 1803, after the collapse of the Peace of Amiens, arrangements governing prisoner exchanges were entirely abandoned, with Napoleon only allowing them on rare occasions. Anyone captured early on was doomed to spend the next decade in prison, unless he escaped. It was generally assumed that prisoner exchanges between the two countries would be reinstated, but negotiations between the British and French failed. Most prisoners were destined to be held in French prisons, well away from the sea, until the peace in 1814. According to Napoleon, when speaking to his surgeon Barry O'Meara on St Helena, the captured seamen did not want to return to the Royal Navy: 'Many of your English sailors did not want to be exchanged. They did not wish to be sent again on board of their floating prisons.'[42] There is no evidence to support his claim – surviving records show that the captured seamen suffered immensely, especially from shortage of food and desperate boredom.

They might not want to rejoin the navy, but that prospect was preferable to life as a prisoner in France.

Many of Napoleon's captives were held in fortresses and walled
towns on the eastern side of France, at places such as Arras,
Valenciennes, Givet, Verdun, Sarrelibre and Besançon, or else were
sent as punishment to the dismal penal depot of Bitche, where many
prisoners were kept in dungeons deep underground. These fortified
strongholds were no longer needed to protect France, because the
Revolutionary and Napoleonic armies had pushed the frontier much
further east by invading neighbouring countries. At the time of
Napoleon's first abdication in 1814 over sixteen thousand prisoners
were being held in France, about three-quarters of whom were
sailors. Most had been taken through the actions of French privateers
capturing merchant vessels, or from naval vessels being shipwrecked.

Guarded by gendarmes, the captured seamen were marched from
the ports where they landed to these prisons, with only the officers
having an opportunity to use wheeled transport. Such marches of
several hundred miles could be gruelling, especially for men who
might not have stepped ashore for months, and each night they were
put into secure lodgings, usually the local gaol. In August 1804
sixteen-year-old Midshipman Robert Bastard James was on board
the *Rambler* brig, which was returning to the squadron off Brest after
a stint of blockading Rochefort. They captured two merchant vessels
carrying wine, and James was put in charge of one of the prize vessels,
with orders to sail to England. The prize was poorly equipped, and
terrible weather (plus his men becoming drunk) in the Bay of Biscay
forced them into the mouth of the River Loire and on to rocks. They
were captured and taken by boat to Nantes, then marched some
five hundred miles to prisons on the other side of France. 'Not being
accustomed to walking,' James lamented, 'we were incapable of any
farther than half way to the town, where we were to rest for the night.
The miserable remains of our money the men spent in brandy – and
four of them so drunk that the soldiers were obliged to procure a cart
to take us.'[43] He went on: 'we looked like a set of half starved miserable
wretches, instead of British seamen . . . guards used to exhibit us as
fine specimens of English sailors – in throwing a ridicule on our

wretched appearance – long beards, half famished, no shoes – they forgot they were casting a severe reflection on their own navy, to be so often beat by such miserable looking wretches.'[44]

After a rest of several days, they continued their journey, this time with money given to them by a wealthy English resident: 'My men, as usual, stopped at every public house on the road and were generally drunk before they entered the prison, and I really think that sailors march better drunk, than sober; in one case, they would stagger and roll along, singing and quarrelling, while on the other hand, they would be as sulky as mules, and only go by driving.'[45]

Robert James was taken to Verdun, the prison where military and naval officers were held, on the left bank of the River Meuse. The majority were held on parole, wherever they wished to live, giving their word of honour – *parole d'honneur* – not to escape. There were also detained civilians – *détenus* – at Verdun, many with their wives and children and often lodging in the town. The place was unlike any other prison and developed into a microcosm of English society. James remarked that

> Verdun resembles a small fashionable town in England. The lodgings were good and not extravagant . . . Horses were brought from England, and came through Germany at a most enormous expense – at last there was a very excellent set of horses, and the course was as fashionable and full of roguery as Newmarket. Drinking and smoaking clubs were established in many parts of the town, for all classes, and it was here that the naval youth spent his time, and money.[46]

Captain Jahleel Brenton of HMS *Spartan* had earlier been a prisoner-of-war at Verdun, after his frigate the *Minerve* grounded off Cherbourg harbour in thick fog in July 1803 and the entire crew was captured. When they finally reached Verdun, most of Brenton's crew was sent on to Givet. In October 1806 Brenton became one of the rare prisoners-of-war to be exchanged (for Captain Infernet, captured at the Battle of Trafalgar) and allowed back to England. When James Bodie, Brenton's coxswain from the *Spartan*, was captured in 1807, he was authorised to stay at Verdun because of his connections with Brenton, rather than being transferred to a prison like Givet.

While the loss of liberty for so many years was terrible to bear, life for the officers at Verdun was pleasant enough compared with conditions in many of the other prisons. Lieutenant John Carslake was captured in early 1809 and what vexed him most at Verdun was the difficulty of sending letters. In one letter to his brother-in-law Lieutenant John Yule in March 1811, he complained:

> Every effort which I have used for some months past to get a letter conveyed to you has proved ineffectual. Four have been returned to me and even this scrap stands a poor chance of succeeding. The difficulties of corresponding are great beyond example, but instead of discouraging me, they add to my anxiety and consequently strengthen my perseverance . . . You have fine boys with prospects of an addition to your family! . . . I cannot bear to reflect on the period of seeing them, because that pleasure is reserved for a time so very remote, in that we have so entirely extinguished the idea of returning that [Lieutenant John] Bingham and myself have taken the lease of a house and garden for economy sake, and it is so pleasantly situated that we are become the envy of all our neighbours.[47]

After writing this letter, Carslake and Bingham were to spend another three years as prisoners, until released at the end of the war.

For those petty officers and seamen who were in prison, with no prospect of escape, conditions could be intolerable. John Finny, a carpenter's mate, was pressed into the navy in May 1805, only to be captured a few months later when on board HMS *Dove* which was taking dispatches to Nelson's squadron off Cadiz. He spent the rest of the war in prison, initially at Arras, until his release in 1814. In November 1806 he wrote in despair: 'During the course of this summer, we experienced all the hardships of captivity, having no subsistence from our native country, but was all along flattered with hopes of getting clear by peace, or a general exchange. This continued for some months but alas, to our mortification, instead of a general release our correspondence with England was shut up in consequence of which our enemies now showed themselves in their true colours.'[48]

Thomas Williams, a merchant seaman from St Ives in Cornwall, was held at Givet prison from April 1804 and described the food that was given to them:

> Our provisions from the French were very mean indeed. We had one pound of brown bread, half a pound of beef (said to be beef, but which consisted of heads, liver, lights, and other offal of the bullock, and that not very fat), a little salt, and about a noggin of peas or calavances, which were served to us every four days, and three farthings in money paid once a week; but they would deduct a certain portion from each person for the repairs of the prison, etc . . . You can easily picture to yourself the state of society in such a place without any restraint. Captain Jahleel Brenton, of the H.M.S. *Le Minerve*, laid down certain rules for the Commandant of the depot to observe with respect to the prisoners before he left our depot for Verdun as to spirits, beer, etc, which was strictly adhered to, as far as could be done in a direct way.[49]

Despite Brenton's strictures, Williams admitted that the naval seamen continued to get drunk as normal: 'the old men-of-war's men found out many inventions. Smuggling was carried on in every possible way, and you can easily guess what followed.'[50]

Conditions in prisons depended very much on local circumstances, such as the gaoler in charge and the wealth of individual prisoners, and from Verdun Captain Brenton helped to improve the conditions of the ordinary seamen. For poorer prisoners, some money was handed out by relief funds administered by charities, like the Lloyd's Patriotic Fund in London, but constant complaints were heard that the money was not finding its way to the needy. Six years after the end of the war, Midshipman Robert James complained bitterly that many people received allowances who were not eligible:

> There was a committee established at Verdun, for the management of the monies, arising from the numerous subscriptions all over England, Ireland, Scotland, for the relief of the prisoners in general, but instead of its being vested in the hands of the naval and military senior officers, it was in the hands of hostages [imprisoned civilians] and distributed among a set of rascals who never dared show their faces in their native land again, for fear of the gallows. One fellow received two guineas per

month, a noted highwayman, whose arm had been broke by a gentleman whom he wanted to rob – and escaped . . . by flight to the Continent.[51]

The Reverend Robert Wolfe was appointed chaplain to all British prisoners-of-war in France and decided to base himself at Givet:

I found the depôt in the most deplorable state. Both in a moral and phys-ical point of view, it would be difficult to conceive any thing more degraded and miserable . . . So great was their distress, at that moment, that, unable to satisfy the craving of hunger, they were seen to pick up the potato peel-ings, that were thrown out into the court, and devour them . . . The little money that was received by the prisoners, instead of being applied to the relief of their wants, and to make them more comfortable in food and clothing, was spent in riot and excess. On these occasions, sailors are, of all other men, most ready to communicate, and never think of to-morrow.[52]

Along with hunger, sickness was dreaded. John Robertson, a seaman from King's Lynn, was held at Arras prison from late 1806 and saw many fall sick: 'A great number of poor fellows are daily carried to the hospital, from 20 to 30 and sometimes 40 of a day; the complaints is fevers, viz the spotted fever, the putrid fever, and the fever and ague, and many others. Complaints brought on by long imprisonment and bad living.'[53] John Finny was also at Arras and wrote of men falling ill all the time. In February 1806, a few months after his capture, he too fell sick:

This day we had an exceeding heavy gale of wind and snow, the deep-est that any of the oldest inhabitants can remember, and several of them were smothered in the snow. I was carried to the hospital this day very bad with the fever and was almost starved with the cold. The storm being begun before I left the Citadel I had about three quarters of a mile to go, the four men that carried me on the barrow was very much fatigued with me, as it blowed and snowed so excessive hard.[54]

Towards the end of the war, Midshipman James was moved to Sarrelibre prison, which he hated more than Bitche, where he had earlier been sent as punishment. He particularly disliked having to share rooms with colliers from Tyneside, whom he regarded as his social inferiors, while the colliers in turn loathed Captain Brenton whom they blamed for ranking them too low – on a par with mere midshipmen. James described his situation:

> This depôt was for fifteen hundred prisoners, chiefly seamen . . . The rooms in which we were confined were about twenty feet square . . . here I was with another midshipman, shut up with a set of coal heavers, mates of Colliers . . . The Navy was every thing that was bad. The Midshipmen a set of trash. And that fellow Brenton was no better, to rate captains and mates of merchantmen with them. Their conversation dwelt chiefly on coals; canny lads; and brigs with pink sterns.[55]

James objected that the French at Sarrelibre gave them insufficient supplies: 'The cloathing was withheld so that the poor fellows used to stalk about in a blanket.'[56] John Tregerthen Short, from St Ives, was captured with his cousin Thomas Williams just a few weeks after the crew of Captain Brenton's *Minerve*, and he was held at Givet with them. According to Short, 'We were paid tenpence per man by Bradshaw, a big rascal, clerk to the Captain of *La Minerve* frigate; this was allowed us by English Lloyds.'[57]

Even though they had the opportunity, British officers could not escape unless their parole was withdrawn through some misdemeanour, because their word of honour was so binding. If any officer dared escape while on parole, he risked being dismissed from the navy and treated like a social outcast. Midshipman Edward Boys, held at Verdun, described the parole conditions:

> Prisoners on their arrival at Verdun were invariably conducted to the citadel, when their names, age, birth place, profession, and description were entered in a book. They were then obliged to sign a paper, promising upon honour to conform to the regulations of the depôt, and not to escape, if permitted to reside in the town. A direct violation of this engagement was so unreservedly condemned by all classes, that during the five first years of the war, I recollect but three who so disgraced their country.[58]

Most prisoners were not officers and were therefore not held on parole, which gave them the freedom to attempt to escape. Throughout the course of the war, only a few hundred prisoners managed to do so, and most of these were midshipmen who had forfeited their parole. It was easier for those who had access to money and who knew the French language or were able to learn it – which excluded most of the seamen. Escape attempts were something new, despite the experiences of George Mackay, because it was an accepted practice of war that, in time, all prisoners would be exchanged. What helped many escaping prisoners in the police state of France was that they were able to pass themselves off as conscripts for the French army. This explained both their wretched appearance and strange accent, as the conscripts were drawn from way beyond the traditional borders of France. Their escape routes were various, some heading off to northern France and the Netherlands, while others went into Germany, Austria and Italy. Thomas Williams wrote of one escape from Givet: 'There happened to be five midshipmen of the English Navy who had broken their parole at Verdun for the express purpose of being sent to a confined depot in order to desert. I had the pleasure of seeing them go over the railings of the prison, some of them dressed in women's clothes with a basket of potatoes on their backs, as was the custom of the women who came to the prison gate to sell.'[59] Williams himself escaped from Givet and reached Ostend where he was recaptured, but happily learned that the midshipmen had all reached England.

Informers were an especial threat – at Verdun alone there were at least fifty. Two midshipmen, William Heywood and James Gale, escaped from Givet in 1808 and hid in a cave, but an informer (apparently their own servant, a marine by the name of Wilson) revealed their hiding place. The guards

went direct to the mouth of the cave where they were concealed. They were ordered to come forward and surrender, which they immediately did, when the first gendarme, with his sabre, cut Mr. Haywood [Heywood] to the ground, and again plunged the sword into poor Haywood's body until life was extinct, Mr. Gale being also severely wounded; but they spared his life, and he afterwards recovered. The information as to their whereabouts was given by a marine named Wilson, belonging to H.M. frigate *La Minerve*, who had lost one of his legs in the service, for which he was sure of a pension for life.[60]

It appalled Edward Boys that Heywood's body 'was afterwards taken into the prison-yard, stripped naked, and exposed to the view of the prisoners, for the purpose of intimidating others from the like attempt'.[61] Midshipman Edward Boys had been a prisoner since 1803, and after he was moved from Verdun to Valenciennes and his parole withdrawn, he became desperate to escape: 'Parole had, hitherto, tended, in some measure, to reconcile me to captivity, but being now deprived of that honourable confidence . . . no obstacle could avert my intention of finally executing, what I now felt a duty.'[62] Eventually he was successful in his escape bid.

Many midshipmen thought that they could not really be considered as on parole, because they had to muster twice a day at Verdun, and after hearing a rumour that they would be moved to Sarrelibre, Midshipman Robert James and Assistant Surgeon William Porteous decided to escape from Verdun. They reached Ulm but were discovered and taken in irons to Bitche in bitterly cold weather. James found the prison as bad as he expected, being forced to live underground:

> The souterrains were kept as clean as the situation would admit of but it was so infested with rats that they would appear in droves and destroy all our cloathing and provisions. We were obliged to burn candles all day. The little light came from the windows [and] was never sufficient to read by. In the forenoon we were allowed two hours to breathe fresh air on deck [the courtyard] and the same in the afternoon. It was in this infernal place many a youth became the victim of all kinds of vices. Drinking raw spirits, gambling and smoking were a continual repetition – and generally ended in boxing matches. The place was so humid that our blankets looked as if a heavy dew had fallen on them [and] consequently ended in giving the strongest constitution rheumatisms for life, and the weak ones became cripples.[63]

James added: 'The Frenchman may say what he pleases against the prison ships [hulks] in England, but the worst of them was a palace compared with the Fort of Bitche.'[64] To John Robertson at Arras prison, it was folly to try to escape. At the end of 1808 he recorded:

> Sent off for Bitche this morning two people for desertion [escaping] . . . and in the evening two more deserters were brought back, and close confined. I am much astonished to see so many people deserting when they have so many sad proofs of an impossibility of effecting their escape, and daily being brought back, and adds sorrow to sorrow, till their troubles are really past bearing . . . We may say that Liberty is sweet, so it is, but it is dear buying it at the hazard of our lives.[65]

Midshipman James related one attempted escape from Bitche:

> Two clever fellows formerly belonging to the *Minerve*, Capt. Brenton, of the names of Cox and Marshall, one was a carpenter, the other a blacksmith. They undertook to open the strong doors and liberate all their fellow prisoners . . . Nine o'clock was the hour to start. Rendezvous were given, and these fine fellows Cox and Marshall were to lead the way. The lights were put out, silence was observed by everyone as they proceeded. About half way in a long, narrow passage, Cox heard some person endeavoring to stifle a cough just before him. He asked Marshall if he did not hear some noise. Shortly after some person touched Cox on the arm. He asked Marshall if it was him. No, says he, Damme get on, don't be afraid. At that moment Cox dropt dead at his feet, a sword had gone through his heart.[66]

French soldiers had been alerted to the escape attempt by spies among the prisoners and were lying in wait. Marshall was also killed, and many of the other prisoners seriously wounded. The next day, James related, 'The bodies of Cox and Marshall were brought into the court yard naked and mutilated as they were, and placed as a spectacle as well as an example to the rest.'[67]

On board the *Minerve*, William Cox had his son with him, too young to be rated a boy. He had previously tried to escape from

Givet with his son, then about five years old, but had been caught and sent to Bitche. On the death of his father, the young boy was sent to Verdun, and actually tried to escape: '[He] was one of four venturous little boys who descended one of the angles of the citadel of Verdun, without a rope: they were taken about five leagues distant, brought back, and whipped for their temerity.'[68]

Despite the informers, there were always officers willing to risk assisting escape attempts, provided that they did not involve breaking parole. Lieutenant George Jackson was taken to Verdun but was actually refused parole as he had tried to escape on the march there, and so he had no qualms about continuing his escape attempts. In the end, he was sent to Bitche and through sheer bravado became one of the few prisoners to succeed in getting out of the impregnable fortress. In December 1812 he made his way to Verdun with his companion, an army officer, who decided to stay in hiding there and not continue to England. This was very awkward, but, Jackson recorded, 'I found a new friend in J. Carslake, who was a perfect stranger to me. He was a Lieutenant in the Navy, and he procured for me a passport as a Swiss clockmaker. Furthermore, he made arrangements with a man to take me a certain distance from Verdun.'[69] This was John Carslake who had leased a house the previous year with his friend John Bingham, being convinced that they would be prisoners for a long time.

Some seamen and officers continued to join the French Navy as a means of escaping prison. When Midshipman James and his drunken seamen (who most likely had been pressed a few months earlier) were shipwrecked on the French shore, James mentioned that 'their insolence to me was beyond bearing. They exulted in the idea of being made prisoners and snapped their fingers at me, saying that on shore Jack was as good as his master.'[70] They tried to join the French Navy, provoking James to fury: 'And as for you, Traitors that you are, and undeserving the name of Britons, can you hesitate between honor and infamy? Return back with me to your prison, and . . . show yourselves worthy of a country like England.'[71]

At Givet prison, Thomas Williams said that when the French

army was in Spain, they were so desperate for troops that prisoners-of-war were recruited: 'They sent officers to each depot of prisoners to recruit men to form an Irish brigade. Accordingly . . . any men who would say they were Irish might go, not regarding what nation they really belonged to on the French books, so that in a very few days, such was the desire to get clear of the prison, they enlisted 400 or 500 men from our depot only.'[72] Late in the war, James related, many of Napoleon's troops passed through Verdun, including the Irish brigade of the French army:

> While I was standing by a coffee-house, two soldiers, one a sergeant, came up to me and asked me how I did. I did not recognise them at first on account of the dress and mustachios. I was too soon convinced they were two of my own men, and because I would not go into the coffee room and drink with them, they loaded me with a deal of abuse. I got away from them, nor did I go out until the regiment was gone. There were also three midshipmen in their service, two of them enlisted at Givet and the other at Bitche!! I have learned since that one of them is now a lieutenant in our own naval service!!!'[73]

A good number of prisoners-of-war never made it back to Britain but died either during escape attempts or in prison itself. At Arras, John Robertson recorded, 'There is only one burying ground belonging to the prison where all is buried, the inhabitants as well as the prisoners without any distinction to sorts of religion . . . it stands a full mile from the town. At the entrance of the ground stands a mount, about sixteen feet high in the imitation of Mount Calvary; and on that is erected a Cross.'[74] George Jackson's family thought he was dead, not realising that he had been captured, and he was one of the few to make a successful escape across the Channel. The day after his arrival at Portsmouth, his brother Caleb was brought to him: 'My brother was greatly affected at this unexpected meeting. He had been summoned by the Flag Lieutenant that morning to appear at the Admiral's office, without being informed for what purpose . . . He had considered me dead long since.'[75] Many others were not so lucky – John Short compiled a list of the deceased at Givet from 1804 until the prisoners' release in 1814, and he reckoned that over three hundred men died there alone, while John Finny at Arras said that 'In the three years and six months we have been in this place there is about six hundred deaths which is a great number in the time.'[76]

Map of Italy, Corsica, Sardinia, Sicily and Malta

EIGHT

————— ◆ —————

INTO BATTLE

We had a most bloody action which lasted from 7 o'clock in the morning till ¼ after 6 at night; however, we knocked all their fleet to atoms almost, and we can boldly venture to say [so] far as the best day that old England ever saw.

Midshipman William Spry on the Battle of the Saintes
on 12 April 1782[1]

Off Chesapeake Bay one cold February morning in 1813, during the war with America, Marine Captain Wybourn was extremely aggravated when the normal routine was thrown into confusion by Vice-Admiral Warren's decision to practise clearing the ship for battle:

> The Admiral suddenly gave orders to clear for action, and all cabins were knocked down, and as great preparation made for fighting as if an enemy had actually been in view. A general exercise took place, and several firing with shots, broadsides of ammunition being ridiculously thrown away. The Admiral says it puts everything in place for real service, but all we have done is to render every officer uncomfortable at a cold, miserable season, for the Chesapeake is colder than England, and nothing but canvas screens to keep out frost and snow, while his own cabin is closed, well-carpeted and a large fire. This put us all out of humour, and dinner not ready till 5 o'clock, the cooks being fighting, and the fire out.[2]

Apart from experience gained from capturing prizes, some of which

put up a determined resistance, efficiency was maintained with training, drills and exercises, though some captains prepared their crews
better than others. Such 'clearing for action' was rarely practised,
since it involved a complete transformation of a warship in readiness
for fighting, much to Wybourn's discomfort.

As soon as one or more strange ships were seen, they were generally hoped to be enemy vessels, with a chance of an easy capture and
prize-money. According to Samuel Leech, when HMS *Macedonian*
spotted the American ship USS *United States* in October 1812, 'a
whisper ran along the crew that the stranger ship was a Yankee
frigate. The thought was confirmed by the command of "All hands
clear the ship for action, ahoy!" The drum and fife beat to quarters;
bulk-heads were knocked away; the guns were released from their
confinement; the whole dread paraphernalia of battle was produced; and after the lapse of a few minutes of hurry and confusion,
every man and boy was at his post.'[3] He added that after the ship
was cleared for action in this way, 'a few of the junior midshipmen
were stationed below, on the berth deck, with orders, given in our
hearing, to shoot any man who attempted to run from his quarters'.[4] A few years earlier the seaman Robert Wilson, on board the
frigate *Unité* in the Adriatic, mentioned how they were called to
action: 'At 9 in the morning, it being very hazy and a perfect calm,
we perceived a number of gunboats close to us, and making for us
with their sweeps [long oars]. The drum was immediately beat,
and every man repaired to his quarters and cleared away for
action.'[5]

In such circumstances, the men invariably pulled together and
demonstrated immense cheerfulness and bravery. According to
Midshipman William Dillon, when Lord Howe gave his squadron
the signal to prepare for battle just before the Glorious First of June
in 1794,

> a state of excitement was manifested totally beyond my powers of
> description. No one thought of anything else than to exert himself to his
> utmost ability in overcoming the enemy. It was also very satisfactory to
> observe the change of disposition in the ship's company of the *Defence*.

All animation and alacrity pervaded these men: no more sulky looks. The enemy was near, and all hands were determined to support their Captain. The ships when near each other were cheered by their crews in succession. Death or Victory was evidently the prevailing feeling.[6]

Similarly at Trafalgar, just as the *Victory* was about to clash with the French, Marine James Bagley said 'about 12 o'clock we gave 3 cheers and then the engagement began very hot on both sides'.[7] It was a common feature of Royal Navy crews especially to cheer – or huzzah – as they went into battle. 'It is a *disputed point*, whether cheering should be allowed,' Midshipman George Elliot commented. 'I say decidedly yes. No other nation can cheer. It encourages us and disheartens the enemy. I still distinctly recollect the stirring feelings of these men's cheers.'[8]

After the Battle of Trafalgar Midshipman Edward Polwhele of the *Tonnant* wrote to his father, at Helston in Cornwall, in admiration of the cheering men:

I leave you to guess what must be the feelings, the resolution, of a person in the capacity of an officer, when he hears men (as I heard) on their way to the surgeon, one in particular, with all his bowels hanging out, encouraging his gunmates, and huzzaing along the decks as he passed below. The only thing that affected me was some of my messmates wishing me well and shaking hands, which was a sort of thing I thought . . . might be dispensed with, as it only tended to cloud and not exhilarate the spirits.[9]

Seeing a potential enemy and raising an alarm could occur at any time, something Midshipman James Scott discovered on the first occasion he heard the signal to prepare for battle:

For the first time my slumbers were invaded by the sound of the hollow drum beating to quarters. My eyes were scarcely unclosed, when I heard the hurried cry of 'Turn out – turn out!' 'Bear a hand there, – move up, men!' At the same time another mid . . . getting under my hammock, nearly capsized me, roaring in my ears, 'Turn out! don't you know an

enemy is nearly alongside?' The bustle between decks, and the anxiety of
every one to ascend the ladder, produced something like a certainty in my
mind that we were about to have a brush with Johnny Crapaud [the
French], and it was confirmed by the flash and dinning report of one of our
main-deck guns at the moment of my stepping over the coamings of the
hatchway. The hurry and bustle of the scene gave me no time for reflection
until I got on the main-deck, where, all bearing evidence of hostile preparation, I began to have some idea that actual fighting was no joke.[10]

The vessel proved to be an English merchantman, but Scott had
gained valuable experience: 'This false alarm was of some advantage to
me, for I experienced all the serious feelings that would have attended
me, had a conflict actually taken place, and I felt a confidence (hitherto doubtful,) that I should do my duty when called upon.'[11]

Once orders were given to clear for action, preparations were much
the same for a fight against a single ship as for a full-scale battle. The
aim was to get everything ready for firing the cannons, as well as to
reduce the effects of damage from incoming shot. On the upper
decks the men's tightly rolled hammocks were lashed into netting
above the sides of the ship to provide protection from missiles, and
on the open decks netting was rigged as an obstacle to boarders and
spread above the main deck to try to prevent debris from falling on
the men. Midshipman Dillon said that while they were chasing the
French, 'a splinter netting was fitted over the quarter deck to receive
the [pulley] blocks that might be shot away aloft, and a cask of water
was hoisted into the main top, to be prepared for fire'.[12] When part of
a mast was shot away in battle, the wood, sails and rigging raining
down on the men below could have a combined weight of many tons.
This netting would not hold such a lethal weight, which formed a
heavy, tangled obstacle that had to be cleared from the deck. Instead,
iron chains were fixed between the masts and the yards, to stop the
yards and sails falling if the rigging was shot away.

On those decks above the water-line, the bulkheads were removed,
along with any other partitions, to provide the maximum amount of
room to load and fire the guns, as well as give an unobstructed view
of each gun deck. This meant that the captain and officers lost their

cabins for the duration of the battle (or the exercise, as Wybourn complained). Any other obstructions, such as the officers' furniture, and chests, boxes and bags containing the belongings of the seamen, were also removed, either to the hold or into boats that were lowered and towed behind the ship, so as to avoid the hazard of them being smashed into splinters by cannonballs. Anything else at risk of producing splinters was also removed, such as animal pens and cages. Items were simply thrown overboard if there was no time to stow them out of the way, as William Richardson described on one occasion off Brest: 'We saw the enemy's fleet in the outer roads at anchor, all ready for a start to sea; and it falling little wind we in the evening brought our fleet to anchor. As an engagement was expected to take place next morning, every ship prepared for battle; the ocean was soon covered with tubs, stools, and other lumber thrown overboard to be clear of the guns.'[13]

Even during the slow approach to the enemy at Trafalgar much was jettisoned while the ships cleared for action, and Captain Harwood of HMS *Belleisle* noted in his journal: 'Made all sail, bearing down on the enemy. Threw overboard unavoidably, in clearing for action, butts in packs 7. Ditto., cut for grog and topsail halliard tubs, 2. Ditto., cut for cook's tubs, 3. Puncheons and harness casks, 2; some beef and pork in harness tubs, iron hoops, 6 parcels, 10 in each; biscuit bags from the different berths, 90 in number.'[14] It was not uncommon after a battle for an officer or seaman to find that he only had left the clothes he was wearing because his box or bag of personal items had been discarded.

Animals were shifted from the ship because they were otherwise likely to add to the confusion. Goats, sheep, chickens, pigs and even cows were stowed in the boats towed behind the warships, but if time was short, the animals might be thrown overboard to fend for themselves. At the Battle of the Nile, when the British fleet sailed straight into the attack as soon as the French ships were sighted, the logbook of HMS *Zealous* records, 'Cleared ship for action, and hove overboard ten bullocks.'[15]

While animals thrown overboard inevitably drowned, those on board or towed behind in the boats were as likely to be wounded or killed in battle as the seamen. Major Thomas Oldfield of the marines told his sister that on board the *Theseus* during the Battle of the Nile, 'Beatty and myself had one shot which knocked the plank from under us. Most of our poultry were killed, and the arm-chests beat to pieces.'[16] James Gardner recalled a running fight to protect a convoy off the coast of Spain in 1782. He was in the *Panther*, which was not expected to take part in the fighting, and so they had not dealt with the animals beforehand. Gardner was near a midshipman who was struck in the leg by a cannonball: 'It was a spent shot that killed him, and weighed 28 pounds, and what was remarkable, it took off at the same time the leg of a pig in the sty under the forecastle.'[17] Livestock were at times kept in the larger ship's boats, which served as ready-made pens, and Gardner said that the sheep were still in one boat on the upper deck, in a very exposed position:

> One of our poor fellows was cut in two by a double-headed shot on the main deck, and the lining of his stomach (about the size of a pancake) stuck on the side of the launch, which was stowed amidships on the main deck with the sheep inside. The butcher who had the care of them, observing what was on the side of the boat, began to scrape it off with his nails, saying, 'Who the devil would have thought the fellow's paunch would have stuck so? I'm damned if I don't think it's glued on!'[18]

Waiting for a battle to start was a nerve-racking time for everyone, especially for first-timers. Marine Lieutenant Samuel Ellis of the *Ajax* at Trafalgar commented on how the seamen prepared for battle as they approached the enemy line:

> I was sent below with orders, and was much struck with the preparations made by the bluejackets, the majority of whom were stripped to the waist; a handkerchief was tightly bound round their heads and over the ears, to deaden the noise of the cannon, many men being deaf for days after an action. The men were variously occupied; some were sharpening their cutlasses, others polishing the guns, as though an inspection were about to take place instead of a mortal combat, whilst three or four, as if

in mere bravado, were dancing a horn-pipe; but all seemed deeply anxious to come to close-quarters with the enemy.[19]

After suffering a false alarm, Midshipman James Scott admitted that he was still afraid before his first battle:

There are few things to be compared to the interest created by the chase of an enemy, but now that the hubbub was over, and the time was absolutely come when we were to smell powder and feel its effects in right good ernest, no Bang-bang without its tell-tale bullet, I began to consider the possibility of my being minus a leg or an arm before night, even if I was so fortunate as to retain my head upon my shoulders. I confess a comical sensation seized me, and the stillness that reigned as we approached the muzzles of the enemy's guns, was productive of no very consolatory or reassuring cogitations. The interval of suspense, though short, was sufficiently protracted to convince me that fighting, however fascinating *à la distance* to a young and ardent mind, as leading to honour and renown, is quite another affair when brought to that precise minimum of time, that ere the warm blood can pursue its appointed course of action through the mazes of the throbbing heart, the angel of death may have done his work, holding in his grasp some beloved companion or well-known form. The coming conflict then assumes an aspect that must ever appear formidable and awful to a young beginner.[20]

Food was a problem before battles, as the fire in the galley had to be extinguished. At the Battle of the Glorious First of June, they had been preparing to fight for three days, and Midshipman Dillon commented: 'His Lordship [Howe] knew that John Bull did not like fighting with an empty stomach; but it was a sorry meal, scarcely deserving the name. We had not had much time for a fire in the range for cooking since the 28th of last month [May]. All the tables and conveniences were stowed below; all the partitions taken down; nothing to be seen on the decks but powder, shot, ramrods and instruments of destruction.'[21] After Trafalgar, William Pryce Cumby, first lieutenant of the *Bellerophon*, described to his son their battle meal: 'At eleven o'clock finding we should not be in action for an hour or more we piped to dinner which we had ordered to be in readiness for the ship's company at that hour thinking that Englishmen would fight all the better for having a comfortable meal, and at the same time Captain Cooke joined us in partaking of some cold meat &c on the rudder head, all our bulkheads, tables &c being necessarily taken down and carried below.'[22] Also at Trafalgar, the Irish seaman John Brown in the *Victory* said that after Nelson had gone round the decks to encourage everyone, they had a rudimentary meal: 'So we piped to dinner and ate a bit of raw pork and half a pint of wine.'[23]

While it is the large battles between two opposing fleets, such as Trafalgar and the Nile, that are most remembered today, the overwhelming majority of conflicts were on a much smaller scale, quite commonly duels between warships like frigates. The fighting between fleets usually only involved line-of-battle ships, but the number of enemy ships captured and destroyed in these major battles was insignificant compared with the number taken in smaller actions, frequently merchantmen or privateers. The large battles reduced the enemy's capacity for warfare, while the majority of British naval ships destroyed enemy trade, so reducing their capacity for continuing the war and (of much more importance to warship crews) providing prize-money and occasional loot. The number of men involved in individual and large-scale battles varied from around a few hundred to many thousand. At the Battle of the Nile in 1798 just over 8000 men and officers took part on the British side, on board fourteen battleships, while at the Battle of Trafalgar in October 1805, around 17,000 men in twenty-seven battleships were on the British side – equivalent to the population of the city of Leicester at the time.

Just before the large-scale battle called the Glorious First of June, William Dillon watched the two fleets drawing closer. 'How shall I describe it?' he wrote. 'A scene of magnificence and importance, not of common occurrence, and not often equalled on the ocean – upwards of 50 sail of the line viewing each other, and preparing to pour out their thunder destructive of the human species, which would decide the fate of either fleet, and probably that of the nation.'[24]

Naval battles were all about firing cannons (guns) and carronades (powerful, large-calibre guns, but with a shorter range). In simple terms, a gunpowder cartridge was exploded inside a cannon, which fired whatever had been rammed down the muzzle on top of it. Solid iron cannonballs – shot – were the main type of missile, and different-sized cannons fired shot of varying weights. A 32-pounder gun, for instance, fired a cannonball weighing 32 pounds, which measured around 6.4 inches diameter. Other missiles could be fired from cannons, even scrap metal. Double-headed shot – two solid lumps of iron linked by a bar or a chain – was fired in order to cripple a ship's rigging and sails. Grape-shot was a collection of iron balls tied up in a canvas bag, and canister comprised a tin filled with musketballs or slightly larger shot. Both these missiles disintegrated on firing, showering the enemy's crew with bullet-like projectiles. On board HMS *Macedonian* in the battle against USS *United States* in October 1812 (which the British lost), Samuel Leech observed the devastation of the different kinds of incoming shot:

> Grape and canister shot were pouring through our portholes like leaden rain, carrying death in their trail. The large shot came against the ship's side like iron hail, shaking her to the very keel, or passing through her timbers, and scattering terrific splinters, which did a more appalling work than even their own death-giving blows . . . grape shot is formed by seven or eight balls confined to an iron and tied in a cloth. These balls are scattered by the explosion of the powder. Canister shot is made by filling a powder canister with balls, each as large as two or three musket balls; these also scatter with direful effect when discharged.[25]

The main aim in all battles, whether against merchant ships, privateers or large enemy fleets, was not to sink ships, but to capture them and take the crew prisoner. That way prize-money could be earned, and any useful warships were incorporated into the Royal Navy. The purpose of firing shot from cannons and carronades was therefore not to hole and sink a ship but to kill and maim the enemy crew, either directly or else indirectly by splinters and falling debris, and to put the enemy cannons out of action and destroy their ability to control their ship.

In wooden sailing ships, splinters – jagged pieces of wood of all sizes – were most feared. When shot smashed through the ship, a shower of splinters was spewed across the deck, which was more than enough to injure or kill anyone in the way, as Dillon witnessed in the *Defence*: 'I had never seen a man killed before. It was a most trying scene. A splinter struck him in the crown of the head, and when he fell the blood and brains came out, flowing over the deck. The Captain went over, and, taking the poor fellow by the hand, pronounced him dead.'[26] At a close range of 30 yards or less, even the relatively small cannonballs from 18-pounder guns could penetrate oak planks 30 inches thick – the approximate thickness of the largest warships just above the water-line. The sides were thinner at the level of the gun decks, and so at close range the seamen had very little protection. When ships were fighting only a few feet from each other, the shot could easily pass through one side of a vessel, spraying deadly wood splinters, before it carried on across the deck and through the opposite wall of the ship, destroying anything and anyone in its path. As opposing ships drew closer, the gunners reduced the amount of gunpowder in the cartridges to try to avoid the shot passing through both sides of the enemy ship, because it did far more damage ricocheting around the cramped space of a gun deck.

One gun crew was assigned to each cannon, and the way they were organised varied from ship to ship. The largest guns weighed nearly three tons and required at least six men to load and fire them. If the cannons on both sides of the ship were being fired, the total number of men available for each gun was halved, and once the fighting started gun crews were depleted by casualties. The seaman Robert Wilson said that on board his ship there was 'a captain, a sponger and boarder, a fireman, and a sail trimmer to each gun'.[27] He explained their roles:

> The captain of the gun has to fight her, or fire her off; the sponger and boarder (one person) has to sponge the gun in action and to be ready to board an enemy vessel; the fireman with his bucket is to attend in case of fire; the sail trimmers are to trim the sails when required. There are also pumpers and swabbers, who pump out the ship, or free her from water, in case of a leak springing in action. The powder men or boys are those who supply the

The *Victory* at the Battle of Trafalgar just after Nelson and others around him on the quarterdeck were shot by French sharpshooters. The poop deck is above

The hold of HMS *Victory*, with the water casks on top of the shingle ballast. One cask is about to be hoisted out of the hold

Layout of the hold of the frigate *Phoebe* in 1806, drawn by Midshipman
William Ffarington, showing the arrangement of wooden casks of salted meat and rum

The cast-iron galley stove of HMS *Victory* with a wooden steep tub to the side

The cots suspended in the sick-bay of HMS *Victory*

Cockpit of the *Victory* during the Battle of Trafalgar showing the dying Nelson. Standing in uniform on the far left is Lieutenant John Yule, the chaplain Alexander Scott is kneeling to the left of Nelson and the surgeon William Beatty is shown squatting on Nelson's right in long coat and boots. Note the lanterns used for lighting ot Capt Demalle the 13 may 1807

Ser J Beg Live to in form you

J James Bodie Quarter Master
Belong to St.M Ship Sparton wnder Comond
of Capt Brenter wos send from the said Ship
on th 13 may wnder Comond of Laftennen Weir
After a Lerg Ship in shor wich at 10 Aim
Went along sid of her and when seing th Bot th
Ememey Called hall hands the sam as a British
mon of war wich Mr Weir hordered muster for th
Rest of th Bots a Cordingly J Did so th yolle
and Cutter was in sight But a good way of then
th Lench Cam hup and it was agreed among th
Offsers to Bord hir on Ever pisson wich all Bots
geve way to her pistel shot of th fire begun
Which J stered th Bot that Mr Weir wos
in and Lead him on th Stabrt Quarter af ord
to his Mdrs which we wos under a veri hot
fire for a Corendrebl time — ——

A letter from James Bodie of HMS *Spartan* describing how he was captured in May 1807
and taken as a prisoner-of-war to Verdun in France

Gravestone of Thomas Williams, a prisoner-of-war in France, in Barnoon cemetery at St Ives, Cornwall

A naval cannon reused as a bollard outside the dockyard at Portsmouth, Hampshire

The memorial plaque to Henry Roberts Carpenter who died on board HMS *Scout* on the notorious Banks of Newfoundland

Greenwich Hospital on the River Thames in 1805

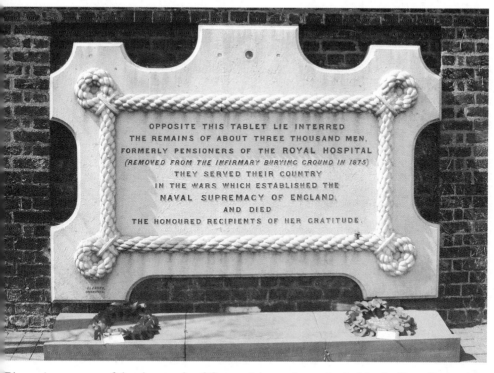

OPPOSITE THIS TABLET LIE INTERRED
THE REMAINS OF ABOUT THREE THOUSAND MEN,
FORMERLY PENSIONERS OF THE ROYAL HOSPITAL
(REMOVED FROM THE INFIRMARY BURYING GROUND IN 1875)
THEY SERVED THEIR COUNTRY
IN THE WARS WHICH ESTABLISHED THE
NAVAL SUPREMACY OF ENGLAND,
AND DIED
THE HONOURED RECIPIENTS OF HER GRATITUDE.

Plaque in memory of the thousands of Greenwich pensioners buried in the East Greenwich
Pleasaunce. Their remains were moved from the original Greenwich Hospital cemetery
during building operations

Greenwich Pensioners Joseph Burgin, James Connell and George French,
all Trafalgar veterans, in 1844

Greenwich Pensioner Daniel Fearall, a marine
and Trafalgar veteran, in 1844

Greenwich Pensioner Henry Stiles, a
Trafalgar veteran, in 1844

guns with powder; there are also some on the lower deck who pass along the powder from the magazine up to the powder men on the upper deck.[28]

The powder men, also called powder monkeys, were responsible for carrying gunpowder cartridges from the magazine to each cannon, a job usually delegated to boys and women.

For gun crews to be effective they needed good training and frequent practice, and it was this above all else that gave the Royal Navy an advantage over most other maritime nations. Each evening the crew was beat to quarters – summoned by beating on a drum to their battle stations. They then went through the routine leading up to the firing of a gun, as Samuel Leech on board the *Macedonian* described: 'When at sea, the drummer beats to quarters every night . . . At the roll of this evening drum, all hands hurry to the guns. Eight men and a boy are stationed at each gun, one of whom is captain of the gun, another sponges and loads it, the rest take hold of the side tackle-falls, to run the gun in and out, while the boy is employed in handing the cartridges, for which he is honoured with the singularly euphonious cognomen of powder-monkey.'[29]

Francis Spilsbury, the surgeon of the sloop *Favourite*, emphasised the importance of training and practice:

Our men were regularly trained, as is customary, to the exercise of great guns and small arms. It is perhaps the great attention to this most useful regulation on board British ships of war, which gives us a decided superiority over our enemies. On the beat of a drum, the men immediately fly to their quarters; and their being so constant in that point of duty, increases their agility, gives them confidence in their own powers, and prevents much of that confusion, which with those less disciplined must necessarily ensue – even the little powder-boy would be ashamed of being reproached by his ship mates, for not knowing his duty. On these occasions a general silence prevails, all attentively listening for the word of command.[30]

On board his new frigate, the *Sybil*, in March 1780, Captain Thomas Pasley noted that 'Today being . . . exercising day, I gave orders that the men should fire three rounds of powder and ball (great guns, tops, and everywhere) to accustom them to sponge, prime, and load, their guns in reality. A little confusion and irregularity there was; but on the whole they performed well, some incomparably so; a real little brush or two would bring them into excellent order.'[31] Pasley referred frequently to such exercises, though he despaired of improving the marines, as on 7 April: 'Exercised great guns and small arms – Damned rascals, those marines.'[32]

Some captains made use of captured gunpowder for live firing exercises, because the Admiralty only allowed a very small amount for this purpose. On 6 November 1781 Captain Pasley, now in the *Jupiter*, wrote in his journal: 'Today being according to my invariable custom exercising day, I resolved to fire both upper and lower deck guns, as they had been long loaded. Besides I had got a quantity of Dutch powder out of the prize which I esteemed greatly superior to our English, and therefore proposed loading the guns with it making use of no other till the whole of it was expended.'[33] The exercise was not carried out properly, with tragic results:

> Great God, how shall I narrate the dreadful shocking accident that happened at the 7th gun on the lower deck? Re-charging the gun, two men were ramming home the cartridge when it caught fire – the gun went off and the two men were never more seen; in a thousand pieces they must have been blown, as some parts of their skulls were found twenty yards distant. The captain of the gun, a clever fellow, had obliged them to sponge the gun twice to prevent accidents. They boisterously called for the cartridge, saying the gun was all clear, and they desired the man who handed it to bite the cartridge that the pricker might more readily get to the powder – to this request alone they, poor fellows, owe their fate. The heat of the gun, or perhaps some triffling invisible spark, touched that part where the powder was laid bare, and fired it – neither exceeded 22 years.[34]

It was just such dangerous short cuts, often leading to accidents, that the exercising of the guns was designed to minimise, by instilling in the gun crews a routine that became a series of natural reflex actions, even in the exhaustion of a prolonged battle. Such exercising was also designed to improved their speed and accuracy without resorting to dangerous practices.

When First Lieutenant Cumby of HMS *Bellerophon* was inspecting everything prior to Trafalgar, he remarked that 'the fifth or junior lieutenant . . . who commanded the seven foremost guns, on each side of the lower deck, pointed out to me some of the guns at his quarters where the zeal of the seamen had led them to chalk in large characters on their guns the words "Victory or Death" – a very gratifying mark of the spirit with which they were going to their work'.[35]

Once the fighting started, despite the removal of wooden and canvas partitions, the officers' unobstructed view of each gun deck did not last beyond the second or third broadside. By this time the whole deck was filled with choking smoke from the guns, which gradually blackened everyone and everything. Because of the smoke-filled atmosphere, James Scott said, drinking water was on hand for the gun crews: 'Water is always distributed along the decks for the refreshment of the men; the smoke of the powder, added to the exertions of the men, causing an intolerable thirst.'[36] The smoke lingered because of the lack of ventilation, which was not helped by the gap between decks being so small. 'After a few minutes' firing,' Basil Hall commented,

> the lower deck becomes so completely filled with smoke that no one can see two yards before him; the noise and apparent confusion swell on the unpractised senses of men, who are brought for the first time into action; and be their courage what it may, they are apt to get so confounded, that their early, and, perhaps, their most precious fire is almost inevitably thrown away. If the men have never been taught the true value of a good aim, nor, theoretically as well as practically, instructed in the method of obtaining it, their only thought will of course be how to blaze away as fast and as indiscriminately as possible.[37]

On board the *Victory* at the Battle of Trafalgar, Marine Lieutenant Lewis Rotely was ordered to fetch reinforcements from those marines helping to fire the guns. He found the scene overwhelming:

I was now upon the middle deck. We were engaging on both sides, every gun was going off . . . A man should witness a battle in a three decker from the middle deck, for it beggars all description, it bewilders the senses of sight and hearing. There was the fire from above, the fire from below, besides the fire from the deck I was upon, the guns recoiling with violence, reports louder than thunder, the decks heaving and the sides straining. I fancied myself in the infernal regions where every man appeared a devil. Lips might move, but orders and hearing were out of the question. Everything was done with signs.[38]

Only two days after seeing a man killed for the first time, fourteen-year-old Midshipman Dillon was in the thick of the fighting at the Glorious First of June: 'The Lower Deck was at times so completely filled with smoke that we could scarcely distinguish each other, and the guns were so heated that, when fired, they nearly kicked the upper deck beams. The metal became so hot that, fearing some accident, we reduced the quantity of powder, allowing also more time to elapse between the loading and firing of them.'[39] Captain Pasley of HMS *Jupiter* was also relieved that his men successfully avoided accidents during a fierce battle against the French at Porto Praya, Cape Verde Islands, on Easter Monday 1781:

It is impossible for me to speak too highly of the intrepid and cool gallantry of my ship's company; the fire they kept up was past all conception – not one accident. Two particulars I cannot help mentioning: on the lower gun deck in the heat of the action half a cartridge of powder was scattered, when half a dozen fellows with all possible coolness gathered round and *personally watered* it to prevent accident; the other my coxswain Harrison . . . brought me one of the enemy's shot, and requested my liberty to return it out of his gun – so reasonable a request I could not refuse.[40]

During a battle, it was only the discipline and training of the men that prevented the inevitable confusion produced by the noise, smoke and streams of blood on the deck from degenerating into chaos. This was an era when naval officers had a paternalistic attitude to their men and a strong sense of honour and chivalry. They led from the front, winning the respect of their crews by an exaggerated disregard for their own safety. At the Battle of Lissa in 1811, Lieutenant O'Brien recorded what happened when one French ship was about to attack his own: 'She succeeded in passing under the stern, and poured in a raking fire, which would have proved most destructive to the men on the main-deck, had I not ordered them to lie down between the guns, as by standing they were uselessly exposed, it being impossible to bring a gun to bear on the enemy at the moment.'[41] This saved unnecessary slaughter, he said, since 'many of the enemy's shot rattled along the decks without doing injury to the men thus protected by lying close between the guns'.[42] Two midshipmen were not so lucky – they were seriously injured because, out of a sense of honour, they chose to remain standing.

The attitude of his fellow officers was something that Captain Edward Codrington cherished. As he wrote to a friend in 1801, 'There is something very fine in the manner of men of courage to each other before going into action, and the memory of this seems almost to repay one for the danger. The little traits of this sort I have witnessed in the few opportunities which chance has thrown in my way I can hardly ever think of without emotion.'[43] A sentence from Nelson's diary entry on the day of his death at Trafalgar, which is likely to have been written with the knowledge that it might become public if he was killed, probably encapsulates his attitude: 'May the Great God, whom I worship, grant to my Country, and for the benefit of Europe in general, a great and glorious victory; and may no misconduct in any one tarnish it; and may humanity after Victory be the predominant feature in the British Fleet.'[44]

In every battle there were at least a few casualties and often scenes of dreadful carnage, even in a short duel between two ships. In his memoirs Samuel Leech recorded details of his first battle, saying that 'it will reveal the horrors of war, and show at what fearful price a victory is won or lost'.[45] Even a single cannonball could be devastating. Although he was busy supplying guns with gunpowder cartridges, at one point Leech was shocked to see two boys injured simultaneously:

One of them was struck in the leg by a large shot; he had to suffer amputation above the wound. The other had a grape or canister shot sent through his ankle. A stout Yorkshireman lifted him in his arms, and hurried him to the cockpit [to the surgeon]. He had his foot cut off, and was thus made lame for life . . . A man named Aldrich had one of his hands cut off by a shot, and almost at the same moment he received another shot, which tore open his bowels in a terrible manner. As he fell, two or three men caught him in their arms, and, as he could not live, threw him overboard.[46]

The dead man was William Aldridge, from London, while the two boys were Jose de Compass and Joaquin Jase, both from Lisbon.

Midshipman Dillon on the lower deck during the Glorious First of June was soaked by sea water coming in through the gunport, but during the laughter that followed, one of his men was killed:

The men cheered me, and laughingly said, 'We hope, Sir, you will not receive further injury. It is rather warm work here below: the salt water will keep you cool.' One of these, John Polly, of very short stature, remarked that he was so small the shot would all pass over him. The words had not been long out of his mouth when a shot cut his head right in two, leaving the tip of each ear remaining on the lower part of the cheek. His sudden death caused a sensation among his comrades, but the excitement of the moment soon changed those impressions to others of exertion . . . The head of this unfortunate seaman was cut so horizontally that anyone looking at it would have supposed it had been done by the blow of an axe.[47]

John Polly was a twenty-six-year-old able seaman from Spitalfields in London, who had joined the ship the year before.

Attacking coastal defences could be just as dangerous as a full-scale battle. In 1809, during the Walcheren expedition, HMS *Blake* ran aground. Now stationary and an easy target, the ship soon came under fire from shore batteries. Marine Captain Wybourn described their perilous position:

We all thought there could be no possibility of escaping. We on the poop, which is the roof of the Captain's cabin, were in such a line with the guns, that it is amazing *any* of us escaped. Almost the first shot killed my best sergeant, a fine fellow, it took off both thighs, left arm and right hand. The poor fellow called out to me, but I could not bear to look at him. Fortunately he died in half an hour, under amputation. Five more men [were] wounded by the same shot and you may judge what were our expectations. When this took place five minutes after we began, I confess I never was more alarmed.[48]

It took an hour to refloat the *Blake*, during which time Wybourn and his marines were constant targets, but overall the men of this ship were lucky to have relatively few casualties.

With no wind, the frigate *Unité* was at a similar disadvantage when attacked by gunboats, each with a single gun, in the Adriatic in December 1806. Robert Wilson witnessed the damage they incurred by cannonballs and splinters:

During the action the enemy certainly kept up a brisk fire, and their shot was well directed; in short we being so good an object for them, several of their shot hulled us, particularly about our quarter and bow on the larboard side, that being the side we engaged on. We shot away one of their lateen yards, and observed one of the gunboats to be in a sinking condition. Lieutenant William Dredge was the first person that fell on our side, he being wounded in the face by a splinter from the 12th gun-port on the main deck, occasioned by a shot striking there. His breast pin was cut in twain, but his bosom escaped unhurt. A shot came on the quarter-deck, through the bulwark between the 2nd and 3rd carronades; the splinters knocked down four men at 2nd gun, *viz.* William Winks, James Berron, Thomas Claxton (three seamen) and William Salter (a marine). I, with others quartered at the 3rd gun, helped them up, the two former were wounded severely, the other two slightly. William Winks suffered amputation of his left leg and died shortly after. The shot split one of our 32-pounder shot and went very close to Lieutenant [Matthew] Grigg of Marines. A shot came through the larboard waist netting, and a hammock, and carried away two iron stanchions and went clean over to the other side . . . One shot struck one of our guns on the main deck and another (spent) struck our rudder. The enemy did not approach within reach of our 32-pounders (carronades) or else, to use a sea-phrase, they would have smelt hell.[49]

After just over an hour, the gunboats retreated to shallow water, where the frigate could not follow.

Even the force of a passing cannonball could maim or kill, and at the very least it caused a severe shock. When the *Defence* began to be pounded by a French ship, Dillon observed that

one of his shot struck the upper part of the quarter deck bulwark, on the larboard side, killed one man and wounded nine. One or two shots passed so close to the Captain [Gambier] that I thought he was hit. He clapped both hands upon his thighs with some emotion: then, recovering himself, he took out of his pocket a piece of biscuit, and began eating it as if nothing had happened. He had evidently been shook by the wind of the shot. He had on a cocked hat, and kept walking the deck, cheering up the seamen with the greatest coolness.[50]

Three days later in the midst of the Glorious First of June battle, Dillon himself experienced a similar shock: 'Two of the men were blown down from the wind of a shot from the ship we were engaging, and I was carried away with them by the shock. I thought myself killed, as I became senseless, being jammed between these men.'[51] After the battle, he went to see the surgeon:

I enquired the fate of the two men I had sent him from my quarters. He told me they were both killed! One of them was without the slightest mark of a wound on any part of his body: the other had a bruise across his loins, supposed to have been occasioned by his having come in contact with the bitts in his fall. It is therefore clear that they were killed by the wind of a shot. Few persons will believe that the wind of a shot can take away life. But here was proof that it could, and the Surgeon was a witness to its having happened.[52]

The most damage was done by broadsides, where all the cannons along one side of a ship were fired at once, or in rapid sequence. On board the *Foudroyant* at the Battle of St Vincent, Midshipman George Parsons observed that 'not, through the whole of that glorious and unprecedented victory, did I hear such a fatal broadside as was poured in the *Foudroyant* by the *Guillaume Tell*.'[53] This was the start of the encounter between the two ships, and the broadside, Parsons thought,

> resembled a volcanic eruption, crashing, tearing, and splintering every-thing in its destructive course. 'Hard up,' said our chief, 'set the jib, and sheet home the fore-top-gallant sail' (for we had shot past the enemy like a flash of lightning). 'The jib-boom is gone, and the fore-topmast is badly wounded,' roared the forecastle officer; 'look out for the topmast – stand from under!' Down it came on the larboard gangway, crushing some to pieces under its enormous weight.[54]

Such broadsides caused so much damage to a ship that they often decided the outcome of a battle. For the seamen in most battles, though, it was more a question of endurance than anything else. Samuel Leech vividly recorded the encounter between the *United States* and his ship, the *Macedonian*. A fierce fight took place that eventually ended with the *Macedonian*'s surrender:

> The battle went on. Our men kept cheering with all their might. I cheered with them, though I confess I scarcely knew what for . . . we kept on our shouting and firing. Our men fought like tigers. Some of them pulled off their jackets and vests; while some, still more deter-mined, had taken off their shirts, and, with nothing but a handkerchief tied round the waistbands of their trowsers, fought like heroes . . . I also observed a boy, named Cooper, stationed at a gun some distance from the magazine. He came to and fro on the full run, and appeared to be as 'merry as a cricket'. The third lieutenant cheered him along, occasionally by saying, 'Well done, my boy, you are worth your weight in gold.' I have often been asked what were my feelings during this

fight. I felt pretty much as I suppose every one does at such a time. That men are without thought when they stand amid the dying and the dead, is too absurd an idea to be entertained for a moment.[55]

Cheering throughout the fighting also had a more practical use, in the view of Midshipman William Millard, who was at the 1801 Battle of Copenhagen: 'When the carnage was greatest he [an army lieutenant] encouraged his men by applauding their conduct, and frequently began a huzza, which is of more importance than might generally be imagined; for the men have no other communication throughout the ship; but when a shout is set up, it runs from deck to deck, and they know that their comrades are, some of them, alive and in good spirits.'[56] It was unacceptable to display fear, Leech remarked:

We all appeared cheerful, but I know that many a serious thought ran through my mind: still, what could we do but keep up a semblance, at least, of animation? To run from our quarters would have been certain death from the hands of our own officers; to give way to gloom, or to show fear, would do no good, and might brand us with the name of cowards, and ensure certain defeat. Our only true philosophy, therefore, was to make the best of our situation, by fighting bravely and cheerfully.[57]

Nevertheless, fear and signs of panic were at times revealed, and Midshipman Dillon of the *Defence* recorded one rare instance: 'A volley of shot assailed the poop, cut away the main brace, and made sad havoc there. Some of the men could not help showing symptoms of alarm: which the Captain [Gambier] noticing, he instantly went up, and, calling the seamen together, led them to set the brace to rights.'[58] During the summer of 1805 the landsman George Price of the *Speedy*, now promoted to ordinary seaman, described to his brother the various actions in which they were involved with the French in the English Channel – this was a time of heightened fear when the French were preparing to invade. On 21 July he wrote: 'I have the honor to say that *Speedy* led the van and [was] greatly applauded by our captain and all the squadron. Our captain is pleased to tell us there is not a coward in the ship. But you may depend upon it there is a number in the ship that would wish to be out of it. But for my part I am determined to do as much as another. But at the same time I don't like it.'[59] A month later he wrote again to his brother, obviously fearful of losing his life, but saying that they were all in the highest spirits. Only a week later he deserted the ship.

In order to prevent the seamen from deserting their posts in battle, the marines were posted at strategic points, although some of them helped out with firing the guns. If opposing ships came close enough, the marines joined in the fighting with small arms, mainly muskets and grenades, and boarders armed with swords, axes and pistols would attempt to cross over to the enemy ship and continue with hand-to-hand fighting. Boarding another ship was a risky strategy because there were too many uncertainties. If the enemy crew was larger than expected, or better trained, more resolute or just lucky, an attempt at boarding might end not only in a confused retreat, but also defeat, with the enemy taking the opportunity to gain the initiative. Usually boarding was only considered as a last resort, or when an enemy ship had ceased firing, but refused to surrender.

During the Battle of Trafalgar, James Spratt, a forty-six-year-old master's mate in the *Defiance*, was in charge of the boarding party. He had been responsible for training the men under his command, and as the cannonfire from the French ship *Aigle* petered out, he urged his captain, Philip Durham, to give the order to board. Later, Spratt described the situation:

Being within pistol shot, about this time the wind had died away and a dead calm ensued . . . both ships boats being shot through and rendered useless and no prospect of closing with the enemy, I asked my Captain leave to board by swimming, as I well knew 50 or 60 of the boarders who I taught for some years could swim like sharks. This request he received with astonishment saying I was too prompt, but finally consented, so I gave the word 'All you, my brave fellows, who can swim follow me'. I plunged over board from the starboard gang way with my cutlass between my teeth and my tomahawk under my belt and swam to the stern of *L'Aigle* where by the assistance of her rudder chains I got into her gun-room stern port *alone*.[60]

To his consternation, nobody followed:

> My men, in the loud clamour of a general engagement not hearing
> what I said, or misunderstood me, did not follow, so I fought my way
> under God's guidance through a host of gallant French, all prepared
> with arms in hand, and through all decks until I got on her poop . . . I
> now showed myself to our ships crew . . . and gave them a cheer, with
> my hat on the point of my cutlass. Our ship at this moment contrived
> to sheer alongside, and now came the tug of war, both ships lashed
> side by side . . . A division of my boarders flew to my support, and a
> timely one indeed, for I was that moment attacked by 3 grenadiers with
> fixed bayonets.[61]

In grappling with them, Spratt fell from the poop deck to the
quarterdeck and was surrounded by Frenchmen:

> I found myself now in a desperate conflict on the French quarter deck.
> The first division of boarders being nearly cut up were just reinforced by
> a fresh division which soon cleared the quarter deck of every soul but one
> officer, who had done his duty well as long as was in his power, and
> trying to escape below, was seized by two of our men with uplifted tom-
> ahawks. He cried for quarter and threw himself at my feet, and I was
> obliged to throw myself on him and cover his body to save him from our
> men . . . when a grenadier from the starboard gangway with fixed bayo-
> net thought to run me through, but I parried his thrust with my blade. He
> then retired a little, levelling his piece [musket] at my breast, which I
> struck downwards with my trusty old friend the cutlass, so that the ball,
> which would otherwise have passed through my body shivered and shat-
> tered the bone of my right leg.[62]

Calling out for help, Spratt was rescued and carried back to the
Defiance, and eventually the French ship was taken.

Once a losing ship was incapable of continuing to fight effectively,
the captain usually surrendered, and after the Glorious First of June,
several French ships were captured, along with their crews. William
Dillon's ship, the *Defence*, took some of the prisoners:

The next day we received 56 Frenchmen from the *Northumberland*, with a few officers . . . Some of their seamen, very fine powerful men, tried hard to be received as volunteers on board the *Defence*. There was no end to their praises of our conduct and of our victory. But their offers were not accepted. Strange to say, all the foreigners we had on board had deserted their guns, except one. As this fact had been ascertained, there was no desire to add to their number by allowing the Frenchmen mentioned to form part of our crew. This conduct of the foreigners made a lasting impression on my mind, never to employ them in any ship I might command. Consequently, when I rose in the Service, my first object in taking the command of any ship of war was to get rid of all of them that happened to be serving on board.[63]

Dillon was extremely prejudiced against the lower classes in general, and found it easy to extend this to the foreigners among their ranks. Nevertheless, he was sympathetic when he encountered several of the French seamen a few months later at Chatham, where they were held on board the notorious prison hulks in the River Medway:

During this severe frost [January 1795], one of the hulks lying here, in which the prisoners of war were confined, required some assistance to set her moorings to rights, and I was sent on that duty. To my astonishment I there met many of the French seamen that we had captured in the *Thetis*. They recognized me, and in the most cheerful manner offered to lend a hand in the work going on. I could not help feeling for them, poor fellows, but they bore their captivity with a lightness of heart peculiar to that nation.[64]

Despite all the propaganda and the undoubted superiority of the British sailors over the vast majority of the crews of their Continental enemies, British ships were sometimes forced to surrender. Lieutenant George Vernon Jackson had to surrender to the French off Guadeloupe in 1809. Outnumbered by four French ships against his own, it was not long before the captain was badly wounded and Jackson had to help him below. Soon after, as Jackson recalled, 'I returned to my post and saw the gunroom steward coming towards me. He said that we had struck. To satisfy myself as to the fact, I went to the quarter-deck ladder, where I was met by a salute of bayonets and the exclamation, "En bas . . ."[65] Jackson was landed at Brest, a prisoner-of-war.

Much worse than being forced to surrender was the prospect of a ship blowing up. Once a fire started in a ship, the abundance of combustible material plus the presence of so much gunpowder ensured that if it was not extinguished immediately it would rapidly become uncontrollable. At Trafalgar, the French ship *Algésiras* caught fire, as Lieutenant Frederick Hoffman in the *Tonnant* witnessed:

> Our severe contest with the French admiral [in the *Algésiras*] lasted more than half-an-hour, our sides grinding so much against each other that we were obliged to fire the lower deck guns without running them out. At length both ships caught fire before the chest-trees, and our fire-men, with all the coolness and courage so inherent in British seamen, got the engine and played [water] on both ships, and finally extinguished the flames, although two of them were severely wounded in doing so.[66]

Once a fire took hold, it was only a matter of time before it reached the powder magazines and the ship blew up. At the Battle of the Nile, the French flagship *L'Orient* caught fire, which caused panic on the British side. From HMS *Swiftsure*, the chaplain Cooper Willyams witnessed what happened next:

> Several of the [French] officers and men seeing the impracticability of extinguishing the fire, which had now extended itself along the upper decks, and was flaming up the masts, jumped overboard; some supporting themselves on spars and pieces of wreck, others swimming with all their might to escape the dreaded catastrophe. Shot flying in all directions dashed many of them to pieces; others were picked up by the boats of the fleet, or dragged into the lower ports of the nearest ships: the British sailors humanely stretched forth their hands to save a fallen enemy, though the battle at that moment raged with uncontrolled fury. The *Swiftsure*, that was anchored within half-pistol-shot of the larboard bow

of *l'Orient*, saved the lives of the commissary, first lieutenant, and ten men, who were drawn out of the water into the lower deck ports during the hottest part of the action.[67]

There was now the fear that the fire could spread from ship to ship, as Midshipman Theophilus Lee, also of the *Swiftsure*, related:

Every moment the dreadful explosion was expected – the least noise could now be heard, where the din of war before raged with such uncontrollable violence, – till at last an awful and terrific glare of light blinding the very sight, showed the *L'Orient* blowing up, with an astounding crash, paralyzing all around her, by which near a thousand brave spirits were hastened into eternity. A large ignited beam fell into the foretop of the *Swiftsure*, and set it on fire, but the flames were soon extinguished; other and heavier pieces bounding against the sides or into the chains, and some even upon decks and booms, but all being speedily prevented from doing mischief, by the active measures employed; the greater portion, as anticipated, passing clear over the mast heads, and falling in the sea a considerable way beyond the tremendous explosion, however it shook the ship more than the whole battle. It was like an earthquake, the air rushing along the decks and below with inconceivable violence, and creating a tremulous motion in the ship, which existed for some minutes, and was awfully grand.[68]

Fire and explosion, though rare since seamen were always alert to fire spreading through a ship, were the main causes of a ship being destroyed in battle. It was unusual for a ship to sink because even when full of holes, many wooden ships continued to float, and the loss of their masts through cannonfire was an advantage since it lowered the centre of gravity. Many more ships were lost through storms, lightning strikes and running on to rocks than were sunk during battles. In this respect the French *Vengeur du Peuple* was unlucky. After the Glorious First of June battle, this ship had a huge hole in the stern and started to take in water rapidly. Midshipman William Parker described what happened next in a letter to his father. The ship, he said, was so much disabled that she could not live much longer upon the water, but gave a dreadful reel and lay down upon her broadside. We were afraid to send any boats to help them, because they would have sunk her by too many poor souls getting into her at once. You could plainly perceive the poor wretches climbing over to windward and crying most dreadfully. She then righted a little, and then her head went down gradually, and she sunk. She after that rose again a little and then sunk, so that no more was seen of her. Oh, my dear father! when you consider of five or six hundred souls destroyed in that shocking manner, it will make your very heart relent. Our own men, even, were a great many of them in tears and groaning . . . I really think it would have rent the hardest of hearts.[69]

Altogether, one hundred and fifty men were saved from the French ship.

Once a battle was over, it was necessary to clean up the ship and carry out essential repairs. James Scott recorded the scene on board the French ship *Guerrière*, which his own ship, the *Blanche*, had captured:

The blood-stained planks of the quarter-deck bore ample testimony to the accuracy of our fire, but on descending to the main-deck a scene of slaughter presented itself which converted our feelings of triumph into those of horror and dismay. The disfigured and mangled bodies of our gallant foes were scattered in many a heap around. The main-deck was slippery with blood and gore . . . At one gun on the main-deck every man was killed or wounded, one of our cannon-shot having taken the upper part of the muzzle of the gun, when in the act of running it out, and, splitting the upper half to pieces as far as the trunnions, it acted with the destructive effects of a shell, destroying gun and men at a blow. The immediate vicinity of the useless piece sufficiently marked the sanguinary effects of this well-told shot, which were confirmed by one of the wounded Frenchmen quartered at the gun.[70]

William Dillon said that after the Glorious First of June, many of the ships started to do repairs: 'But the ship that astonished us all by her extraordinary exertions was the *Queen*. She had lost her main mast. This was replaced in a most able manner before the evening of this day: all her sides were scrubbed, her paintwork looking as clean as if nothing had happened – a good proof of what can be done with good discipline and management.'[71] When a battle between two ships had been fierce, it was often difficult to tell from their condition which side had won. When George Watson arrived at Lissa in 1811, he saw the French ship *Rivoli*, which had just been captured by the *Victorious*. He was sent on board both ships to help unload some stores:

> They had both suffered severely in the conflict, and there was hardly a whole plank on either of their sides to be seen, so many balls had passed through them. The *Rivoli*, of the two was the worst: she was under jury masts [temporary masts], her proper ones having tumbled overboard in a breeze after the action, in consequence of their shattered condition. The *Victorious*'s masts were also severely wounded, and obliged to be fished, (that is, secured by planks extended up and down the mast to connect the weak parts). The guns in both ships had many of their muzzles broken off, by the shot taking them in a raking position. The carnage had been extensive in both, but in the *Rivoli*, dreadful; the marks of which yet remained, for I saw on the ceiling of the gun room, and cabin decks, part of the blood, brains, &c. of the slain adhering, as it had been scattered in the battle.[72]

After the tension, fear and exhaustion of a battle, various emotions took over, and the men reacted in different ways. In a letter to his brother, Captain Codrington reflected on his recent experiences at Trafalgar: 'The battle after all, as I warned my officers, is nothing compared with the fatigue, the anxiety, the distress of mind which succeeds [it], more particularly in the case of such horrible weather as we had to encounter on this occasion.'[73] On board the captured *Macedonian* in 1812, Leech regretted what happened when the fighting was over:

> Most of our officers and men were taken on board the victor ship [*United States*]. I was left, with a few others, to take care of the wounded. My master,

the sailing-master, was also among the officers who continued in their ship. Most of the men who remained were unfit for any service, having broken into the spirit-room and made themselves drunk; some of them broke into the purser's room, and helped themselves to clothing; while others, by previous agreement, took possession of their dead messmates' property. For my own part, I was content to help myself to a little of the officers' provisions, which did me more good than could be obtained from rum. What was worse than all, however, was the folly of the sailors in giving spirit to their wounded messmates, since it only served to aggravate their distress.[74]

On other occasions the men could appear light-hearted after a battle, as Wilson witnessed in 1806 on board the *Unité*:

By way of showing how careless sailors are about any thing when fighting, while we were at dinner, says one, 'Why Tom, how many bells is it?' (*i.e.* what time is it). 'About 2' (*i.e.* 5 o'clock). 'Why, damn my eyes, we dine at quality hours today.* But never mind, double allowance of grog, my boy! I'll be damned to hell if I would not willingly kick up such a smoke every day for a double allowance, would not you?' To which the other readily assented.[75]

Many men found the sheer scale of the devastation and carnage resulting from a battle quite shocking. The end of the fighting was a time for reuniting with friends and mourning those who had been killed, as Leech discovered:

Some who had lost their messmates appeared to care nothing about it, while others were grieving with all the tenderness of women. Of these, was the survivor of two seamen, who had formerly been soldiers in the same regiment; he bemoaned the loss of his comrade with expressions of profoundest grief. There were, also, two boatswain's mates, named [George] Adams and [William] Brown, who had been messmates for

* The later dining hours of the officers.

several years in the same ship. Brown was killed, or so wounded that he died soon after the battle. It was really a touching spectacle to see the rough, hardy features of the brave old sailor streaming with tears, as he picked out the dead body of his friend from among the wounded, and gently carried it to the ship's side, saying to the inanimate form he bore, 'Oh Bill, we have sailed together in a number of ships, we have been in many gales and some battles, but this is the worst day I have seen! We must now part!' Here he dropped the body into the deep, and then, a fresh torrent of tears streaming over his weather-beaten face, he added, 'I can do no more for you. Farewell! God be with you!'[76]

Even experienced officers, like Lieutenant John Yule of Nelson's flagship the *Victory* at Trafalgar, had trouble coming to terms with events. Nearly a month after the battle he wrote to his wife Eliza about his mixed emotions in the days that had followed:

The horrors of an action during the time it lasts, and for a short time afterwards, makes everything around you appear in a different shape to what it did before, and though the heart may for a moment be rendered callous by the dreadful carnage around him and though they may call us sea brutes for not feeling so acutely as they would do on shore, believe me my dearest Girl we are not void of sympathy. The mind is made up to fall, before the conflict commences, and each man when he sees his neighbour fall thanks God that it was not himself – Self, dear Self, occupies most of our thoughts, and yet Eliza believe me I thought of only half of myself. I wished to live for the better, and best beloved, half. The dear Infants engrossed not a little of my thoughts, and if I should fall!! – I felt more for my poor widowed Eliza than I did for myself – Heaven spared my Eliza's husband and my children's father. I return [still only] a Lieutenant after all my golden dreams, but am content. My Eliza, I am sure, will be equally so.[77]

He then set down his feelings about the wider effect of the battle:

The action will be, by the nation, conceived a glorious one, but when the devastation is considered, how can we glory at it? How many widows, orphans and fatherless has it made? How many has it made sad, and how few . . . has it made glad? In the *Victory* we do not feel it a victory. The loss of our Chief has thrown a gloom around that nothing but the society of our friends and families can dispel. That quarter deck, which was formerly crowded with courtiers, an hour after the combat was totally neglected. The happy scenes we formerly witnessed are now laid aside. The theatre, the music, the dancing which occupied the dull part of our time is laid aside. We look to the seat of an old messmate and find he is gone – we ask for such a man – he was killed Sir in the Action; another, he was wounded, he lost a leg. We ask for no-one for fear of a similar reply – *One hundred and fifty* killed and wounded, and *I am* alive without a wound – ought I not to thank the Almighty?[78]

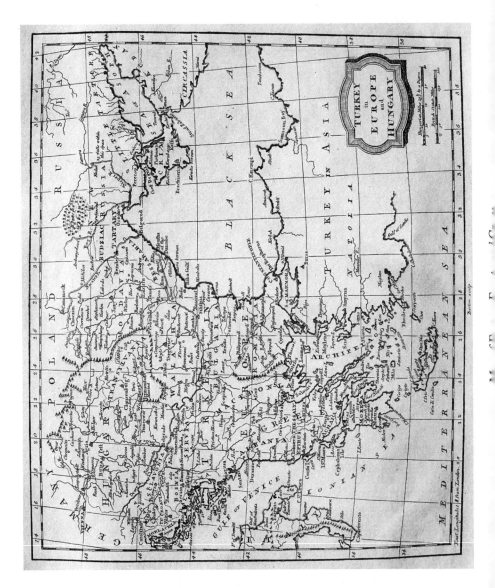

NINE

·◆·

UNDER THE KNIFE

After being maimed in battle to be obliged to suffer the slow and erroneous amputation of a doubting, unskilful surgeon by the light of a purser's short dip [candle].

One of Captain Rotheram's 'Growls of a Naval Life'[1]

It was during and after battles that the surgeon was most occupied, mainly in cutting off wounded limbs. The recurring phrase in eye-witness descriptions of where the surgeon worked during battle was a vision of hell' – in almost the deepest part of the ship, down below the water-line, with no natural light, no ventilation, constantly shaken by broadsides, and with the noise of the battle raging above. It was an area dark, deafening and drenched in blood.

Several hundred surgeons were employed by the Royal Navy as warrant officers, many of them Scotsmen or Irishmen, and all approved by the Company of Surgeons in London. Most had not been to university, but had learned their craft as apprentices to other surgeons. The Scotsman Peter Cullen left a description of his examination at Surgeon's Hall in 1789:

> The examiners were seated at a semi-circular table, where were two, three or more candidates standing before it, and answering such questions as were put to them. Mr. Cullen having walked up to the table, and made his bow, was asked his name, from whence he came, and for what purpose he meant to be examined? On answering that it was for the Naval Service,

one of the examiners arose, and taking Mr. Cullen to the side of the room, inquired his age, his apprenticeship, studies, and practice in his profession. To all these Mr. Cullen having returned a satisfactory reply, the examiner proceeded to question him on anatomy, physiology, and surgery. Then stated some of the most important surgical cases, or diseases, and how he would treat them. This gentleman was quite satisfied with Mr. Cullen's proficiency, and taking him to the centre of the table, where the President was sitting, said 'I find this young gentleman fully qualified as an Assistant Surgeon for His Majesty's Navy'. The President bowed to Mr. Cullen, and desired him to pay one guinea.[2]

Physicians were higher in status than surgeons and were graduates of Oxford or Cambridge universities and fellows of the College of Physicians. Graduates of universities perceived to be inferior, such as Edinburgh or Leiden, were only admitted as associates. Virtually no physicians were employed by the Royal Navy, except in the naval hospitals and one assigned for each major overseas squadron.

Within the navy many shared the view of Aaron Thomas who considered surgeons lazy and drunken, 'the business being entirely done by surgeon's mates. The surgeons themselves rarely know more of the men's diseases than what they take from the sick list or the verbal word of their mates, they, poor souls, being employed in the more *important* concern of catering for the wardroom or gun room mess.'[3] Marine Lieutenant Wybourn was very ill at Naples on board HMS *Madras*, but considered his life was saved by the surgeon's mate, as he told his sister Matilda: 'The Surgeon [is] such a brute that had I not had more fortitude than many, [he] would have hastened my end . . . To the skill and attention of the Mate, a very attractive young man, I may attribute my recovery . . . I put myself entirely under this young man and you see, my love, I am able to write though very weak.'[4]

On board the *Defence* in 1794, Midshipman William Dillon rated the surgeon a disaster:

He was a most amiable man. It was he who was the cause of introducing flannel for the use of the seamen in the Navy, to protect them against

the effects of rheumatism. But, with all his humane intentions, he unfortunately could not perform the operation of amputating a limb, the
consequence of which threw double labour upon his assistant, Mr.
Youhall [William Yowell], an Hibernian . . . Mr. [James] Malcolm, the
Surgeon, was so sensible of his failing, being also extremely nervous, that
he left the *Defence* a few days after her arrival in port.[5]

Before Malcolm's departure, Yowell was the only surgeon's mate, but
fortunately he was exemplary, in Dillon's view:

He turned out to be a most zealous and able practitioner, or the result
might have been very fatal to many. It was to him that the wounded
looked up for relief [after the Battle of the Glorious First of June]. There
were upwards of 60 severely wounded. The slight ones were, of course,
not of such importance. His attention in dressing these patients occupied
22 hours out of the 24. Many a time did I go the rounds with him and
have witnessed his skill, and kindhearted care of those brave men. I have
known him come on to the Quarter Deck at 2 o'clock in the morning
after terminating his labours to breathe some fresh air. He would then say,
'I have only two hours to rest myself. After that, I must recommence my
visits.'[6]

On the other hand, the surgeon James Ker was certainly not over-
worked on board HMS *Elizabeth*, which left Portsmouth in
November 1778 to reinforce the fleet in the West Indies:

Until we get into warm weather my time for rising is seven or half after
seven o'clock. Breakfast at eight. At nine I see my patients which takes up
half an hour or an hour. From that to eleven [I] generally read or write in
my cabin, then take a walk on deck, give the captain an account of the
sick. After having stretched my limbs, seen what the admiral is doing and
what the fleet, how we steer and how the wind blows, I come down to my
cabin again and take up a book till the drum beating The Roast Beef of
Old England warns me to dinner . . . After dispatching this necessary
piece of business and the grog being finished, the remainder of my
time till supper is spent variously in reading, writing, card-playing,

backgammon, walking or conversation as humour leads. From supper
time at 8 o'clock till bed-time is spent in chit-chat over our grog drinking.[7]

In 1805 surgeons received a substantial pay rise, along with entitlement to half-pay and a pension, and surgeons' mates were renamed
assistants. The surgeon's cabin was on the dark orlop deck, alongside
the midshipmen, while the assistants had to mess with the midshipmen. Instruments were the responsibility of the surgeon, though
medicines were supplied by the Admiralty following the 1805 reforms.
The sick-bay varied from ship to ship, often being a row of hammocks on the lower deck or next to the galley (where the smoke was
believed to be beneficial), so that invalids could be cared for by their
messmates. By the end of the eighteenth century the sick-bay was
situated on one side of the upper deck, under the forecastle, where
the pigs were once kept, which gave better access to the heads.
Conditions in the sick-bay of the *Rainbow* in the West Indies in
1773 were revealed by the surgeon Robert Robertson, who took
for granted that insects were commonplace when referring to one
seaman, who eventually died. Lewis Campbell, he said, 'expectorated
moderately; the pus was no longer fetid or offensive to his taste . . .
He remarked that the flies and insects which, before he began to
take the bark, always devoured the pus, would not now touch it.'[8] The
chaplain Edward Mangin was appalled by the sick-bay of the
Gloucester in 1812 when they were anchored off Holland:

> The apartment referred to [the sick-bay] is forward on the half-deck,
> and close to the ship's head, which is the general water-closet for the
> crew. Add to this, that, whenever it blows fresh, the sea, defiled by a
> thousand horrible intermixtures, comes, more or less, into the hospital;
> and on the above occasion [a severe gale], passed completely through it;
> augmenting most severely the misery of the patients who amounted to
> the usual number of eighteen or twenty men, labouring under the
> common afflictions to which seamen are liable . . . The scene presented
> by this crowd of sufferers, to be conceived, must be beheld . . . The
> place less than six feet high; narrow, noisome and wet; the writhings,

sighs, and moans of acute pain; the pale countenance, which looks like
resignation, but is despair; bandages soaked in blood and matter; the
foetor of sores, and the vermin from which it is impossible to preserve
the invalid entirely free! Yet – to get put on the Doctor's list is considered an indulgence; as it exempts the sick man from that more dreaded
state of toil and servitude to which, when fit for duty, he is necessarily
exposed.[9]

During battles the sick-bay was of no use to the surgeon, being
cleared for action and exposed to enemy fire, and so the cockpit,
where the midshipmen lived, was converted to an operating theatre,
with surgery performed by candlelight. When fighting was fierce,
the injured men brought to the cockpit were so numerous that
they overflowed into other parts of the ship. During the Battle of
Camperdown against the Dutch, the surgeon Robert Young of HMS
Ardent had little assistance and was overwhelmed by the number of
wounded. He graphically related the scenes in the cockpit that day, 11
October 1797:

> I had no mate, having been without one for three months before. I was
> employed in operating and dressing till near four in the morning, the
> action beginning about one [in the] afternoon. So great was my fatigue
> that I began several amputations, under a dread of sinking before I should
> have secured the blood vessels. Ninety wounded were brought down
> during the action, when the whole cockpit deck, cabins, wing berths,
> and part of the cable tier, together with my platform, and my preparations
> for dressing, were covered with them, so that for a time, they were laid on
> each other at the foot of the ladder where they were brought down, and
> I was obliged to go on deck to the Commanding Officer to state the sit-
> uation and apply for men to go down the main hatchway, and move the
> foremost of the wounded further forward into the tiers and wings, and
> thus make room in the cockpit.[10]

About sixteen men died before Young was able to treat them, and
another man was so severely injured that little could be done for
him:

Joseph Bonheur [Joseph Bonier, a landsman from London] had his
right thigh taken off by a cannon shot close to the pelvis, so that it was
impossible to apply a tourniquet; his right arm was also shot to pieces,
the stump of the thigh . . . presented a dreadful and large surface of
mangled flesh. In this state he lived near two hours, perfectly sensible
and incessantly calling out in a strong voice to assist him. The bleeding
from the femoral artery, although so high up, must have been very
inconsiderable, and I observed it did not bleed as he lay. All the service
I could render the unfortunate man was to put dressings over the parts
and give him drink.[11]

In the battle between the frigates HMS *Macedonian* and USS
United States in 1812, there were so many casualties that the surgeon,
Michael O'Brien, and his assistants could barely cope. After the
battle, Samuel Leech went to help: 'The surgeon and his mate were
smeared with blood from head to foot: they looked more like butchers than doctors. Having so many patients, they had once shifted
their quarters from the cockpit to the steerage; they now removed to
the ward-room, and the long table, round which the officers had sat
over many a merry feast, was soon covered with the bleeding forms of
maimed and mutilated seamen.'[12]

The process of amputation under battle conditions was by today's
standards horrific, and terrified many of the men who were waiting to
see the surgeon. Amputation was usually the only solution for badly
injured limbs, as otherwise infection, primarily gangrene, was liable
to set in, and the sooner the operation was performed, the more
successful its outcome. Few operations other than amputations of
limbs could be performed until anaesthetics were used. The first operation under anaesthesia did not take place until 1846, in London,
though occasionally opium was administered beforehand to dull the
pain. Patients were held in place by the surgeon's assistants while
he operated.

The first task was to apply a tourniquet above the wound to reduce
the flow of blood. This also helped the surgeon to see the wound a
little better in the dim candlelight. He next cut through the skin, tis-
sues and muscle right down to the bone with a knife, after which the

flesh was pulled back so that the bone could be cut higher up. Nelson's right arm was amputated by the surgeon Thomas Eshelby after being struck by a musketball just above the elbow in the disastrous attack in 1797 against the Spanish town of Santa Cruz on Tenerife in the Canary Islands. He could not forget the shock of the cold instruments, as George Magrath, his surgeon on board the *Victory* in 1803–4, learned from him: 'Of all the sufferings of the operation . . . he complained most of "the coldness of the knife," in making the first circular cut through the integuments and muscles. So painfully and deeply was the recollection engrafted on his feelings, that I had general instructions, in consequence, whenever there was a prospect of coming to action, to have a hanging stove kept in the galley, for the purpose of heating water, in which to immerse the knife.'[13]

Leech helped with the amputation on a Swedish messmate, Able Seaman Jacob Logholm: 'We held him while the surgeon cut off his leg above the knee. The task was most painful to behold, the surgeon using his knife and saw on human flesh and bones, as freely as the butcher at the shambles does on the carcass of the beast!'[14] He added: 'Such scenes of suffering as I saw in that ward-room, I hope never to witness again.'[15]

Next, the arteries and smaller vessels would be tied with silk or waxed thread ligatures, the tourniquet was released, and finally the skin was folded back over the stump of the bone and taped, with the ligatures hanging out. The ligatures were believed to help drain the wound, and eventually fell out, but they were actually a source of infection. One of Nelson's ligatures took months to fall away, and he suffered considerable pain for a long time afterwards, possibly because a nerve had been tied up with the artery.

Towards the end of the war in France, in July 1815, Midshipman Robert Barrett of the *Hebrus* frigate was also horrified at the process of amputation after an accident to the carpenter's mate, twenty-three-year-old George Huntley from South Shields:

The poor fellow's jacket was quickly ripped off, and it was a lamentable spectacle to behold his mutilated frame: his only words were, 'Doctor, bear a hand.' The most stern and iron nerve, I am sure, must give a momentary shudder, when the surgeon [David Boyter], after having made the first incision, and drawn back sufficient skin to cover the stump, grasps the knife with firmness, and cuts determinedly through the quivering flesh, severing the arteries and muscles down to the bone . . . poor Huntley winced at this terrible period, but afterwards continued only to mutter as before, 'Bear a hand, good doctor.' 'Tis a mistake, I doubt not, to believe the suffering either severe or excessive, in comparison, when the bone is severed, and the marrow touched by the saw; but the most courageous heart will flinch when the arteries are hooked out until the ligatures are fastened.[16]

In 1789 the surgeon Lionel Gillespie proposed covering the stump with a pig's bladder, a procedure that does not seem to have been adopted:

In reflecting on the improvements amputation has undergone and those it is capable of, it strikes me as an easy and plausible method of dressing that . . . after the vessels have been secured and the soft parts have been drawn down, to apply immediately over the face of the stump a hog's bladder, prepared in such a manner as to soften it and prevent it becoming stiff from the heat of the body. To the mouth of this straps of adhesive plaster might be attached, which would stick to the skin previously shaved, and supported by a few turns of bandage. The bottom of the bladder being then laid hold of and drawn down so as to bring the circumference of the stump into contact, may be tied so as to preserve this situation of the parts and effectually exclude air.[17]

One of the keys to a successful operation was speed, because if it went on too long the patient could die of shock or bleed to death. With Huntley's amputation, Barrett noted that 'The operation on his arm was skilfully completed in little more than twelve minutes, but the agony he suffered was excruciating when the splinters were extracted from his face and breast'.[18] At the Battle of Camperdown, Henry Spence, a seaman aged about twenty-five years, was brought down to the cockpit of the *Russell* in a bad way, as the surgeon George Magrath recorded: 'Being in the act of running out one of the forecastle guns, a large cannonball from the opponent's ship struck him a little above the ankle joints, and carried away both legs.'[19] Magrath was so short of skilled help that he had to attend to another patient: 'During the time that I was examining the legs, another man came to the cockpit with profuse hemorrhages from a large artery that was divided by a splinter. I was therefore necessitated to leave Spence (previously applying the tournequet) to staunch the man's bleeding, which was soon done, and afterwards he [Spence] was laid on the table.'[20]

Apart from the surgeon's mates, during a battle surgeons also had assistance from unskilled seamen, called loblolly men, and from any available women. Examples of women performing such duties come to light in chance remarks, as with Magrath, who accepted it as normal that women were on board during the battle, and only mentioned them in passing during his description of the operation on Spence:

> He was laid on the table and the operation was performed in the usual way, which he bore very well indeed, so much so, that he did not require an assistant to hold him on the table; lucky it was that he bore it so well, as a shot at this time came into the cockpit and passed the operating table, close, this startled all the women who formed the chief of my assistance . . . The Tournequet being applied in the ham, the operation was finished in the usual way by bringing the muscles and teguments over the face of the stump, so as to form a longitudinal line down the face of the stump, the lips being laid neatly together, they were retained in that state of contact with each other by adhesive straps, the bandage being applied, a cordial was administered, and he was laid on a platform, in the cable tier, erected for the accommodation of the wounded men. When the action was over, he was put into a cot.[21]

Magrath commented that 'The man's legs were amputated in the heat of action, which I am happy to say did not retard the case, indeed when he was first carried to the cockpit, there were little hopes of success.'[22] The following year another woman is known to have helped in the surgeon's cockpit, this time at the Battle of the Nile. She was Christiann White, who claimed that 'during the action I attended the surgeon in dressing the wounded men, and like wise attended the sick and wounded during their passage to Gibraltar, which was 11 weeks on board his Majesty's ship *Majestic*'.[23]

Like Magrath's experience, the surgeon Robert Young painted a picture of torment in the cockpit of his ship at the Battle of Camperdown, forcing himself to remain detached yet compassionate:

> Melancholy cries of assistance were addressed to me from every side, by wounded and dying and piteous moans and bewailings from pain and despair. In the midst of these agonising scenes I was enabled to present myself firm and collected, and embracing in my mind the whole of the situation to direct my attentions where the greatest and most essential services could be performed. Some with wounds, bad indeed and painful but slight in comparison with the dreadful condition of others, were most vociferous for my assistance. These I was obliged to reprimand with severity as their noise disturbed the last moments of the dying. I cheered and commended the patient fortitude of others, and sometimes extorted a smile of satisfaction from the mangled sufferers amidst so many horrors. The man whose [right] leg I first amputated, Richard Traverse [Richard Travese, a landsman from Manchester], had not uttered a groan or complaint from the time he was brought down, and several, exulting in the news of the victory, declared they regretted not the loss of their limbs.[24]

Despite the surgeons' best efforts, many patients developed fevers and died, quite often of tetanus or gangrene. Huntley, whose amputation was witnessed by Barrett in the *Hebrus*, only survived a few days after surgery. Hygiene was simply not understood, and even though surgeons strived after cleanliness, they did not know that bacteria from their instruments and elsewhere caused infection. On board the *Macedonian*, Leech thought that alcohol was responsible for the death of another shipmate:

Among the wounded, was a brave fellow named [John] Wells. After the surgeon had amputated and dressed his arm, he walked about in fine spirits, as if he had received only a slight injury. Indeed, while under the operation, he manifested a similar heroism – observing to the surgeon, 'I have lost my arm in the service of my country; but I don't mind it, doctor, it's the fortune of war.' Cheerful and gay as he was, he soon died. His companions gave him rum; he was attacked by fever and died. Thus his messmates actually killed him with kindness.[25]

One survivor of amputation was sixteen-year-old Midshipman William Rivers, a native of Portsea and the son of the *Victory*'s gunner, also called William Rivers. Midshipman Rivers had his left foot badly injured and three teeth knocked out by shot during the Battle of Trafalgar. He related what happened after he had been helped to the cockpit: 'The foot hung by a piece of skin about 4 inches above the ankle. When in the cockpit I called for Putty Nose (the nickname for the purser's steward) for a knife to cut the foot off. M'Beatty the surgeon stopped it, saying "what are you going to do with a knife?" "Cut my foot off, it is of no use," I say. "Doctor – when will you take me in hand?" Answer "very shortly".'[26]

Midshipman Rivers had to wait some time before Surgeon Beatty dealt with him, as his father, Gunner Rivers, later heard: '[It was] about an hour after when the doctor took him in hand, told him to lay down on the table. His answer was, "I will sit on the table, you may cut where you please." During his amputation, [he] said to the ship's company that was wounded, "My men, it is nothing to have a limb off, you will find pleasure when you come here, men, to get rid of your shattered limb."'[27]

The action over, Gunner Rivers described how he went down into the cockpit to look for his son: 'Here I am Father, nothing is the matter with me; only lost my leg, and that in a good cause. He requested that I would get him up. The Doctor granted [permission]. I got him in my cabin.'[28] His father later remarked that it was customary at midnight to throw dead men overboard, as well as amputated limbs, and that when his son realised what was happening, he heard him call out, '"Ask the men, what they were doing at the port." Answer, "Nothing Sir." "I suppose you are throwing legs and arms overboard" "Yes Sir" "Have you got mine?" "I don't know Sir" "I understood old Putty Nose was to have them for fresh meat for the sick".[29] The man they called Putty Nose was the purser's steward, James Cosgrove, a native of Dublin. Rivers made a remarkable recovery, returned to duty after a few weeks, and four years later married and had several children.

The surgeons were far more proficient than their Continental naval counterparts, and at Trafalgar the surgeon William Shoveller of HMS *Leviathan* was horrified at the sight of Spanish prisoners, as he wrote in his report:

> The *Leviathan* has been much crowded with Spanish prisoners (about 500), 90 of whom were wounded, several with tourniquets on their different extremities, and which had been applied since the action, four or five days elapsing, consequently most of the limbs in a state of mortification or approaching it. In four of these cases I amputated – two arms, and two thighs – the two former did well and were sent on shore at Algeziras, the latter died on the third day of the operation, the stumps becoming mortified.[30]

Nevertheless, the physician Gilbert Blane saw many men bleed to death or lose so much blood that they could not undergo an operation, and he was in favour of the men carrying tourniquets during a battle: 'It has been proposed, and on some occasions practiced, to make each man carry about him a garter, or piece of rope-yarn, in order to bind up a limb in case of profuse bleeding. If it be objected that this, from its solemnity, may be apt to intimidate common men, officers should at least make use of some precaution.'[31]

Another common battle injury that was often fatal was being burned by the accidental explosion of loose gunpowder and cartridges, such as when the wads that held the shot and gunpowder in place were not wetted when firing cannons, which, as Blane explained, 'prevents their inflaming and blowing back when they fight the weather side of the ship [into the wind]; a circumstance which, without this precaution, gives occasion to a number of accidents by the burning parts catching the loose powder, or setting fire to the cartridges'.[32] On board the *Leviathan* at Trafalgar, William Shoveller recorded that Andrew Pheling, a seaman, was 'Burnt in the face, neck, breast and thighs, by an explosion of one of the main deck guns, the breach of which flew out'.[33] Under Shoveller's care, he was fit enough to return to duty a month later. Less fortunate was David Morris, a thirty-year-old seaman, who was fatally injured in the same accident, 'severely burnt over his forehead, face, neck, and over the whole of the breast and belly'.[34] Although he was given opium, and dressings and ointments were applied, some of Shoveller's treatment was not helpful. From the start 'he was bled and an enema ordered immediately',[35] and after a fortnight, Morris died.

It was not death or injury in battle, but everyday accidents and disease that took their toll on ship's crews, and there was an assumption that on top of those who might die in battle or shipwreck, one sailor in thirty might die from accident or disease during a voyage. Experienced seamen were not exempt from accidents, and although many were due to unnecessarily dangerous working methods, where safety was sacrificed to speed, numerous incidents were undoubtedly due to too much alcohol. Appalling accidents were continually recorded, many of which were falls from high in the rigging on to the deck or into the sea, or falls down open hatchways, as with Joseph Lawrance, an ordinary seaman of the *Canopus*, at Plymouth in July 1806: '7 oClock P.M. Fell from the main deck into the hold in the act of taking his hammock down and fractured the seventh rib of the left side. He was immediately bled to the amount of sixteen ounces.'[36] Because the *Canopus* was being repaired, they were all being held on board a hulk (rather than being given leave), and so the surgeon Abraham Martin added: 'Was sent to the hospital after taking his purge. We are at this time in the *Yarmouth* hulk in a great state of confusion and noise.'[37]

Robert Bailey, a landsman from Somerset, blamed the negligence of the boatswain for the death of an able seaman, James McCartney, when their ship the *Audacious* was heading for Palermo in Sicily to rejoin Nelson towards the end of May 1799: 'His death was occasioned in getting the sheet anchor over the side – by too much noise and hurry of the boatswain which is too common on those occasions.

The flue [fluke] of the anchor pitched on both his feet. One lay cut off and part of the other foot. He survived near a week in this calamitous situation.'[38] Off Valletta in Malta some months later, in January 1800, Bailey noted further incidents: 'A melancholy accident took place this evening. Wm Lewis belonging to the main top unfortunately fell out of the top in to the launch; fortunately he only broke his thigh.'[39] Just two days later, at ten in the morning during a gale, Bailey recorded, 'close reefed topsails, sent down top gt [gallant] yards and struck top gt [gallant] mast. Two lads [Thomas] Hatch and a Maltese boy in furling the mizen topsail was knocked off the yard; the Malta lad fell on the poop and was dead in an instant; Hatch fell overboard and was fortunately picked up but much hurt.'[40] The Maltese boy was Vincenzo Bonefatso, who had joined as a volunteer.

By October 1806 the *Canopus* was at sea, and the surgeon reported another accident, the casualty being Stephen Kennedy, a seaman: 'This unfortunate patient in the act of going down the fore ladder when it was blowing hard and the ship rolling very much slipped off and pitched upon a quart bottle on the lower deck which broke and made a very extensive wound in the sole of his right foot.'[41] Gangrene rapidly set in, and strangely the surgeon monitored its progress rather than instantly amputate, which was the general procedure. By the fourth day he noted: 'This morning he appeared refreshed having had a good night. The gangrenous appearance has extended all over the leg up to the knee and a swelling . . . up to the groin. Tongue foul. Pulse weak and tremulous. Answers sensibly when spoken to but his eyes have an unusual languor in them.'[42] By four in the afternoon, Kennedy was dead.

Someone falling overboard usually galvanised the crew into action, particularly as most seamen could not swim. Archibald Sinclair depicted the scene:

There is no call or cry can be heard at sea that elicits such instantaneous alacrity, rouses the dormant faculties of sleepers, and stimulates the active energies of all hands, like 'A man overboard' . . . In a well ordered ship, after the first rush on deck, a stranger not accustomed to our ways would be struck with the unusual silence, and the calm determined energy with which a few commonplace manoeuvres are performed . . . Under these circumstances the ship's way has soon been stopped, boats are manned, lowered and away. The rigging, tops and yards are clustered with officers and men, indiscriminately gazing around the horizon, in hopes of being the first to catch a glimpse of one who, for the moment, is the object of such intense and general anxiety.[43]

In August 1810, on board the *Nisus* frigate, the surgeon James Prior witnessed Matthew Reilly from Dublin fall overboard as they approached the Cape of Good Hope:

A fine sailor-lad, who had been in a former ship with me, doing duty aloft with some companions, missed his hold and was precipitated into the sea. The alarm was instantly given, and every effort made to arrest the rapid progress of the ship; but before this could be effected, the poor sufferer was left at a considerable distance behind. Still we could trace him in the undulation of the waves, struggling for existence; our eyes were rivetted upon him to direct the boat in endeavouring to save him, yet with no other effect than to witness the last struggles of human nature, – for just when it had arrived within arm's length, he sunk to rise no more. To increase the general regret on this occasion, it was discovered that the poor boy allowed half his pittance of pay for the support of an aged mother.[44]

When rescue was not possible, they set sail again, as Sinclair sadly noted: 'For a very short time the memory of the lost one is spoken of with regret, but soon fades away, and his only epitaph will be the two letters opposite to his name in the ship's books, – D.D. – discharged dead.'[45]

Other accidents occurred because of the physical strain involved in many aspects of work on board, in particular when filling and lifting water casks. Seamen were frequently afflicted by hernias, also referred to as ruptures, in which an organ protrudes into another part of the body – usually part of the intestine protruding through the abdominal wall of tissue. Trusses were frequently supplied to the seamen to keep organs in place, but they were not always effective. In March 1804, William Shoveller, surgeon of the *Leviathan*, described the suffering of George Barnes, a twenty-seven-year-old seaman: 'The hernia was reducible and supported by a truss; but from his inattention to its application, has allowed the rupture to slip into the scrotum, and his bowels to remain for some days in a state of constipation. Bleeding, enemas, drastic purges and fomentations have been used, without effect. [Sent to] Haslar Hospital.'[46]

Hernias were so commonplace that men were not admitted into the navy with a pre-existing condition. Because seamen could obtain a pension from the Chatham Chest for injuries sustained, it was specifically decreed that 'The Directors of the Chest having reason to believe that many persons having obtained Pensions for Ruptures which they had upon them before entering into His Majesty's Service, the Surgeons are desired in all cases for the above complaint to be careful in examining whether such injury has recently happened.'[47] George Wheeler, also twenty-seven years old and an able seaman from the *Phaeton*, was deemed worthy of a pension, 'by a considerable portion of intestine and omentum being forced down into the left side of the scrotum, which was with difficulty returned; and has been down several times since; from making too great an exertion on the twenty seventh of June eighteen hundred and eleven . . . training one of the main deck guns when at his quarters off the coast of Borneo in the East Indies'.[48]

It is not surprising that the men also suffered from a whole host of other conditions, such as rheumatism, respiratory problems and bowel complaints, but the difficulty for the surgeon was that most illnesses were not understood. Disease was the invisible terror, because virtually nothing was known about the real causes or identifications of sickness, which was believed to fall into three main categories – 'fevers, fluxes, and the scurvy'.[49] Most physicians thought that disease was due to noxious smells or 'miasmas', while the more pious believed it was caused by sin. Some also believed that disease was linked to the phases of the moon and weather conditions. The surgeon Lionel Gillespie repeatedly linked the weather and the moon to the condition of his patients, as at the Nore on 8 December 1787: 'The wind came to the S.W. last night and blew fresh with rain. It continued in that quarter. Heavy dark clouds and a moist air. The restlessness and watchfulness of several, patients as well as others, on the nights of the 6th and 7th seemed to predict variation in our atmosphere coinciding with the approaching phase of the moon – one or two were attacked with arthritis.'[50] Over a decade later George Magrath admitted: 'Notwithstanding the great advances which of late years have been made in the science of medicine, we are not yet sufficiently acquainted with the laws which govern the system in a state of health.'[51] Nelson, writing to another physician, commented: 'The great thing in all military service is health; and you will agree with me, that it is easier for an officer to keep men healthy, than for a physician to cure them.'[52]

Sometimes the seamen recovered in spite of, rather than because of, the surgeon's intervention. If a disease was identified imprecisely, the treatment could be unhelpful if not dangerous, with much blood-letting, deliberate blistering of skin, purgatives and emetics. On 20 December 1805 at Plymouth, the surgeon William Shoveller recorded that Robert Leister, a twenty-four-year-old seaman, 'complains of cough, pain in his breast affecting his respiration and headache and general pains'.[53] For what may have been a severe cold or influenza, Shoveller carried out drastic initial treatment: 'Bled, purged, blistered.'[54] By the 30th Leister was discharged to duty, though no thanks to his medical care.

George Magrath was mystified by one illness that spread rapidly through the *Russell*. Soon after leaving Yarmouth in March 1801, under Captain William Cuming, to join in Nelson's bombardment of Copenhagen, many were laid low, and the illness only abated when they went to the Mediterranean three months later, but it returned on their way back to England in September. Magrath likened it to typhus and scurvy, and wrote in frustration that 'I am not really in possession of language sufficiently emphatical or expressive to describe the distressed situation of the *Russell*'s crew, during the prevalence of this scourge, without feeling and lamenting for the poor sufferers who underwent more human misery than even the imagination can conceive.'[55]

On arriving in port, ships' crews were frequently forced to remain on board for a while in a period of quarantine, in order to minimise the risk of diseases like yellow fever and plague being brought ashore. Generally, the seamen and officers hated this period of quarantine and felt that it served no purpose.

As soon as ships put to sea, many new recruits suffered from seasickness, though this could afflict old hands as well. James Scott, who in 1803 at the age of thirteen had just joined the *Phaeton* frigate as a volunteer recruit, suffered badly from seasickness at first and reckoned that 'Sea-sickness I found worse than the doctor's emetics at home'.[56] The surgeon Lionel Gillespie wrote in nauseating detail in his journal about seasickness, which he experienced when his ship, the *Vanguard*, sailed from Woolwich to Portsmouth in May 1787:

> The ship pitched most intolerably. Most of our people were more or less affected with seasickness. 25 [May] – blowed hard. About noon I became sick, could not eat any all day, vomited at first an acid, then an insipid phlegm. Slept badly, but about 6 o'clock of the 26th A.M. the ship pitching much, I became affected with insufferable nausea, spitting, dizziness . . . and at length vomited two or three times yellow bile. At noon got better . . . for 24 hours my sickness continued. I eat or drink nothing. About the time the bilious vomiting occurred I had a stool after being costive for some days. My sickness as well as that of several others on board regularly observed the period of a day occurring at noon and going off about the same time. Found some benefit from chewing of ginger.[57]

Eight months later, during another bout of seasickness, this time on board the *Racehorse*, Gillespie was more analytical about the condition:

> The consent between the brain, stomach and vessels of the skin in seasickness is remarkable. A vertiginous sensation is first perceived, followed by anxiety and nausea. The face becomes pale, the extremities chilly, and the whole surface shrivelled. A few quick motions of the ship produces a straining and vomiting. The contents of the stomach are thrown up and

the subsequent straining . . . of the respiratory organs proves a stimulus to the organs of the circulation. The blood being also forced up to the head perhaps stimulates the brain. The vessels of [the] surface become relaxed and filled with blood. The depressing nausea is relieved and spirits return for a time. I have to remark with regard to seasickness that it is proper to prepare for it by opening the belly previously, by avoiding all cause of indigestion, avoiding the use of fluids, to be abstemious, when at sea to keep in the air and if possible to work, to pull and haul; or when the stomach has been emptied, to avoid drinking and support a warmth of surface lying abed with much clothing. I've sometimes met with persons who are never affected with seasickness, an instance of this sort I have now before me in a boy. I think that most of those I have seen thus happy have been of a thin rather delicate habit with a long neck and consumptive make.[58]

New recruits were also responsible for the deaths of hundreds of seamen, because after being seized by the press-gang, the men came on board in their filthy clothes, bringing with them lice that rapidly spread what is nowadays called epidemic typhus. The crowded conditions on board led to the rapid spread of such diseases, and the surgeon Thomas Trotter reckoned that 'There is no situation where so large a number of human beings are confined in so small a space as in a man of war.'[59] Typhus in particular was so common in overcrowded places with inadequate or dire standards of hygiene that it was often called jail, hospital, camp, ship or war fever. When lice suck the blood of an infected person, the bacteria multiply inside them and are excreted in their faeces. Seamen scratching lice bites became infected by rubbing infected lice faeces into their wounds, and the disease was also spread by coming into contact with lice faeces on the clothing and bedding of sufferers.

The main symptoms of this potentially fatal disease are a prolonged high fever, severe headache and a rash. Although the causes of the disease would not be discovered for decades, it was realised that impressed seamen were a prime cause, and Gilbert Blane commented that 'a single infected man, or even any part of his cloathing, may spread sickness through a whole ship's company . . . and when the cause of the sickliness of particular ships is traced to its source, it will generally be found to have originated from taking on board infected men at Spithead, or wherever else the ship's company may have been completed'.[60] The response was to attempt to have impressed men stripped, washed and provided with new clothes, and Blane also advocated strict hygiene and ventilation on board ships, because of the belief that typhus and other diseases were caused by foul smells and poor-quality air. This reduced the cases of typhus, but the disease was never eradicated.

The 'flux' was a common complaint that included dysentery, gastroenteritis and food poisoning. Dysentery (an intestinal infection caused by eating or drinking contaminated food or water) was also described as 'the bloody flux', and patients suffered from diarrhoea, often with blood, abdominal cramps and dehydration. On board the *Rainbow* in the West Indies in 1773, the surgeon Robert Robertson commented that dysentery had hit them hard: 'The dysentery still continued to rage amongst the people, attacking young and old; but none of the officers were seized with it. However, this is not much to be wondered at, if it be considered that they lived better in every respect, and were not exposed to so many hardships as the people were . . . All the attendants of the sick were affected with the flux.'[61] He added:

> Of all the diseases which attack a ship's company, the dysentery, if not the most fatal, is in my opinion equally so with any other; and by far the most loathsome. The constant doleful complaints from the various violent pains of the bowels; from gripes, and tenesmus; from the continual noxious fetor about the sick, as well as from that of the necessary [toilet] buckets . . . What renders the dysentery on board of ships most distressing, is, that no *certain method* of curing it has yet been discovered.[62]

The disease sailors feared most was yellow fever, which had a very high mortality rate, and they dreaded hearing that their destination was the West Indies, where it was so prevalent. In 1794 at Port Royal in Jamaica, Midshipman Frederick Hoffman described its spread on board his own ship: 'The yellow fever was now making lamentable havoc among the crew. Six were either carried to the hospital or buried daily. After losing fifty-two men, one of the lieutenants, the captain's clerk, and four mids, the captain requested the admiral's permission to go to sea, for, although we had more than thirty cases of the fever on board, the surgeon thought the pure sea-breeze might be the means of preserving their lives.'[63]

The surgeon's assumption that they were safer at sea was correct, though he had no idea that by leaving land, they also left behind mosquitoes which carried and spread the yellow fever virus. It was often called 'yellow jack' because of the yellow quarantine flag flown on ships where men had contracted the disease, but it was also known as 'the vomits' or 'black vomits' because sufferers became feverish and vomited dark bloody liquid. Their skin and eyes also turned yellow through jaundice caused by the breakdown of the liver. The progress of the disease was rapid. A few days after being bitten by a mosquito, the fever rapidly took hold, with either death less than a week later or else a prolonged period of convalescence. The real cause of yellow fever was unknown, and some surgeons used bark,* while others distrusted its use and favoured a mercury purgative (in the form of calomel pills) and bleeding. This terrifying disease frequently overwhelmed ships' crews, leaving only a handful of survivors out of several hundred previously healthy men. Those who recovered had a lifelong immunity.

Once Hoffman's ship was finally rid of yellow fever, the crew next suffered from scurvy, and 'one hundred and forty of the seamen were obliged to keep their beds. Their legs, hands, feet and gums became almost black, and swollen to twice their natural size.'[64] Scurvy was a slow and insidious disease caused by vitamin C deficiency and had truly appalling effects. It was probably the worst disease caused by poor diet, and yet by far the easiest to prevent and cure. It was very much a plague of sailors confined on board ship, with no easy access to fresh fruit and vegetables – more seamen died from scurvy than all other causes of mortality combined. Those falling prey to scurvy would

---

* The Peruvian cinchona tree bark, also known as Jesuit's bark, from which quinine was derived years later.

gradually experience listlessness and depression, aching and stiff joints, old wounds opened and previously healed bone fractures separated. In addition, new injuries such as bruises, cuts and fractured bones failed to heal, gums became sore and swollen, teeth loosened and fell out, while the breath stank. On the skin, haemorrhages caused purple blotches and spots, which eventually turned black. Without effective treatment, sufferers became totally lethargic and eventually died.

When Hoffman's ship reached the island of St Domingo, some scurvy sufferers were taken on land, because burying them in the ground was (bizarrely) considered a cure:

> Immediately, on anchoring, by the advice of the surgeon, we sent a party on shore with spades to dig holes in the softest soil they could find for the purpose of putting the worst scurvy subjects into them . . . Twenty men, who looked like bloated monsters, were removed on shore, and buried in them up to their chins. Some of the boys were sent with the sufferers to keep flies and insects from their faces. It was ridiculous enough to see twenty men's heads stuck out of the ground. The patients were kept in fresh earth for two hours, and then put into their hammocks under a large tent. On the fourth day they were so much benefited by that treatment and living on oranges, shaddocks, and other antiscorbutic* fruits, that they were able to go on board again.[65]

Scurvy was such a serious hazard of long sea voyages that many doctors searched for a cure, and by the mid-eighteenth century it was established – but not universally accepted – that citrus fruits and fresh green vegetables dramatically reversed its course in a matter of days. The crew on board Hoffman's ship could have been simply treated with the fresh fruit, without undergoing burial in soil, but ignorance prevailed. Scurvy was much more a disease of the ordinary seaman, as their diet was more basic than that of most officers.

In 1795 the physician Sir Gilbert Blane resigned from St Thomas's Hospital in London and became a commissioner for the Board of the

---

* Scorbutic means suffering from scurvy.

Care of Sick and Wounded Seamen (Sick and Hurt Board). He straightaway ordered that lemon juice should be issued daily, mixed with rum, sugar and water. When in the West Indies, limes were often substituted, so that the seamen came to be called 'limeys', yet lemons contained twice as much vitamin C and were far more effective at combating scurvy. Citrus fruits had been shown to be effective decades earlier, when James Lind advocated lemon juice, but he had recommended rob, a boiled lemon syrup that loses its vitamin C. With Blane's intervention, this once appalling disease was virtually eradicated. In the years afterwards it occurred only sporadically, as in 1801 on board the *Russell*, when the surgeon George Magrath was greatly affected by the torment of the seamen:

> Several of the scorbutic cases were truly the most deplorable I ever beheld, exhibiting the most aggravated symptoms of malignancy and distress. It first invaded with much languor and torpor the body; the countenance became pale and bloated . . . respiration was much disturbed, nay, in many, quite suspended on the slightest exertion or motion of the body. Soon after the appearance of these unfriendly precursors, the gums acquired a softness and considerable tumour, from which arose hemorrhage . . . the teeth in many instances became loose and the breath evicted a most offensive and foetid smell.[66]

Magrath did say they had no deaths, 'as the citric acid performed a cure in every instance'.[67] Nevertheless, throughout the Napoleonic Wars scurvy was a minor complaint for British sailors, in contrast to earlier times, and at long last Royal Navy ships could remain at sea effectively for long periods of time.

Blane observed that crews were more prone to illness when anchored close in to shore, but thought this was because of the bad air ('mal aria') from nearby marshes. The surgeon James Prior on board the *Nisus* in 1811 agreed that it was far healthier at sea than on land: 'The sea is without doubt the healthiest place in a tropical climate. The breeze, pure, fresh and invigorating, untainted by pestiferous effluvia, and uninterrupted by obstructions, revives the drooping frame from the effects of heat or laborious avocations.'[68] He

added: 'In all the detested spots that conspire against human life –
and America has her West-Indies and Guiana, Africa her Gambia
and Senegal, Asia her Java and Banda, and parts of Europe are yet
scourged by plague, the best preservative is to keep embarked. Here
we may often bid defiance to the grim fiend – Death, and his ruthless agents, marsh and animal effluvia.'[69]

Mosquitoes were a nuisance for their bites, but nobody realised
that they were carriers of disease and of malarial parasites, which are
transferred to humans when bitten. Men frequently went on shore to
search for firewood and to fill up water casks, where they encountered
mosquitoes, and Blane's advice was that 'The duties of wooding and
watering are so unwholesome, that negroes, if possible, should be
hired to perform them.'[70] This was not because he thought black
Africans were expendable, but because it was thought they were more
resistant to such diseases. Blane knew that in most cases seamen
would have to be employed in wooding and watering, and so his
advice was that they should not stay on shore overnight and to swallow some Peruvian bark, commenting that

> the fever produced by the impure air of marshes may not appear for many
> days after the noxious principle, whatever it is, has been imbibed; men
> having been sometimes seized with it more than a week after they had
> been at sea. It naturally occurs, therefore, that something may be done in
> the intermediate time to prevent the effects of this bad air; and nothing
> is more advisable than to take some doses of Peruvian bark, after clearing
> the bowels by a purgative.[71]

Without understanding malaria, they had discovered that bark
was effective at preventing and treating the disease. In November
1805, the surgeon Francis Spilsbury was on board the *Favourite* sloop,
which was accompanying a convoy to Africa. When they went on
shore in what is today Senegal, the men were given bark, but
Spilsbury was unconvinced, thinking that it used up their supplies far
too quickly: 'Here we first began to give our men bark in wine; a glass
before they went, and another when they returned, under the idea of
preventing fever. Whatever medical gentlemen may think of this

practice, I shall call it a *hocus-pocus* mode of driving away fever.'[72] In his opinion it was much better to give the men bark once they had fallen ill. Many years before, in 1774, Surgeon Robert Robertson on board the *Rainbow* in the West Indies took a different view: 'Employed in watering the ship. The waterers get the tincture of bark in the morning',[73] and for the next two days: 'Gave the waterers tincture of bark'.[74] He used bark to prevent illness and to treat sick seamen and concluded that it was often effective, but such new remedies that were not understood were slow to be accepted.

So poor was the comprehension of the causes of diseases that a single remedy was believed to be capable of treating all manner of unrelated illnesses like scurvy and venereal disease. Local and national newspapers frequently carried advertisements such as one in a West Country newspaper in 1809 that proclaimed the wonders of Wessels Jesuit Drops:

IN HIS MAJESTY'S NAVY, these Drops have for near 100 years past maintained their Character as a specific for the Scurvy, Gravel, Dropsy, Stranguary, Weakness and Obstruction, in the Urinary Passage; and general debility; but particularly for their absolute and speedy Cure on the first attack of the Venereal Disease. Wessels Jesuit Drops and Specific Remedy, are the *only safe* and *expeditious Cure* from the first stage of Venereal Infection to the last stage of confirmed Lues, and are so innocent in their nature, as to require little or no restraint. As a restorative for general Debility, Wessels Jesuit Drops have been long known and esteemed whether the debility arises from too copious use of Mercury, from excess of Venery, or intense heat of climate, they are equally serviceable: – such as have the misfortune to be troubled with old *stubborn Gleets, Seminal Effusions*, or any *weakness* of the *Kidneys, Ureters* or *Bladder Diabete*, or difficulty in making water, will experience a compleat cure by due perseverance. Shaw and Co. 66, St. Paul's Church Yard, having purchased these medicines of Mr Wessel, none can possibly be genuine unless a black Stamp engraved Shaw and Edwards, successors to Joseph Wessels, appears on the out-side of every bottle. Ask for Wessel Jesuits Drops with a black stamp. Price 2s 9d. – 11s. and 22s per bottle.[75]

Surgeons' journals are full of records of men suffering from venereal disease ('the itch' or 'the pox' to the seamen) along with the
remedies, such as John De Venner, a seaman aged twenty-one, who
was recorded as having 'Swelled testicle and gonorrhoea. Bled.
Purged. Fomentations. Nitrous draught. Astringent injections.'[76] Up
to 1795 infected men were charged 15 shillings by the surgeon for
treatment, which frequently involved mercury, but payment was abolished as it deterred them from reporting their condition. Writing in
1773, the *Rainbow*'s surgeon Robert Robertson reckoned that 'Seamen
on board of his majesty's ships are so desirous to save their fifteen
shillings, that by taking medicines of each others prescriptions, and
putting off time, three out of every four who complained on board
the *Rainbow* had lues venera.'[77] With their recourse to prostitutes, the
men would have suffered all manner of conditions, including syphilis
(usually referred to as lues venera) and gonorrhoea. When surgeons
apparently cured patients, this more frequently reflected the natural
progress of the disease.

At Spithead in May 1798, on board HMS *Russell*, the surgeon
George Magrath despaired of the captain of marines, whom he calls
Robert J—— and who was suffering from gonorrhoea. This was
Marine Captain Robert Johnson, and Magrath described his condition
in detail, along with his treatment, with the comment: 'This gentleman
has a girl on board, the same that communicated this disease, and
although he is well aware that she is injured, he still continues to sleep
with her, notwithstanding I have put him in the remembrance of what
mischief she may do him. However he was deaf to all my arguments
and still persists in keeping [her] on board.'[78] Surgeon Lionel Gillespie
witnessed something similar on board the *Racehorse* in 1787:

> At this time there is on board here four prostitutes who have affected three
> or four persons, two with gonorhea and the rest with chancres and one has
> a crystalline – yet these women are seemingly well in health, are in good
> spirits and having been turned over from their first paramours are enter-
> tained by others who seem to remain unaffected by any syphilitic
> complaints. This seems to confirm me in the idea which I have formed of
> Lues Venera, that it depends on the state of the body of the person infected.[79]

On board the *Unité* in 1808, Robert Wilson was saddened by the death of William Thompson 'who died this day after lingering for some time with the venereal which wore him down to a skeleton and then killed him. I am sorry to say, that previous to this man's death, I myself heard him exclaim, "Well, I'll get well soon, time enough at any rate by the time we go again to Malta and then I'll have another rattle at a b—— of a w——."'[80]

As well as venereal disease, all kinds of ulcers were a constant concern of surgeons. Captain Edward Brenton wrote a few years after the Napoleonic Wars that 'The ulcer, when it has once got possession of a ship, is one of the most contagious and serious complaints to which seamen are liable. During the late war, the *Northumberland* had it to such a degree, that I think they were compelled to pay her off, that she might be cleansed from the infection. The loss of a limb was a very common occurrence from this complaint.'[81] The men often had leg ulcers, which were open sores, inflamed and painful, and difficult to heal. In 1812 Edward Mangin was perturbed by some men in the sick-bay of the *Gloucester* suffering from 'hideous ulcers (a general complaint) arising from bruises received in the course of their hard work, and exasperated by the damp in which they lie'.[82]

———•———

Men who were very ill or badly wounded could be transferred to hospital ships or hospitals on land. This was not necessarily in their best interests, according to Blane, who admitted they were then exposed to other diseases: 'Crowding, filth, and the mixture of diseases, are the great causes of mortality in hospitals.'[83] The two major hospitals in England were at Plymouth and Haslar at Portsmouth, with smaller establishments at other key coastal places like Yarmouth, Deal, Paignton, Dartmouth and Sheerness – Greenwich Hospital was an almshouse for pensioners, not a medical hospital. Overseas there were hospitals in the major ports like Gibraltar, Malta, Port Mahon at Minorca, Halifax in Canada, Cape of Good Hope, Madras, Antigua, Barbados and Bermuda. In addition, old ships were converted to hospitals in ports, while others were seagoing vessels that accompanied the fleets.

When the physician George Pinckard was shown round Haslar Hospital in 1796, he was greatly impressed:

> I felt it an honor to England that so noble an institution should offer, to our brave tars, the comforts required in sickness . . . The hospital, like many others of this island, from the grandeur of the edifice, might be mistaken for a palace. It is built in an open, airy situation near the sea, at a short distance from Gosport. The sick are brought in boats, from the ships at Spithead, and, conveniently, received on shore at a landing place at the hospital. This great building, fitted for the accommodation of two thousand patients, together with houses for officers and the medical attendants, a chapel, a laboratory, a variety of offices, and thirty-eight acres of good pasture land, belonging to the institution, is enclosed within a high brick wall, with iron-gates, and a porter's lodge at the entrance, which no stranger is permitted to pass, without the leave of one of the resident lieutenants.[84]

More to the point, none of the sick seamen was able to abscond from this secure hospital building.

Surgeons discharged to hospital those they could not deal with on board, and so Surgeon Robert Young of HMS *Ardent* let several men go to sick quarters at Great Yarmouth in June and July 1797, since they lacked 'any prospect of being cured on board'.[85] His discharged men had all manner of conditions, such as Alexander Mitchell, a seaman suffering from insanity, Charles Cain, a seaman with a maimed hand, John Halloran, a marine with venereal disease, and even the surgeon's mate, John Todd, with scurvy – increasing Young's shortage of assistants during the Battle of Camperdown a few months later. After that battle Young was understandably proud of his achievements, since he was able to discharge to hospital several men whom he had successfully treated: 'I have the satisfaction to say that of those who survived to undergo amputation or be dressed, all were found next morning in the gun room, where they were placed, in as comfortable state as possible, and on the third day were conveyed on shore in a keel in good spirits cheering the ship at going away, smoking their pipes and jesting as they sailed along and answering the cheers of thousands of the populace who received them on Yarmouth key [quay].'[86]

———•———

Men who died were rarely accorded special treatment like Nelson, whose body was brought back to England in a barrel of alcohol (spirits of wine topped up with brandy). Keeping a body on board until it could be buried in consecrated ground was generally not practical in the days before refrigeration. Nelson's body fared badly, as the surgeon William Beatty described in a private letter written to Reverend Scott in December 1805 while still on board the *Victory*:

> The remains of the late Lord Nelson are perfectly plastic, and in such a state of preservation from being completely saturated with the strong spirit in which they have been so long immersed, that embalment is rendered not only unnecessary, but the process if undertaken may be attended with the unpleasant circumstance of the skin coming off the body when the wrappers and bandages with which it is surrounded are removed. The features being lost, the face cannot with propriety be exposed during the time which the body may lay in state.[87]

A few weeks after the failed Dardanelles attack in 1807, Rear-Admiral Sir Thomas Louis died suddenly on board the *Canopus* off Alexandria in Egypt. It was decided to send his body to Malta, and the surgeon Abraham Martin described his embalming process: 'The stomach, intestines and spleen were removed and other sound viscera as well as the abdomen were well washed with spirits and sprinkled with nitre and camphor. Hemp soaked in spirits was also put in the cavity in place of the unsound viscera that were removed and the abdomen sewn up with the glover's suture.'[88] Louis's body was taken to Malta, where he was buried on Manoel Island. Vice-Admiral Collingwood, Nelson's second-in-command at Trafalgar, died at sea on 7 March 1810, and his body was brought back to England to be buried near Nelson in St Paul's Cathedral in London. Lord Eldon was moved by the emotions he observed: 'I attended his funeral at St.

Pauls, and was much affected by the grief manifested by some seamen who had served under him. I was a bearer, and a poor black sailor in tears laid fast hold of my arm, and attended almost the whole ceremony.'[89]

Sir Peter Parker's body was also embalmed after he died during an attack on a camp near Baltimore on 31 August 1814. He was captain of the *Menelaus* frigate, and Midshipman Robert Barrett said that he 'was adored by his officers and crew, [and] fell a victim to his unbounded zeal and devotion in the service of his country . . . he died as a British captain should do, cheering on his men against the enemy'.[90] Barrett was from the *Hebrus* frigate, and after the failed attack on Baltimore the following month, he said,

> it was arranged by the Commander-in-Chief . . . that the body of the late Capt. Sir Peter Parker, Bart., should be conveyed to the Island of Bermuda on board our ship the *Hebrus* . . . Having been ordered to the *Menelaus* on duty, previous to the removal of the corpse, I shall never forget how mournful and dreary was the appearance of all on board upon this melancholy occasion. It was reported, that it was with considerable reluctance the crew could be brought to acquiesce in the propriety of resigning the remains of their beloved commander to the custody of another ship. The body, having been embalmed, lay in state in the after-cabin . . . When I came forth from this melancholy scene, I beheld the stern and rugged visage of many a veteran tar moistened by a tear.[91]

When they reached Bermuda in October, Barrett recorded, 'I had the honour of being midshipman of our launch, which conveyed the remains of Sir Peter Parker on shore, where they were interred at St. George's, with the most distinguished military honours. His coffin was followed to the vault by all the public authorities in the island.'[92] His body was subsequently taken to London and buried in the family vault at St Margaret's Church at Westminster. This burial took place in mid-May 1815, as the *Morning Post* related:

> Sir Peter had received in October last the honours of a public funeral at Bermuda, to which island his body had been carried from the Chesapeake

in the *Hebrus* frigate . . . but it having subsequently been found to have been the wish of Sir Peter Parker, if he fell on service abroad, that his remains should be brought home and deposited in the vault of his family, the *Hebrus* was again entrusted with this melancholy freight . . . On the arrival of the *Hebrus* at Portsmouth, she was ordered round to Sheerness, from whence in the Admiralty barge the corpse was brought to Deptford on Saturday evening, attended by Captain Palmer, his officers, and a proportionate body of seamen, where it was received in the dock-yard with appropriate attention by the officers of government; and at half past five yesterday morning the Admiralty barge, with the Union Jack up, bearing the body on a military bier, resting on a platform surmounted by black feathers, appeared off Westminster-stairs, followed by three government barges, with pennants, containing the officers and seamen appointed to attend the ceremony. At six the boats drew up to the stairs, when the whole landed, and being met by the attendants and friends waiting on shore to join the naval procession, they proceeded to St. Margaret's Church in the following manner:

Four Mutes.

Plumes of Black Feathers, with Pages to assist.

THE BODY

on a bier, carried on the shoulders of thirty seamen, preceded by Captain Palmer, in full uniform, and naval mourning; his lieutenants on each side, dressed in the same way, attended by three of Sir Peter's late midshipmen, and his brave lieutenant Mr. Pearce.[93]

After listing various other mourners, the newspaper added: 'Before reaching the church, they were received and joined by the Rev. Mr. Groves, who, heading the procession, conducted it to the church, where the ceremony was performed in a very impressive manner, and rendered additionally interesting by the novel and affecting sight of thirty-six British seamen ranged up the centre of the church on both sides of the bier, on which lay the sword and hat of the deceased, surmounted by the colours of the navy.'[94]

Officers were buried on land if at all possible, as happened with Lieutenant Lawry in November 1794. Aaron Thomas recorded the event in his journal:

Mr Lawry was buried in St John's churchyard [Newfoundland] on the
Monday after he was murdered. His body was removed from the *Boston*
to the shore in the same boat in which he went to lose his life. His corpse
was attended on the water by a boat from the *Monarch*, one from the
Amphion, one from *Pluto*, one from *Bonette*, one from *Lutine* and two of
our own boats. They contained every officer of the squadron. The boats
took a circuitous route in the harbor and moved in a slow and solemn
manner. On his coffin was placed his uniform hat, his sword and dirk. On
landing at the King's Wharf all the marines of the different ships, who
had been previously landed, [and] the three companies of St John's
Volunteers received his body, which was carried to the place of interment
in a great funeral parade, attended by all the captains of the squadron and
the principal officers, several gentlemen of the town, and all the officers
and troops stationed here.[95]

Ordinary seamen who died were not accorded such special treatment. Instead, they were sewn up in their hammock, which was
weighted with one or two cannonballs, and tipped into the sea with
a short funeral service. Cornelia Knight recalled that Nelson
referred to such a burial when he was asked what should be done
with his amputated arm: 'the Surgeon asked, if he should not
embalm it, to send it to England to be buried; but he [Nelson]
said, "throw it into the hammock, with the brave fellow that was
killed beside me" – a common seaman'.[96] Basil Hall explained the
entire process:

Very shortly after poor Jack dies, he is prepared for his deep-sea grave by
his messmates, who, with the assistance of the sail-maker, and in the
presence of the master-at-arms, sew him up in his hammock, and having
placed a couple of cannon-shot at his feet, they rest the body (which now
not a little resembles an Egyptian mummy) on a spare grating. Some
portion of the bedding and clothes are always made up in the package,
apparently to prevent the form being too much seen. It is then carried
aft, and, being put across the after-hatchway, the union jack is thrown
over all. Sometimes it is placed between two of the guns, under the half
deck; but generally, I think, he is laid where I have stated, just abaft the

main-mast. Next day, generally about eleven o'clock, the bell on which
the half-hours are struck is tolled for the funeral by one of the quartermasters of the watch below, or by one of the deceased's messmates; and all
who choose to be present assemble on the gangways, booms, and round
the main-mast, while the fore-part of the quarter-deck is occupied by
the officers.[97]

The actual funeral ceremony was simple and short, as the chaplain
Edward Mangin described after conducting the burial at sea of the
coxswain Thomas Flynn:

> The body was brought at 10 o'clock in the forenoon, to the starboard
> gangway; sewed in a hammock, with a couple of 32 lb. shots at the feet,
> extended on a grating, and covered with a ship's ensign. The crew and
> officers, bare-headed, surrounded it, and I read the funeral service. When
> I pronounced the words, 'we commit his body to the deep', a seaman
> standing by took off the colours, and turning the grating, launched poor
> Tom into the bosom of the German ocean [North Sea], into which he
> sunk sullenly and for ever. The multitude of stern looking men standing
> round; and preserving a profound silence; the splash of the corpse as it
> dropped; the untimely fate and fair character of the man . . . impressed me
> with very mournful feelings.[98]

Even if close to land, the seamen were still buried at sea. When the
Lapwing was anchored at St Kitts in July 1798, one seaman's death
was documented by Aaron Thomas:

> Peter Bird, a seaman aged twenty-three, departed this life. He had been
> ill of a flux about nine days . . . So I see this poor youth was boasting in
> his strength, but the Lord has told us of this folly, by taking one away
> from amongst us who has been in the ship more than 4 years, and during
> all that period, has never been in the sick list until nine days before his
> death . . . Bird is the first man that has died *aboard*, since I came into this
> ship. At daylight the body of Peter Bird was sewed up in his hammock
> with a ninepounders [cannonball], and put into the jolly boat; carried 2
> cable length from the ship, and committed to the deep.[99]

However, when a woman died on board the frigate *Hussar*, within sight of Harwich, the crew thought Captain Wilkinson was inhumane to order her body to be cast overboard, as John Wetherell witnessed:

> Our Corporal of Marines Richd Wright . . . had his wife on board, a fine young woman. She took sick and died on board. The boat was ordered to be manned next morning, her body put in a shell made by the ship's joiner, taken out to sea and sunk, at the same time the ship lay within three miles of Harwich . . . This morning several of our married men's wives left the ship and went on board the tender and landed in the evening at Harwich. They would not remain on board where such an unfeeling monster commanded.[100]

In 1799 Aaron Thomas was still in the West Indies and writing to one of his brothers in England: 'Yet the dread of the hurricane's month suddenly coming on, and the fever and fluxes which we are all so liable to here, makes me think it right in me to say, that if I make my earthly exit in this country, you will find my will, either at Mrs. Wainwright's or at Thomson & Co in Basseterre in St Kitts.'[101] In the entry for the end of September, he jotted in his journal, 'This evening I was taken very ill – remained on board until the 22 October when I was obliged to go to sick quarters ashore at Basseterre St. Kitts.'[102] He subsequently wrote: 'I this day and last night for the first time felt the effects of severe flux – at 8pm felt better, this brings me to say that the lessening of a pain is a pleasure and that the diminishing of pleasure is pain.'[103] This was his last journal entry, and on 13 December 1799, Aaron Thomas died in the hospital at St Kitts.

During battle there was no time for ceremonies or shrouds, and bodies were immediately thrown overboard. In April 1801, fourteen-year-old John Finlayson, who was a signal midshipman on board the *St George*, witnessed his first battle at Copenhagen. He was with several other seamen in a boat rowing to the *Elephant*, 'when in a moment a spent shot, a twelve-pounder, struck the Sergeant [of Marines] in the back and knocked the breath out of him. He fell in the bottom of the boat and never either spoke or moved. This was

a great shock to me. I scarcely knew what I said or did.'[104] His lieutenant told him to check his pulse: 'I tried the wrist, and pronounced
him dead, quite dead. As this was no time to think about burying
the dead as we should have wished, we threw the Sergeant overboard, wishing him a safe passage to the Other World.'[105] The first
battle Midshipman William Dillon experienced was the Glorious
First of June, in 1794, and he lamented that 'The number of men
thrown overboard that were killed, without ceremony, and the sad
wrecks around us taught those who, like myself, had not witnessed
similar scenes that War was the greatest scourge of mankind.'[106]

It appears callous to have treated the dead in this way, but there
was no room for sentimentality, and Sir Gilbert Blane was appalled
by what he perceived to be the lack of hygiene on board French ships
that the British captured, complaining that filthy water and worse
ended up in the hold,

> for the blood, the mangled limbs, and even whole bodies of men,
> were cast into the orlop, or hold, and lay there putrifying for some
> time. The common sailors among the French have a superstitious
> aversion to the throwing of bodies overboard immediately after they
> are killed, the friends of the deceased wishing to preserve their
> remains, in order to perform a religious ceremony over them when
> the hurry and danger of the day shall be over. When, therefore, the
> ballast, or other contents of the holds of these ships, came to be
> stirred, and the putrid effluvia thereby let loose, there was then a
> visible increase of sickness.[107]

Basil Hall asserted that crews wanted to dispose of bodies rapidly for
superstitious reasons:

> Independently of any personal interest, the sailors are always very desirous
> that no one should die on board; or rather, they have a great objection
> to the body of any one who has died remaining amongst them. This is
> a superstition easily accounted for amongst men whose entire lives
> are passed, as it were, on the very edge of the grave, and who have quite
> enough, as they suppose, to remind them of their mortality, without the

actual presence of its effects. An idea prevails amongst them, that sharks will follow a ship for a whole voyage which has a corpse on board; and the loss of a mast, or the long duration of a foul wind or any other inconvenience, is sure to be ascribed to the same influence. Accordingly, when a man dies on board ship, there is an obvious anxiety amongst the crew to get rid of their late shipmate as speedily as possible.[108]

When the *Victory* was returning to England after the Battle of Trafalgar, Marine Lieutenant Robert Steele observed that the men were very uneasy: 'In crossing the Bay of Biscay we had very bad weather, and the wind was constantly heading us; which the sailors ascribed to a corpse [Nelson's] being on board, and some of them supposed that till the noble Admiral was buried (as they thought he ought to be) in his own empire, the Ocean, with due honours, we should never pass the chops of the Channel.'[109]

Henry Walsh is not likely to have been the only one disturbed by the fact that many seamen were buried at sea without any of their relations ever learning of their death: 'There is thousands of worthy men buried in the boundless ocean unknown to any of their parents or relations, the thoughts of which often grieved my heart full sore.'[110] Such burials were a particularly sad end for men who had been forced from their families by the press-gang.

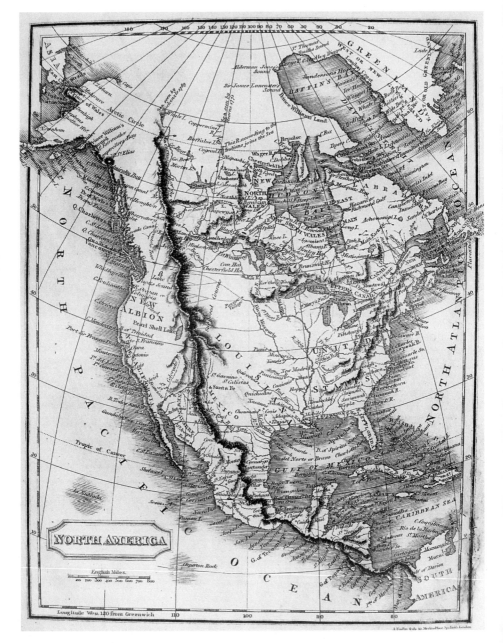

Map of North America

TEN

—•◆•—

AT LEISURE

Two evenings each week is devoted to amusement, then the Boatswain's mates, with their pipes summons 'All hands to play'. In a moment the scene is truly animating. The crew instantly distribute themselves, some dancing to a fiddle, others to a fife.

Observation of the soldier William Wheeler while a passenger in the *Revenge* in 1811[1]

Except in times of danger, such as during bad weather or faced with imminent action, daily life for sailors was not a constant round of working, eating and sleeping. There were times specifically set aside for leisure activities, when they could relax, as Daniel Goodall remembered of the *Temeraire* in 1802:

Our Captain would pipe all hands to amusement – a certain mode, under proper regulation, of keeping Jack out of mischief, and in health and spirits. We had an excellent band on board, whose services were brought into constant requisition on such occasions, and regular 'sets' for dancing were formed with as much decorum, but with far more freedom, than in the stateliest ball-room – the officers not disdaining to set an example of sharing in the general amusement. Those of the men who thought themselves not sufficiently qualified to join in the regular public ball, or who preferred a rollicking jig or hornpipe in presence of a more select circle, could find plenty of fiddlers amongst their shipmates, only too glad of the opportunity to display their skill in extracting sound from catgut.[2]

Music and dancing were always popular at various levels. Many officers preferred what would now be termed 'classical' music and 'ballroom dancing', and if they could afford it captains built up their own bands or small orchestras, deliberately taking on sailors who could play instruments. The pressed American seaman James Durand admitted that 'I joined the musicians thinking it easier to play an instrument in the ship's band than to do ship's duty. There was a first rate instructor and for three weeks while we chased French privateers, my chief work was blowing on a flute. Gradually I gained some proficiency at it. The Captain now purchased new instruments equal to a full band. I learned the clarinet.'[3] Samuel Leech felt that the band of the *Macedonian* was an asset to the ship:

> The captain procured a fine band, composed of Frenchmen, Italians and Germans, taken by the Portuguese from a French vessel. These musicians consented to serve, on condition of being excused from fighting, and on a pledge of exemption from being flogged. They used to play to the captain during his dinner hour; the party to be amused usually consisting of the captain and one or two invited guests from the wardroom; except on Sundays, when he chose to honour the ward-room with his august presence. The band then played for the ward-room. They also played on deck whenever we entered or left a port. On the whole, their presence was an advantage to the crew, since their spirit-stirring strains served to spread an occasional cheerful influence over them.[4]

In foreign ports warships not only supplied military support for British diplomats, but often served as cultural ambassadors, providing entertainment for the local gentry. Dances on board ship were popular, and Elizabeth Ham recorded a guest's view of such events when she was living in Guernsey in 1804:

> Oh, these naval balls, they were *so* enjoyable! The measured sweep of the eighteen oared barge! A coach and six is nothing to it! Then being hoisted on deck enveloped in flags taken from the enemy, their capture aided, perhaps, by the two young heroes who always stand ready to

unmuffle and hand you out of the chair. I never went on board a King's
Ship in my life without having each hand taken by a Navy Officer,
which, by the by, they always take care to retain as long as they reasonably can.[5]

Sadly, not all these occasions were universally enjoyed, and after a ball
held on board the *Immortalité* in the summer of 1802, some of the
ladies who were invited complained to a midshipman 'that the lieutenants – alas! for poor human nature! – were both tipsy, and so
redolent of onions were your own messmates, that they were quite
unapproachable'.[6]

Ready-made orchestras were extremely rare, but most ships contained quite a few amateur musicians, since most people on land
created their own amusements, including singing, dancing and playing musical instruments. Most ships had at least one fiddle player,
and frequent references are made to black fiddlers, who seem to have
been particularly valued. On board HMS *Gibraltar* in 1811, one passenger observed that the seamen 'never seemed to dance with any
spirit unless they had an old Black to fiddle to them, of the name of
Bond. He is a most curious fellow, and cannot play on his instrument
unless it be accompanied by his voice or rather his throat, which
makes a rumbling noise, growing louder and louder as the longer he
fiddles.'[7] Samuel Bond, from America, was a thirty-three-year-old
gunner and probably a former slave.

In 1804, the *Culloden* was commanded by Captain Christopher
Cole and was part of the fleet of Rear-Admiral Sir Edward Pellew.
According to the seaman Robert Hay,

> The Admiral and Captain Cole both well knew the advantages of cheer-
> fulness in a ship's crew, and embraced all opportunities of bringing it
> into play. In the evening the instrument of black Bob, the fiddler, was in
> almost constant requisition, giving spirit to the evolutions of those who
> were disposed to trip it a little on the light fantastic toe. Invigorating and
> enlivening games were going on in all quarters, and if there happened to
> be more dancers than could get conveniently within the sound of Bob's
> fiddle, the Admiral's band was ordered up.[8]

Pellew took pride in the orchestras that he formed and was ruthless in acquiring suitable musicians. When he was captain of the *Indefatigable* in 1795, he heard Joseph Emidy play the violin in an opera house at Lisbon and decided he was an ideal addition for his band. Many years later James Silk Buckingham became a music pupil of Emidy and was struck by the story of his life:

> He was born in Guinea on the west coast of Africa, sold into slavery to some Portuguese traders, taken by them to the Brazils when quite a boy, and ultimately came to Lisbon with his owner or master. Here he manifested such a love for music, that he was supplied with a violin and a teacher; and in the course of three or four years he became sufficiently proficient to be admitted as one of the second violins in the orchestra of the opera at Lisbon. While thus employed, it happened that Sir Edward Pellew, in his frigate the *Indefatigable*, visited the Tagus, and, with some of his officers, attended the Opera. They had long wanted for the frigate a good violin player, to furnish music for the sailors' dancing in their evening leisure, a recreation highly favourable to the preservation of their good spirits and contentment. Sir Edward, observing the energy with which the young negro plied his violin in the orchestra, conceived the idea of impressing him for the service.[9]

To Buckingham's disgust, Pellew directed a press-gang from the *Indefatigable* to seize Emidy:

> He accordingly instructed one of his lieutenants to take two or three of the boat's crew, then waiting to convey the officers on board, and, watching the boy's exit from the theatre, to kidnap him, violin and all, and take him off to the ship. This was done, and the next day the frigate sailed, so that all hope of his escape was in vain. In what degree of turpitude this differed from the original stealing [of] the youth from his native land, and keeping him in slavery, these gallant officers, perhaps, never condescended to consider ... yet all England was roused ... to protest against the African slave trade, while peers and commoners, legislators and judges, not only winked at, but gravely defended, in the legislature and from the bench, the crime of man-stealing for the British Navy.[10]

Emidy now had to adapt his music to his new environment:

> Poor Emidy was thus forced, against his will, to descend from the higher
> regions of the music in which he delighted – Glück, Haydn, Cimarosa,
> and Mozart, to desecrate his violin to hornpipes, jigs, and reels, which he
> loathed and detested: and being, moreover, the only negro on board, he
> had to mess by himself, and was looked down upon as an inferior being –
> except when playing to the sailors, when he was of course in high
> favour . . . [he] was only released by Sir Edward Pellew being appointed
> to the command of a line-of-battle ship, *L'Impetueux*, when he was per-
> mitted to leave in the harbour of Falmouth.[11]

Emidy served in the Royal Navy for nearly five years before being
discharged a free man at Falmouth in 1799. He lived the rest of his
life in Cornwall, becoming a virtuoso violin player, music teacher
and celebrated composer, and his tombstone still stands in Kenwyn
churchyard near Truro.

For many of the crew, dancing was what would now be called
'country dances', such as jigs and reels, and ones like the hornpipe
were adapted by the seamen and effectively became sailors' dances.
Although a band was preferred, these dances only required a single
instrument, usually a fiddle or flute, and so were easily arranged by a
small group of seamen without needing the ship's band. Despite
most men being engaged in hard physical work every day, exercise
such as dancing was regarded as beneficial for their health, something
the surgeon Sampson Hardy noted in his medical journal for the
Maidstone: 'There also appeared a disposition in the people to inter-
mittent fevers, the effects of which I could easily remark were in a
great measure obviated by the salutory exercise of dancing which
was encouraged in the ship's company every evening, Captain
Mowbray kindly allotting the space under the half deck on the starboard side for that purpose.'[12] A passenger on board HMS *Gibraltar*,
previously unacquainted with the navy, noted that 'of an evening the
men generally amuse themselves by dancing on the main deck, and
the boatswain's mate summons them to this mode of diversion by
piping "all hands to dance, hoy!" It is an entertaining spectacle to

watch them on these occasions, for they dance in a manner quite peculiar to themselves, without paying much attention either to figure or step."[13]

Other physical activities were also permitted, as James Scott in the *Phaeton* recalled:

> In fine weather, when the retreat from quarters was beaten [at the end of the day], the band was ordered up for those who preferred the amusement of dancing. Buffet the bear, leap-frog, wrestling, &c. were pursued by others; in short, every one was at liberty to amuse himself as he thought fit, the quarter-deck being alone kept sacred. This temporary relaxation of the bonds of discipline was as much enjoyed by the captain and officers as by the crew themselves.[14]

Singing, with or without a musical accompaniment, was favoured. The Royal Navy did not allow the singing of sea shanties while the men worked (long spells at the capstan* were accompanied by tunes on a fiddle or a flute), but the sailors sang forebitters when off duty. The name 'forebitter' comes merely from the fact that they were sung on the forecastle, where the sailors were allowed to congregate, and this space was in front of ('afore') the bitts. The songs themselves might be traditional, memorised from music hall and theatre performances, bought as ballad sheets from street hawkers, or composed by the men themselves. Forebitters dealt with subjects with which seamen were familiar – pirates, long and difficult voyages, battles, strange incidents and, above all, women. One song from this era begins:

> Farewell and adieu to you Spanish Ladies
> Farewell and adieu to you Ladies of Spain
> For we have new orders to sail for old England
> But I hope in a short time for to see you again

---

* A drum mounted on a vertical axle with removable wooden bars that many men would push against to rotate. It acted like a winch and was mainly used for hauling in anchor cables.

We'll rant and we'll roar like true British heroes
We'll rant and we'll roar all on the Salt Sea
Until we strike soundings in the channel of Old England
From Ushant to Scilly is thirty-five leagues.[15]

This was originally a Royal Navy song, mostly sung on homeward-bound ships from the Mediterranean, but was later adopted by merchant seamen, who used it as a capstan shanty.

Songs enlivened all aspects of life ashore and afloat, such as 'The Sea Fight', described as 'a catch written by Captain Thompson':

Boatswain! Pipe all hands hoy!
Turn out every Man and Boy!
Make Sail – give Chace.
Then splice main brace!
A Gallant Ship! my boys she's French!
In Grog and Flip here's to each wench
Loos Boys, higher
Stand by – Fire!
She strikes! she strikes! ours is the day.
A Glorious Prize! belay – belay![16]

Captain Edward Thompson was well known for his poetry and songs, some of which were published in 1767 under the title of *Sailor's Letters, written for his Select Friends in England.*

Another song, collected by Richard Blechynden in 1781, begins:

We are the Boys that fear no noise
When Thundering cannons roar.
We Sail for Gold and Silver Bright,
And spend it when on Shore.
Foll de roll – de roll &c.

We eat Salt Beef for our relief
Salt Beef and Biscuit Bread
Whilst you on shore and numbers more

Are on dainty dishes fed
Foll de roll etc.[17]

The song ends with the verse,

When our Goodly Ships are sinking down
We know not Good from Evil
There's the Parson a Praying and the Boatswain a swearing
So we serve both God and Devil.[18]

Many songs were bawdy or straightforwardly obscene, as the seaman George Watson remarked: 'The poet you might see employed composing sea-songs, or odes on naval exploits; sometimes also smutty, or amorous rhymes to gratify the youthful midshipmen, and other lusty members of his auditory.'[19] Today, many of the more popular songs have survived as traditional songs or folk songs, and where these sound rather trite in their sentiments and bland in their words, it is often the inevitable censorship of the Victorian folk-song collector who bowdlerised the original bawdy version.

Good singers were admired, but one performer on board the *Macedonian* attempted to desert. On discovering that the merchant ship he boarded was actually delivering gunpowder to his old ship, he gave himself up and was pardoned. Samuel Leech described how he was welcomed back:

The crew were all delighted at his return, as he was quite popular among them for his lively disposition and his talents as a comic singer, which last gift is always highly prized in a man of war. So joyous were we all at his escape from punishment, that we insisted on his giving a concert, which went off well. Seated on a gun, surrounded by scores of men, he sung a variety of favourite songs amid the plaudits and encores of his rough auditors. By such means as these, sailors contrive to keep up their spirits amidst constant causes of depression and misery . . . But for these interludes, life in a man of war, with severe officers, would be absolutely intolerable; mutiny or desertion would mark the voyages of every such ship.[20]

Because many of the men were pressed into the navy, Leech thought that anything to alleviate their situation was welcome:

> A casual visitor in a man of war, beholding the song, the dance, the revelry of the crew, might judge them to be happy. But I know that these things are often resorted to, because they feel miserable, just to drive away dull care. They do it on the same principle as the slave population in the South [United States], to drown in sensual gratification the voice of misery that groans in the inner man . . . so, in a man of war, where severe discipline prevails, though cheerfulness smiles at times, it is only the forced merriment of minds ill at ease; minds that would gladly escape the thraldom of the hated service to which they are bound.[21]

Daniel Goodall of the *Temeraire* mentioned that the amusements went beyond music and dancing, and included theatricals: 'Independent of the numerous sea games wherewith we diversified our dancing, the midshipmen got up very enlivening, if not critically correct, dramatic entertainments, which their audiences, more inclined to be pleased than critical, always took in the best spirit possible, and thus afforded encouragement to perseverance on the part of the young gentlemen.'[22] Several years later, when he was a marine on board the *Amelia* anchored at Corunna, Goodall again found that the midshipmen were fond of amateur dramatics:

> Our 'middies', by way of contributing their quota to the general amusement, got up a dramatic representation, to which everybody of importance in the place was invited, for they judged rightly that nautical amateurs would be regarded as quite a novelty, if not a treat. Our principal manager in this affair was Mr Coulson, a native of Quebec, who had joined as a midshipman when we were out there as convoy. He certainly had some histrionic talent, and that is more than I would venture to assert for his coadjutors. A Glasgow man, one of the crew, was scene painter . . . All our actors were midshipmen, with the exception of one, a marine, required to make up the roll of *dramatis personae*. We had six ladies on board, wives of seamen and petty officers, who had got leave to accompany their husbands on the cruise, but none of these had a

vocation for the boards, and were of no farther use than as they lent their aid in getting up the young gentlemen in their parts, and in supplying some needful articles from their wardrobes for our female characters.[23]

The schoolmaster, an Irishman named O'Donnell, was persuaded to deliver the prologue, but he suffered from stage fright:

> O'Donnell was well qualified to have done justice to this part of the proceedings, for he was an excellent elocutionist, but he also laboured, unfortunately, under the disadvantage of being a very nervous man, and to counteract this constitutional defect he endeavoured to brace himself up with a tumbler or two of grog. He succeeded in this only too well, for before anyone could notice the extent to which he had imbibed, he rushed on to the stage and into the prologue in such style as never before was witnessed. After roaring half through the piece with an emphasis, accent, and gesticulation most wonderful and amusing, he fairly broke down.[24]

While trying to read a scribbled copy of the prologue stuck inside his hat, O'Donnell lost his balance and sat down on the stage, but Goodall was relieved that the production was saved when 'one of the "middies" rushed out half-dressed, and, seizing the schoolmaster by the collar of the coat, dragged him off, still seated, and roaring lustily at the unlucky prologue, amid shrieks of laughter. The best of the joke was that our foreign visitors, though they joined in the general mirth, seemed to take it for granted that it was all in due course.'[25]

Musical shows and plays were a method of impressing the local dignitaries, and in 1807 Vice-Admiral Cuthbert Collingwood wrote home to his wife about the reaction of an official from the North African province of Tetuan to the sailors taking women's roles in the plays:

> We have an exceedingly good company of comedians, some dancers that might exhibit at an opera, and probably have done so at Sadlers Wells, and a band consisting of twelve very fine performers. Every

Thursday is a play night, and they act as well as your Newcastle company. A Moorish officer, who was sent to me by Hadgi Abdrahman Ash Ash, the Governor of the province of Tetuan, was carried to the play. The astonishment which this man expressed at the assembly of people, and their order, was itself a comedy. When the music began, he was enchanted; but during the acting, he was so transported with delight, that he could not keep his seat. His admiration of the ladies was quite ridiculous; and he is gone to his Prince fully convinced that we carry players to sea for the entertainment of the sailors: for though he could not find the ladies after the entertainment, he is not convinced that they are not put up in some snug place till the next play-night.[26]

Apart from their varied entertainments, sailors' spare time was spent repairing and making clothes, shoes and other items, using skills from previous occupations. 'Here in one place may be seen a tailor,' observed Robert Wilson,

in another a shoemaker, a tinker, a brazier, a glazier, a plumber, a painter, a seamster, a draftsman, a twine-maker, stocking and glove makers, hat makers, hat coverers, button makers, knife makers, book binders, coopers; nay, every trade almost that you can mention, even to a watch maker, and all at their different occupations . . . Those who are not employed sewing or mending, you'll see them either learning to read or write, or cyphering, or instructing others. Some are playing the violin, flute or fife, while others dance or sing thereto. Others are relating awful stories of what happened in awful times, while their hearers are listening with respectful silence.[27]

The seamen manufactured all kinds of things from materials they acquired, from bone knitting needles to carved wooden boxes. Some of the handicrafts were for their own use, while others were presents for friends and family at home. Fancy ropework was popular, as were pictures of ships in a variety of techniques, and coins were sometimes engraved as love tokens. One such silver coin was apparently engraved by John Walsh, with a picture of a ship on one side and the inscription 'Foudroyant 1781', while on the other side are the names

Jn° [John] Walsh and Elizabeth Manah above two hearts, pierced with two arrows, encircled by the inscription 'When this you see remember me.'[28]

With the ship's company isolated for weeks or perhaps months at a time, any news was at a premium, and in the absence of news, gossip was rife. As Aaron Thomas put it, 'No person who has not been in a ship can credit the various reports which are flying about every day, or rather every hour. These are termed Galley Packets.'[29] When blockading the port of Brest, Daniel Goodall said that they craved excitement and latched on to any rumours: 'Before we had been a month at sea, a report circulated amongst the crew that we were to have an entire change of officers, and . . . at first the news was set down as a mere "galley packet," by which name unfounded reports are known on shipboard.'[30] Aaron Thomas occasionally noted such gossip in his journal: 'At dinner yesterday, Ridgeway tells me, that [Captain] Harvey said, that in every bawdy house in Portsmouth, he had very often noticed, very general indeed, that when they brought him wine, there never was any stopper in the wine decanter, but always an old cork – by which remark I must infer that he has been a visitor general, to all the [brothels] . . . in Gosport, Portsmouth and Portsea.'[31]

Anything and everything might constitute an item of interest, such as one incident that Thomas recounted:

> The Captain sent his servant out of the cabin to desire the officer of the watch to keep his luff and hold his wind.* The servant went on deck, and told the officer, that it was the Captain's desire that he would *hold his wind*. Bless me says the officer, I broke wind so gently that I did not think that the Captain could have heard me: Oh, I have it now; it is very true that I was standing near the cabin skylight. I did not think of that. Pray make my humble respects to the Captain and assure him that I shall not be guilty of the like again. Servant came from off the quarter deck, and told the Captain that Mr. P was very sorry for what had happened,

* That is, to maintain course and speed.

but that he would take care not to be guilty of the like again. This led to an explanation, and this little affair ended in a laugh amongst all parties.[32]

Doubtless real-life incidents formed the kernel of various stories passed on from sailor to sailor, as Thomas was well aware:

In a ship, some transaction is every half hour arising for comment. The foremast man ingratiates himself with the wardroom boys; every word he hears the officer speak is brought out and immediately told at the breechen of every gun in the waist, to this is always added a thousand falsities. Everyone who relates the story adds something. If a servant says the chaplain and the purser broke a wine glass today at hob nob, the story goes the purser cut the slit in his tongue with a piece of flint glass which chaplain put in his rice pudding. The most trifling disaster which occurs in the captain's cabin is magnified to the galley as a most momentous calamity for the sake of laughing at the misfortunes which attend their superiors.[33]

In this way gossip formed the basis for many of the 'yarns' narrated by sailors to pass the time and which the soldier William Wheeler observed: 'Those who are fond of the marvellous, group together between two guns and listen to some frightful tale of ghost and gobblin, another party listens to some weather beaten tar who "spins a yarn" of past events, until his hearers sides are almost cracked with laughter'.[34] Samuel Leech considered that many of the stories were 'of things most rare and wonderful; for your genuine old tar is an adept in spinning yarns, and some of them, in respect to variety and length, might safely aspire to a place beside the great magician of the north, Sir Walter Scott'.[35] Archibald Sinclair, recalling events many years later, was rather more cruel in his assessment of storytelling:

It would scarcely be credited in the present day the almost total want of anecdotal power, or the faculty of telling a story, which pervaded all hands. Not only was there little or no invention, but even repetition did not seem to improve the original fault of bad telling. The same anecdotes or stories were repeated over and over again, with little or no variation, and the listeners were like children, who, when once you have told them a story, do not like the smallest deviation, either in word or deed, from the original text. It is at once and for ever stereotyped into their brain. If I have heard the story of a distinguished admiral and the midshipman's pig once, I have heard it a thousand times. It seemed a never-failing source of amusement and interest.[36]

Aaron Thomas heard a story that appealed to the men's dark humour:

Hilliard [William Hilliard, boatswain's mate] told me this day that he was on board the *Bellona* of 74 guns in the year 1759, and on the ship being paid, a woman had leave to come on board and sell three barrels of ale. But two of them contained gin, which the Master at Arms found out, and stove in the head of both, so that the liquid run about the decks, and the ship having a small heel at this time, the gin run to leeward, which the ship's company perceiving, lay down on their bellies and drank as much as they could lick up; but fifteen or twenty, who were more alert and *deeper* [more thoughtful] than the rest, jumped overboard, and put their mouths to the scupper holes from whence the gin was running out in a spout. Here they swallowed so much that nine men lost their senses in 3 minutes ... and were drowned. The rest were picked up by the ship's boats, but in so drunken a state that they were hoisted in with a whip [a simple hoist for bringing ladies aboard].[37]

Gossip and yarns were a constant distraction, but could rarely compete with news from the outside world. While his ship was cruising off the coast of Newfoundland in 1794, Thomas found they had an unusual amount of news:

From the circumstance of our falling in with a number of American vessels and getting newspapers from them we used, jocosely, to call these latitudes our coffee room – here we come to read the news. Very few vessels we boarded from Europe but what gave us newspapers. As soon as a sail was discovered the cry on the quarter deck was 'I see a newsman two points to our larboard beam, I wonder if she is from Europe or America'. After she had been boarded and the officer returned, the buzz of 'What news?' would be as violent on deck for some minutes as . . . the appearance of a *Gazette Extraordinary* [in a coffee house].[38]

Thomas was exceptional in being well educated and had been in business in London and possibly elsewhere, which is probably why he was employed as the captain's coxswain and steward. He made the most of newspapers when they came his way, and noted in his journal on 30 August 1798: 'Spent the whole day on board, in reading the *Star*, *Sun* and *Morning Post* London newspapers which came out by the last packet: yet the newest paper was dated on June the first of this year.'[39]

The number of seamen who could read inevitably varied from ship to ship, and there is evidence that where the majority were illiterate, some of those who could read and write pretended they could not, while others who were poor readers and writers lost what little skill they once had. The seaman Richard Greenhalgh wrote apologetically to his parents that 'my old writer Thomas Brown is drafted on board of the *Ann* . . . Excuse my bad writing as I have not practiced it much lately, but now I have lost my writer, and so I believe I shall write myself for the future.'[40] There was always a demand for literate men to read and write letters, according to Samuel Leech: 'I now experienced the advantage of the primary education I had received when a boy. Many of my shipmates could neither read nor write, and were, in consequence, either altogether deprived of the privilege of intercourse with their friends, or were dependent on the kindness of others, to read and write for them. For these I acted as a sort of scribe.'[41]

The seamen had a concessionary cheap postage rate of one penny, prepaid, which was introduced in 1795. This was subsequently believed by some officers to have been partly responsible for the serious mutinies that occurred two years later, at a time of revolution in France, since the men were being encouraged to read and write. In Captain William Hotham's view,

in granting additional privileges and advantages to the seamen of the
Fleet, the temper of the times does not appear to have been sufficiently
considered, in which every spark of innovation, however trifling, was
likely to burst into a flame. Amongst the most ill-judged of these
impolitic indulgences which were gratuitous, was that of giving the commissioned officers the power of franking the seamen's letters and thereby
giving encouragement to an extent of epistolary communication never
known before and palpably injurious to discipline and order. Fancied
grievances were generated by these means, in addition to real ones, and
opportunity given to ill-disposed men to institute comparisons and test
the different modes officers had of preserving their authority. This circumstance of franking, insignificant as it may appear *per se*, was
nevertheless one great assistant, if not cause, of the general spirit of insub-
ordination that existed.[42]

Not everyone could afford this cheap rate – of his seven surviving letters, George Price only paid the penny rate on three of them. His
brother paid the postage on delivery for the rest, costing him between
six and seven pence each.

Letters from home, and the opportunity to send letters, were inter-
mittent because they were totally dependent on the ship carrying
the letters meeting up with the ship the letters were bound for, while
avoiding the hazards of shipwreck, sinking in bad weather or capture
by an enemy. Frequently, letters were taken to the nearest friendly
port, where they waited to be picked up. On 27 August 1807, William
Wilkinson began a letter to his wife from the *Minotaur* off
Copenhagen: 'My dear wife, This is the fourth letter to you and I
cannot scold you for not writing because I know you have written,
but I have not received any. I have just been looking over the last dear
letter I received from you which you wrote when we were off the
Texel and it is a great comfort to me to have anything belonging to
you.'[43] The further the ship was from Britain, the more problems
there were with communications, and just two months earlier, at
Palermo, Marine Captain Wybourn complained to his sisters:

At length an opportunity offers to send letters to England, which we have been anxiously looking for this long time. I fear you will think it long since the date of my last, but I assure you no ship has sailed for England, and to send by *land* might cost 16 shillings, which would exceed by, at least, 15 times the value of my scrawl, thus have I accounted for my silence, but what excuse can all my dear friends at home advance? Two letters are all I have received in ten months.[44]

With no news from home, Marine Lieutenant John Fernyhough was feeling lonely during the blockade of Cadiz in October 1805. In a letter to his parents he confided:

I wrote to my brother Robert [also in the marines] during our short stay in the Channel (only two days), after our return from the West Indies. I have yet received no answer, which I can only attribute to his not having received my letter, as I think he had sailed from Spithead before it arrived in England. Sometimes I fancy myself deserted by all the world, every ship brings letters to all except myself. I wrote to my brother to procure me a flute, to beguile a few tedious hours.[45]

This was the last letter he wrote, because he was drowned a few days later when trying to save a Spanish ship after Trafalgar.

When letters did arrive it was a cause for rejoicing, which Leech observed: 'The arrival of the mail-bag is a season of peculiar interest on board a man of war . . . The men crowd around, as the letters are distributed, and he was pronounced a happy fellow whose name was read off by the distributor; while those who had none, to hide their disappointment, would jocularly offer to buy those belonging to their more fortunate messmates.'[46] On another occasion, when blockading Cadiz, Wybourn told his sister Emily: 'To my joy the other day I saw the well known characters on the back of your letter as it was tumbled out of a large bag of letters from England; it was the more acceptable as the day before the general packet [Post Office ship] had arrived, and I perceived everyone happy round me by the receipt of letters, and had to deplore my hard fate not having received one line since I left England now many, many months since.'[47]

George Price was likewise desperate to receive letters from his brother in Southwark, and wrote to him in March 1805:

> I take this opportunity of writing, hoping to find you in health as it leave me at present, bless God for it. I think it very hard that I cannot get no letter from you and you know I have nobody else to write to, therefore I should be very happy to hear how you do and your wife and my sister Ann. You must suppose that my case is very hard to be on board of a man of war exposed to the greatest dangers and not a soul in the world that I can get letters from to hear of my relations or anybody that I know.[48]

In the total absence of other forms of communication, such as are now taken for granted, letters from home were precious items that were read and reread, and frequently treasured. Soon after writing to his brother, Price received a much-coveted letter, yet he was still anxious for more family news. 'I am very glad my Aunt Stammers has not quite forgot me,' he replied to his brother, 'and please to remember me to her the next time you write. I am very sorry I cannot hear whether my sister Ann is alive and well or not, but let me know this time if you have heard anything about them . . . Please to remember me to your wife and child and my sister if you should hear of her and to all inquiring friends.'[49]

Frederick Hoffman recalled a letter that was addressed to a young midshipman:

> He had, among others, received a letter from his mother, and to be more retired had gone abaft the mizzenmast to read it. The sea-breeze was blowing fresh, when just as he had opened it and read the first words, it blew from his hands overboard. Poor little fellow! The agonised look he gave as it fell into the water is far beyond description. He was inclined to spring after it. Had he known how to swim he would not have hesitated a moment. Unfortunately all the boats were on duty, or it might have been recovered.[50]

Another leisure activity was the reading of books, common among officers, as well as a few educated seamen, but a warship was at best damp and often wet, as Aaron Thomas found: 'Books are truly perishable things. What numbers have I had spoiled since I came afloat. This day I sent ashore to Mrs Wainwrights, the history of Corsica, printed in Italian in Naples. My Turkish and Italian grammar, Horace's Odes, and several other books, all spoiled by salt water getting into the chest in which they were kept.'[51] Some commanders, including Nelson, distributed among their crews Bibles and prayer books provided by the Society for the Promotion of Christian Knowledge, and in a few ships other books might be provided, as Joseph Bates in the *Rodney* remembered:

> To improve our mental faculties, when we had a few leisure moments from ship duty and naval tactics, we were furnished with a library of two choice books for every ten men. We had seventy of these libraries in all. The first book was an abridgement of the life of Lord Nelson, calculated to inspire the mind with deeds of valor, and the most summary way of disposing of an unyielding enemy. This, one of the ten men could read, when he had leisure, during the last six days of each week. The second was a small church-of-England prayer book, for special use about one hour on the first day of the week.[52]

Sunday was marked out as special in most warships, and Basil Hall observed that many men took the opportunity to rest:

> Even were it not an affair of duty, sheer weariness would generally enforce the fourth commandment on board a man-of-war, and the delicious day of rest be most fully enjoyed at sea. It must be owned, indeed, on the lower deck of a man-of-war on Sunday afternoon, between dinner-time and the hour of tea, or evening grog, a cast of idleness is the most characteristic feature. Groups of men may be seen sitting on the deck chatting over very old stories, a few are reading, and many are stretched out flat on their backs fast asleep, or dosing with their heads on their arms on the mess-table.[53]

Although the seamen were only occasionally given shore leave, they were generally permitted to visit other nearby ships on Sundays, as Archibald Sinclair described:

As little or no leave was ever granted to the sailors, to have a run on shore, partly from the uncertainty of their ever returning on board again, and also when, by any chance, they did get on shore, either on duty or otherwise, they did not know very well how to behave themselves, and generally got themselves, and others, into serious trouble, the habit was established of allowing 'ship visiting,' on a Sunday, and on no other day . . . in foreign ports particularly, but occasionally at home.[54]

Sinclair thought the scheme was terrible, since it was simply an excuse for the men to get uncontrollably drunk:

After dinner on Sunday, at one o'clock, the word was passed through the ship that leave would be granted, upon application, to visit certain ships which were named . . . Lists were made out and signed; boats were manned, and a respectable lot of sailors and marines, all clean and sober, were mustered upon the quarter-deck, to see that they were so, and taken on board various ships. What took place below, from that hour till sunset, and how the sinews of war were supplied [with alcohol], was a mystery . . . At sunset the boats were sent from the various ships to bring back the absentees. The boatswain piped, and called, 'Away there, Royal Sovereigns!' 'Away there, Princess Royals!' 'Away there, Constances!' This would be done in a tolerably respectful manner while dealing with the men of the large ships, but it was different when he came to the men of the small fry of vessels. 'Tumble up there, you Badgers, Teasers, and Scorpions,' was the very mildest form in which they would be invited to take their departure.[55]

The next stage was the most difficult as invariably the returning seamen were in a drunken state:

Two or three 'Royal Sovereigns,' the same number of 'Princess Royals,' and a 'Constance,' would be got on deck, each between two very unsteady friends, but comparatively sober, and placed in their boats alongside. Next come, perhaps, the fighting, or bumptious lot . . . and they are, with some difficulty, stowed away in the boats. Then come the last lot, or the dead ones, as they were called; who were hopelessly, helplessly dead drunk, and had to be hoisted out of the ship, or down the side, like a sand-bag, and to be got on board their own ship in the same manner. Their messmates then took charge of them, and they were kept as much out of sight and hearing as possible. No notice of missing muster, or unusual noises, was taken. The commanding officer became hard of hearing, and took to hard winking, to cure it; and like the two magical words in the Arabian Nights, 'open sesame,' two other words passed everything, 'liberty men.'[56]

In the long absences from home, the officers especially took some consolation in their pets, and even became attached to the livestock. In his journal entry for 26 March 1781, Captain Pasley lamented: 'Today my favourite pet sheep, who had been my companion to and from the Cape of Good Hope, to my no small regret died. His disorder poison, by constantly licking the washings or scrapings of the copper [from the galley stove], he having the liberty of the deck at all times.'[57] Animals were readily acquired, occasionally to sell for a profit, but mostly as pets. The officers frequently had dogs, which were sometimes the spoils of war, such as one rescued by Captain Fremantle from the *Santissima Trinidad* after the Battle of Trafalgar: 'My pug dog is called Nympha ... and is a great favorite,' he told his wife, 'she sleeps in the bed with me and is solaced every morning from the warm blankets into a large tub of cold water, this keeps her clear of fleas, and she is at this instant worrying an unfortunate kitten that is her companion. I mean to buy a parrot at Gibraltar and perhaps a monkey to amuse myself.'[58] In a letter written later that year he admitted that 'If it was not for my poor little dog that I worry all day and who is so good that I allow him to sleep in my bed, I should be more miserable than I am.'[59]

Dublin-born Hercules Robinson attributed his early promotion to his kindness towards Vice-Admiral Collingwood's pets:

When Collingwood promoted me from his own ship to be Lieutenant of the *Glory*, he sent a commendation with me, which, when my new

Captain Otway read to me, made my cheek tingle, knowing how undeserved it was, and feeling that my having been discovered playing with
and petting 'Bounce,' the Admiral's dog, 'Poor Bouncey, good dog, dear
Bouncey,' &c.; and feeding 'Nanny,' his goat, with biscuit, when she
butted her head at me, had effected more than I cared to acknowledge in
my promotion.[60]

Dogs were habitually taken on board by the ships stationed at
Newfoundland. In 1785 Midshipman James Gardner was in the
Salisbury at St John's, and he related what happened when the ship
was about to sail for home:

The Admiral having given permission for any person that pleased to take
home a dog, 75 were actually embarked . . . I messed in the main hatchway berth on the lower deck, with four midshipmen and a scribe. We had
eight of those dogs billetted on us. One of them had the name of
Thunder. At dinner I once gave him a piece of beef with plenty of mus-
tard rolled up in it. The moment he tasted it, he flew at me and I was
obliged to run for it. He never forgot it, and whenever I offered him victuals he would snap at me directly. Another of those dogs used to sleep at
the foot of Charley Bisset's cot, and when the quartermaster would call
the watch this dog would fly at him if he came near Bisset, who would
often plead ignorance of being called, and by that means escape going on
deck for the first hour of the watch.[61]

James Scott reminisced about how such a dog on board the
Barfleur was renowned for his life-saving:

Whenever the weather would permit, the ship's company were allowed to
bathe alongside, in a sail suspended from the fore and main yard-arms.
We had on board a valuable Newfoundland dog of great size: Boatswain
was not only the pet and delight of the middies' berth, but equally enjoyed
the goodwill of the whole crew; the animal richly merited the affection
and attentions showered upon him. His station, while the men were
sporting in the water, was always on the gangway, couchant, with his
fore paws over the gunnel, and his head so far advanced that he could

obtain a clear view of all that was passing under him. Did the cry for assistance reach his ear, Boatswain would instantly distinguish it from amidst the hubbub of the multitude, prick up his ears, jump overboard, and swim to the person who appeared to require his assistance . . . This noble quadruped had saved several lives. Whilst lying in Hamoaze, a shore-boat pulling athwart the ship's hawse in a strong ebb tide, took the cable amid ships, and was upset: he was overboard in a moment, and succeeded in saving a woman and a man.[62]

Considering the livestock that was carried to provide fresh food during the voyage, some of which was allowed to roam freely through the ship, to which were added sailors' pets of all descriptions, warships must at times have resembled floating menageries. The *Culloden*, returning to Plymouth from India in 1809, was probably in this category. The arrival of the ship was reported in the local newspaper: 'Vice-Admiral Sir Edward Pellew, Bart. landed last week, from the *Culloden*, a beautiful full-grown hunting-tiger. It was so tame, that a seaman led it through the streets with a small rope, and the children stroked it over the back without the least danger of being hurt. The Admiral also landed a turtle of nearly five hundred weight.'[63]

Towards the end of the war, in 1815, Abraham Crawford described how they brought back a young bear captured in the Pyrenees that had been presented to their admiral:

These kind of rough pets . . . are not much to be desired on board ship; for, besides the difficulty, if not impossibility, of teaching them cleanly habits, they are at times extremely mischievous, and even dangerous . . . From being petted and kindly treated by the sailors, Bruin was in the habit of paying a visit to the different messes, when they were at their meals. One day he lingered on the lower deck after the men had finished their dinners, and kept prowling about, and going from mess to mess, to see and pick up a few scraps more. In his perambulations, he thrust himself in the way of one of the cooks, whose business it is to put things to rights after all the others have dined. This man, to get rid of the interruption, gave the animal a sharp kick, when Bruin turned round, and not seeing from whence the blow came, seized the first thing he laid his eyes upon. This happened to be the hand of some poor fellow that hung below the stool upon which he had stretched himself to take a nap after dinner, and before it could be released from the brute's jaws, the man's hand was much lacerated, and one of his fingers had to be amputated.[64]

Officers like Crawford were also plagued by the bear: 'It not unfrequently happened that, in attending to some duty on deck, the first intimation one had of Bruin being at hand, was finding your leg tightly clasped in the arms of the brute. This was by way of play; but it was a rough and unseasonable interruption, and sure to set Jack grinning, who chuckled to see the officer in limbo.'[65]

Among those animals specifically bought as pets, monkeys were perennially popular because of their antics. In Basil Hall's opinion,

A dog is the most obvious and natural pet for a gentleman, but still, a dog, with all his familiarity, is a selfish sort of companion, for he generally bestows his whole sociability either upon his master, or his master's servant who feeds him . . . No dog, therefore, can ever become a very general favourite of the crew, for it is so completely his nature to be exclusive in his regards that were a whole pack of hounds on board, they would not be enough, nor afford a tenth part of the amusement – I may almost call it occupation – which a single monkey serves out to a ship's company.[66]

Monkeys were frequently the subject of anecdotes repeated by the seamen, and aboard the *Sceptre* in 1812, John Boteler recalled the rivalry between the first lieutenant's dog and the ship's monkey, which rather mimicked the social hierarchy:

Our first lieutenant had a spaniel on board: the animal was well aware of the standing and authority of his master, and it was ridiculous to notice the difference of the dog's behaviour when his master was on or off deck. When on, the dog would strut about the midshipmen, now and then showing his teeth at them, very different when off deck, then it was to get away from the mids for fear of a kick, and to make himself scarce.

We had also a long-tailed monkey. I don't know if anyone owned him, but he was a general favourite, especially with the ship's company. His tail was prehensile, and he could hang by it. The dog and he were at drawn daggers; the dog would fly at him whenever he shewed himself on the quarter-deck. One day the dog was asleep by the topsail haulyard rack, when the monkey was coming up the companion hatch . . . The men saw him – 'What's Jacko up to now, I wonder?' The monkey soon solved the doubt: he mounted the main rigging, till from rope to rope he reached the topsail haulyards, and by this he descended till just over and within reach of the dog. Then hanging by his tail and his hind legs he caught the dog by both ears, lifting him up and shaking him soundly, chattering and apparently laughing the whole time, the dog howling all the while; when well shaken the monkey ceased, hauled himself up a little, well pleased. Strange, ever after this, the two were excellent friends.[67]

Of all the pets commonly adopted by sailors, parrots were perhaps the most exotic, and in December 1809 William Wilkinson wrote to his wife about one that he had acquired from a captured French ship:

The parrot is at present doing pretty well. I was fearful at first it would not live, the weather being so cold, and it just coming from a hot climate. Besides, an hour after I had it on board the prize some sailors frightened it overboard which hurt it very much. But it is now recovered and by keeping it warm I hope to preserve it. They are very likely to die coming suddenly from a hot country into a cold one, which is the case with it as it is just come from Rio De Janeiro in South America. I never saw a bird so handsome. Sir J says it is worth ten or fifteen guineas in England. I think it is one of last year's birds as it is scarcely tame yet. It is now sitting on its perch close to me. The whole of its head, neck and breast is scarlet, its wings of different shades of green, with some yellow feathers. Its tail is black and between its wings is a most beautiful purple. I don't think it is the kind of parrot that talks, but its plumage makes up for more than that.[68]

Perhaps it was just as well that Wilkinson's parrot did not talk, for those capable of mimicry were likely to cause trouble, as Thomas

Cochrane recalled. In 1794 his ship the *Thetis*[69] was stationed at Norway and allowed visitors:

> On board most ships there is a pet animal of some kind. Ours was a parrot, which . . . had learned to imitate the calls of the boatswain's whistle. Sometimes the parrot would pipe an order so correctly as to throw the ship into momentary confusion, and the first lieutenant into a volley of imprecations, consigning Poll to a warmer latitude than his native tropical forests . . . One day a party of ladies paid us a visit aboard, and several had been hoisted on deck by the usual means of a 'whip' on the mainyard. The chair had descended for another 'whip', but scarcely had its fair freight been lifted out of the boat alongside, than the unlucky parrot piped 'Let go!'. The order being instantly obeyed, the unfortunate lady, instead of being comfortably seated on deck, as had been those who preceded her, was soused overhead in the Sea![70]

Fortunately for the parrot, the first lieutenant was ashore at the time.

For entertainment, the crews of warships relished shore leave above all else, but all too often it was denied them, as Marine Captain Wybourn observed in port at Syracuse in 1807:

> The usual routine of business going on in the fleet, all bustle, confusion and hurry to get water, provisions, repair ships, set rigging to rights, painting etc., etc. This generally lasts for some days; the poor sailors, fagged to death from daylight till after dark and frequently all night, and when all is complete, *they* are the *only* class not permitted to enjoy a few hours on shore. So much for the brave fellows who are so *conspicuous* in their country's cause – how these undaunted men submit is a matter of astonishment.[71]

Even the officers did not always obtain leave, and William Wilkinson wrote to his wife about his distress at being unable to see her and their new baby when his ship was at Spithead: 'You will know what I must have felt at my not being able to leave the ship, and I well knew my dearest how anxiously you must have expected me. But I most frequently pray that we may have peace, when all these troubles are over. If we do not, I still think that I may be with you, for I cannot bear the life of uncertainty which I have been subject to since I have been absent.'[72]

When shore leave or liberty was granted, it was generally the officers who benefited most, particularly when their ship was in a foreign port, though they were not always welcome, as Midshipman George Allen saw at Tangiers:

The place in its outward show is tolerably decent but inwardly I cannot inform you of, not having seen one door open the whole of the time we were on shore . . . The inhabitants are much more cleanly than those of Portugal, but they have a great antipathy to Englishmen – indeed they saluted us when we went on shore with Christian Dogs, Hereticks, &c, one of them carried his zeal for his religion rather too far, for as Captain Stephens was coming into town after an excursion on horse-back he lifted up a large stone and threw it with all his force against, *at* him I should have said, but fortunately it missed, and the fellow was obliged to run for it, or otherwise he would have been bastinadoed to death.[73]

Sightseeing, sketching and acquiring souvenirs were popular pastimes ashore, which were even done during military operations. After Copenhagen surrendered in September 1807, several officers obtained permission to go ashore and look round the devastated city. William Wilkinson described the scenes to his wife:

I was on shore at Copenhagen two days ago . . . We went away at ten o'clock and returned at five, after seeing everything that was to be seen, which was not very much. We went to the exchange, museum, and to the observatory. From the latter place we had a view of everything at a considerable distance from the town . . . And we were all over the church that was burnt, the inside of which must have been amazingly beautiful from the great number of marble monuments we saw there. I brought a small piece of one of them (that had been broke off either by a shot or cracked by the fire) away with me.[74]

In more peaceful locations, archaeological sites were a favourite attraction. Anchored off the North African coast in 1793, Midshipman James Gardner accompanied a lieutenant on a visit to the ancient ruins of Carthage:

> [I] saw several remains of antiquity, broken columns, underground passages, pieces of frieze, and the remarkable arches supposed to be the stables of elephants. I went into a room like a cellar and got a piece of flooring, of beautiful green and white marble, which I brought home, but some thief in England stole it from me – the devil do him good with it. The ground about the ruins was covered with reptiles of almost every description, which made it dangerous to explore. I carried a piece of frieze several miles intending to bring it home also, but was obliged to leave it from fatigue.[75]

While his ship was at Naples, Marine Captain Wybourn made an excursion to some of the first excavations at the Roman cities of Pompeii and Herculaneum:

> These two cities were destroyed about 60 years after Christ, and not discovered till 57 years ago, but a nobleman accidentally digging a well to his house, the workmen came directly upon the seats of the theatre which led to the discovery. How it is possible, that a rich and extensive city should have remained swallowed up for nearly 1,700 years, without some attempts to find it, is most wonderful. We proceeded to Pompia [Pompeii] and arrived over fields of lava, at that part of the city called the barracks; the pillars, piazza, rooms and parade, are quite perfect, and the paintings in stucco in as good preservation as if only done yesterday with even the names and various scribblings of the soldiers in their barrack rooms.[76]

Wybourn added: 'We were most highly gratified and wrote our names where many other travellers had, as a memento of our having visited these antiquities, on the marble and in conspicuous places'[77] – nowadays even *his* graffiti has some historic value.

To Marine Lieutenant Robert Fernyhough, sightseeing at Malta in 1810, some graffiti had an altogether different value, as it was the work of his late brother John. He told his brother William about the discovery: 'On visiting St. Paul's cave, can you imagine my dear brother, the excess of my feelings, in observing the name of our dear brother John cut in the roof, he having visited it when at Malta in the *Donegal*. I have cut out the piece of the rock, with the imprint of his much-loved name, and will bring it to England for you.'[78]

Boys who were servants to officers had frequent opportunities to accompany them on shore, as fourteen-year-old Robert Hay experienced at Madras:

Mr Dunsterville, my master [the ship's chaplain], went often ashore at this port and on some occasions took me with him. This, not withstanding his keeping me very bare of pocket money, I was exceedingly fond of and never missed an occasion that offered. He was a frequent visitor at the house of the Governor, and while he was getting regaled inside I had liberty to roam about the garden, from the luxuriant produce of which I also got well regaled. All the trees, bushes, shrubs and flowers were new to me and I was never tired gazing on them. Cocoanuts, pumpions [pumpkins], water melons, shaddocks, mangoes, oranges, lemons, limes, pineapples, bananas, cashoo nuts, beetle nuts, chillies etc. etc., grew in the greatest abundance . . . Leaves, blossoms, green and yellow fruit blended their various hues and greatly enhanced its beauty.[79]

What struck officers and men alike was the difference in the people and way of life in a foreign country. Having more experience of the world and having met people of many nations, seamen were generally less narrowly xenophobic than those who lived in Britain, but they still had their prejudices and preconceptions, tempered by their own experiences. Nelson certainly despised the French, and in a letter in 1803 to Hugh Elliot, ambassador to Naples, he insisted that 'I would not, upon any consideration, have a Frenchman in the fleet, except as a prisoner. I put no confidence in them . . . I think they are all alike. Whatever information you can get me, I shall be very thankful for; but not a Frenchman comes here. Forgive me; but my mother hated the French.'[80] William Dillon had an aversion to Americans, and when he was a midshipman on board the *Defence* in 1794, he declared that 'The Purser's steward . . . was a Yankee, a person I could never bear.'[81] Other officers and men might not have hated foreigners, but were frequently appalled by their customs, and Captain Pasley, after transferring some French prisoners to another vessel with all their belongings, commented: 'Let any man convince me of such a sight proceeding from a French man-of-war with English prisoners and I'll alter my opinion of a French man . . . we parted apparently good friends; *I had the honor of being not only hugged but kissed and slabbered by them.* Nasty Dogs – I hate a man's kiss.'[82]

While George Watson wandered round the town of Colonia in Uruguay, he noticed the similarities and differences between the people of Spanish descent there and those he had met in Spain:

> We lay in this port above six months, and during that period, I had ample opportunity, owing to my intercourse with the shore, to reflect upon the character of the people. I could observe little difference between them and the inhabitants of Old Spain, only what might arise from the distance from each other, their costume was much the same, but more negligent, and the self consequence of the home bred Spaniard was much diminished. Notwithstanding they were as lazy as other Spaniards, lousey, superstitious, and lascivious, and consequently cowardly – there is nothing so likely to enervate the mind, as a licentious, and immoral course of conduct. As far as I could judge by dealing with them, they were honest, and not disposed to overreach. The women were pretty but very dark complexioned; the symmetry of their bodies is beautiful, they are so much lighter made than English women, and so exceedingly well formed is their clothing that you would take an old woman for a girl till you saw her face. They are of a grave and apparently contemplative countenance, but for all that very volatile and gay, which is the natural effect of a warm climate. There are a great many negro girls in the town, who have been brought from Africa, who conform to the manners of the Spaniards, and seem also to enjoy a tolerable share of liberty.[83]

Lisbon in Portugal was one port that visitors invariably found unpleasant. The first time Samuel Leech had shore leave there he was aware of an alien culture:

> I was one day walking leisurely along the streets, quite at my ease, when the gathering of a noisy multitude arrested my attention. Looking up, I was shocked at seeing a human head, with a pair of hands beneath it, nailed to a pole! They had just been taken from a barber, who, when in the act of shaving a gentleman, was seized with a sudden desire to possess a beautiful watch which glittered in his pocket. To gain this brilliant bauble, the wretched man cut his victim's throat. He was arrested, his hands were cut off, then his head, and both were fastened to the pole as I have described them. Upon inquiry, I ascertained that this was the ordinary method of punishing murder in Portugal; a striking evidence that civilization had not fully completed its great work among them.[84]

James Scott, on his first visit to Lisbon, was equally disgusted by this practice. A human head, he said, was

> stuck on a pole by the arsenal wall, opposite to the house where the crime was committed, and in one of the most public and frequented streets of the town . . . On passing the spot near midnight, the only individuals I perceived in the street were some of my countrymen collected around the pole: they were all of the medical department; their zeal for the practical part of their profession had determined them to walk off with the exposed head of the murderer. I presume they effected their object, for the police were not a little surprised the following morning to find the pole divested of its head ornament.[85]

Some seamen like Aaron Thomas made a conscious study of the places they visited, and extracted as much information from the local people as they could. At Antigua in the West Indies, a woman hired to wash Thomas's clothes explained to him the importance of shades of skin colour to the slaves:

> A black infant might have its freedom bought for ten joes [a local coin]

or thirty-three pounds currency. That a mulatto child was to be bought for the same price, but that a mustee infant would have his freedom for seven joes, [and] that a dustee infant could have his freedom for six joes. A dustee is as white and fair as the most delicate European. Their hair when infants is generally as white as cream, and when they grow up, were they in Europe, they would not be known to be [West] Indians, did not their drawling soft and effeminate voice betray them. The reason why a dustee is to be bought cheaper than a mulatto is that a mulatto when grown up would find it a very difficult matter to get out of an island in the West Indies, but a dustee could get off without any difficulty at all, his white skin would avoid suspicion.[86]

Thomas also talked to one of the elderly slaves:

[I] had a long conversation with an old Negro woman who, about 40 years ago, came from Makoko, near the Lake of Zambra in the eastern shore of Africa . . . She had not forgot her native tongue, but told me the names of many things in the African tongue. I asked her if she did not wish to go back again to her own country, she answered me – Who will carry me back master: nobody durst carry me back, unless they wish to lose 2 hundred pounds – I shall die a slave, master, nobody will carry me back, master – I shall be a slave all the days of my life.[87]

Most seamen's view of foreign places was confined to what they could see from their ship, since shore leave was a rare commodity, especially in America, as Samuel Leech explained:

The principal draw-back on the enjoyment of our stay at Norfolk [Virginia, USA] was the denial of liberty to go on shore. The strictest care was taken to prevent all communication with the shore, either personally or by letter. The reason of this prohibition was a fear lest we should desert. Many of our crew were Americans: some of these were pressed men; others were much dissatisfied with the severity, not to say cruelty, of our discipline; so that a multitude of the crew were ready to give 'leg bail' as they termed it, could they have planted their feet on American soil. Hence our liberty was restrained.[88]

They made up for it, Leech added, when given shore leave on their return to England:

> When a man of war is in port, it is usual to grant the crew occasional liberty to go on shore. These indulgences are almost invariably abused for purposes of riot, drunkenness and debauchery; rarely does it happen, but that these shore sprees end in bringing 'poor Jack' into difficulty of some sort; for, once on shore, he is like an uncaged bird, as gay and quite as thoughtless. He will then follow out the dictates of passions and appetites, let them lead him whither they may.[89]

He summed up their experiences in one short comment: 'Bad as things are at sea, they are worse in port.'[90]

It did not matter to most seamen what port they were in, because any leave they were given was spent in finding women and getting drunk. At Spithead in 1809, George King had the opportunity of going ashore at Portsmouth:

> We now commenced having leave on shore by watches for forty eight hours and having but little money I soon found out where the bum boat woman lived, where she supplied me and others with a few pounds till pay day, taking care she had good interest by paying five shillings extra for each pound. Three of my shipmates with myself determined to have a regular spree. We commenced drinking grog at the three legs a man [brothel] in High Street and it was not long before we suited ourselves with a girl each and when we had well bowsed up our gibs [drunk enough liquor] we called a coach and swore we would be gentlemen for one day. Accordingly we desired the coachman to drive to Portsea and back. Occasionally . . . [we] cried out 'avast' when we wanted to wet the whistle at different houses. About three in the afternoon we had some dinner and the coachman bore us company. From thence we drove backward and forward till dusk, when we alighted at the house we started from. We paid the fare and then completely sewed the coachman up, he being a complete tippler. We then repaired with our doxies homeward and the following day our leave was expired, but as our money was not all gone we staid on shore another day and night reserving as

much as would give us a good stifter [drink] the next morning, and pay
the boat hire, as [it] was customary when men went on shore on leave
never to come off sober.[91]

The amount of money that seamen managed to waste in a very
short time is well documented. At Malta in 1812 George Watson's
ship was overhauled, and they were allowed leave while the work
continued: 'One watch at a time were sent on shore on liberty, that is,
as a sailor thinks, to do as you like. Each division was allowed to
remain out of the ship forty eight hours, which was time enough for
a man of war's man to waste as much rino [money] as he could earn
in half a year. We had prize money paid us previous to our landing,
which made our jaunt more agreeable.'[92]

At Nevis in October 1798, Aaron Thomas watched some seamen returning late from leave: 'at 6pm the three liberty men came
aboard in a boat, in a dismal pickle, the serjeant of marines having
been looking for them all day. Hilliard the boatswain's mate had
lost his hat, jacket, shoes, waistcoats and six joes – half of sailors are
truly asses when ashore.'[93] Whether Hilliard lost the clothes or
sold them is not recorded, but selling possessions to buy drink and
women was a frequent occupation of the sailors and represented a
brisk trade in most ports. While at Minorca for some time, with
several opportunities for leave, George Watson soon spent his
money: 'Being often on shore I naturally run out of cash, having so
many ways to get rid of it, I had almost disposed of every article of
dress which anybody would buy, and still I was hard run.'[94] Watson
commented that the people of Gibraltar 'appear on all occasions
ready to buy poor Jack's clothes, which are generally disposed of at
a very low rate to procure wine &c. I sold a waistcoat here, I paid
half a guinea for at Portsmouth, for the small sum of half a crown,
and I have no doubt they would get as much again for it, when they
sold it to another having plenty of money, and wanting such an
article.'[95]

Frederick Hoffman was of the opinion that it was almost impossible to change the attitudes and habits of the seamen, and
consequently they would always end up poor or destitute:

Sailors possess shades like other men, but when you reflect that they are on board their ships for months in an open sea, exposed to all weather, privation, and hardship, which they bear with philosophic patience, you will agree with most people and admit that they deserve indulgence when they get on shore, but you may wish for their sakes that they knew the value of money better. You cannot change the Ethiopian's skin without boiling him in pitch, which you know is a dangerous experiment. Sailors seldom arrive at the age of reflection until they are past the meridian of life, and when it is almost too late to lay by anything considerable to make them comfortable in their old age.[96]

Apart from the spendthrift ways of the seamen, part of the problem was paying out their wages and prize-money in lump sums in arrears, with intervals of many months or more between each pay day. Daniel Goodall commented on the situation in 1801:

The custom at that time prevalent in the navy was, that no person got any pay until he had been over six months in the service. If at any time the ship in which a new hand served was in course of pay after the expiry of his six months' service, he received whatever balance was due to him beyond that period, but the first six months' was always retained until the ship was paid off – a provision meant for Jack's benefit in order that he might not be cut adrift at the last without some means in hand, but which Jack, with his proverbial improvidence, too frequently turned to but poor account. Formerly, when a vessel-of-war was first commissioned, her crew received no pay whatever until they had been twelve months aboard of her; she was then said to be in the course of pay, and they got what was due for six months the first time they went into port after the expiry of the year's service. In the case, however, of a ship being ordered on a foreign station, the crew received two months' pay in advance, and this was ultimately adopted as the rule with all ships when first commissioned, whether for home or foreign service.[97]

Transferring or 'turning over' seamen from one ship that had just entered a home port to another one about to sail, without giving them any shore leave or their full back pay, also caused a great deal of resentment, as Nelson noted in 1783: 'My time, ever since I arrived in Town, has been taken up in attempting to get wages due to my *good fellows*, for various ships they have served in the war. Disgust of the seamen to the Navy is all owing to the infernal plan of turning them over from ship to ship, so that men cannot be attached to their officers, or the officers care two-pence about them.'[98]

Inevitably even careful seamen could run out of cash because of the way they were paid, and then they resorted to borrowing. On board ship it was often the purser who acted as financier, but he was usually regarded by the men as a swindler. Samuel Leech certainly had a grudge against pursers:

> The practice of paying seamen at long intervals is the source of many evils. Among these, is the opportunity given to pursers to practise extortion on the men . . . The spendthrift habits of most sailors leave them with a barely sufficient quantity of clothing, for present purposes, when they ship. If the cruise is long, they are, consequently, obliged to draw from the purser. This gentleman is ever ready to supply them, but at ruinous prices. Poor articles with high prices are to be found in his hands; these poor Jack must take of necessity, because he cannot get his wages until he is paid off. Hence, what with poor articles, high charges and *false* charges, the purser almost always says he has a claim which makes Jack's actual receipts for two or three years' service, woefully small. Were he paid at stated periods, he could make his own purchases as he needed them.[99]

When in port seamen found plenty of opportunities of spending their money even if they were not given shore leave. In 1801 the *Temeraire* was at Plymouth, and Daniel Goodall described the scene on board when the sailors were paid:

> As soon as the ship was refitted and provisioned for another cruise, and reported ready for sea, the commissioner and pay-clerks came on board and paid the ship's company. The fact of pay being delayed until all the preliminary work was got through had made no difference on the score of Jack's having all the delights of spending, for the money being sure, a

great deal of it could be got rid of by anticipation. From the time we had cast anchor, all who had cash, either in possession or reversion, were quite in a position to command the luxuries most in request among seamen, for the Plymouth bum-boat women took good care to fetch alongside regular supplies of legs of mutton, geese, turkeys, hams, sausages, red herrings, soft bread, butter, eggs, tea, sugar, coffee, and tobacco. On all of those good things they, of course, charged a very handsome profit, for they had to leave a margin for the risks attending the short credit before pay-day, and the still greater risks after it, as the ship seldom remained more than two days at most after the men were paid. The actual risk, to be sure, was but small, for Jack considered his debts of this kind as debts of honour, so that the bum-boat women had a thousand-fold better chances in their favour than even bum-bailiffs.[100]

Many traders who sold goods to the seamen in British and Mediterranean ports were described as Jews and were not highly regarded. According to Goodall, they were seen as legitimate targets for any cruel jokes the seamen could devise:

Jack had a totally different code of morals to guide him in his dealings with the Jew slop-merchants, whom he esteemed it a highly creditable achievement to cheat – an achievement of which he, however, could but rarely boast, so preternaturally was their native cunning sharpened in their dealings with the sea-going Gentiles, who were so alive to every chance of giving them the worst of a bargain. In Jack's creed a belief in a Jew's honesty found no place, and the extortionate price they in general demanded for all their wares certainly afforded some small ground for the seamen's heterodoxy in regard to Judiacal probity. It did happen at times that the Children of Israel got worsted in their dealings with the men of war.[101]

Goodall described how the warships were transformed into floating markets:

I should mention here that the slop-merchants were accustomed to bring their goods on board in large hampers, lined inside with oilcloth,

and bound outside with iron hoops – these receptacles answering the purpose much better than boxes, as being so much lighter, whilst they were
hardly less secure, the lid being firmly padlocked until the merchant was
ready to display his goods, which he simply did by folding back the capacious lid and spreading the more attractive articles thereon. These
hampers were capacious enough to contain a stock of wearing apparel
worth sixty or seventy pounds, so it may well be believed that their owners
took no inconsiderable care of them and felt no small amount of anxiety
in regard to their safety when they ventured for the purpose of traffic on
board of a ship in course of pay.[102]

As usual, when the seaman George King was paid a substantial
sum, most of his money went to buy drink:

On our arrival in Spithead in the month of June [1806] we were ordered
to join Sir Samuel Hood off Rochfort. We then received our proportion
of wages for the first time since 1804 which was a new scene to me. The
Jews crowded on board with their baskets and bales of slops besides the
bum boat women with quarts of rum tied up in paper similar to pounds
of sugar, and we all in the ship was eager to obtain that drug. I purchased
such articles I was in need of and then looked out for grog having a few
pounds to splice. I was soon supplied by the bum boat women. Elated by
the success of obtaining of it, I went below to my mess where we soon
got through that quantity. In the meantime some of my messmates had
got two or three more quarts of the same, only paying seven shillings a
quart, and we thought that very reasonable as we had been in the habit
of paying one shilling for one pint of three water grog from our shipmates. On the following day we were ordered to sea. About 12 pm we
unmoored, shortened in, and at two weighed and made sail to join the
commodore off Rochfort. The same evening at sunset we beat to
quarters as is customary and I being a little elevated was reported for
being drunk and on the following morning at seven bells received one
dozen lashes.[103]

For seamen like John Powell who were careful with their money,
pay day was a time for observing the foolishness of the sailors in

wasting their hard-earned cash. From Powell's comments it would seem that George King's purchases of grog were among the better bargains to be had:

> On the day appointed for payment about two hundred Jews came on board bringing with them all sorts of slops, watches, hats, rings, jackets, telescopes etc. it was exactly like a fair. There was also provisions of all sorts to be sold, together with gingerbread and cakes, which many of the men were fools enough to buy. One man gave eight guineas for a watch and the next morning he found it was good for nothing; another gave thirty shillings for a hat that was not worth 12, so that is the way that they are always so poor as they usually are.[104]

Apart from drink and food, the seamen also bought items to adorn their living space in the ship, which Samuel Leech noted: 'Most of the men laid out part of their money in getting new clothing; some of it went to buy pictures, looking-glasses, crockery ware, &c., to orna-ment our berths, so that they bore some resemblance to a cabin.'[105] The desire to make the ship comfortable might even stretch to com-missioning paintings. The officers routinely had their cabins decorated with pictures, among which portraits of loved ones were particularly popular, but as George Watson remarked, the crew of a large warship usually included men from various professions who used their talents to entertain other crew members in their spare time, such as the artist, who 'suiting himself to the manners of his patrons, attracted the eye with scenes similar to those used by the poet, to affect the passions and delight the ear. There were "Jack on a cruise", capering, drinking, fighting, &c. always attended with "Poll" or "Bess" and the like, with many other most obscene and lascivious representations . . . all which helped to cheer the heart of "poor Jack", and beguile the weary hours of a long blockade.'[106]

Basil Hall commented that it was the 'domestic character, indeed, [which] gives the Navy of England its peculiar distinction, and mainly contributes to its success. For English naval men, and they alone, so truly make the sea their home. When afloat, they have no other thoughts of professional duty or of happiness but what are connected with the vessel in which they swim.'[107] Since Hall was an officer his point is made rather more smugly than how many of the seamen might have expressed it, but his view remains valid, and later he noted that 'It is impossible to describe the degree of regret, I might almost dignify it by the name of sorrow, with which some of us left the *Leander*, whose good old wooden walls had formed our house and home.'[108] This is not so surprising when it is remembered that the warships were not just war machines, but the only home that serving sailors knew, often for many years.

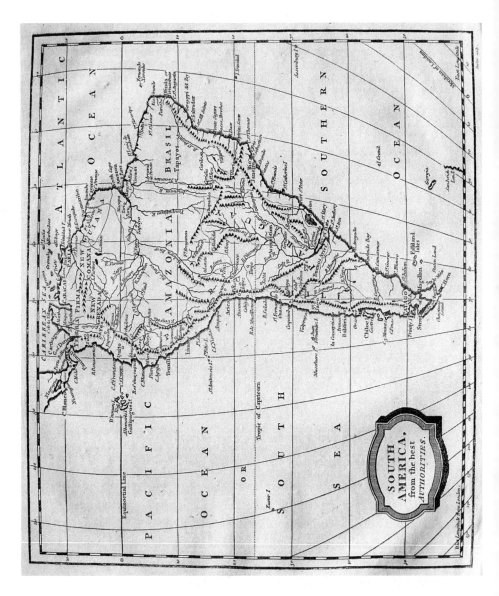

SOUTH AMERICA, from the best AUTHORITIES.

ELEVEN

——•◆•——

GLORY AND HONOURS

Having been some thirty years at sea, sitting down to reflect what sort of life you have spent and asking yourself whether you wish to pass such another.

One of Captain Rotheram's 'Growls of a Naval Life'[1]

From when Nelson joined the Royal Navy in 1771 to his death in 1805, a period of thirty-four years, Britain was at war for two-thirds of that time – and another decade would elapse before peace was finally secured. As the war dragged on, year after year, everybody loved to hear of victories, even if the casualties were high, because such news lifted the spirits and made people feel more secure from foreign invasion. William Richardson was in the West Indies when his ship, the *Prompte*, received the news about the defeat by Nelson in 1798 of Napoleon's fleet off Aboukir in Egypt:

Here we first heard of the glorious battle of the Nile, fired a salute on the occasion and in the evening illuminated the ship, our noble 1st and only Lieut. made a large bowl of good punch and we drank the health of the gallant Nelson with six more guns, then the health of our noble captain, who was on shore dining with the Governors, with four guns and then to the officers and crew of the *Prompte*, set off sky rockets and burnt blue lights and concluded the night merry and cheerful.[2]

This was nothing compared to the celebrations in Britain, and

even that staid newspaper *The Times* adopted a light-hearted
approach:

> It is but justice that his Country should *grant arms* to Lord Nelson, since
> he has so gallantly lost one in her service . . . In their boasted Expedition
> to the East, the French had taken care to get the start of Nelson; but he
> shewed his superior skill by *crossing the line* before them. Captain Berry
> and his Hearts of Oak distinguished themselves so nobly, that every
> Briton sincerely hopes our English Oak may always bear such a *Berry* . . .
> It was observed after the action, that most of the French were miserably
> cloathed, and many nearly naked, although our gallant Admiral had given
> them so *handsome a dressing*.[3]

Already the journalists were referring to 'Lord' Nelson, although no
announcement had yet been made about a peerage, and when it did
come many felt that being created a baron, when Admiral Jervis had
been created an earl for a lesser victory, was an insult.

Although Nelson and his officers received many gifts and rewards
for the victory, relatively little filtered down to the crews. Rewards for
such victories were presented particularly by organisations of busi-
nessmen whose goods travelled by sea and needed naval protection,
or by those involved in insuring ships and their cargoes. Trophies in
the form of ceremonial swords and silver plate were common, as
were gifts of money. Officers also aspired to promotion and social
advancement, and they certainly looked for awards of orders of
chivalry, such as the Order of the Bath, or peerages as recognition of
their services.

It was rare for medals to be awarded, either for individual gallantry
or for campaigns. Gold medals were issued to the admirals and captains involved in the battles of St Vincent and the Glorious First of
June, and all officers and men were awarded privately minted medals
for the battles of the Nile and Trafalgar, but it was not until the reign
of Queen Victoria that an attempt was made to recognise the heroic
efforts of the navy at this time. In 1848 the Naval General Service
Medal was issued to the survivors of over two hundred naval actions
that took place between 1793 and 1815.

The seaman always looked to prize-money as his reward, but shares of prize-money from large battles like the Nile and Trafalgar were low, because the enemy ships were much more likely to be destroyed or badly damaged, and had no valuable cargoes to sell, while any prize-money was shared between crews of the whole fleet. After the island of Martinique was taken from the French in 1794 Midshipman James Scott had great hopes of his share of the prize-money from the expedition. Being wounded he was transferred from his ship, the *Pompée*, and sent back to Britain in the *Belleisle* with an expectation that he would receive his money soon after arrival:

> Before we set sail, Mr. Maxwell, the Agent who had followed the expedition to Martinique, gave us bills upon England for the amount of prize-money (a considerable sum) due to those officers and men of the *Pompée* who had accompanied the Commodore into the *Belleisle*. The bills were protested [rejected], and sent back to the West Indies; and the first news we heard in return was, that Mr. Maxwell had departed this life, and had died insolvent . . . I had now lost all that I had gained.[4]

On board Aaron Thomas's ship, the *Lapwing*, able seaman Francis Kirnan from London also kept a journal filled with biting comments. On 5 November 1797, he wrote, 'the agent's clerk came on board and paid 10 dollars, 6 bitts and 3 dogs, being as he tells us the remainder of our due – it is astonishing the swindling and roguery practised by agents.'[5] Two months later he added that 'no species of knavery is left out in paying sailors prize money'.[6]

On the other hand, the marine Daniel Goodall, serving in the *Amelia* in 1809, was lucky to have no problems with his prize-money:

> Before we left the coast of Spain we had a small supplement of good luck in the shape of a capture of three large decked boats, laden with stores and military clothing for the 119th regiment of the line of French infantry. They were attempting a passage from Bayonne to Gijon when we descried them along shore, and our boats being sent in pursuit of the

crews in charge of them, run the boats on the beach and escaped up the country. There were complete suits for a thousand men, a plentiful supply of shirts and shoes, and several casks filled with hams and soap. The boats we broke up for firewood, a pair of shoes and a shirt was given to every man and boy in the ship, and the hams and soap also were distributed, so we had a foretaste of our share in the captures. When we reached Plymouth a few weeks after, a fair distribution of all the prize-money due to us was made, and we had, besides the treasure taken at St. Andero, something very handsome to receive for the value of vessels cut out at Sables d'Oloune, the crew of the *Amelia* had long reason for speaking exulting of the thumping luck they had experienced in their cruise off the coast of Spain.[7]

Because of all the potential pitfalls surrounding the payment of prize-money, it was appreciated when their officers did all they could to speed up payments. Theophilus Lee remembered that Henry Digby, when captain of the *Aurora*, always tried

to sell his prizes in the lump to the Jews at Lisbon; and as soon as the gallant and active Captain . . . appeared there, he was surrounded by competitors for the purchase of them, – the amount being invariably paid down in cash, and divided before another cruize commenced. This gave an eclat to the *Aurora* which brought all the best seamen of the transports to enter on board her; and she had a ship's company, for a vessel of her class, perhaps unrivalled in the service. Her crew became great dandies, having the gold Crusadoes made into buttons, and sown so thick on their jackets, that many thousands of this coin were thus distributed in the ship. At the bottom of their trowsers they had also broad lace of fine quality, and, in fact, the *Aurora*'s men were known from all the other seamen of the fleet by these costly decorations, as well as by their large silver buckles, handsome silk handkerchiefs, and other indications of 'lots of prize money'.[8]

Much more than their wages, prize-money was the tangible reward that the majority of sailors from humble or impoverished backgrounds dreamed of. Although captures of Spanish treasure ships were the exception rather than the rule, when they happened the captains became rich enough to buy country mansions and estates, while some crew members might fulfil their dream of buying an inn and retiring on the proceeds. Henry Digby was later captain of the *Alcmene* when the Spanish ships *Thetis* and *Santa Brigida* were captured in the Bay of Biscay in 1799, loaded with treasure. Like Nelson, Digby was the son of a clergyman, and although he did not rise so high or become nearly so famous as Nelson, he was extremely successful in capturing enemy shipping. While in the *Aurora*, he captured fifty ships from January 1797 to September 1798, of which the majority were Spanish. Digby's share of the prize-money from these and other captures, plus the fortune he received for his role in taking the *Thetis* and *Santa Brigida*, made him a very rich man, and he used part of his wealth to restore the family home at Minterne Magna in Dorset. As well as being lucky with prize-money, Digby had a distinguished career, commanding the *Africa* at the Battle of Trafalgar, and the following year he married the daughter of the Earl of Leicester. He was awarded various honours and had reached the rank of admiral by the time he died in August 1842 at the age of seventy-two.

At the other end of the scale was John Smith Cowan, who never became a post-captain. James Scott served under him in 1810 when he was acting captain of the *Barfleur* and was surprised by his experience:

> Capt. Cowan astonished me not a little by observing that he had never witnessed a shot fired in anger during the whole of his active career. I forget the number of years it embraced, but the singular part of the business was, that he had been constantly in sea-going ships, ever in search of enemies, and had never encountered any capable of resistance. Yet how far more deserving of promotion was this officer than the many who, with not a third part of his knowledge and abilities, had by mere good luck been so placed and circumstanced as to enable them to push their claims with success. The service is a lottery in this respect: it was the fate of Captain Cowan to experience all the real fag and hardships of the profession without receiving an adequate reward.[9]

Towards the end of the war, in 1813, William Dillon was irritated by false reports of the amount of prize-money awarded to officers:

> It was whilst in company with five naval Captains that our attention was drawn to an article in one of the newspapers, attempting to prove what a lucky set of men the Captains of the Navy were in taking prizes and making fortunes. This article was so pointed, and so false in its assertions, that we drew up a reply to it which was signed by the whole six. We stated that we had been so many years serving our Country, that we had commanded ships a long while, that the whole of us had been wounded, and that none of us had, up to that period, received £100 Prize Money.[10]

Not quite true in his case, since earlier in his career Dillon had gained substantial prize-money. When he was lieutenant of the *Aimable* in 1797, they captured 'a fine ship called the *Teneriffe*, from the Caracas, deeply laden with cocoa . . . We were soon in Tortola with our prize. My share of her amounted to £500 – the greatest share of prize money I ever received. I instantly sent it to my father.'[11]

The line between pursuit of prizes, glory and strategic need was ambiguous. The battle in 1794 that became known as the 'Glorious First of June' was acclaimed as a great British triumph because Lord Howe's fleet defeated the French warships that were commanded by Rear-Admiral de Villaret de Joyeuse. Yet from the French side it was a brilliant defensive victory. Bad harvests had produced almost famine conditions in some parts of France, and the French warships were escorting a fleet of over a hundred transports carrying grain from the United States. While the British warships were occupied with the French fleet, the grain reached France safely, and although the battle provided propaganda to boost British morale, the arrival of the much-needed grain had the same effect in France.

Both officers and seamen hoped for prizes as a reward, and the strategic effect of the prize system was to disrupt and curtail the enemy's trade, crippling their economy and reducing their power and will to continue the war. In the long term, the cumulative effect was more important than those clashes between warships, or the battles between great fleets, that caught the imagination of the public. Nelson was exceptional in that, although not insensitive to the need for prize-money, he always put the pursuit of glory and honour first. He gained many honours from his successes in battle, including a knighthood, and was then created Baron Nelson of the Nile by George III and made the Duke of Bronte by the King of Naples. Above all, Nelson took over from Sir Francis Drake the position of Britain's best-known and best-loved sailor, and people still toast his 'immortal memory'.

———•———

As well as being distanced by rank and discipline aboard ship, a gulf persisted between officers and men when the war came to an end. All commissioned officers (lieutenants and above) were entitled to half-pay when they were not actively employed, and a few obtained pensions. For post-captains and higher ranks, even being laid off on half-pay did not stop their automatic promotion by seniority when officers above them died off, but for those under the rank of post-captain peace often meant the end of their career. For officers who did manage to stay on in the navy, the prospects for promotion and social advancement were greatly diminished. Archibald Sinclair summed up the plight of midshipmen: 'When this ship [the *Morgiana*] was paid off (with many others) at the close of 1814, every mate and midshipman went through the ordeal of what was then styled "passing for a gentleman". If you could not show that you were of gentle blood; or, what was of far more consequence, get some political influence to bear, you were simply discharged, and were considered to have no further claim upon the service.'[12]

Another midshipman, John Bluett, who had just returned from a voyage to Quebec, was somewhat happier at the prospect of being laid off, because he found he had been promoted to lieutenant and so was eligible for half-pay, as he confided in his diary on 17 August 1815:

Once more, with pleasure I leap on the blest shores of Old England; rendered additionally gratifying by the improvement in my condition since I left it. I find I am confirmed Lieutenant since 28th Feby. 1815. I shall now thank God be able to relieve my beloved parents, from the immense expense they have been at to support me as a gentleman since I have been at sea. The peace will for the present throw me out of employ, and frugally indeed must I live to make my half pay (of £90 a year) support me. To what distant period must I look before I can be happy with my beloved Margaret and dare I hope she will preserve herself disengaged for a period so indefinite, for the sake of one so little worthy of her; the thoughts being no present comfort. I must dismiss it.[13]

Sadly the relationship with Margaret did not last, but in 1821 Bluett married Sophia White.

For some men, leaving the navy was an opportunity to return to family and friends. Captain Fremantle had been away from his family for a considerable period, but on 6 March 1814, with peace in prospect, he wrote from Trieste to his wife Betsey:

Please God I shall sail tonight in the *Eagle* for England where I hope soon to meet all I hold dear in the world, for every place [held by the enemy] has been taken and nothing remains to be watched but Corfu and Vienna which do not so much depend upon naval operations. I am in hopes to enjoy some years of quiet. Nothing could have been more unkind to me than the present Admiralty, but thank God I have no occasion for their assistance. I have been made Commander of the Order of Maria Theresa, which no other English officer except Lord Wellington has ever received. I am told that it also makes me and my heirs Counts of the Empire; so my little Countess hold up your head until I come to England and then you will be a good girl. I frequently look at some children here and endeavour to calculate the height of my own: it seems to me so unnatural to have a child 3½ years old that I have never seen.[14]

For some officers an end to the war was the point at which they turned to a different career on land, but many had known no other life except the navy and languished in poverty or scraped by on their half-pay. Of these, some doubtless hoped for a renewal of war because peace had proved short-lived in the past, and might do so again, but by 1821 the situation was clear. In May of that year Napoleon's death in exile put an end to fears of a resurgence of hostilities from France.

Just the previous month, in his diary entry for 5 April, the naval surgeon Guy Acheson had written a poignant poem called 'The Half-pay Officer':

Mark well that haggard eye, that brow of care,
Where Pride seems nobly struggling with despair,
That sullen look, that dignity of mien,
Which e'en these faded garments cannot screen;
Such is the man, who lately led his crew,
To fight, to conquer, and to bleed for you;
Such is the man, who late in proud array,
Shone with the Proud, the Great, the Fair, the Gay.
But who alas! now scans with wary eye
Each group, each equipage, that passes by;
Alert to turn, if haply he should meet
Thou whom his pride forbids him now to greet.
The meagre wretch who begs from door to door
Is blest compared with the genteely poor;
No stubborn pride assails his callous breast,
No thoughts of past disturb his nightly rest.
The Cottager, his daily labour o'er,
Has still the blessings of a home in store
Though poor that home, though scant and coarse his fare,
His wife's, his children's smiles await him there;
Not for him who early leaves his home
Through boundless seas and foreign climes to roam;
Inspired by zeal, disease and death to dare
To guard the wealth he ne'er, alas! must share.
His attic home receives his wasted form,
No wife to greet, no lisping babes to charm,
His meal before him oft untasted lies
While tears of bitter care bedim his eyes;
To him alas, one only hope is given;
A page in History! a place in Heaven!
Is this my country, the chill reward
For these thy boasted, darling sons prepared?

These, who so oft thy blood'ned Flag unfurled,
Who fixed thy Empire o'er the watry world.
These who first checked the mighty Tyrants sway,
First opn'd for Wellington his glorious way;
This the reward? Alas, too plainly true,
Yet still they'll fight, they'll bleed, they'll starve for you.[15]

For over six years since the war had ended, Acheson had observed the fate of officers surviving on half-pay only and naturally he sympathised most closely with them, but despite his assertions to the contrary, the situation was generally worse for the seamen and those officers too low in rank to be entitled to half-pay. Yet for many men the initial prospect of leaving the navy was one of euphoria, as Daniel Goodall depicted:

> For all that has been said and sung about Jack's strong attachment to his profession, I must say that the prospect of freedom from its obligations thus opened up to us by the news from France produced a delirium of joy amongst the whole of the men in the fleet very much at variance with the assumption that Jack preferred nothing better than his ship, his messmates, and 'a life on the ocean wave'. Nor can this rejoicing at the prospect of a release from service be at all wondered at, considering that by far the greater number of hands were forced into it, and retained there much against their wills, and that many of them had not set foot on land for years – liberty to go on shore, even for a day, being then but rarely granted, so great was the dread of desertion.[16]

At the peak of the war the navy employed up to 145,000 men, but by 1817 the estimate of manpower required had fallen to around 19,000. A few laid-off sailors had enough money to live on, and some found places on merchant ships, whalers and fishing vessels, which were still short-handed after losing many of their crew to the press-gang, but for the majority the future was bleak. At the end of hostilities many warships were decommissioned, and their cannons scrapped – more would be scrapped as developments in technology made them obsolete. A number of these cannons were reused as bollards – with the muzzle upwards and a cannonball fixed in the mouth. They became so familiar that iron bollards were specially manufactured to resemble these cannons, and the design is now an accepted part of street furniture. The old warships, stripped of anything useful, were converted to supply depots, floating work platforms in the docks and prison hulks. It is a sad irony that some starving ex-seamen who turned to crime would find themselves as convicts on board a converted warship, and just as the cannons ended up on the street, so too did many impoverished sailors.

When the seamen were discharged they tended to behave exactly the same as they had previously done on shore leave – they spent their money fast and freely until within a few days, or weeks at the most, they were penniless. Where they had been used to returning to their ship, or serving on board another one, they now found that no ship would take them. Even at the time, some people felt that it was a mistake to pay off so many seamen at once, as a letter in the *Naval Chronicle* noted: 'I am aware that the Admiralty were anxious to release the seamen after so many years service in the defence of their country, both from a sense of justice to the men and to the country; yet, from the state in which we have seen the poor fellows at every port, so soon after getting their discharge, it is quite obvious that, for their own good, they might have been gradually paid off.'[17]

It did not take long to separate these seamen from their back pay and prize-money, and as James Scott grieved, 'How often doth the reckless sailor escape the perils of mighty ocean's din – the greedy monsters of the deep – the cannon's roar – the battle fight – the fire – the wreck, to be finally stranded on his native land – to feel he hath grappled with the omnipotent works of a mighty God, only to fall a prey to the grasping clutches and devouring passions of his fellow men!'[18]

The first thought of many of the laid-off seamen was to demand work, as in September 1815 when *The Times* reported:

A large body of seamen, lately discharged from on board of men of war, attempted to obtain admission yesterday into the London Docks, for the avowed purpose of driving from thence all the foreigners they might find employed on board of vessels lying there. By letters received yesterday from Newcastle, we learn, that for some days past the seamen in that quarter had assembled in a body, with a view to obtain employment at an advanced rate of wages. They had taken the means of preventing any ship leaving Newcastle and the neighbourhood with coals, by dismantling the shipping in the trade. The seamen demand to be paid after the manner of the transports, – namely, to have £5 per month, and five men and a boy to be allowed for every 100 ton. This day a general meeting of the seamen, it was understood, would be held on the sands, in the vicinity of Newcastle, to consider what further proceedings they ought to adopt under existing circumstances.[19]

However much they might protest, there were not enough seafaring jobs for all the laid-off sailors, and wages were kept low. Most of the men had no other skills and stood no chance in competition with all the returning soldiers for a dwindling number of labouring jobs that were being gradually replaced by machines. With no pensions or social security systems, and faced with starvation, many sailors turned either to begging or to crime – a situation summed up in two terse verses of a contemporary song:

> Says Jack, 'There is very good news;
> There is peace both by land and by sea;
> Great guns no more shall be used
> For we all disbanded must be.'

> Says Jack, 'I will take to the road,
> For I'd better do that than do worse;
> And everyone that comes by, I'll cry:
> "Damn you, deliver your purse!"'[20]

Since many of the men had no experience of crime but were forced to steal to support themselves, they were more likely to be caught, and exceptional cases were reported in the newspapers:

SOUTHWARK SESSIONS. GEORGE NICHOLA was indicted for stealing a pair of pantaloons, the property of Saml. Knight, on the 25th of February last [1815]. The prisoner, who is Portuguese, and could not be understood but through the medium of an interpreter, pleaded guilty, and said it was distress, and absolute want of food, which had induced him to commit the offence with which he was charged. He had served his Majesty in the navy for ten years, but was discharged in October last, since which time he had subsisted almost entirely on the bounty of a poor Irish woman; he had made repeated applications for a passport to return to his own country; but all his efforts had been unsuccessful. He threw himself on the mercy of the Court; at the same time expressing his readiness again to enter the navy, if they would receive him. Papers were produced by the prisoner which proved the truth of his statement, and the Court sentenced him to be imprisoned one month. Sir Wm. Leighton, the presiding Alderman, humanely declaring that he would, during that time, make inquiries as to what could be done to assist him.[21]

Others fared little better when begging:

MANSIONHOUSE. – Tuesday *John Sanderson*, a sailor, was charged with stopping passengers in the street, and abruptly demanding of them to supply his wants. One of the complainants, a young man, stated, that on Monday last, between ten and eleven at night, he was stopped by the prisoner in Fenchurch street, on pretence of begging, but in a manner that surprised him much, it resembling the conduct of a foot-pad: he called the watchman, and gave him in charge. The prisoner stated, that he had been paid off from a King's ship about two months, when he was possessed of 59l. [£59] of which he was robbed the same night at a house where he slept in Little Russell-street, Bloomsbury: he was in great distress, and afflicted with disease, and had no place of abode ever since. He had a brother in Liverpool, whom he wished to join, and had repeatedly applied for a pass, which he now solicited. Another complainant stated, that he had frequently seen the prisoner commit the same offence, and in particular towards a lady and gentleman, whom he undertook to bring forward. The LORD MAYOR

observed, that if it should be clearly made out against the prisoner
that he had obtained money under the influence of compulsion, it
would amount to highway robbery. – Remanded for further examination.[22]

Inevitably many of the destitute seamen congregated around the
ports, and in 1821, when Acheson was lamenting the fate of half-pay
officers, the port of Hull put the 'Hull Sailor Poor Bill' before
Parliament. The shipowners resisted the proposed tax, arguing it was
unprecedented, but as a letter to *The Times* pointed out, 'the
Sunderland sailor poor acts, the decisions of the courts of law in various cases which have come before them, and the fact that shipping
is now directly assessed in many places to the relief of the poor, completely contradict this statement'.[23]

Thousands of officers and seamen alike never returned home, but
were lost or buried at sea, and there were established charities for
widows and dependants of officers who were killed in action. For
famous battles like the Nile and Trafalgar public charities were organised to make payments to the wounded, widows and orphans. For
distressed ex-seamen, though, it was only the long-standing charity
called the Chatham Chest and Greenwich Hospital that provided
help. The Chatham Chest was moved to Greenwich in 1803, and the
two funds were amalgamated in 1814. Greenwich Hospital, whose
proper title was The Royal Hospital, Greenwich, was not a medical
hospital but a retirement home or almshouse for naval seamen and
marines with sea service, in operation since 1705. For those considered
eligible the fund paid a fixed sum as compensation for a wound or
disability or a pension to enable an ex-seaman to live in his own
accommodation, perhaps with his wife and children. Alternatively, it
could provide a place for him to live as a Greenwich Pensioner at the
hospital, complete with distinctive blue uniform. As the amount of
money was limited, there were always more applicants for funds and
hospital places than could be supported.

Even for the men who managed to stay on in the navy after 1815,
life was not easy when they did eventually leave the service. George
King was finally invalided out in 1831 with a small pension, and rather

than stay in Britain he sailed to America, where he obtained a post as a teacher. He did not settle and soon returned to Britain, where he tried various jobs, but competition for work was fierce. He found he could not survive, and as his pension entitled him to apply for a place in Greenwich Hospital, he attempted to gain admittance:

> I now began to turn my thoughts towards making an application to the Lords Commissioners of the Admiralty and accordingly I went to their office on the following Board day, there being upwards of three hundred applicants waiting for Admission. I tendered my Pension Ticket to the porter and my name was taken down and sent in but the number admitted into Greenwich Hospital that day was thirteen. The rest was ordered to attend on a future day so that I was obliged to trust again to St. Katharines Dock where I had several days [work] afterwards, now and then trying the London and West India Dock, then turning again to St. Katharines and got two or three days work just before Christmas Eve.[24]

After many years of service, King had prize-money owing to him from various battles and skirmishes, the payment of which was a trickle rather than a stream, but he 'once more visited Somerset House if haply there might be any proportion of prize money become due, but I was on my application answered in the negative'.[25] Without work and income, he tried for Greenwich Hospital once more:

> It being Board day at the Admiralty Office [I] produced my pension ticket with a hundred more [men]. We had to wait out in the court yard till our names was called to appear in the inner office. At eleven their lordships arrived and the number called in was about fifty but only nine vacancies. I did not expect to be admitted but one of the lords asked me my service and also my pension to which I answered him twenty four years and sixteen pounds pension when he ordered my ticket to be taken away and I was ordered into the outer office to sit down. When the nine was accepted the remainder went away and each of us received a note to repair down to Greenwich Hospital and produce that note to the Regulating Boatswain at the main guard of Greenwich hospital. I immediately set

off accompanied [by] another man and arrived there at four o'clock and went to the main guard, produced the note and [was] placed on the books upwards of seven years since.[26]

In April 1844, to coincide with the Easter holidays, the *Illustrated London News* presented a patriotic yet naive portrayal of some of the Greenwich seamen. '"The Old Pensioners," as they are somewhat irreverently termed by light-hearted holiday folks,' the reporter commented,

> are great personages in the amusements of Easter Week at Greenwich . . . Hurrah for the sons of the ocean, the old boys who are fond of their jacket to the last! hurrah for the gallant heroes who led them on from victory to victory! and hurrah for our naval fame, that stands pre-eminent over that of all the nations of the earth . . . And who more nobly performed this duty than our gallant tars, who with the flag that they loved, were ever ready to brave 'the battle and the breeze?' A time-honoured band are the veteran pensioners of Greenwich, who fought and shed their blood to maintain inviolate the freedom of their native land against foreign aggressors, and vindictive foes. Three cheers in remembrance of our naval chiefs of other days, and one cheer more for the living memorials of our proud achievements on the ocean! Hurrah for Lord Nelson and his glorious deeds![27]

Seven veterans were next likened to living memorials:

> Hurrah for Greenwich Hospital! Monuments have been erected to the memory of departed greatness – statues dedicated to dead heroes hold a prominent situation in the great temples of the land – but the proudest testimonial of national gratitude to the living, stands on the Thames Bank, at Greenwich . . . Nelson's name is imperishable. Cape Trafalgar will always occupy a prominent page in the records of naval history; and now be it our task to rescue humbler, though not less brave individuals, from obscurity, by presenting the portraits of seven who fought on the memorable occasion (when England triumphed, but Nelson fell).[28]

Descriptions, with pen-and-ink sketches, were given of seven seamen, and although George King was still alive (he died in 1857 at the age of seventy), those chosen for the feature were veterans who had fought at Trafalgar. They included Joseph Burgin,

> about sixty years of age, first drew his breath at Bishop Stortford, and believes himself to be the senior pensioner in the hospital, which he entered in the year 1806. He served in the *Vanguard*, Nelson's flag ship, in the battle of the Nile – was paid off at the peace of Amiens, but subsequently impressed, and again served with Nelson in the *Victory* in the battle of Trafalgar. He was stationed at the 13th gun on the middle deck, and lost his left leg in the middle of the fight through a shot from the *Bucentaur*. Enjoys a pension of £14 per annum. He is a fine specimen of the sturdy class, and could tell many a tale of war by flood and field.[29]

When Burgin was serving in the *Vanguard*, as a landsman, he used the false name of James Coxhead. He was laid off at the Peace of Amiens, but was taken during the hot press of May 1803 and served on board the *Victory* as an ordinary seaman until severely injured at Trafalgar in 1805. He died at Greenwich Hospital in 1862, almost ninety years old, after being resident there for over half a century.

Another of the veterans was David Fearall, who had enlisted with the marines in 1799. 'This gallant veteran,' it was stated,

> now seventy-two years of age, is a native of Lewes in Sussex, was sergeant of marines in the *Victory* at Trafalgar, and nobly responded to the last telegraphic signal of her chief; he afterwards served in the *Milford* at Trieste; has been engaged in numerous boat actions and cutting-out the enemy's vessels from under batteries; but though repeatedly in the thickest of the fight never received a wound. After fifteen years in various ships he retired upon a pension of £17 4s. per annum; is still hale and hearty, and well remembers incidents in which he bore a prominent share.[30]

Although not luxurious, Greenwich Hospital provided the basics for retired seamen and marines, with a higher standard of living and greater freedom than the average parish workhouse, where so many of Nelson's seamen ended their days. In most cases the plight of such men went unnoticed, but those who had served at the most famous battles occasionally came to public attention, as in a letter to *The Times* of 1872: 'When visiting the Chorley Union workhouse last week, I found an inmate named Joseph Swindlehurst, who was a sailor in the *Victory* at Trafalgar, and who is now 89 years. I merely venture to lay his case before the public, hoping that some means may be found to help this old sailor pass his last days out of "the house".'[31] Nobody by the name of Joseph Swindlehurst is recorded as having fought at Trafalgar, but like Burgin he may have used an alias, or he was simply an old seaman embellishing his tales of the sea. Certainly his life in retirement was not one of leisure, as the medical officer of the workhouse attested: 'Joseph Swindlehurst, aged 89, is . . . an inmate of the Chorley (Lancashire) Union Workhouse . . . He is at present more than earning the cost of his maintenance by working as a tailor.'[32]

However they fared in the peace, the thousands of men and women who were caught up in the navy during the wars with France and America could not be robbed of their experiences and their memories – people like Mary Sperring, who 'never tired of telling that she washed the blood from the shirt which the gallant Admiral [Nelson] wore when he received his fatal wound'.[33] There were also many men like the marine David Newton, who died in 1878 at the age of ninety-two, who were fond of reliving the past. A few years before he died the vicar of Cholesbury, Buckinghamshire, where Newton retired after his sea service managed to obtain a Greenwich pension for him. The vicar later related one of the stories that the old man had told him:

> In one of our chats I happened to ask in what way his ship went into action at Trafalgar. His reply was, 'You see, Sir the enemy was drawn up in a kind of half moon shape, two deep, and close together; so we went spank into them' – the old man's countenance brightened at the thought – 'and broke their line, But just as we had done so, were getting into position, our tiller rope was shot away, and four ships at once set upon us, two taking us fore and aft.' 'It was very hot work, Sir' he added, 'while it

lasted, and our second lieutenant, Mr. Little, came down between decks and ordered all the men to lie down flat on the decks. Fortunately the "Billyruffian," (the old sailor will persist in so styling her; he knows the *Bellerophon* by no other name) and another ship came to our aid, and it ended in two or three. I forget which of the captains that had attacked us having to deliver up their swords on our deck to Captain Moresom [Moorsom]'.[34]

Such stories, sometimes written down, sometimes dictated to newspaper reporters, and sometimes passed on from generation to generation, form the building blocks of family history – and it is the sum of the histories of all the families that forms the history of the nation.

Ordinary people generally favoured the Jack Tars, not least because the Royal Navy remained Britain's main defence, and as the seaman William Robinson commented, 'a British seaman has a right to be proud, for he is incomparable when placed alongside those of any other nation. Great Britain can truly boast of her hearts of oak, the floating sinews of her existence, and the high station she holds in the political world'.[35] The monarch and the British government were always less sympathetic than the people, though, and Nelson's words, written in 1797, would ring true for seamen and marines for a very long time: 'We are a neglected set, and, when peace comes, are shamefully treated.'[36]

NOTES

———— ◆ ————

Abbreviations
BL – British Library
NMM – National Maritime Museum
RMM – Royal Marines Museum
RNM – Royal Naval Museum
TNA – The National Archives

INTRODUCTION: SCUM OF THE EARTH

1 Watson 1827, p. v
2 Wathen 1814, p. 5
3 Wellington 1838, p. 496. In a letter to Earl Bathurst he said, 'We have in the service the scum of the earth as common soldiers'
4 Petrides and Downs 2000, p. 38
5 The tune was by William Boyce
6 Many thanks to Dr Mike Duffy for this lead
7 Gentleman 1770, p. 209; he was reviewing a comedy called *The Provok'd Husband*
8 Firth 1908, p. 235
9 Watson 1827, p. 120
10 Goodall 1860, p. 59
11 Watson 1827, p. 156
12 Hall 1846, series 2, pp. 152–3
13 Hawker 1821, pp. 6–7

A FEW FACTS AND FIGURES

1 Watson 1827, p. viii
2 Dillon 1953, vol. 1, p. 18
3 Tiverton Library manuscript GM/1805/1128/86
4 Price 1984, p. 28

ONE: LEARNING THE ROPES

1 Watson 1827, p. 114
2 Dibdin 1844, p. 108 – from 'The True English Sailor' by Charles Dibdin
3 Goodall 1860, p. 5
4 National Maritime Museum manuscript SPB/15
5 Scott 1834, vol. 2, p. 296
6 Hall 1846, series 1, p. 7
7 Moody 1959, p. 230
8 Moody 1961–2, p. 248
9 Thomas 1968, p. 45
10 Thursfield 1951, pp. 243–4
11 Wheeler 1951, p. 25
12 Gardner 1906, pp. 124–5
13 Thursfield 1951, pp. 23–4
14 Royal Naval Museum manuscript 1986/537/50
15 The National Archives ADM 1/2507
16 NMM manuscript LBK/38
17 Hay 1953, p. 72
18 Thursfield 1951, p. 35. This was July 1812
19 Analysed by David Cordingly (2003, p. 209)
20 Oxford Archaeology 2007, p. 47
21 Aaron Thomas Papers, Special Collections, University of Miami Libraries

22 Aaron Thomas Papers
23 Aaron Thomas Papers, written in 1799
24 Aaron Thomas Papers, written in September 1798
25 Thomas 1968, p. 115
26 Royal Marines Museum manuscript 11/12/41: letter dated 13 February 1799
27 Raigersfeld 1929, p. 14
28 Raigersfeld 1929, p. 14
29 Aaron Thomas Papers
30 Aaron Thomas Papers, written in 1799
31 Aaron Thomas Papers
32 Crawford 1851, vol. 1, p. 272
33 NMM manuscript SPB/15
34 Hay 1953, pp. 43–4
35 Hay 1953, p. 44
36 Millard 1895, p. 84
37 NMM manuscript LBK/38
38 TNA ADM 1/5346
39 Hay 1953, pp. 44–5
40 Thursfield 1951, p. 243
41 Crawford 1851, vol. 1, p. 169
42 Thursfield 1951, p. 244
43 Thursfield 1951, p. 245
44 Fraser 1896, p. 272
45 Thursfield 1951, pp. 245–6
46 Thursfield 1951, p. 246
47 Goodall 1860, pp. 20–1
48 Thursfield 1951, p. 247
49 Leech 1844, pp. 36–7
50 Hall 1846, series 1, p. 137
51 Smyth 1867, p. 478
52 Goodall 1860, p. 21
53 Robinson 1836, p. 12
54 Forester 1954, p. 28
55 Hay 1953, p. 51
56 Thursfield 1951, p. 31
57 Brewer 1805, p. 433
58 Hay 1953, pp. 70–1
59 Raigersfeld 1929, p. 36
60 Bonner-Smith 1942, p. 51
61 Crawford 1851, vol. 1, p. 35
62 Morrice 1801, pp. 5–6
63 Crawford 1851, vol. 1, p. 37
64 Crawford 1851, vol. 1, pp. 34–5
65 Crawford 1851, vol. 1, p. 37
66 Scott 1834, vol. 1, p. 8
67 Scott 1834, vol. 1, p. 13
68 Robinson 1911, p. 114, from 'The Jolly Sailor's True Description of a Man-of-War' of the late eighteenth century
69 Watson 1827, pp. 115–16
70 Robinson 1836, p. 27
71 Robinson 1836, p. 28
72 Goodall 1860, pp. 18–19
73 Goodall 1860, p. 65
74 Hall 1846, series 1, p. 74
75 Gardner 1906, p. 241
76 Aaron Thomas Papers
77 *The Naval Chronicle* 3, 1800, p. 159
78 Nicolas 1846, p. ccxiv
79 Hall 1846, series 1, p. 82
80 Dillon 1953, vol. 1, p. 164
81 Dillon 1953, vol. 2, p. 124
82 Scott 1834, vol. 1, p. 41
83 Aaron Thomas Papers
84 Goodall 1860, pp. 59–60
85 Rees 1822, pp. 3–4
86 Goodall 1860, pp. 63–4
87 Goodall 1860, p. 64
88 Hall 1846, series 1, p. 82
89 Bates 1868, p. 42
90 Gardner 1906, p. 178
91 Bates 1868, pp. 42–3
92 Watson 1827, p. 89
93 Dillon 1953, vol. 1, p. 101
94 Dillon 1953, vol. 1, p. 104
95 Thursfield 1951, p. 14
96 Goodall 1860, pp. 50–1
97 Hoffman 1901, pp. 72–3
98 Glascock 1826, pp. 138–9
99 Robinson 1836, pp. 54–5
100 Robinson 1836, p. 55
101 Susan Lucas collection
102 Marryat 1872, pp. 36–7
103 Glascock 1826, pp. 141–2
104 Gardner 1906, p. 199
105 Glascock 1826, p. 143
106 Hay 1953, p. 164
107 Hoffman 1901, p. 24

108 Scott 1834, vol. 1, pp. 72–3
109 O'Meara 1822, vol. 1, p. 177

TWO: PRESSED

1 *The Times* 16 August 1790
2 Bates 1868, p. 85
3 Bates 1868, p. 85
4 Boteler 1942, p. 44
5 Lincoln and McEwen 1960, p. 14
6 *Middlesex Journal: or, Chronicle of Liberty* 3–5 Jan 1771
7 *The Times* 23 October 1787
8 *Hampshire Chronicle* 21 March 1803
9 Pasley 1931, p. 61
10 Letter of 10 December 1815 from 'An Englishman', in *The European Magazine* February 1816, p. 122
11 O'Meara 1822, vol. 2, p. 381
12 Lovett 1876, pp. 2–3
13 National Maritime Museum manuscript JOD/156
14 Fyfe 1942, p. 51
15 Jackson 1927, pp. 26–8
16 Wyndham-Quin 1912, pp. 121–2
17 Rattenbury 1837, p. 15. German Phillips was identified by Eileen Hathaway (1994, p. 37)
18 *Naval Chronicle* 9 1803, pp. 243–4
19 *Naval Chronicle* 9 1803, p. 247
20 *Naval Chronicle* 9 1803, p. 329
21 Leyland 1899, pp. 1–2
22 The National Archives ADM 1/5128
23 NMM manuscript LBK/38
24 Kelly 1925, p. 251
25 Waterhouse 1911, pp. 187–8
26 Price 1984, p. 17
27 Price 1984, p. 18
28 Lovett 1876, p. 3
29 *The Hampshire Courier, or, Portsmouth, Portsea, Gosport, and Chichester Advertiser* 2 March 1812
30 *Blackwood's Edinburgh Magazine* 10, 1821, p. 444. This was published by Thomas Doubleday, an early folk song collector in Northumberland, using his alias Josiah Shufflebotham
31 Goodall 1860, pp. 2–3
32 Goodall 1860, pp. 3–4
33 Goodall 1860, p. 3
34 Robinson 1836, pp. 2–3
35 *The Times* 8 October 1790
36 *Naval Chronicle* 9 1803, pp. 331–2
37 Royal Naval Museum manuscript 1996/31/1 – these are the final words of a journal written in 1820. Mackay also wrote a near-identical journal five years earlier (1996/31/2), which ended with his arrival at Yarmouth
38 *The Times* 19 November 1793
39 Kelly 1925, pp. 270–1
40 Thomas 1968, p. 178
41 TNA ADM 51/1146
42 Thomas 1968, p. 179
43 *The Times* 25 July 1798
44 *Gentleman's Magazine* 50, 1780, p. 72
45 *Gentleman's Magazine* 50, 1780, p. 73
46 *The Times* 2 October 1787
47 TNA ADM 1/2676: letter of 23 July 1781
48 Stirling 1919, vol. 1, pp. 94–5
49 Moody 1959, p. 229
50 Moody 1959, p. 230
51 TNA ADM 51/1146
52 Rattenbury 1837, p. 15
53 Price 1984, p. 7, written on 18 December 1803
54 *Naval Chronicle* 12, 1805, pp. 453–4
55 Pettigrew 1849, vol. 1, p. 410
56 *Naval Chronicle* 9, 1803, p. 247
57 Royal Marines Museum manuscript P/9/14
58 RMM manuscript P/9/14
59 RMM manuscript 591/76(B)
60 RMM manuscript 591/76(B)
61 Rees 1822, p. 1
62 RMM manuscript 11/19/93
63 RMM manuscript 11/19/93
64 Aaron Thomas Papers, Special Collections, University of Miami Libraries
65 Aaron Thomas Papers
66 Nicolas 1845, vol. 5, p. 45
67 Nicolas 1845, vol. 5, p. 45

68 TNA ADM 1/2507
69 Leech 1844, p. 71
70 Thursfield 1951, p. 159
71 TNA ADM 52/3804

THREE: SALT JUNK AND GROG
 1 Aaron Thomas Papers, Special
     Collections, University of Miami
     Libraries
 2 Gardner 1906, pp. 244–5
 3 Dillon 1953, vol. 1, p. 386 fn
 4 Leech 1844, p. 46
 5 Nicolas 1844, p. 297
 6 Upton collection, Wilkinson
     060228wdww, letter of 28 February
     1806
 7 Goodall 1860, p. 67
 8 Goodall 1860, p. 67
 9 Aaron Thomas Papers. This was 25
     July 1798, at Basseterre, St Kitts
10 Watson 1827, pp. 126–7 – this was in
     1811
11 Blane 1785, p. 292
12 Thursfield 1951, p. 246
13 Thursfield 1951, pp. 246–7
14 Goodall 1860, pp. 132–3
15 Robinson 1836, p. 7
16 Hall 1846, series 1, p. 137
17 Royal Naval Museum manuscript
     1986/537/50
18 RNM manuscript 1986/537/50
19 Hall 1846, series 1, p. 137
20 Hall 1846, series 1, p. 138
21 Thursfield 1951, p. 247
22 Thomas 1968, p. 190
23 Aaron Thomas Papers
24 Pemberton 1843, p. 161
25 Pemberton 1843, p. 145
26 Raigersfeld 1929, pp. 11–12
27 RNM manuscript 1986/537/23 – this
     was December 1811 on board HMS
     Queen
28 Barrett 1841a, p. 15
29 Sinclair 1857, pp. 37–9
30 Hall 1846, series 1, p. 137
31 Watson 1827, pp. 125–6. This was in
     1811

32 Griffiths 1824, p. 158
33 Aaron Thomas Papers. This was 8
     July 1798
34 Fremantle 1940, p. 94
35 Pasley 1931, p. 69
36 Pasley 1931, p. 69
37 Dillon 1953, vol. 1, p. 397
38 Fremantle 1940, p. 176
39 Fremantle 1940, p. 212. He was still
     in the Neptune
40 National Maritime Museum
     manuscript JOD/156
41 Barrett 1841a, p. 15
42 Gardner 1906, p. 139
43 Aaron Thomas Papers
44 Trotter 1804, vol. 3, p. 279
45 Thomas 1968, p. 93
46 Thomas 1968, p. 190
47 Thomas 1968, p. 190
48 Price 1984, pp. 17–18: letter of 25
     May 1804
49 Trotter 1804, vol. 3, p. 280
50 Raigersfeld 1929, p. 18
51 Trotter 1804, vol. 3, p. 279
52 Aaron Thomas Papers. This was 17
     April 1799
53 Hay 1953, p. 170
54 Hay 1953, pp. 170–1
55 NMM manuscript JOD/156
56 Hay 1953, p. 171
57 Trotter 1804, vol. 3, p. 129
58 Royal Marines Museum manuscript
     11/19/93
59 Hall 1846, series 1, p. 31
60 Barrett 1841a, p. 15
61 Raigersfeld 1929, p. 24
62 Raigersfeld 1929, p. 25
63 Watson 1827, p. 148
64 Raigersfeld 1929, p. 39
65 RMM archive 'John Whick
     Musician – Royal Marines, Letters
     from HMS Victory 1808–1812',
     ACQ 2004/0075
66 Blane 1785, p. 211
67 Thursfield 1951, p. 26
68 Thursfield 1951, p. 31
69 Thursfield 1951, p. 32

70 Crawford 1851, vol. 1, p. 134
71 Prior 1820, p. 76.
72 Fremantle 1940, p. 245. This was 1806
73 Pasley 1931, p. 217
74 Pasley 1931, p. 217
75 Blane 1785, p. 283
76 Nicolas 1845, vol. 5, p. 438
77 NMM manuscript JOD/148
78 Prior 1820, p. 49
79 Aaron Thomas Papers
80 Sinclair 1857, p. 6
81 The National Archives ADM 1/5346
82 TNA ADM 1/5346
83 TNA ADM 1/5362
84 Jackson 1927, pp. 37–8
85 Fremantle 1940, p. 128. He was on board the *Ganges* in Aris Bay in July 1804
86 Fremantle 1940, p. 245. He was in the *Neptune*
87 William Ffarington logbook in Brixham Museum
88 NMM manuscript GRE/15
89 Petrides and Downs 2000, p. 73. This was 1 April 1805
90 Raigersfeld 1929, p. 23
91 NMM manuscript JOD/156. He was on board HMS *Minerva* in 1793
92 Bates 1868, pp. 20–1
93 Bates 1868, p. 21
94 Petrides and Downs 2000, p. 66
95 Scott 1834, vol. 1, p. 21. This was in 1803 under Captain Cockburn
96 Thursfield 1951, p. 29
97 Sinclair 1857, p. 59
98 Spilsbury 1807, p. 6
99 Thomas 1968, pp. 35–6
100 Blane 1785, p. 300
101 Thursfield 1951, p. 173
102 Jackson 1927, p. 5
103 Blane 1785, p. 301
104 Thomas 1968, p. 77
105 Fremantle 1940, p. 209
106 Watson 1827, p. 61
107 Hall 1846, series 2, p. 98
108 Sinclair 1857, pp. 57–8

109 Watson 1827, p. 106
110 Leech 1844, p. 65. This was in 1810 off Lisbon
111 Thursfield 1951, p. 141
112 Thursfield 1951, p. 153
113 Thursfield 1951, p. 154
114 Goodall 1860, p. 23
115 NMM manuscript MSS/73/075
116 Price 1984, p. 31: letter of 8 May 1805
117 William Ffarington logbook
118 NMM manuscript JOD/156
119 Trotter 1804, vol. 3, p. 129. He was writing in 1801
120 Leech 1844, pp. 65–6
121 Letter in Yule-Booth collection
122 Aaron Thomas Papers
123 Raigersfeld 1929, p. 32
124 Aaron Thomas Papers
125 Aaron Thomas Papers
126 Aaron Thomas Papers
127 Aaron Thomas Papers
128 Aaron Thomas Papers
129 Aaron Thomas Papers
130 Aaron Thomas Papers
131 Aaron Thomas Papers
132 Rees 1822, p. 10
133 Leech 1844, p. 66
134 Watson 1827, pp. 108–9
135 NMM manuscript MSS/73/075

FOUR: FACING THE ELEMENTS

1 Watson 1827, p. 134
2 Bourchier 1873, p. 73. His brother was William Bethell, not Codrington
3 Prior 1820, p. 55
4 Prior 1820, pp. 54–5
5 Petrides and Downs 2000, p. 117
6 Petrides and Downs 2000, p. 117
7 Petrides and Downs 2000, pp. 117–18
8 Thomas 1968, p. 35
9 Thomas 1968, p. 189
10 Thomas 1968, p. 45
11 Thomas 1968, pp. 45–6
12 Royal Marines Museum manuscript 11/19/93
13 Plaque inside St Mary's church at

Bridport. Charlotte Carpenter had already lost her second son in 1787, aged eight years, and three other sons died in infancy. She herself was buried in the churchyard in 1815, and the plaque was erected by her youngest and only surviving son

14 Gardner 1906, p. 220
15 Fremantle 1940, p. 31
16 Millard 1895, p. 82
17 Moody 1961–2, p. 108
18 Watson 1827, p. 133. He was on board HMS *Eagle*
19 Scott 1842, pp. 85–6
20 Moody 1961–2, p. 246. This was April 1815
21 Petrides and Downs 2000, p. 49
22 Hay 1953, pp. 184–5
23 Rees 1822, p. 23. This was December 1809
24 RMM manuscript 11/19/93
25 RMM manuscript 11/19/93
26 TNA ADM 52/2359
27 TNA ADM 52/2359
28 TNA ADM 52/2359
29 Inglefield 1783, pp. 6–7
30 Inglefield 1783, pp. 7–8
31 Inglefield 1783, pp. 14–15
32 Inglefield 1783, pp. 21–3
33 Inglefield 1783, p. 24
34 Inglefield 1783, pp. 24–5
35 Inglefield 1783, p. 27
36 Inglefield 1783, p. 32
37 *Annual Register* 1782, p. 228
38 Hay 1953, p. 214
39 Pemberton 1843, p. 84
40 Trotter 1804, vol. 1, p. 446
41 Regulations 1808, p. 365
42 *The Royal Cornwall Gazette, Falmouth Packet and Plymouth Journal* 19 March 1808
43 Hay 1953, pp. 99–100
44 Leech 1844, p. 35. He is two years older in the muster books than in his memoirs
45 National Maritime Museum manuscript JOD/156

46 William Ffarington logbook, Brixham Museum
47 William Ffarington logbook
48 NMM manuscript RUSI/ER/3/11
49 NMM manuscript RUSI/ER/3/11
50 Thursfield 1951, pp. 257–8
51 Hay 1953, p. 190
52 Regulations 1808, p. 425
53 RMM manuscript 11/12/42
54 Regulations 1808, p. 427
55 RMM manuscript 11/19/93
56 RMM manuscript 11/12/42. The letter dates to 14 August 1805
57 Beatty 1807, p. 33
58 Beatty 1807, p. 68
59 Nicolas 1844, p. 89
60 NMM manuscript WQB/40
61 Beatty 1807, pp. 80–1
62 William Ffarington logbook
63 TNA ADM 1/5399
64 Leech 1844, pp. 125–6
65 Gardner 1906, p. 107
66 Tucker 1844, pp. 427–8
67 RMM manuscript 11/12/42: two letters written at Portsmouth dating to 14 and 29 August 1805
68 Hay 1953, p. 71
69 Newnham Collingwood 1829, p. 124
70 Beatty 1807, p. 28
71 Beatty 1807, p. 81
72 Hay 1953, p. 167
73 NMM manuscript JOD/156
74 Petrides and Downs 2000, p. 117
75 William Ffarington logbook
76 Trotter 1804, vol. 1, pp. 443–4
77 William Ffarington logbook
78 Moody 1959, p. 230
79 Royal Naval Museum manuscript 2001/57
80 Moody 1959, p. 230
81 Moody 1959, pp. 230–1
82 NMM manuscript GRE/15
83 Trotter 1804, vol. 1, pp. 444–5
84 Dillon 1953, vol. 1, p. 104
85 Blane 1785, p. 145
86 *The Times* 12 September 1806
87 *The Times* 12 September 1806

88 William Ffarington logbook.
    Barlow was captain of the *Phoebe*
    from 1795 to 1801
89 William Ffarington logbook
90 Bates 1868, pp. 45–6
91 Bates 1868, p. 46
92 NMM manuscript WQB/39
93 Lovell 1879, p. 31
94 Letter in Upton collection
    07119wwsp
95 Letter in Upton collection
    071123wwsp 23 November 1807
96 Aaron Thomas Papers, Special
    Collections, University of Miami
    Libraries. This was 1798
97 Spilsbury 1807, p. 16
98 Letter of John Yule to his wife 20
    March 1802, Yule-Booth collection
99 TNA ADM 1/5126
100 Dillon 1953, vol. 1, pp. 428–9
101 William Ffarington logbook
102 William Ffarington logbook
103 William Ffarington logbook
104 Cockburn 1815, p. 2
105 Cockburn 1815, p. 8. This was July
    1810
106 Lowry 2006, p. 93
107 Trotter 1804, vol. 1, p. 444
108 Regulations 1808, p. 139
109 RMM manuscript 11/12/42
110 Cooper 1869, pp. 124–5
111 Dillon 1953, vol. 1, p. 429
112 Petrides and Downs 2000, p. 184
113 Gardner 1906, pp. 89–90
114 *The Times* 7 December 1785
115 *The Times* 7 December 1785
116 Fremantle 1940, pp. 118–19
117 British Library manuscript Add.
    38,886
118 NMM manuscript MSS/73/075
119 TNA ADM 1/181
120 RNM manuscript 2001/57. This was
    January 1811
121 Crawford 1851, vol. 2, p. 220
122 Davis 1815, p. 12 (first published in
    1805)
123 TNA ADM 1/5346

124 Aaron Thomas Papers
125 Aaron Thomas Papers
126 Aaron Thomas Papers
127 Aaron Thomas Papers
128 Robertson 1807, pp. 432–3
129 Blane 1785, p. 53
130 Petrides and Downs 2000, p. 101
131 Yule-Booth collection
132 O'Meara 1822, vol. 2, p. 252
133 Trotter 1804, vol. 1, p. 444
134 Trotter 1804, vol. 1, p. 444
135 Cockburn 1815, pp. 32–3
136 Prior 1820, p. 48
137 Raigersfeld 1929, pp. 29–30
138 Hay 1953, p. 101
139 Prior 1820, p. 48
140 Prior 1820, pp. 48–9
141 Prior 1820, p. 49 fn
142 Hay 1953, p. 102
143 Prior 1820, p. 49
144 Cockburn 1815, pp. 31–2
145 Regulations 1808, p. 137
146 Thursfield 1951, p. 249
147 Regulations 1808, p. 137
148 Thursfield 1951, p. 335
149 TNA ADM 1/5346
150 TNA ADM 1/5346
151 TNA ADM 1/5346
152 TNA ADM 1/5346
153 TNA ADM 1/5442
154 Fremantle 1940, p. 174. This letter
    was written on 22 June 1805 on
    board the *Neptune* off Ushant
155 Thursfield 1951, p. 11
156 Hall 1846, series 1, p. 31
157 Wyndham-Quin 1912, p. 144. He is
    also called Chevers
158 Smyth 1829, pp. 223–4
159 Thomas 1968, p. 185. Journal entry
    for 8 November 1794

FIVE: A WIFE IN EVERY PORT

1 Watson 1827, p. 135
2 Griffiths 1824, p. 95. This was
   written in 1811
3 Thursfield 1951, p. 8
4 Moody 1959, p. 233

5 Moody 1959, p. 233
6 Gardner 1906, p. 16, where a bowdlerised version is given
7 Pillet 1818, p. 218
8 Goodall 1860, pp. 25–6. This was in 1801
9 Steele 1840, p. 235
10 National Maritime Museum manuscript WIL/1/21: letter of 4 February 1809
11 The National Archives ADM 102/163
12 Dillon 1953, vol. 1, p. 96
13 Greig 1924, p. 174
14 NMM manuscript AGC/P/17. This letter was written on 12 June 1805
15 Goodall 1860, p. 26
16 Goodall 1860, pp. 26–7
17 Hawker 1821, p. 2
18 Hawker 1821, p. 4
19 Hawker 1821, p. 5
20 Forester 1954, p. 48
21 Letter from an anonymous officer in *United Services Journal* 1839 part 3, pp. 419–20
22 *Penny Magazine* 3 May 1834, pp. 175–6
23 *Penny Magazine* 3 May 1834, p. 176
24 *Parker's General Advertiser and Morning Intelligencer* 2 September 1782
25 Pinckard 1806, p. 38
26 Watson 1827, pp. 22–3
27 Watson 1827, p. 82
28 Watson 1827, pp. 83–4
29 Watson 1827, p. 84
30 Watson 1827, pp. 82–3
31 Nicol 1822, pp. 19–20
32 Aaron Thomas Papers, Special Collections, University of Miami Libraries
33 Aaron Thomas Papers
34 Aaron Thomas Papers
35 Aaron Thomas Papers
36 Anon 1806, p. 51
37 Royal Naval Museum manuscript 1985/323
38 RNM manuscript 1985/323
39 Watson 1827, pp. 201–2
40 RNM manuscript 1992/442
41 RNM manuscript 1992/442
42 TNA ADM 37/596
43 TNA ADM 27/19. Thanks to Mick Davis for finding this
44 RNM manuscript 1992/442
45 TNA ADM 1/5345
46 NMM manuscript SPB/15
47 Griffiths 1824, pp. 109–10. This was written in 1811
48 Letter of John Yule to Eliza Yule, 16 November 1805, Yule-Booth collection
49 Letter of John Yule to Eliza Yule, 9 December 1805, Yule-Booth collection
50 Letter of John Yule to Eliza Yule, 9 December 1805, Yule-Booth collection
51 NMM manuscript JOD/156
52 Watson 1827, p. 98
53 Watson 1827, pp. 71–2
54 Watson 1827, pp. 89–90
55 NMM manuscript WQB/39
56 NMM manuscript GRE/15
57 Tucker 1844, p. 414
58 TNA ADM 36/14817 (2nd entry)
59 TNA ADM 36/14817 (2nd entry)
60 Wellcome Institute Library, vol. 10 Western Ms. 3676
61 Nicol 1822, pp. 186–7
62 Aaron Thomas Papers
63 NMM manuscript MSS/77/148. He was in the *Audacious*
64 Leech 1844, pp. 94–5
65 Chronicle of the *Annual Register* 54 for 1812 (1813), p. 93
66 Chronicle of the *Annual Register* 54 for 1812 (1813), p. 93
67 TNA ADM 53/1242
68 Rowbotham 1937, p. 366
69 TNA ADM 82/124
70 Portsmouth City Museum and Record Office manuscript 11A/S/1
71 *The Naval Chronicle* 17, 1807, p. 309
72 See Cordingly 2001, pp. 85–6

73 *Woolmer's Exeter and Plymouth Gazette* 11 May 1809
74 *The Times* 2 September 1815
75 Boser 2002
76 Smyth 1829, p. 201
77 Chronicle of the *Annual Register* for 1807 (1809), p. 463
78 *Morning Chronicle* 6 October 1807
79 NMM manuscript WQB/40
80 TNA ADM 1/5383
81 TNA ADM 1/5383
82 *The Times* 22 October 1807
83 TNA ADM 1/5428
84 TNA ADM 1/5428
85 Thursfield 1951, pp. 9–10
86 Thursfield 1951, p. 10
87 Thursfield 1951, p. 10
88 TNA ADM 1/5331
89 TNA ADM 1/5331
90 TNA ADM 1/5331
91 TNA ADM 1/5331
92 Leech 1844, pp. 43–4
93 Hall 1846, series 1, pp. 40–1
94 Hall 1846, series 1, p. 8
95 TNA ADM 101/93/1. The surgeon was Abraham Martin
96 NMM manuscript RUSI/ER/3/11
97 Hall 1846, series 1, p. 9
98 NMM manuscript GRE/15
99 NMM manuscript MSS74/074
100 NMM manuscript MSS74/074
101 Upton collection, Wilkinson 091217spww

SIX: BELLS AND WHISTLES
1 National Maritime Museum manuscript SPB/15
2 Leech 1844, pp. 39–40
3 Thursfield 1951, p. 243
4 Dillon 1953, vol. 2, p. 84
5 Thursfield 1951, p. 244
6 Goodall 1860, p. 19
7 Goodall 1860, pp. 19–20
8 Goodall 1860, p. 20
9 Hall 1846, series 1, p. 138
10 Portsmouth City Museum and Record Office manuscript 11A/S/1

11 Hay 1953, p. 45
12 Leech 1844, pp. 42–3
13 Hay 1953, p. 46
14 Leech 1844, pp. 43–4
15 Pasley 1931, p. 63
16 Leech 1844, pp. 83–4
17 Bates 1868, p. 44
18 Bates 1868, p. 45
19 Robinson 1836, p. 6
20 Royal Marines Museum manuscript 11/19/93
21 Griffiths 1824, pp. 192–3
22 Watson 1827, pp. 67–8
23 Hall 1846, series 1, p. 66
24 Gardner 1906, p. 108
25 Thomas 1968, p. 99
26 NMM manuscript WQB/40. Prince William was the captain
27 NMM manuscript WQB/40
28 Hall 1846, series 1, p. 5
29 Thursfield 1951, p. 248
30 Leech 1844, p. 42
31 Thursfield 1951, p. 249
32 O'Loghlen 1766, pp. 112–13
33 O'Loghlen 1766, p. 113
34 Regulations 1806, p. 163
35 Hall 1846, series 2, p. 96
36 Leech 1844, p. 49
37 Leech 1844, pp. 49–50
38 Leech 1844, pp. 50–1
39 Goodall 1860, pp. 22–3
40 Aaron Thomas Papers, Special Collection, University of Miami Libraries
41 Jackson 1927, p. 11
42 NMM manuscript JOD/148
43 Watson 1827, pp. 138–9
44 NMM manuscript MSS/73/075
45 Aaron Thomas Papers
46 NMM manuscript JOD/156
47 NMM manuscript JOD/156
48 Dillon 1953, vol. 1, p. 97
49 Sinclair 1857, p. 52
50 Goodall 1860, p. 22
51 Scott 1834, vol. 1, p. 37
52 Thursfield 1951, p. 146
53 Goodall 1860, p. 16

54 Aaron Thomas Papers
55 Thursfield 1951, p. 171, from the journal of Robert Wilson
56 *Mariner's Mirror* 7, 1921, p. 343
57 Goodall 1860, p. 31
58 Goodall 1860, pp. 31–2
59 Aaron Thomas Papers
60 Aaron Thomas Papers
61 Aaron Thomas Papers
62 Aaron Thomas Papers
63 *Flindell's Western Luminary* 13 August 1813
64 Scott 1834, vol. 2, p. 62
65 Scott 1834, vol. 1, pp. 15–16
66 Scott 1834, vol. 1, p. 14
67 Dillon 1953, vol. 1, p. 105
68 Royal Naval Museum manuscript 1995/48
69 Delafons 1805, pp. 271–2
70 The National Archives ADM 1/5124
71 Lincoln and McEwen 1960, p. 20
72 Robinson 1836, p. 1
73 Dillon 1953, vol. 1, p. 327
74 Goodall 1860, p. 37
75 Goodall 1860, p. 40
76 Goodall 1860, pp. 43–4
77 TNA ADM 1/5442. Wardocks was from Ireland and Buckhawson from Germany
78 TNA ADM 1/5442
79 Thursfield 1951, p. 36
80 Moody 1959, p. 238
81 Goodall 1860, pp. 34–5
82 Watson 1827, pp. 111–12
83 TNA ADM 1/5442
84 Scott 1834, vol. 2, p. 158
85 Scott 1834, vol. 2, pp. 160–1
86 Scott 1834, vol. 2, p. 162
87 Scott 1834, vol. 2, p. 163
88 Goodall 1860, p. 46
89 Goodall 1860, p. 49

SEVEN: CONVOY AND CAPTURE

1 National Maritime Museum manuscript SPB/15
2 Malcolm 1828, p. 239. In later life John Malcolm was a poet
3 Malcolm 1828, pp. 237–8
4 Malcolm 1828, pp. 239–40
5 Watson 1827, p. 23
6 Moody 1961–2, p. 112
0 Moody 1961–2, pp. 114–15
8 Aaron Thomas Papers, Special Collections, University of Miami Libraries
9 Whitfeld 1900, pp. 209–10
10 Hall 1846, series 1, p. 64
11 Aaron Thomas Papers
12 NMM manuscript JOD/156
13 NMM manuscript JOD/156
14 NMM manuscript JOD/156
15 NMM manuscript MSS/74/074
16 NMM manuscript MSS/74/074
17 NMM manuscript MSS/74/074
18 Fremantle 1940, p. 205
19 British Library manuscript Add. 38,886
20 O'Meara 1822, vol. 1, p. 177
21 Sinclair 1857, p. 62
22 NMM manuscript MSS/73/075
23 NMM manuscript MSS/73/075
24 NMM manuscript MSS/73/075
25 Dibdin 1844, p. 101
26 NMM manuscript MSS/73/075
27 Watson 1827, p. 170
28 Watson 1827, p. 169
29 Tiverton Library manuscript GM/1805/1128/86
30 James 1859, p. 257
31 Tiverton Library manuscript GM/1805/1128/86
32 James 1859, p. 257
33 Royal Naval Museum manuscript 1996/21/2
34 RNM manuscript 1996/31/2
35 RNM manuscript 1996/31/2
36 RNM manuscript 1996/31/2
37 RNM manuscript 1996/31/2
38 RNM manuscript 1996/31/2
39 Report on Treatment of Prisoners of War 9 May 1798, p. 12 in Lambert 1975
40 Report on Treatment of Prisoners of War 9 May 1798, pp. 58–9 in Lambert 1975

41 Report on Treatment of Prisoners of War 9 May 1798, p. 59 in Lambert 1975
42 O'Meara 1822, vol. 2, p. 28
43 British Library manuscript Add. 38,886
44 BL manuscript Add. 38,886
45 BL manuscript Add. 38,886
46 BL manuscript Add. 38,886
47 Letter of 26 March 1811 in Yule-Booth collection. Bingham had been a prisoner since October 1807
48 NMM manuscript JOD/224. His journal is anonymous, but was almost certainly written by Finny (see TNA ADM 37/384)
49 Short and Williams 1914, p. 76
50 Short and Williams 1914, p. 76
51 BL manuscript Add. 38,886
52 Wolfe 1830, pp. 62–4
53 NMM manuscript JOD/202
54 NMM manuscript JOD/224
55 BL manuscript Add. 38,886
56 BL manuscript Add. 38,886
57 Short and Williams 1914, p. 33
58 Boys 1864, p. 45
59 Short and Williams 1914, p. 94
60 Short and Williams 1914, p. 35
61 Boys 1864, p. 113
62 Boys 1864, p. 94
63 BL manuscript Add. 38,886
64 BL manuscript Add. 38,886
65 NMM manuscript JOD/202
66 BL manuscript Add. 38,886
67 BL manuscript Add. 38,886
68 Ellison 1838, p. 78
69 Jackson 1927, p. 210
70 BL manuscript Add. 38,886
71 BL manuscript Add. 38,886
72 Short and Williams 1914, pp. 78–9
73 BL manuscript Add. 38,886
74 NMM manuscript JOD/202
75 Jackson 1927, p. 219
76 NMM manuscript JOD/224

EIGHT: INTO BATTLE

1 National Maritime Museum manuscript AGC/14/8
2 Petrides and Downs 2000, p. 169
3 Leech 1844, p. 127
4 Leech 1844, p. 127
5 Thursfield 1951, p. 154. This was December 1806
6 Dillon 1953, vol. 1, p. 122
7 NMM manuscript AGC/B/18
8 Elliot 1863, pp. 12–13
9 Polwhele 1826, p. 578
10 Scott 1834, vol. 1, pp. 26–7
11 Scott 1834, vol. 1, p. 28
12 Dillon 1953, vol. 1, pp. 122–3
13 NMM manuscript JOD/156
14 Jackson 1900, p. 238
15 The National Archives ADM 52/3550
16 Field 1924, p. 143
17 Gardner 1906, p. 30
18 Gardner 1906, pp. 31–2
19 Fraser 1913, pp. 215–16
20 Scott 1834, vol. 1, pp. 86–7
21 Dillon 1953, vol. 1, p. 128
22 NMM manuscript JON/7
23 Thursfield 1951, p. 364
24 Dillon 1953, vol. 1, p. 128
25 Leech 1844, p. 135
26 Dillon 1953, vol. 1, p. 125. This was Captain Gambier
27 Thursfield 1951, p. 253
28 Thursfield 1951, p. 253
29 Leech 1844, pp. 41–2
30 Spilsbury 1807, p. 6. This was in 1805
31 Pasley 1931, pp. 72–3
32 Pasley 1931, p. 77
33 Pasley 1931, p. 195
34 Pasley 1931, pp. 195–6
35 NMM manuscript JON/7
36 Scott 1834, vol. 1, p. 295
37 Hall 1846, series 3, p. 128
38 Royal Marines Museum manuscript 11/12/42
39 Dillon 1953, vol. 1, p. 131
40 Pasley 1931, p. 138

41 O'Brien 1839, pp. 209–10
42 O'Brien 1839, pp. 210–11
43 Bourchier 1873, pp. 39–40
44 Nicolas 1846, p. 139
45 Leech 1844, p. 130
46 Leech 1844, p. 131
47 Dillon 1953, vol. 1, p. 130
48 Petrides and Downs 2000, p. 141
49 Thursfield 1951, p. 155
50 Dillon 1953, vol. 1, pp. 124–5. This was 29 May 1794
51 Dillon 1953, vol. 1, p. 131
52 Dillon 1953, vol. 1, p. 139
53 Parsons 1905, p. 26
54 Parsons 1905, pp. 26–7
55 Leech 1844, pp. 132–4
56 Millard 1895, p. 88
57 Leech 1844, p. 134
58 Dillon 1953, vol. 1, p. 125. This was 29 May 1794
59 Price 1984, p. 37
60 NMM manuscript MSS/77/163
61 NMM manuscript MSS/77/163
62 NMM manuscript MSS/77/163
63 Dillon 1953, vol. 1, p. 142
64 Dillon 1953, vol. 1, pp. 181–2
65 Jackson 1927, p. 143
66 Hoffman 1901, p. 213
67 Willyams 1802, p. 53
68 Lee 1836, pp. 92–3
69 Moorhouse 1910, p. 172
70 Scott 1834, vol. 1, pp. 306–7
71 Dillon 1953, vol. 1, p. 139
72 Watson 1827, p. 143
73 Bourchier 1873, pp. 72–3
74 Leech 1844, p. 144
75 Thursfield 1951, p. 155
76 Leech 1844, p. 145
77 Letter in Yule-Booth collection
78 Letter in Yule-Booth collection

NINE: UNDER THE KNIFE

1 National Maritime Museum manuscript SPB/15
2 Thursfield 1951, p. 49 (written by Cullen in the third person)
3 Thomas 1968, p. 36
4 Petrides and Downs 2000, pp. 57–8
5 Dillon 1953, vol. 1, p. 144
6 Dillon 1953, vol. 1, p. 144
7 Boog Watson 1969, p. 215
8 Robertson 1807, p. 309
9 Thursfield 1951, pp. 28–9
10 The National Archives ADM 101/85/7
11 TNA ADM 101/85/7
12 Leech 1844, p. 142
13 Nicolas 1845, vol. 2, p. 444
14 Leech 1844, p. 143
15 Leech 1844, p. 143
16 Barrett 1841b, p. 24
17 TNA ADM 101/102/6. This was a journal entry of 15 February 1789
18 Barrett 1841b, p. 24
19 TNA ADM 101/118/1
20 TNA ADM 101/118/1
21 TNA ADM 101/118/1
22 TNA ADM 101/118/1
23 Wellcome Institute Library, vol. 10 Western Ms. 3676
24 TNA ADM 101/85/7
25 Leech 1844, p. 144
26 Royal Naval Museum manuscript 1998/41/1
27 RNM manuscript 1998/41/1
28 RNM manuscript 1998/41/1
29 RNM manuscript 1998/41/1
30 TNA ADM 101/106/1
31 Blane 1785, pp. 498–9
32 Blane 1785, p. 498
33 TNA ADM 101/106/1
34 TNA ADM 101/106/1
35 TNA ADM 101/106/1
36 TNA ADM 101/93/1. Lawrance was twenty-five years old
37 TNA ADM 101/93/1
38 NMM manuscript MSS/77/148. His surname is McCarty in the ship's muster book (TNA ADM 36/13758)
39 NMM manuscript MSS/77/148
40 NMM manuscript MSS/77/148
41 TNA ADM 101/93/1
42 TNA ADM 101/93/1
43 Sinclair 1857, pp. 47–8

44 Prior 1820, p. 5
45 Sinclair 1857, p. 49
46 TNA ADM 101/106/1
47 RNM manuscript 1986/537
48 RNM manuscript 1986/537/14
49 Blane 1785, p. 210
50 TNA ADM 101/102/4
51 TNA ADM 101/118/2
52 Nicolas 1845, vol. 5, p. 437: letter from Nelson to Dr Moseley of Chelsea Hospital, 11 March 1804
53 TNA ADM 101/106/1
54 TNA ADM 101/106/1
55 TNA ADM 101/118/2
56 Scott 1834, vol. 1, p. 21
57 TNA ADM 101/102/3
58 TNA ADM 101/102/4. This was 19 January 1788
59 Trotter 1804, vol. 3, p. 274
60 Blane 1785, p. 242
61 Robertson 1807, p. 301
62 Robertson 1807, pp. 432, 435
63 Hoffman 1901, pp. 53–4
64 Hoffman 1901, p. 79
65 Hoffman 1901, p. 80
66 TNA ADM 101/118/2
67 TNA ADM 101/118/2
68 Prior 1820, p. 49
69 Prior 1820, p. 54
70 Blane 1785, pp. 222–3
71 Blane 1785, p. 224
72 Spilsbury 1807, p. 17
73 Robertson 1777, p. 80
74 Robertson 1777, p. 80
75 *Woolmer's Exeter and Plymouth Gazette* 18 May 1809
76 TNA ADM 101/118/1. This was February 1804 on board the *Leviathan*
77 Robertson 1807, p. 479
78 TNA ADM 101/118/1
79 TNA ADM 101/102/4
80 Thursfield 1951, p. 226
81 Brenton 1838, p. 256 fn
82 Thursfield 1951, p. 29
83 Blane 1785, p. 338
84 Pinckard 1806, pp. 42, 43–4
85 TNA ADM 101/85/7
86 TNA ADM 101/85/7
87 NMM manuscript AGC/30/6
88 TNA ADM 101/93/1
89 Lincoln and McEwen 1960, p. 14
90 Barrett 1841a, p. 457
91 Barrett 1841a, pp. 13–14
92 Barrett 1841a, p. 15
93 *Morning Post* 15 May 1815, in Dallas 1815, pp. 103–4
94 *Morning Post* 15 May 1815, in Dallas 1815, pp. 104–5
95 Thomas 1968, p. 179
96 Nicolas 1845, vol. 3, p. 475
97 Hall 1846, series 1, p. 148
98 Thursfield 1951, pp. 356
99 Aaron Thomas Papers, Special Collections, University of Miami Libraries
100 Forester 1954, p. 43
101 Aaron Thomas Papers
102 Aaron Thomas Papers
103 Aaron Thomas Papers
104 Finlayson 1952, p. 130
105 Finlayson 1952, p. 130
106 Dillon 1953, vol. 1, p. 138
107 Blane 1785, pp. 109–10
108 Hall 1846, series 1, p. 147
109 Steele 1840, p. 9
110 Moody 1959, p. 235

TEN: AT LEISURE

1 Wheeler 1951, p. 47
2 Goodall 1860, pp. 51–2
3 Durand 1926, p. 59
4 Leech 1844, pp. 90–1
5 Gillett 1945, p. 67
6 Crawford 1851, vol. 1, p. 78
7 National Maritime Museum manuscript JOD/148
8 Hay 1953, p. 94
9 Buckingham 1855, p. 167. He calls him Emidee
10 Buckingham 1855, pp. 167–8
11 Buckingham 1855, pp. 168–9
12 The National Archives ADM 101/108/3

13 NMM manuscript JOD/148

14 Scott 1834, vol. 1, p. 40

15 British Library manuscript 45580 Blechynden Papers Vol. III 'A Collection of Naval Songs, Odes, Cantatas Poems, &c. Compiled by Richard Blechynden 1781'

16 BL manuscript 45580 Blechynden Papers Vol. III

17 BL manuscript 45580 Blechynden Papers Vol. III

18 BL manuscript 45580 Blechynden Papers Vol. III

19 Watson 1827, p. 88

20 Leech 1844, pp. 72–3

21 Leech 1844, p. 74

22 Goodall 1860, pp. 51–2

23 Goodall 1860, p. 116

24 Goodall 1860, p. 117

25 Goodall 1860, pp. 117–18

26 Newnham Collingwood 1829, pp. 269–70

27 Thursfield 1951, p. 257

28 Comfort 2004, p. 44

29 Thomas 1968, p. 195

30 Goodall 1860, p. 32

31 Aaron Thomas Papers Special Collection, University of Miami Libraries

32 Aaron Thomas Papers

33 Thomas 1968, pp. 195–6

34 Wheeler 1951, p. 47. This was in 1811, on board the *Revenge*

35 Leech 1844, pp. 124–5

36 Sinclair 1857, p. 84

37 Aaron Thomas Papers

38 Thomas 1968, p. 154

39 Aaron Thomas Papers

40 Royal Naval Museum manuscript 1984/546, letter dated 20 May 1800

41 Leech 1844, p. 105

42 Stirling 1919, pp. 118–19

43 NMM manuscript WIL/1/4. He was master of the ship

44 Petrides and Downs 2000, p. 109

45 Fernyhough 1829, p. 57

46 Leech 1844, p. 104

47 Petrides and Downs 2000, p. 98. This letter was written in January 1806

48 Price 1984, p. 28

49 Price 1984, p. 31

50 Hoffman 1901, pp. 134–5

51 Aaron Thomas Papers

52 Bates 1868, p. 41

53 Hall 1846, series 2, p. 66

54 Sinclair 1857, pp. 28–9

55 Sinclair 1857, pp. 29–30

56 Sinclair 1857, p. 30

57 Pasley 1931, p. 128

58 Fremantle 1940, pp. 250–1

59 Fremantle 1940, p. 261

60 Robinson 1858, p. 49

61 Gardner 1906, pp. 42, 47

62 Scott 1834, vol. 2, pp. 233–6

63 *Woolmer's Exeter and Plymouth Gazette* 27 July 1809

64 Crawford 1851, vol. 2, pp. 339–40

65 Crawford 1851, vol. 2, p. 340

66 Hall 1846, series 2, p. 73

67 Bonner-Smith 1942, p. 29

68 Letter in Upton collection, 09121wwsp. He was master of the *Christian*

69 Not the *Hind*, as Cochrane recorded in his memoirs

70 Dundonald 1861, p. 58

71 Petrides and Downs 2000, p. 122

72 Letter in Upton collection, 071123wwsp, dated 23 November 1807

73 NMM manuscript MSS/74/074: letter from Gibraltar Bay, 2 June 1808

74 NMM manuscript WIL/1/9: letter of 9 October 1807

75 Gardner 1906, pp. 133–4

76 Petrides and Downs 2000, pp. 90–1

77 Petrides and Downs 2000, p. 91

78 Fernyhough 1829, p. 151

79 Hay 1953, p. 96

80 Nicolas 1845, vol. 5, p. 238

81 Dillon 1953, vol. 1, p. 111

82 Pasley 1931, p. 215. This was December 1781

83 Watson 1827, pp. 37–8
84 Leech 1844, pp. 57–8
85 Scott 1834, vol. 2, p. 223
86 Aaron Thomas Papers
87 Aaron Thomas Papers
88 Leech 1844, p. 102
89 Leech 1844, p. 109
90 Leech 1844, p. 112
91 NMM manuscript MSS/73/075
92 Watson 1827, p. 149
93 Aaron Thomas Papers
94 Watson 1827, p. 92
95 Watson 1827, pp. 59–60
96 Hoffman 1901, pp. 32–3
97 Goodall 1860, p. 25
98 Nicolas 1844, p. 76
99 Leech 1844, p. 116
100 Goodall 1860, pp. 27–8
101 Goodall 1860, p. 28
102 Goodall 1860, p. 29
103 NMM manuscript MSS/73/075
104 NMM manuscript AGC/P/17: letter
     to his mother, 12 June 1805
105 Leech 1844, pp. 115–16
106 Watson 1827, pp. 87–8
107 Hall 1846, series 1, p. 17
108 Hall 1846, series 1, p. 74

ELEVEN: GLORY AND
HONOURS
1 National Maritime Museum
   manuscript SPB/15
2 NMM manuscript JOD/156
3 *The Times* 13 October 1798
4 Scott 1834, vol. 2, p. 167
5 NMM manuscript PHB/12
6 NMM manuscript PHB/12
7 Goodall 1860, pp. 113–14
8 Lee 1836, p. 50
9 Scott 1834, vol. 2, pp. 226–7
10 Dillon 1953, vol. 2, p. 237
11 Dillon 1953, vol. 1, p. 306
12 Sinclair 1857, p. 10
13 Royal Naval Museum manuscript
    1995/48
14 Fremantle 1940, vol. 3, p. 369
15 RNM manuscript 2001/57. Acheson

    died at Dublin in 1849/50
16 Goodall 1860, pp. 35–6
17 *Naval Chronicle* 34, 1815, pp. 480–1
18 Scott 1834, vol. 3, p. 372
19 *The Times* 19 September 1815
20 Firth 1908, p. 228
21 *Morning Chronicle* 31 March 1815
22 *Bell's Weekly Messenger* 16 October
    1814
23 *The Times* 19 February 1821
24 NMM manuscript MSS/73/075
25 NMM manuscript MSS/73/075
26 NMM manuscript MSS/73/075
27 *Illustrated London News* 13 April
    1844, p. 233
28 *Illustrated London News* 13 April
    1844, p. 233
29 *Illustrated London News* 13 April
    1844, p. 233
30 *Illustrated London News* 13 April
    1844, p. 233
31 *The Times* 11 December 1872
32 *The Times* 18 December 1872
33 *Bristol Mirror* 17 December 1864
34 *The Times* 6 January 1873, letter from
    the vicar (H.P. Jeston) with the
    headline 'A Trafalgar Veteran'
35 Robinson 1836, p. 105
36 Nicolas 1845, vol. 2, p. 402

BIBLIOGRAPHY

Anon 1806 *Tour Through England Described in a Series of Letters from a Young Gentleman to his Sister* (London)

Barrett, R.J. 1841a 'Naval Recollections of the late American War' *United Service Journal and Naval and Military Magazine*, part 1 pp. 455–67, part 2 pp. 13–23

Barrett, R.J. 1841b 'The passage of the Gironde in 1815' *United Service Journal and Naval and Military Magazine*, pp. 13–25

Bates, J. 1868 *The Autobiography of Elder Joseph Bates; embracing a long life on shipboard* (Battle Creek, Michigan)

Beatty, W. 1807 *Authentic Narrative of the Death of Lord Nelson: with the circumstances preceding, attending, and subsequent to, that event; the Professional Report on His Lordship's Wound; and several interesting anecdotes* (London)

Blane, G. 1785 *Observations on the diseases incident to seamen* (London)

Bonner-Smith, D. (ed.) 1942 *Recollections of My Sea Life From 1808 to 1830 by Captain John Harvey Boteler, R.N.* (London)

Boog Watson, W.N. 1969 'Two British Naval Surgeons of the French Wars' *Medical History* 13, pp. 213–25

Boser, R. 2002 'The Creation of a Legend' *History Today* 52 (10), pp. 36–7

Boteler, J.H. 1942 (ed. D. Bonner-Smith) *Recollections of My Sea Life from 1808 to 1830* (London)

Bourchier, J. 1873 *Memoir of the Life of Admiral Sir Edward Codrington, volume 1* (London)

Boys, E. 1864 (4th edn) *Narrative of a captivity, escape, and adventures in France and Flanders during the war* (London) .

Brenton, E.P. 1838 *Life and Correspondence of John, Earl of St. Vincent, G.C.B., Admiral of the Fleet, &c. &c. &c. vol. II* (London)

Brewer, G. 1805 'Account of the Battle of Trafalgar: In a Letter from Jack Handspeck, on board the Temeraire, to his landlord, Bob Spunyarn, at the Common Hard, Portsmouth' *European Magazine and London Review* 48, pp. 433–5

Buckingham, J.S. 1855 *Autobiography of James Silk Buckingham including his voyages, travels, adventures, speculations, successes and failures, vol. 1* (London)

Cockburn, G. 1815 *A Voyage to Cadiz and Gibraltar, up the Mediterranean to Sicily and Malta, in 1810, & 11, including a description of Sicily and the Lipari Islands, and an Excursion in Portugal vol. 1* (London)

Comfort, S. 2004 *Forget Me Not: a study of naval and maritime engraved coins and plate (1745–1918)* (London)

Cooper, J.S. 1869 *Rough Notes of Seven Campaigns in Portugal, Spain, France and America during the years 1809–1815* (Carlisle)

Cordingly, D. 2001 *Heroines & Harlots: Women at Sea in the Great Age of Sail* (London)

Cordingly, D. 2003 *Billy Ruffian: The Bellerophon and the Downfall of Napoleon. The Biography of a Ship of the Line, 1782–1836* (London)

Crawford, A. 1851 *Reminiscences of a Naval Officer during the late war with sketches and anecdotes of distinguished commanders, vols. 1 and 2* (London)

Dallas, G. 1815 *A Biographical Memoir of the late Sir Peter Parker, baronet* (London)

Davis, J. 1815 (new edn) *The Post-Captain; or, the Wooden Walls Well Manned; comprehending a view of naval society and manners* (London)

Delafons, J. 1805 *A treatise on naval courts martial* (London)

Dibdin, C. 1844 *The Songs of Charles Dibdin Chronologically Arranged, with notes, historical, biographical and critical* (London)

Dillon, W.H. 1953 (ed. M.A. Lewis) *A narrative of my professional adventures (1790–1839) by Sir William Henry Dillon, K.C.H., Vice-Admiral of the Red, Volumes I and II* (London)

Dundonald, T. 1861 *The Autobiography of a Seaman, volume 1* (London)

Durand, J. 1926 (ed. G.S. Brooks) *James Durand An Able Seaman of 1812: His Adventures on 'Old Ironsides' and as an Impressed Sailor in the British Navy* (London)

Dye, I. 1987 'American Prisoners of War, 1812–1815', pp. 293–320 in *Ships, Seafaring and Society: Essays in Maritime History* (ed. T.J. Runyan) (Detroit)

Elliot, G. 1863 (reprinted 1891) *Memoir of Admiral the Honble Sir George Elliot written for his children* (London)

Ellison, S. 1838 *Prison Scenes; and Narrative of Escape from France, during the late war* (London)

Fernyhough, T. 1829 *Military Memoirs of Four Brothers engaged in the service of their country* (London)

Field, C. 1924 *Britain's Sea-Soldiers: A History of the Royal Marines and their predecessors* (Liverpool)

Finlayson, J. 1952 'A Signal Midshipman at Copenhagen' *Blackwood's Magazine* 271, pp. 121–37

Firth, C.H. (ed.) 1908 *Naval Songs and Ballads* (London)

Forester, C.S. (ed.) 1954 *The Adventures of John Wetherell* (London)

Fraser, E. 1896 'The Battle Honours of the British Fleet. The Temeraire' *The Navy and Army Illustrated* vol. 2 no. 24, pp. 271–80

Fraser, E. 1913 *The Sailors Whom Nelson Led: Their Doings Described by Themselves* (London)

Fremantle, A. (ed.) 1940 *The Wynne Diaries vol. III 1798–1820* (Oxford)

Fyfe, J.G. (ed.) 1942 *Scottish Diaries and Memoirs 1746–1843* (Stirling)

Gardner, J.A. 1906 (ed. R.V. Hamilton and J.K. Laughton) *Recollections of James Anthony Gardner* (London)

Gentleman, F. 1770 *The Dramatic Censor; or, Critical Companion* (London)

Gillett, E. (ed.) 1945 *Elizabeth Ham by Herself 1783–1820* (London)

Glascock, W.N. 1826 *Naval Sketch-Book; or, the Service Afloat and Ashore; with characteristic reminiscences, fragments and opinions, vol. 1* (London)

Goodall, D. 1860 *Salt Water Sketches; Being Incidents in the Life of Daniel Goodall* (Inverness)

Greig, J. (ed.) 1924 *The Farington Diary by Joseph Farington, R.A., vol. 6* (London)

Griffiths, A.J. 1824 *Observations on some points of seamanship: with practical hints on naval economy* (Cheltenham)

Hall, B. 1846 (new edn) *Fragments of Voyages and Travels (Series 1, 2 and 3)* (London)

Hathaway, E. 1994 *Smuggler: John Rattenbury and his Adventures in Devon, Dorset and Cornwall 1778–1844* (Swanage)

Hawker, E. 1821 *Statement Respecting the Prevalence of Certain Immoral Practices Prevailing in His Majesty's Navy* (London)

Hay, M.D. (ed.) 1953 *Landsman Hay: The Memoirs of Robert Hay 1789–1847* (London)

Hoffman, F. 1901 (ed. A.B. Bevan and H.B. Wolrhyche-Whitmore) *A sailor of King George: the journals of Captain Frederick Hoffman, RN, 1793–1814* (London)

Inglefield, J.N. 1783 *Captain Inglefield's Narrative, concerning the loss of his Majesty's Ship the Centaur, of Seventy-four guns* (London)

Jackson, G.V. 1927 (ed. H. Burrows) *The Perilous Adventures and Vicissitudes of a Naval Officer 1801–1812: Being Part of the Memoirs of Admiral George Vernon Jackson (1787–1876)* (Edinburgh, London)

Jackson, T.S. (ed.) 1900 *Logs of the Great Sea Fights 1794–1805, vol. 2* (London)

James, W. 1859 (new edn) *The Naval History of Great Britain vol. IV* (London)

Kelly, S. 1925 (ed. C. Garstin) *Samuel Kelly: An Eighteenth Century Seaman whose days have been few and evil, to which is added remarks etc. on places he visited during his pilgrimage in this wilderness* (London)

Lambert, S. (ed.) 1975 *House of Commons Sessional Papers of the Eighteenth Century. Volume 118. George III. Land Revenue, Prisoners of War, Fisheries 1797–98* (Wilmington)

Lee, J.T. 1836 *Memoirs of the life and service of Sir J. Theophilus Lee, of the Elms, Hampshire* (London)

Leech, S. 1844 *Thirty Years from Home, or A Voice from the Main Deck being the experiences of Samuel Leech, who was for six years in the British and American Navies, was captured in the British frigate Macedonian: afterwards entered the American Navy, and was taken in the United States Brig Syren, by the British ship Medway* (Boston)

Leyland, J. (ed.) 1899 *Dispatches and letters relating to the blockade of Brest 1803–1805 vol. 1* (London)

Lincoln, A.L.J. and R.L. McEwen (ed.) 1960 *Lord Eldon's Anecdote Book* (London)

Lovell, W.S. 1879 (2nd edn) *Personal Narrative of Events, from 1799 to 1815, with anecdotes* (London)

Lovett, W. 1876 *The Life and Struggles of William Lovett in his pursuit of bread, knowledge and freedom* (London)

Lowry, J. 2006 (ed. J. Millyard) *Fiddlers and Whores: The Candid Memoirs of a Surgeon in Nelson's Fleet* (London)

Malcolm, J. 1828 'Reminiscences of a Campaign in the Pyrenees and south of France in 1814', pp. 235–307 in *Memorials of the Late War vol. 1* (Edinburgh)

Marryat, F. 1872 *Life and Letters of Captain Marryat* (London)

Millard, W.S. 1895 'The Battle of Copenhagen' *Macmillan's Magazine* 72, pp. 81–93

Moody, T.W. (ed.) 1959 'An Irish Countryman in the British Navy, 1809–1815: The Memoirs of Henry Walsh' *Irish Sword* 4, pp. 228–45

Moody, T.W. (ed.) 1961–2 'An Irish Countryman in the British Navy, 1809–1815: The Memoirs of Henry Walsh' *Irish Sword* 5, pp. 107–16, 236–50

Moorhouse, H. (ed.) 1910 *Letters of the English Seamen: 1587–1808* (London)

Morrice, D. 1801 *The Young Midshipman's Instructor; with useful hints to parents of sea youth, and to captains and schoolmasters in the Royal Navy* (London)

Newnham Collingwood, G.L. 1829 *A Selection from the Public and Private Correspondence of Vice-Admiral Lord Collingwood: interspersed with memoirs of his life* (London)

Nicol, J. 1822 *The Life and Adventures of John Nicol, Mariner* (Edinburgh, London)

Nicolas, N.H. 1844 *The Dispatches and Letters of Vice Admiral Lord Viscount Nelson*, volume 1 (London)

Nicolas, N.H. 1845 *The Dispatches and Letters of Vice Admiral Lord Viscount Nelson*, volumes 2, 3 and 5 (London)

Nicolas, N.H. 1846 *The Dispatches and Letters of Vice Admiral Lord Viscount Nelson*, volume 7 (London)

O'Brien, D.H. 1839 *My adventures during the late war: comprising a narrative of shipwreck, captivity, escapes from French prisons, etc. from 1804 to 1827, vol. 2* (London)

O'Loghlen, T. 1766 *The Marine Volunteer: Containing the Exercise, Firings, and Evolutions of a Battalion of Infantry. To which is added Sea-duty and a Supplement* (London)

O'Meara, B.E. 1822 *Napoleon in Exile; or, a Voice from St. Helena. The Opinions and Reflections of Napoleon on the most important events of his life and government, in his own words, vols. 1 & 2* (London)

Oxford Archaeology 2007 *The Royal Hospital Greenwich London Archaeological Report* (Oxford)

Parsons, G.S. 1905 *Nelsonian Reminiscences: Leaves from Memory's Logs* (London)

Pasley, T. 1931 (ed. R.M.S. Pasley) *Private Sea Journals 1778–1782* (London, Toronto)

Pemberton, C.R. 1843 *The Life and Literary Remains of Charles Reece Pemberton* (London)

Petrides, A. and J. Downs (ed.) 2000 *Sea Soldier: An Officer of Marines with Duncan, Nelson, Collingwood and Cockburn. The Letters and Journals of Major T. Marmaduke Wybourn RM, 1797–1813* (Tunbridge Wells)

Pettigrew, T.J. 1849 *Memoirs of the Life of Vice-Admiral Lord Viscount Nelson, K.B., vol. 1* (London)

Pillet, R.-M. 1818 *Views of England, During a Residency of Ten Years; Six of Them as a Prisoner of War* (Boston)

Pinckard, G. 1806 *Notes on the West Indies: written during the expedition under the command of the late Sir Ralph Abercromby, vol. 1* (London)

Polwhele, R. 1826 *Traditions and Recollections; domestic, clerical and literary, vol. 2* (London)

Price, G. 1984 *Pressganged: The Letters of George Price of Southwark alias George Green* (Royston)

Prior, J. 1820 *Voyage in the Indian Seas, in the Nisus Frigate, to the Cape of Good Hope, Isles of Bourbon, France, and Seychelles; to Madras; and the Isles of Java, St. Paul, and Amsterdam, during the years 1810 and 1811* (London)

Raigersfeld, J., Baron de 1929 *The Life of a Sea Officer* (reprint of the edition privately printed c.1830) (London)

Rattenbury, J. 1837 *Memoirs of a Smuggler, compiled from his diary and journal* (Sidmouth)

Rees, T. 1822 *A Journal of Voyages and Travels by the Late Thomas Rees, Serjeant of Marines* (London)

Regulations 1806 and 1808 *Regulations and Instructions Relating to His Majesty's Service at Sea. Established by His Majesty in Council* (London)

Robertson, R. 1777 *A Physical Journal Kept on Board His Majesty's Ship Rainbow, During Three Voyages to the Coast of Africa, and West Indies, in the Years 1772, 1773, and 1774* (London)

Robertson, R. 1807 *Observations on Diseases Incident to Seamen vol. 1* (London)

Robinson, C.N. 1911 *The British Tar in Fact and Fiction: The Poetry, Pathos, and Humour of the Sailor's Life* (London, New York)

Robinson, H. 1858 *Sea Drift* (Portsea)

Robinson, W. 1836 *Nautical Economy; or, forecastle recollections of events during the last war dedicated to the brave tars of Old England by a sailor, politely called by the officers of the navy, Jack Nasty-Face* (London)

Rowbotham, W.B. 1937 'The Naval General Service Medal 1793–1840' *The Mariner's Mirror* 23, pp. 351–70

Scott, A.J. 1842 *Recollections of the Life of the Rev. A.J. Scott, D.D., Lord Nelson's Chaplain* (London)

Scott, J. 1834 *Recollections of a Naval Life* vols. 1, 2 and 3 (London)

Short, J.T. and T. Williams 1914 *Prisoners of War in France from 1804 to 1814, being the adventures of John Tregerthen Short and Thomas Williams of St. Ives, Cornwall* (London)

Sinclair, A. 1857 *Reminiscences of the Discipline, Customs, and Usages in the Royal Navy in 'The Good Old Times' – 1814 to 1831* (London)

Smyth, W.H. 1829 *The Life and Services of Captain Philip Beaver, late of His Majesty's Ship Nisus* (London)

Smyth, W.H. 1867 *The Sailor's Word-Book: An Alphabetical Digest of Nautical Terms, Including Some More Especially Military and Scientific, but Useful to Seamen; As Well as Archaisms of Early Voyagers, Etc.* (London)

Spilsbury, F.B. 1807 *Account of A Voyage to the Western Coast of Africa; Performed by His Majesty's Sloop Favourite, In the Year 1805* (London)

Steele, R. 1840 *The Marine Officer; or, sketches of service, vol. I* (London)

Stirling, A.M.W. 1919 *Pages & Portraits from the Past being the private papers of Sir William Hotham, G.C.B. Admiral of the Red* vol. 1 (London)

Thomas, A. 1968 (ed. J.M. Murray) *The Newfoundland Journal of Aaron Thomas Able Seaman in H.M.S. Boston* (London)

Thursfield, H.G. (ed.) 1951 *Five Naval Journals 1789–1817* (London)

Trotter, T. 1804 (2nd edn) *Medicina Nautica: an Essay on the Diseases of Seamen* vols. 1 and 3 (London)

Tucker, J.S. 1844 *Memoirs of Admiral the Right Hon. the Earl of St. Vincent, G.C.B. &c.,* vol. 1 (London)

Waterhouse, B. 1911 'A journal of a young man of Massachusetts by Benjamin Waterhouse, M.D. (1754–1846)' *Magazine of History with notes and queries* 18 (New York)

Wathen, J. 1814 *Journal of a Voyage in 1811 and 1812 to Madras and China; returning by The Cape of Good Hope and St Helena; in the H.C.S. The Hope, Capt. James Pendergrass* (London)

Watson, G. 1827 *A Narrative of the Adventures of a Greenwich Pensioner written by himself* (Newcastle)

Wellington, A.W. 1838 *The Dispatches of Field Marshal the Duke of Wellington during his various campaigns in India, Denmark, Portugal, Spain, the Low Countries, and France, from 1799 to 1818, vol. 10,* compiled by Lt-Col. Gurwood (London)

Wheeler, W. 1951 (ed. B.H. Liddell Hart) *The Letters of Private Wheeler 1809–1828* (London)

Whitfeld, H.F. 1900 *Plymouth and Devonport in Times of War and Peace* (Plymouth)

Willyams, C. 1802 *A Voyage up the Mediterranean in his majesty's ship the Swiftsure, one of the squadron under the command of Rear-Admiral Sir Horatio Nelson, K.B. now viscount and Baron Nelson of the Nile, and Duke of Bronte in Sicily with a description of the Battle of the Nile on the first of August 1798* (London)

Wolfe, R.B. 1830 *English Prisoners in France containing observations on their manners and habits* (London)

Wyndham-Quin, W.H. 1912 *Sir Charles Tyler, G.C.B. Admiral of the White* (London)

INDEX